Religious Response to
Social Change in Afghanistan 1919-29

Religious Response to Social Change in Afghanistan 1919-29

King Aman-Allah and the Afghan *Ulama*

ఆ౪ఎౘ

Senzil K. Nawid

MAZDA PUBLISHERS

1999

Mazda Publishers, Inc.
Academic Publishers
P.O. Box 2603
Costa Mesa, California 92626 U.S.A.
www.mazdapublishers.com

Library of Congress Cataloging-in-Publication Data

Nawid, Senzil K., 1945
Religious Response to Social Change in Afghanistan;
King Aman-Allah and the Afghan Ulama,
1919-1929/ Senzil K. Nawid.
p.cm.
Includes bibliographical references and index.

ISBN:1-56859-072-5
(cloth:alk. paper)

1. Islam and state—Afghanistan. 2. Afghanistan—Politics and government— 20th century. 3. Afghanistan—Social conditions—20th century. 4. Amanullah Khan, Amir of Afghanistan, 1892-1960.
I. Title.
BP63.A54N38 1998
297.2'72'0958109042—dc21
98-22602
CIP

To the Memory of My Parents
G. Ahmad Nawid
'Ayesha Nawid
and
Professor G. Faruq E'temadi

Contents

viii

Preface

Since the mid-nineteenth century there has been an attempt in various parts of the Muslim world to redefine traditional Islamic institutions to meet the exigencies of the modern world. Efforts to change the medieval picture of Muslim societies have been met with resistance from traditional sectors, who fear the impact of change on the Islamic family structure and Islamic culture generally. Reformist trends in the Muslim world have thus generated debate on the interpretation of the *shari`at*, the divinely-inspired Islamic law, and its role in contemporary Islamic societies. This study is an example of such contention in the 1920s in Afghanistan.

This volume has undergone a number of metamorphoses. Many years of research, rethinking, and rewriting have led to the book in its present form. The original source of inspiration was my mother. Product of a government-sponsored female emancipation movement in the 1920s, her dream of achieving higher education was shattered when the outbreak of clergy-led revolts in 1928 resulted in the closing of girls' schools in Kabul. My father, a liberal nationalist inspired by reformist politics of the 1920s, was also a force leading me farther along this path.

A number of individuals and institutions have been instrumental in making this work possible. I am indebted to Professor Ludwig Adamec for reviewing the manuscript and sharing with me his remarkable collection on Afghanistan, particularly materials from the National Archives of India. The American-Pakistan Research Organization provided a travel grant in 1994 that enabled me to study documents relating to tribal religious leaders of the Khyber region who were actively involved in Afghan politics during the 1920s and to interview several Afghan religious leaders now residing in Pakistan. I would like to express my gratitude to members of the Area Studies Centre at Peshawar University, particularly to Dr. `Azmat Hayat Khan, director, and to Dr. Fazl ur Rahim Marwat, who assisted me in Peshawar. My thanks also go to Rasul Amin and other members of the Writers Union for Afghanistan who helped arrange interviews. Solaiman Gailani facilitated every aspect of my stay in Peshawar, and `Abd al-Wali Sorush Wali, the son of Mohammad Wali Khan, the Regent, shared with me invaluable unpublished documents from the Amani era.

I am grateful also to the International Program and the Research Institute of the College of Social and Behavioral Sciences at the University of Arizona for helping me complete my research at the India Office Library in London. Thanks as well to Patricia, Countess Jellicoe for her generous hospitality during my several research trips to London, and to the staff of the India Office Library for facilitating my research. I would like as well to thank May Schinasie for providing items pertinent to my research from her magnificent collection of Afghan historical materials. I am obliged also to Rawan Farhadi and Nancy Hatch Dupree for reviewing an early version of the manuscript and making useful suggestions, to Vivien Hamley of *Illustrated London News* for providing copies of the pictures of King Aman-Allah and Queen Soraya's visit to London, the staff of Wellcome Institute of History of Medecine in London for providing photographs of the earlier period, and the staff of the Nehro Library in New Delhi, who facilitated my research in India in the summer of 1989.

Distinguished Afghan scholars contributed valuable information: Ne'mat-Allah Shahrani, former professor of theology at Kabul University; `Aziz al-Din Wakil Fofalzai; and the late Mir Gholam Mohammad Ghobar. I am especially grateful to Sayyid Qasem Reshtia for reading the entire manuscript and providing insightful criticism and guidance.

In legal and theological matters, I was assisted by the late Musa Shafiq, former prime minister of Afghanistan. As the son of one of the ulama who figured prominently in the politics of the Amani era, himself an expert in Islamic theology, he provided valuable assistance. I am indebted also to Fatema Gailani, who arranged my interview with Dr. Shafiq, then under house arrest. I am also grateful to Gholam Nabi Chaknawuri, Fazl Ghani Mojaddadi, `Abd-Allah Mojaddadi, and Mohammad `Aziz Mojaddadi for sharing with me family documents and pictures.

Parts of chapters 2 and 3 have appeared in *The International Journal of Middle East Studies* (29, no.4, 1997, pp. 581-605), and parts of chapter 5 have been published in *Annali* (56, no. 3. 1996, pp. 311-319).

Finally, I would like to thank my husband, David Hoyt Johnson, for his help and forebearance throughout the period of research and writing.

Note on Transliteration and Dates

The transliteration of Arabic and Persian words follows the system adopted by the journal of the Middle East Studies Association of North America. Two exceptions are (1) words of Arabic origin which appear without diacritical marks, and (2) short vowels which appear as "e" and "o" instead of "i" and "u." Both the Persian short vowel (a) and long vowel (ā) are represented by "a" to avoid the use of diacritical marks. The two Persian diphthongs are represented by "ai" and "aw," as they are pronounced in the Dari dialect of Afghanistan. The exact transliteration of Persian and Arabic words appears in the glossary in brackets. Proper names are not italicized, but common nouns are. Words such as ulama which have entered into English usage are not italicized. All transliteration of Persian and Arabic words is based on this system, except in quoted texts where a different system was used.

Dates are given according to the Islamic calendar and the Christian calendar, separated by a slash.

Abbreviations

ANA	Afghan National Archives
BACSOA	Biographical Accounts of Chiefs, Sardars, and Others in Afghanistan
FIBD	Frontier Intelligence Bureau Diaries
FPD	Foreign and Political Department
IOR	India Office Records
NAI	National Archives of India
NWFP	North-West Frontier Province

Map 1

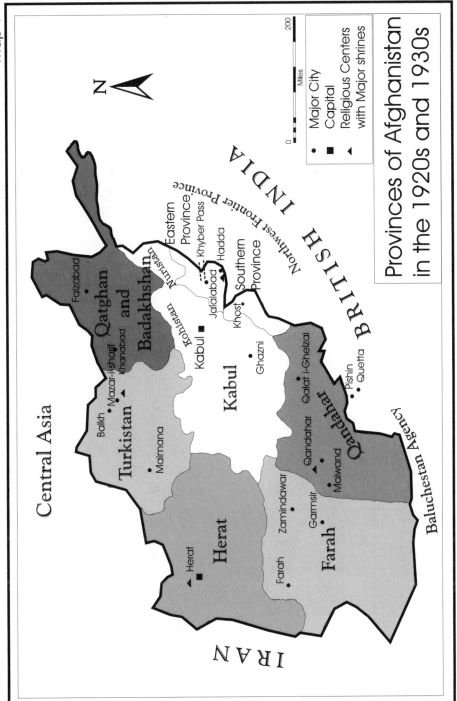

Provinces of Afghanistan
in the 1920s and 1930s

Map 2

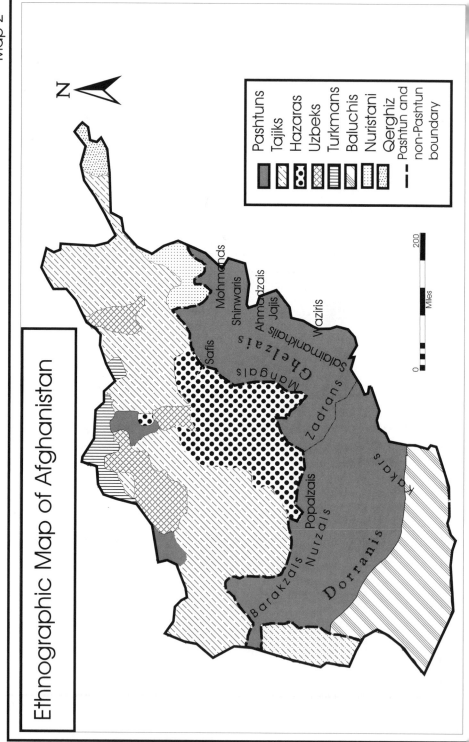

Ethnographic Map of Afghanistan

N

Pashtuns
Tajiks
Hazaras
Uzbeks
Turkmans
Baluchis
Nuristani
Qerghiz
Pashtun and
non-Pashtun
boundary

Mohmands
Shinwaris
Ahmadzais
Jajis
Waziris
Safis
Mangals
Ghelzais
Salarmankhails
Zadrans
Kakars
Popalzais
Barakzais Nurzais
Dorranis

0   Miles   200

Map 3

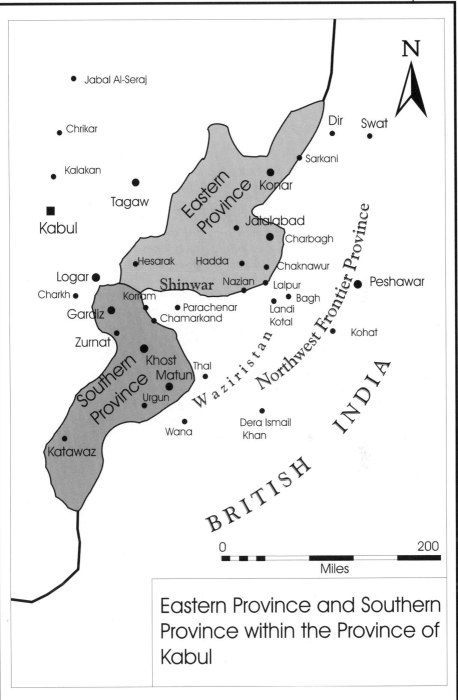

N

Jabal Al-Seraj

Chrikar

Kalakan

Tagaw

Kabul

Eastern Province

Dir   Swat

Sarkani

Konar

Jalalabad

Charbagh

Northwest Frontier Province

Logar

Charkh

Gardiz

Zurnat

Hesarak   Hadda

Shinwar   Nazian   Lalpur

Korram

Parachenar

Chamarkand

Southern Province

Khost   Thal

Matun

Urgun

Wana

Katawaz

Chaknawur

Bagh

Landi
Kotal

Peshawar

Kohat

Waziristan

Dera Ismail
Khan

BRITISH INDIA

0   200

Miles

Eastern Province and Southern
Province within the Province of
Kabul

INTRODUCTION

The accession of Aman-Allah to the Afghan throne in 1919 symbolized the victory of the nationalist reformist groups in Afghanistan. Aman-Allah emerged as the hero of Afghan independence and one of the most dynamic modernizers of the post-World War I period in the Middle East. When he gained power, he had two primary objectives: to achieve Afghanistan's external independence and to lead the country in rapid development. Broadly, he envisioned an independent, nationalist, liberal state based on a constitutionally determined, centralized government; that sustained itself with centrally imposed taxation; that defended itself with a conscripted, centralized army; that regulated itself with a professionally trained cadre of jurists; and that recognized the equality of women by reforming traditional legal customs of family, marriage, and dress, as well as by making education available to women. During the nine years of his reign, he concentrated his efforts on securing Afghanistan's independence and promoting its rapid development.

Afghanistan was a traditional Islamic state when Aman-Allah ascended the Afghan throne. The dual goals of independence and reform had a significant impact on relations between the state and the clergy during the 1920s; interactions between the government and the *ulama* (religious scholars) were more intense and complex during the Amani period than at any other time in Afghan history. They resulted in an array of conflicts and compromises between the clergy and the state. Twice, first in 1924, and then again in 1928, the Afghan clergy became involved in widespread uprisings against Aman-Allah's regime. The antigovernment forces backed by the clergy eventually brought about the king's downfall in 1928.

The clash between Islam and modernism, in all its forms, has been a major theme of political development in the Middle East. Religious opposition to change has surfaced in different Muslim societies at various degrees of intensity, depending on the particular social and political conditions of each society. The Islamic revolution in Iran in 1979 was, in large measure, a clash between a modernizing regime and the religious establishment. As the Shah lost credibility with the religious establishment, he lost legitimacy, and his regime was eventually toppled. Similar kinds of conflicts are now occurring in Algeria, Egypt, Pakistan, Afghanistan, and elsewhere in the Muslim world. This work is a study of the conflict between Islam and a modernizing regime in Afghanistan that was brought down by a challenge to its legitimacy led by the clergy.

Resistance to social change in the Middle East originates from the Islamic perception of law and order and epistemological view of the Qur`an. Muslims believe that all that exists in heaven and on earth belongs to God. All aspects of human conduct are determined by the divinely-aspired religious law (the *shari`at*), which prescribes the rights and duties of an individual in this world and sets forth rules to prepare him for the world to come. As opposed to secular modern law, which is shaped by historical experience, the *shari`at*, the all encompassing law of Islam, is based on the Qur'an, which is considered to be the last word of God, the sayings and the example of the life of the Prophet Mohammad (*sonnat*). As such, the *shari`at* is immutable and cannot be altered according to human will. Any attempt to change the social order of Islam can be construed as the rejection of divine ordinances and hence blasphemy. "The religious order of Islam," twentieth-century Muslim philosopher Mohammad Iqbal stated, "is organically related to the social order which it has created. The rejection of the one will eventually involve the rejection of the other."[1]

Muslim religious law developed during the first century of Islam. Sunni jurisprudence (*feqh*), covering all aspects of religious, political and civil life, took form in the course of the ninth century A.D. through the work of four medieval jurists, Mohammad Al-Shafe`i (d. 820), Abu Hanifa (d. 867), Ahmad bin Hanbal (d. 855), and Malek bin Anas (d. 795). Four separate schools of jurisprudence (*mazaheb*, plural of *mazhab*), each named after its founder, came into being. After the completion of their work, the medieval jurists banned independent interpretation (*ejtehad*) of the *shari`at* to prevent confusion and conflicting opinions regarding its rules.

It was not until the mid-nineteenth century that Muslim reformist jurists began to try to make Islam adaptable to requirements of the modern world by reinterpreting the sacred law—by going back to the original sources (Qur`an and *sonnat*) and by relying on the consensus of the Muslim community of scholars (*ejma`*). Jamal al-Din Afghani and Sheikh Mohammad `Abduh of Egypt emphasized the role of reason in the interpretation of the *shari`at*. They argued that change was necessary to remedy the problem of backwardness among Muslims and to enable them to meet the military and technological challenges of the West. `Abduh justified reforms by stressing the principle of *maslahat*, or legal argument denoting that "good" is "lawful." The rationalism of nineteenth-century Muslim reformers encouraged reforms in Egypt and in Ottoman Turkey, and from there the spirit of reform spread to other parts of the Middle East. The rational ideas of the reformists did not, however, change the views of the majority. The traditional groups—the ulama of the old school, the members of the sufi orders, and their mass following—dismissed all ideas outside the framework of medieval interpretations of the law and remained opposed to change.

For a political authority to be recognized, it must be legitimized according to the *shari`at*. Rulers exist only to enforce divine ordinances. The power wielded

---

[1.] Aziz Ahmad, *Islamic Modernism in India and Pakistan*, 160.

by the ulama, the guardians of the *shari`at*, lay in their duty to apply the law in evaluating the regime's ability to implement and defend the *shari`at* and thus to determine whether the government is legitimate. This power of the ulama to give or withhold legitimacy has made implementation of social or political reforms difficult for all Muslim political leaders. The relative success or failure of modernizing ruling elite has depended on the strength of a central army, the makeup of the society, and its susceptibility to change.

In Afghanistan, a combination of factors—such as militant tribalism, the power of the clergy and their resistance to change, characterized by strong devotion to holy war (*jehad*), and the lack of strong loyalty to the central government—has made rulers even more vulnerable to religious scrutiny than they have been elsewhere in the Muslim world and has created additional burdens for those trying to implement social change. Another factor also influenced the reception of reform. During the nineteenth century Afghanistan became the meeting ground of rivalry between two Western imperial powers, Russia to the north, and British India to the south. This ongoing conflict between the imperial ambitions of the British and those of the czarist, and later, the Soviet Russians often had a direct bearing on events in Afghanistan. Related to the British-Soviet rivalry is the long-standing conflict between Afghanistan and the British, a sub-theme of this book.

The Anglo-Afghan wars molded the militant character of Islam in Afghanistan and increased the social and political influence of the ulama as instigators and leaders of *jehad* against the British. The ulama's leadership in *jehad* reinforced their alliances with tribal groups. In the Pashtun tribal regions bordering British India, pockets of resistance were formed under the leadership of local religious leaders, in practice the political as well as the spiritual leaders of their communities. The adoption of the title *padshah* (king) by some of these leaders suggested not only a noble religious ancestor but also the extent of their political power in their region. By 1880, the end of the Second Anglo-Afghan War, the ulama had become the most powerful group with whom the rulers had to reckon. With the exception of Amir `Abd al-Rahman, Aman-Allah's grandfather who consolidated his authority by means of a strong army, the rulers of Afghanistan depended on the good will of the religious leaders to maintain power. Destructive wars during the nineteenth century along with British control of Afghanistan's foreign policy impeded contact with the outside world. In turn, isolation from the outside world reinforced the "inward-looking" nature of Afghan society and made it more resistant to change.

During the last part of the nineteenth century, Amir `Abd al-Rahman established order and secured compliance with central authority by military means. He laid the foundation of a united state with a strong central government, well-defined boundaries, and a strong standing army. In the time of King Habib-Allah, `Abd al-Rahman's son and successor and Aman-Allah's father, new ideas began to infiltrate the country and a small-scale modernization program was implemented. The reign of Habib-Allah coincided with the rise of Asian nationalism, pan-Islamism, and the Bolshevik Revolution in Russia, all of which had an impact on Afghan political thought in the years leading to Aman-Allah's accession to the throne.

A small group of liberals, led by Mahmud Tarzi, advocated liberal nationalism, pan-Islamism, and social and political reforms. Through provocative articles in *Seraj al-Akhbar* (a newspaper he edited), Tarzi attracted a group of ulama in the capital and several members of the ruling class to the cause of liberal nationalism. Among the most important supporters of the movement was Prince Aman-Allah, who soon became the soul and symbol of the movement. The liberal nationalists strengthened their position by establishing contacts with Turkish and Indian pan-Islamic activists and, through them, with the Bolsheviks and by forging alliances with powerful tribal religious leaders, with all of whom they shared a common goal: the overthrow of British control. *Jehad* swept up diverse Pashtun tribes in the region in a collective expression of "ethnonationalism." Still based on Islamic principles, *jehad* found a new expression in the context of Afghan nationalism.

At the beginning of his regime, Aman-Allah's aspirations and actions did not deviate drastically from what the ulama regarded as the true path of Islam. A coincidence of interest between the regime and the clergy resulted in harmonious relations between them. The potent force in bringing an alliance between Aman-Allah and the clergy was the War of Independence. In 1919, Aman-Allah effectively used Islamic *jehad* to gain Afghanistan's complete independence. At a time when the issue of royal succession was still in question, Aman-Allah's declaration of *jehad* gained him the support of the ulama, most of whom would otherwise have challenged his succession in favor of that of his uncle, Sardar Nasr-Allah Khan. The latter, a devout Muslim, was greatly revered by religious groups.

Aman-Allah's relations with the ulama were further strengthened by his support of pan-Islamism. Through his victory over the British, his support of the caliphate in Turkey, and other pan-Islamic activities, Aman-Allah achieved enormous stature and legitimacy. As the champion of independence and an active exponent of the Islamic cause, he was able to obviate religious opposition to his early reforms. A group of liberal ulama were even inclined to cooperate. The state-clergy alliance, however, began to deteriorate when the reforms began to threaten the orthodox beliefs of the ulama and their traditional influence in the society.

Aman-Allah's reforms fall into two distinct stages: those of 1919-1923 and the radical reforms of 1928. The reaction of the clergy differed to these two stages of reforms. Opposition to the first stage of reforms was led by the lower-ranking ulama in the countryside. In 1928, religious groups of every rank and from every quarter combined in a united front against the government and began a counterattack by allying with militant tribes, dissident groups, opposition leaders and adventurers, and by issuing provocative declarations, denouncing the king as an apostate who had overstepped the bounds of the *shari`at*. The nation lacked a strong army and an urban middle class, the one an effective counterforce to revolt, the other a customary stronghold of support for the sort of reforms Aman-Allah was proposing. Antigovernment forces, spurred on by the ulama, quickly gained strength, becoming a serious threat to the regime. The clergy-inspired rebellion of 1928 ultimately resulted in the abdication of King Aman-Allah on January 14, 1929, and failure of the first concerted effort at modernization in Afghanistan.

King Aman-Allah's dramatic rise to power in 1919 as one of the most dynamic early twentieth-century modernizers in the Muslim world and his equally dramatic fall in early 1929 have been interpreted in various ways. The Afghan historian Mir Gholam Mohammad Ghobar attributes Aman-Allah's failure partially to covert activities of the British against the Amani regime.[2] Leon Poullada focuses on the "dramatic clash between a tradition-encrusted society, dominated by flinty and xenophobic codes of tribal politics, and an idealistic, uncompromising modernizer, whose ideas in many important respects preceded and overlapped those of better-known historical figures in neighboring countries, such as Ataturk of Turkey and Reza Shah of Iran."[3] A third interpretation attributes Aman-Allah's failure to lack of a definite plan of priorities and the absence of a strong financial base: "in face of a tribal-feudal-religious-traditionalist coalition in opposition, he [Aman-Allah] was unable to find the necessary support in a strong urban middle class or in an economically healthy peasant class."[4] Ludwig Adamec attributes Aman-Allah's downfall primarily to neglect of the army.[5] In *Fire in Afghanistan*, Rhea Stewart elaborates on a statement made on June 4, 1919 by Sir George Roos-Keppel, the British High Commissioner in Baluchistan: "Aman-Allah has lit a fire that will take us a long time to put out."[6] Although Stewart does not attribute Aman-Allah's loss of power to the British directly, she does imply British involvement in his downfall.

While each of these theories has merit, none gives sufficient attention to state-clergy relations and the determined opposition of religious forces to Aman-Allah's reforms. In contrast, this study concentrates on the relationship between Aman-Allah and the ulama during the critical years 1919-1929. I have based the bulk of the study on official publications of the Afghan government, including original codes and statutes, *jerga* (assembly) debates, royal declarations gathered from the Afghan National Archives and private collections, newspapers and periodicals, most of which have not been seen by Western scholars. Indeed, most of them have not been seen by Afghan scholars, either. I have also relied on British archival materials, personal interviews, along with data from Afghan and Western historians.

---

[2] Ghobar, *Afghanistan dar Massir-i-Tarikh*, 806.
[3] Poullada, *Reform and Rebellion in Afghanistan*, xvii.
[4] Gregorian, *The Emergence of Modern Afghanistan*, 296.
[5] Adamec, *Afghanistan's Foreign Affairs*, 138.
[6] Stewart, *Fire in Afghanistan*, title page.

Most studies, while mentioning religious protest during the 1920s, have failed to emphasize its significance in relation to the events that took place, have ignored the doctrinal aspect of the opposition ulama, and have characterized the religious establishment as a monolithic reactionary force. This study shows, in contrast, how at the beginning of Aman-Allah's reign some high-ranking ulama cooperated with the reform programs and supported Aman-Allah, and how other factions of the ulama reacted to the changes differently. The main question this work seeks to answer is, why did Aman-Allah, hailed among Muslims as a pan-Islamist and a conqueror who had repelled infidels (*ghazi*), gradually lose legitimacy among the ulama. The answer to this question will help us to better understand the forces that continue to create so much tension in response to change in Afghanistan in particular and in the Muslim world in general.

1

The State and the Religious Establishment

Afghanistan is a traditional society composed of various tribal groups, rather than a consolidated modern state as generally conceived by Westerners. The political framework derives from Islam. At the core of its value system, Islam is the common cultural denominator that binds together diverse ethnolinguistic groups of Afghanistan. More than 99 percent of Afghanistan's population is Muslim, and the overwhelming majority adheres to Hanafi Sunni (orthodox) Islam. Islam made inroads into the northern parts of Afghanistan (then Khorasan) during the first century of Islam (A.H. 25-96/A.D. 645-714). In the following two and a half centuries, Islam became the dominant religion in the regions surrounding the Hindu Kush Mountains, the areas that form present-day Afghanistan. The only region remaining outside the domain of Islam was a remote corner in the northeast known as Kafaristan (Land of the Infidels). Later called Nuristan, its inhabitants accepted Islam or were forcibly converted in the late nineteenth century.

During the nineteenth and early twentieth centuries, Islam was the most potent force behind Afghanistan's struggle against British and Russian imperialism. Religious interest groups and leaders were prominent in the struggle against foreign encroachment and played a major role in all Afghan politics.

SOVEREIGNTY IN SUNNI POLITICAL IDEOLOGY

In Islam, sovereignty belongs to God alone. The concept of the state is based on the *shari`at*, the sacred law of Islam, which determines not only the way of worship but also norms for daily living, principles of statehood, interactions between state and community, and relations among individuals. According to Rosenthal, the *shari`at* is "the core of the faith, the terrestrial expression of di-

1

vine message to and demand upon society," and provides "through its universality a bond much stronger and more enduring than any other loyalty."[1]

The Prophet's rule in Medina, where the first community of believers was established, constitutes the model for government in Islam. The Prophet taught his followers that all that existed in the heavens and on earth belonged to God and that the community of Muslims as vice-regents of God held all things in trust for him. According to the Qur`an and the tradition of the Prophet (sonnat), which are the bases of the shari`at, authority is a sacred trust to be exercised by the members of the Muslim community for the enforcement of the will of God and the improvement of the community.[2] The government is considered legitimate only if it functions within the limits and in accordance with the precepts of justice prescribed in the Qur`an.[3]

In early Islam, temporal leadership was determined by election. The first leaders of the Muslim community, the four "Rightly Guided Caliphs" were, with the exception of the second caliph, `Omar, elected by a body of qualified voters known as ahl al-hal wa al-`aqd (literally, those who have the ability to tie and untie, learned and elite). Temporal authority was vested in the caliph through an oath of allegiance (bai`at). This oath of allegiance was in essence a contractual agreement between the caliph and the community that consisted of a promise by the caliph to rule in accordance with the religious law and an oath by the community to obey his commands. The caliph or the leader (imam) of the community could not define or interpret religious dogma. The main function of the caliph was to lead the community during times of war and act as its executive in times of peace.

With the rise of the Umayyads to power (661-749), the caliphate became hereditary. Legitimate political authority was, however, still attained only through securing the oath of allegiance of the learned and the elite. Eventually, it came through military dominance.

Sunni political ideology developed over several centuries. In the time of the `Abbasids (749-1258), theologians defined the functions of the caliph or the imam and determined the requisites for leadership. `Abd al-Qadir al-Baghdadi (d. 1037) listed the conditions for holding the office of imamate-caliphate: knowledge, probity of character, good judgment, and descent from Quraish.[4] Later, Abu al-Hasan Al-Mawardi (d. 1058) listed the duties of the caliph: to implement the shari`at, to execute and preserve justice, to protect the territory of Islam, to declare jehad, to take full responsibility for administration of finances, and to supervise public affairs.[5] The ruler was also responsible for the defense of Muslim territory against non-Muslim intrusions and the enforcement of the

---

[1] Rosenthal, Islam in the Modern Nation State, 10.
[2] Ka Ka Khel, "Legitimacy of Authority in Islam," 169.
[3] Ibid.
[4] Gibb, Shorter Encyclopedia of Islam, 9; Lambton, State and Government in Medieval Persia, 79-80.
[5] Rosenthal, Political Thought in Medieval Islam, 35-36.

Qur'anic verse commanding good and forbidding evil (*al-amr bi al-ma`ruf wa al-nahy `an al-monkar*).[6]

To preserve the sanctity of the state, classical jurists encouraged the community to disobey orders of the ruler that were repugnant to the ethical principles of Islam, and even to attempt his overthrow.[7] This privilege originated with Abu Bakr, the first caliph, who said,

> I was appointed over you and I am not the best one among you. If I perform my duty properly, support me and if I am at fault criticize me....Let no one among you abandon the *jehad* for the path of God...obey me as long as I obey God and his messenger. If I violate the injunctions of God or Prophet, no obedience is due to me.[8]

Medieval Muslim theologians elaborated this topic. Al-Mawardi, while advocating obedience to the ruler, gave two ways a ruler may be disqualified from being political head of the Muslim community: first, if there is a flaw in his system of justice, that is, if he acts according to his own whim and is corrupt; and second, if he has a major physical defect, mental disorder, or loss of one of the senses.[9]

At the same time, theologians established the doctrine of obedience to the ruler (*eta`at-i-uli al- 'amr*) to prevent anarchy and promote order. They justified this doctrine by quoting the Qur'anic verse, "O ye faithful, Obey God and the Apostle and those set in command amongst you"[10] and numerous sayings of the Prophet enjoining obedience to the ruler only so long as he is righteous and just.

With the breakup of the Islamic empire into independent kingdoms, the temporal power of the caliphs declined, but they were still recognized by Sunni Muslims as the legitimate source of authority. Although rulers were autonomous within their region, their political authority had to be validated by the caliph.[11] After the Mongol occupation of Baghdad in 1258, the caliphate was transferred to Cairo. When in 1517 the Ottoman Sultan Selim II occupied Cairo, he shifted the seat of the caliphate to Constantinople, and the Ottoman sultans virtually claimed for themselves the title of caliph along with its symbolic religious authority.

After the establishment of semi-independent local amirates and sultanates in parts of the Islamic empire from the ninth century on, it became necessary to define the functions and limitations of local rulers: the amirs and sultans. According to classical theologians such as Al-Mawardi, the local princes were entitled to the same obedience from their subjects as was the caliph.[12] Later, the

---

[6.] Enayat, *Modern Islamic Political Thought*, 2.

[7.] *Ibid.*; Ka Ka Khel, "The Theory of Impeachment in Islamic Polity," 100.

[8.] Tabari, 1829.

[9.] Al-Mawardi, *Al-Ahkam al-Sultaniyya*, 17.

[10.] Qur'an, 4:58.

[11.] Gibb, *Shorter Encyclopedia of Islam*, 17-18.

[12.] *Ibid.*

rulers of Transoxiana, Khorasan, and Fars maintained the tradition of seeking the caliph's endorsement for their authority. As time went by, the sultanate established its own power by military operations, taking over not only the temporal but most of the religious functions performed by the caliphs.[13] Toward the end of the eleventh century, Nizam al-Molk, a famous statesman of the Seljuq period, ignored the spiritual authority of the caliph and maintained that the king is the spiritual as well as the secular head of the state.[14] He advocated unconditional loyalty to the kings on the grounds that destruction of monarchy results in chaos and corruption in the society: "[T]he wrath of The Truth [God] overtakes those people and He forsakes them for the vileness of their obedience; kingship disappears altogether, opposing swords are drawn, blood is shed and...many innocent people too perish in the tumults."[15] His statement echoed the philosophy of a famous theologian of the same period. Mohammad Al-Ghazali (d. 1111) maintained that if an evil-doing and barbarous sultan is supported by such strong military force that the attempt to defeat him would create unendurable civil strife, this sultan must be left in his position and obedience rendered to him.[16] The rulers became absolute. The power of kings depended on the extent to which they succeeded in centralizing authority, but it was not until the mid-nineteenth century that forces of modernization prompted both modernists and fundamentalists to question the limits of political leadership and return to the Islamic precept of political legitimacy.[17]

In Afghanistan, in theory, the people acknowledged the authority of a ruler with an oath of allegiance. In practice, his right to the throne was regarded as "temporary and alienable." The survival of the regime depended largely upon the allegiance of two relatively independent forces: the tribal chiefs (*khan*s) and the religious leaders. Alliance with the *khan*s was normally secured by delegating to them important powers. The ruler bargained for the support or at least acquiescence of the religious groups by granting them concessions. When a political leader transgressed these arrangements, the religious leaders evoked religious principles to challenge his power.

According to Ahady, a ruler's political legitimacy in Afghanistan is based on the approval of the ulama and tribal chiefs; the ability of the ruler to implement

---

[13.] Siddiqi, *The Caliphate and Kingship in Medieval Persia*, 104.

[14.] "It is for the kings to observe His pleasure (His name be Glorified) and the pleasure of The Truth [one of the ninety-nine names of God] is the charity which is done to His creatures and in the justice which is spread among them....The Master of the World (May Allah perpetuate his reign) should know that on that great day he will be asked to answer for all those of God's creatures who are under his command, and if he tries to transfer his [responsibility] to someone else he will not be listened to. Since this is so it behooves the king not to leave this important matter to any one else." Nizam al-Mulk, 12-13.

[15.] *Ibid.*, 9.

[16.] Gibb, *Shorter Encyclopedia of Islam*, 19.

[17.] Jamal al-Din Afghani, Mohammad `Abduh, Rashid Ridha, `Abd al-Razeq, and more recently Sayyid Qutb and Abu `Ala Mawdudi, among others, were involved in this process.

the *shari`at* and to wage *jehad* for territorial expansion or defense of Afghanistan against foreign aggression; and the character of the ruler, who is expected to be pious, generous, and courageous.[18] Given Afghanistan's long struggle with the British, holy war (*jehad*) became a recurring theme in Afghan history during the nineteenth and early twentieth centuries. The legitimacy of a ruler was often determined by his courage and ability to lead a successful *jehad* in defense of the country. *Jehad* has served as a unifying force against foreigners even across "Sunni-Shi`a boundaries." The concept of the divine sanction of authority determined the legitimacy of the regime and also the legitimacy of rebellion. According to Oleson,

> from this springs, in the Afghan context, the centrality of the concept of *jihad* first of all; because central power as such was not firmly entrenched in the Afghan society, and hence, the legitimacy of the state and of the ruler was continuously at issue, and secondly also because of Afghanistan's position as a buffer state, between two Christian powers, where the call for *jihad* was used over and again to mobilise the population against enchroachments from the *kafer* [nonbeliever] forces.[19]

The concept of social justice is based in Islam, blended with traditional norms (*rawaj*). In areas dominated by the Pashtuns, the dominant ethnic group in Afghanistan until recent years, the Pashtun code of ethics (*pashtunwali*) held sway side by side with the *shari`at*. In this context, the Pashtuns identified Islam with Pashtunism.

STRUCTURE OF AUTHORITY AND CONCEPT OF LEADERSHIP

Afghanistan's modern age begins in 1747, with the rise to power of Ahmad Shah Dorrani, head of the Sadduzai clan of the greater Abdali tribe and with the ascendence of the Pashtuns, one of four major ethnic groups in the country (the others are the Tajiks, the Uzbeks and the Hazaras). Present-day Afghanistan was formed from fragmented political entities in existence at that time: Qandahar, Herat, and Sistan under the Saffavids; Kabulistan, consisting of all southern and southeastern regions, under the Moguls of India; and Balkh, Takharistan, Badakhshan, and Maimana in the north, under the Uzbek princes. In the sixteenth and seventeenth centuries, the Pashtuns rose up first against the Moguls and then against the Saffavids. The Pashtun campaign against the Moguls was led by Bayazid Ansari, known as the Pir-i-Roshan (d. 1579), and later Pashtun nationalist campaigns were led by the poet-warrior Khoshhal Khan Khatak. In 1707, Hajji Mir Wais Hotaki, of the greater Ghelzai Pashtun tribe, defeated the Saffavids and ended their rule in Qandahar. About the time of Mir Wais's death

---

[18.] Ahady, "Afghanistan: State Breakdown," 170.
[19.] Oleson, "Islam and Politics in Afghanistan," 116.

in 1715, Asad-allah, of the Sadduzai branch of the Abdali (Dorrani) tribe, de-feated Persian rule in Herat and extended his domain to greater Khorasan.

In 1722, Shah Mahmud, Mir Wais's son, overthrew the Saffavids in Iran and occupied their capital in Esfahan. Although the Hotakis of Qandahar were soon overthrown by Nader Afshar of Iran, their short-lived rule prepared the way for the establishment of a central state in Afghanistan. In October 1747, after the death of Nader Shah (1736-1747), a grand intertribal assembly (*Loya-Jerga*) of Ghelzai, Abdali, Tajek, Uzbek, Hazara, and Baluch chieftains met in Qandahar and elected Ahmad Khan Sadduzai (later called Ahmad Shah Baba) as their sov-ereign. The tribal chiefs pledged their allegiance, thus establishing the Sadduzai dynasty (1747-1842) in Afghanistan and ushering in two and a half centuries of Pashtun rule. Under Ahmad Shah Dorrani (1747-1773), the region gradually came together to form modern Afghanistan.[20]

State-Tribal Coalition under the Auspices of Islam

Pashtun tribes constituted the military force and hence the basis of central authority. Although Ahmad Khan was elected *shah* (king) and given the title *baba* (intertribal patriarch), tribal leaders regarded him as not more than a chief. This dichotomy in power structure existed from early on. The ruler's actions and decisions were to comply with the precepts of the *shari`at,* as well as with the principles of *pashtunwali,* the tribal code of honor that defined individual be-havior within the community and the procedures of conduct between tribes. Although legitimacy of power was determined by the *shari`at,* it was negotiated with tribal leaders. Because of the absence of a formulated procedure for suc-cession, the claimants to the throne relied heavily on the goodwill of tribal lead-ers. Political leadership "depended much more on personal qualities of the ruler than obedience or loyalty to authority."[21]

Ahmad Shah solidified and expanded his authority by military conquest and by co-opting the Islamic doctrine of governance. His military expeditions, which built an empire,[22] established him as a leader of *jehad*; for example, the battle of Panipat (1761), the high point of Ahmad Shah's military feats in the Indian subcontinent, was deemed a *jehad* against the Maharata Hindus in de-fense of the Muslim Mogul dynasty. His military expeditions, which resulted in the annexation of parts of northern India, eastern Persia, and Transoxiana, de-

---

[20.] Ahmad Shah's domain, the outline of present-day Afghanistan, consisted of Qandahar, Herat, and Sistan, which had been under the control of the Saffavids; Kabulistan, con-sisting of the southern and southwestern regions ruled by the Moguls of India; and Balkh, Takharistan, Badakhshan, and Maimana in the north, which were ruled by Uzbek princes.
[21.] Olesen "The Political Use of Islam in Afghanistan," 63.
[22.] Ferrier delimited the Afghan empire at this time as follows: the Oxus River and mountains of Kafaristan at the north, the Sea of Oman at the south, the mountains of Ti-bet and the Sutlej and the Indus Rivers at the east, and Khorasan, Persia proper, and Kir-man at the west. Ferrier, *History of the Afghans,* 94.

flected the militant tribes' activities from internal strife to territorial expansion. Victory in various battles enhanced Ahmad Shah's image, both as a military commander and a Muslim ruler. By relinquishing to the Mogul rulers all the conquered territories in India up to the Sind River, Ahmad Shah showed that the purpose of his military campaign in India was intended as a *jehad* in defense of Islam, not for territorial gains.

Afghan historians characterize Ahmad Shah as a genuinely religious man. According to `Abd al-Haiy Habibi, he was a staunch Hanafi Sunni, well versed in the *shari`at*. With consolidation of power under Ahmad Shah, Hanafi doctrine—one of the four recognized schools of law in Sunni Islam, founded by Abu Hanifa (d. 767)—became the official rite of Afghan legal procedure.[23] Ahmad Shah developed an elaborate justice department, based on the Hanafi school of law, along with a religious council headed by a supreme ecclesiastic judge (*khan molla khan,* or *molla-bashi*) to advise him on important state affairs. The justice department was headed by a chief magistrate. Subordinate officials ranged from a chief of legal tribunals and a chief justice to lower-echelon legal officials, such as executers of bodily penalties, religious judges (*qazis*), providers of legal opinion (*moftis*), and supervisors of public morality (*mohtasibs*).[24]

A number of other state-sponsored clerical positions were created during the time of Sadduzai rulers, including head of ecclesiastical education (*khan-i-`olum, modarres-bashi,* or *molla-bashi*); *imam* of the grand mosque in the capital; head preacher (*mir wa`ez*); and head of the clerical groups (*sadr-i-shahr)* in charge of religious endowments.[25] Ahmad Shah expanded the central authority by stressing the Islamic character of the state, and within the limits of the *shari`at,* he enacted regulations concerning everyday matters of state. This body of "ordinary law" (`*orf*) was subject to modification. State laws took the form of *farmans* (royal proclamations) or *fatawa* (plural of *fatwa,* judicial decision). Typical of such legislation was a set of rules compiled by the ulama in a volume entitled *Fatawa-i-Ahmad-Shahi* that was based on Hanafi law and provided the groundwork for administration of the state. Ordinary law was administered through the justice department.

The elaborate legal system did enhance the religious image of the state. It did not, however, totally offset the importance of the tribal code of ethics (*pashtunwali*). The tribal code, which determined the norms for matters related to honor and hospitality, female chastity, vengeance, and blood feud, continued to exist, with its jurisdiction often overlapping that of the *shari`at.* Its enforcement often posed a challenge to the central authority.

Timur Shah (1773-1793), Ahmad Shah's son and successor, was also a devoted adherent of Hanafism. During the latter's reign, all courts in Afghanistan

---

[23.] `Abd al-Haiy Habibi, *Tarikh-i-Mokhtasar-i-Afghanistan,* 2:99.

[24.] Fofalzai, *Dorrat al-Zaman fi Tarikh-i-Shah Zaman,* 272-273; Fofalzai, "Dar al-Qaza-i-Hozor-i-Lame` al-Nur-i-Fakhera-i-Ahmad Shahi Waqe` dar Qandahar," 9-27.

[25.] Elphinstone, *An Account of the Kingdom of Caubul,* 2:277.

were required to abide by tenets of the Hanafi school in every detail.[26] Timur Shah was also the founder of the *Tasbih-Khana*, a center for religious scholarly activities in Kabul.

RELIGIOUS GROUPS AND THEIR POWER

Religious groups in Afghanistan fell into two major categories, the ulama (plural of `alem, a learned man or religious scholar), who received training in religious schools and performed various services in society as professional experts in religious law, and the religious dignitaries, who were revered for piety and spiritual leadership. Both of these groups, and particularly the latter, exerted great influence over the masses.

The Ulama

In Islam there is no equivalent of the Christian priesthood. There are no rituals performed by religious leaders that cannot legitimately be performed by a faithful layman. Nevertheless, over time there emerged a group of religious scholars, the ulama, who held a certain degree of authority over the laypeople. As experts in religious law, the ulama became the spokesmen for the Qur'anic verse commanding good and forbidding evil and religious guides to the community of believers on all matters concerning the *shari`at*. Their members included jurists, teachers, legal advisors, judges, leaders of prayers, and preachers.

Although the ulama were never a cohesive body, their position as intermediaries between the ruler and the ruled, as administrators of justice, and as legal experts on state matters made them a powerful force in Islamic society. Their power as a group began to emerge during the early `Abbasid period. Their role expanded with the development of *mazaheb* (schools of jurisprudence), at which time it became exceedingly difficult for the layman to understand the intricacies of the *shari`at*. As interpreters of religious law, their influence was pervasive. The ulama's influence increased significantly during the rule of the Seljuqs and toward the end of the `Abbasid caliphate. The jurist Mohammad Al-Ghazali ranked "an eagerness to visit the ulama and to hear their advice as the next most important quality or characteristic of the ruler after justice"[27] and maintained that the best ruler "was he who associated with the ulama."[28] His near contemporary Ibn Jama`a (b. 1241) emphasized the ulama's explicit role in the state. Ibn Taymmiyya considered them to be "the heirs of the prophet."[29]

The degree of power among the ulama varied according to the individual `alem's rank, knowledge, piety, position, and relationship to other important ulama (an `alem benefitted from being the son, student, or close associate of a

---

[26.] Fofalzai, *Timur Shah Dorrani*, 1:41.

[27.] Al-Ghazali, *Nasihat al-Muluk*, 27, quoted in Lambton, 119.

[28.] Lambton, *ibid.*

[29.] *Ibid.*, 139.

prominent `alem`). Those ulama who served the state held high religious positions and were directly answerable to the central civil authority. The lower-ranking rural ulama had a much greater degree of autonomy. They did not exert the same influence over state matters as their urban counterparts, but because of their intimate association with the grassroots population, they exercised great influence over the people. As spokesmen for the masses, the lower-ranking clergy have been pivotal in almost all religious rebellions throughout the Muslim world.[30] Whenever the central authority has been weakened and has lost broad popular support, both the lower-ranking and higher-ranking ulama have assumed great political power. A main source of the ulama's power in Afghanistan was their influence with militant tribes.

Divisions among the Ulama

The group structure and authority of the ulama in Afghanistan were typical of that of the ulama in other Sunni Muslim communities. The ulama held three major roles: 1) administrators of Islamic law, 2) instructors in *madrasa*s, and 3) mosque functionaries. Mosque functionaries included callers to prayer, leaders of prayers, and preachers (*khatib* or *wa`ez*). The ulama's importance was reinforced by other functions, such as guarding shrines, collecting alms, certifying documents, and conducting marriages and funerals. Within the Afghan ulama, there were three distinguishable groups: 1) the state-employed, high-ranking ulama, 2) the lower-ranking ulama, mostly local mosque functionaries, and 3) the ulama affiliated with sufi (mystic) orders. This last group was independent of state control.

To become an `alem`, one must acquire religious knowledge under one or several recognized scholars at a *madrasa* in Afghanistan or another Muslim country. The curriculum of the *madrasa* consisted principally of religious studies: commentary on the Qur'an (*tafsir*), the sayings and actions of the Prophet (*hadith*), principles of jurisprudence (*feqh*), logic, philosophy, and Arabic grammar. Sometimes nonreligious studies such as geometry, Arabic and Persian literature, traditional medicine, and mathematics were added to religious studies, and in those cases teaching was shared by two teachers, one specializing in religious and the other in nonreligious studies. Teachers were trained in Afghanistan, Egypt, Turkey, Hejaz, India, and Bokhara.[31]

Prominent religious schools in Afghanistan in the nineteenth and early twentieth centuries were the *madrasa*s of Qal`a-i-Qazi Beig in Kabul, Tagab (or Taqaw), Qandahar, Qunduz, Rustaq, Peshawar (a part of Afghanistan until the

---

[30.] For examples of revolts instigated by lower clergy see Baer, "The Ulama in Modern History," 23.

[31.] Upon completing their studies, students received diplomas signed by a board of examiners consisting of seven ulama. Graduation involved the ceremony of wrapping the turban (*dastar-bandi*), wherein seven ulama each tied a portion of a seven-yard-long turban around the graduate's head. Ne`mat-Allah Shahrani, Oct. 1976.

mid-nineteenth century), Shilgahr in southwest Ghazni and Hadda, near Jalalabad. The Kokaltash *madrasa* in Bokhara, which specialized in Hanafi law, attracted scholars from Kabul, Qandahar, Herat, Balkh, and Badakhshan and received princely subsidies from the Dorrani rulers.[32] Later, the religious school
founded in 1867 in Deoband, India, acquired a comparable reputation as a Hanafi *madrasa* and drew many students from the southern and eastern provinces
of Afghanistan. At the beginning of the twentieth century, some of the most influential ulama in Afghanistan were graduates of Deoband College, which may
in part explain the close bond between the Indian and Afghan Islamists during
the first three decades of the twentieth century.

The prestige an `alem enjoyed depended in large measure on the scholarly
reputation of his chief master. For example, the celebrated Molla Din Mohammad (known as Moshk-i-`Alam) owed his fame as much to the reputation of his
renowned master Mia Mohammad Aslam as to his own scholarly achievements.
The master honored him with the name Moshk-i-`Alam (Scent of the World) to
reflect his intimate acquaintance with all matters of religion. Later Moshk-i-
`Alam was able to establish his own *madrasa* in Shilghar in Ghazni for training
the sons of *molla*s, and he attracted many students from the Logar, Ghazni,
Wardak, Jalalabad, and Hotaki districts.[33]

In the time of Ahmad Shah and his successors (1747-1842), the *madrasa*s in
Afghanistan were supported by land grants from the crown and wealthy bureau-
crats.[34] Thereafter, until the time of Amir `Abd al-Rahman (1880-1901), the
*madrasa*s of Afghanistan were independent of the government and were supported by religious endowments and public donations in cash or in kind, which
paid the teachers' salaries and the students' room and board. Most of the *zakat*
(alms) and other charities also supported the students.[35]

Founded in Kabul by Amir `Abd al-Rahman (1879-1901) to improve the
quality of religious training,[36] the Royal Madrasa was the first state-sponsored
madrasa. Specializing in Islamic law, the Royal Madrasa (Madrasa-i-Shahi)
attracted about two hundred students, whose expenses were paid by the state.[37]
Its graduates constituted the majority of the high-ranking state-employed ulama
under Amir Habib-Allah (1901-1919) and King Aman-Allah (1919-1929).

The ulama usually carried titles indicating the level of their scholarly
achievement and the school where they studied. The title *sheikh* referred to outstanding scholars who had completed their education in one of the leading *madrasa*s in Hejaz or in Egypt and to the leaders of sufi orders. According to the
Hedayat al-`Orfan, a nineteenth-century Naqshbandi text, *sheikh* referred to an
expert in the *shari`at*, a firm believer, a spiritual leader, and a recipient of per-

---

[32] Fofalzai, *Dorrat al-Zaman*, 402.

[33] BACSOA, 13-44.

[34] *Ibid.*

[35] Ne`mat-Allah Shahrani, Oct. 1976.

[36] Kateb, *Seraj al-Tawarikh*, 1913-14, 3:942.

[37] Kakar, *Government and Society in Afghanistan*, 162.

mission to preach from the leader of a sufi order.[38] The title *Mawlawi* (my master), denoting a specialist in Islamic law, was originally borne by a graduate of a religious school in India; later, high-ranking state-employed ulama often adopted this title. *Dahmolla* (*dah* meaning ten, and *molla* meaning learned man or scholar who can guide ten *molla*s) was used in northern Afghanistan for religious scholars who had received their training in Bokhara. *Molla* (learned man) was used for a graduate of a local *madrasa*. Until the beginning of the twentieth century, all religious scholars were called *molla*s, but the term was later restricted to mosque functionaries.

The high-ranking clergy were government-employed ecclesiastic judges, jurists, teachers in government-sponsored *madrasa*s, courtiers who interpreted the law and advised the king, leaders of congregational prayer, and preachers at major mosques in the capital and other large cities. As the most highly educated citizens, they filled important administrative positions in the government, and as custodians of Islam, it was their responsiblity to guide the state on a righteous course. The *qazi*s (ecclesiastical judges) and the *mofti*s (legal advisors) ranked high in the religious hierarchy and composed the most powerful group of ulama. Although appointed by the government, they exercised full jurisdiction within the bounds of the *shari`at*.  The source of the *qazi*'s power was the right to determine the type of or discretionary (*ta`zirat*) punishments meted out, which gave them a broad scope of legal power. Several small important families dominated the upper echelons of the ulama hierarchy.[39]

[38.] `Omarjan, *Hedayat al-`Orfan*, 59.

[39.] A prominent Barakzai family from Qandahar produced several generations of great *qazi*s. From the time of Ahmad Shah (1747-1773) until the War of Independence in 1919, the office of head of ecclesiastical education was occupied exclusively by the Barakzai family. (See Table 1) According to the author of *Tarikh-i-Mazarat-i-Kabul*, this priestly family left behind close to 12,000 unpublished manuscripts and an enormous estate. Khalil, *Tarikh-i-Mazarat-i-Kabul,* 111.

Another important clerical family descended from Qazi Faiz-Allah, the Grand Qazi (*qazi al-qozat*) under Timur Shah, who enjoyed great power and prestige and possessed a large estate. The office of head preacher was held for several generations by a priestly family from Chahardehi, near Kabul. The first prominent member of this family was Mir Esma`il, an important Naqshbandi *sheikh* and head preacher under Timur Shah.  Mir Esma`il was the son of Mir Abu Qasim, a Naqshbandi sheikh who settled in Kabul after spending several years in Kashmir, Bokahra, and Samarqand. The family claimed descendance from the Prophet through Ebrahim bin Musa Kazim. Mir Esma`il succeeded his father as a leader of the Naqshbandiyya order and established headquarters (Khaneqah-i-Islamabad) near Kabul. (Sayyid Makhdom Rahim, 1993)

Mir Esma`il's son, Mir Ahmad, was an eminent `alem who held the same position under Timur Shah's successors, enjoyed enormous prestige, and had thousands of followers in the region. `Ata Mohammad Shekarpuri, *Nawa-i-Ma`arek*, quoted in Fofalzai, *Dorrat al-Zaman fi Tarikh-i-Shah Zaman*, 274.

The latter's son, Mir Mohammad Ma`sum, also known as Hafezji or Mir Hajji, and his grandson, Mir `Atiq-Allah, were among the most influential ulama of Afghanistan in the second half of the nineteenth century.

The increase in the ulama's political influence was accompanied by increased economic power. The higher ulama obtained a share of land revenues and even acquired large parcels of land in the capital. By 1879, about a third of the revenue of each province was dedicated to the upkeep of the religious establishment.[40] The extended estate of Sayyid Ahmad Mir Wa`ez, for example, comprised almost one third of the city of Kabul.[41]

Apparently, marriages between royalty and families of ulama were quite common. In his autobiography, Amir `Abd al-Rahman proudly describes the union of his son Habib-Allah with the daughter of Qazi Sa`d al-Din as a marriage by which he succeeded in establishing a blood relationship with influential families in Afghanistan.[42] Such marriages strengthened the political position of the parties involved and increased the influence of the high-ranking ulama at the official level.

As well as holding influence in political and economic spheres, many ulama played an active role in promoting the study of philosophy, history, and literature. In fact, most Afghan literary works written during the eighteenth, nineteenth, and early twentieth centuries was produced by religious scholars. Hazrat Baqi Qayyum Jahan Mojaddedi was one of the greatest poets of the later centuries. Although his complete works of poetry have not been preserved, his scattered poems have been published in various Afghan newspapers and magazines.[43] His father, Shah Saffih-Allah, was the author of five books, and another member of this clerical family, Shah Fazl-Allah, was the author of `Omdat al-Moqamat, the history of the Mojaddedies up to the time of Shah Saffi-Allah (1126-1212/1748-1833).

The lower-ranking mollas served in the mosques of small towns and villages and in the more remote or smaller districts of the large cities. They led daily prayers, conducted marriages and funerals, and taught in the mosque schools. In the absence of a qazi, they registered documents as notaries and issued judicial opinions on matters related to marriage and inheritance; their activities also were interwoven with the daily life of the people, among whom they exercised great influence. Unlike the high ulama, who depended on royal appointments, the local mollas were supported by their communities and were largely free from government control. Sources of income were alms, fees from marriages and funerals, and grants of land from tribal leaders and villagers.

[40.] Ghani, "Islam and State-building in a Tribal Society," 271.

A district, a park, and a fortress in Kabul were among the extensive property holdings of the descendants of Qazi Faiz-Allah.

[41.] The part of Kabul that once belonged to the descendants of Mir Ahmad was referred to as the awqaf-i-mir wa`ez in the official listings of the revenue office.

[42.] Mir Munshi, The Life of Abdur Rahman, 2:11. Amir `Abd al-Rahman himself was married to Bibi Halima (alias Bobojan), the daughter of Mir `Attiq-Allah, a grandson of the famous Mir Wa`ez. Similarly, Mir `Attiq-Allah was married to Shams-i-Jahan, the daughter of Amir Dust Mohammad Khan.

[43.] Dar'ert al-Ma`aref-i-Afghanistan, 3:587.

Mosques were centers of news and local discussion, and *molla*s played a role in informing the community of important local or national issues, thus maintaining communications between the mosques and the local people. In tribal areas, the *molla*s were especially influential because of their role as mediators in the tribal *jerga*s.

The majority of the lower- and higher-ranking ulama were concentrated in the eastern and southern provinces, where, due to the shortage of farm land, clerical occupation formed the most common means of livelihood.

Spiritual Leaders (*Ruhaniun*)

Roy Mottahedeh distinguishes two types of religious leadership in Islam: "leadership in piety" and "leadership in religiously defined local functions."[44] He argues that because of the great importance attributed by Muslim theologians to piety as the only lasting virtue, men who devoted their lives to God and lived exemplary religious lives were greatly revered. Even kings solicited the intercession of such pious men, for both spiritual and political reasons.[45] In Afghanistan, the leaders of sufi orders, their devout adherents, and pious men who claimed noble religious lineage exercised "leadership in piety." Generally referred to as the *ruhaniun*, they commanded great respect among the people and some were even regarded as friends of God (*awliya'*) who had reached the highest level of spirituality. They usually bore appellations such as *sayyid, hazrat, padshah, shah, shahzada, naqib, mir, mian, ishan, khwaja, akhundzada*, or *sahebzada*, that denoted their noble ancestry. A late-nineteenth-century report on tribal affairs in the North-West Frontier, prepared by British political agents, included explanations of some of these appellations: *Sayyid* (singular for *sadat*) is "the term given to the descendants of the Prophet," who, "owing to their large number and varying circumstances, are not given precedence over other spiritual leaders"; *mian*s are the descendants of spiritual leaders of past centuries "who have acquired a wide reputation among many tribes, and not a merely local reputation"; *akhundzada*s, sometimes also known as *pirzada*, are the offspring of religious leaders "of merely local reputation"; *sahebzada*s are descendants of *molla*s "who have gained a reputation for learning or sanctity."[46]

Leaders of the Sufi Orders (*Ahl-i-Tariqat*)

The Afghan ulama enjoyed a compatible relationship with the leaders of sufi orders. Most of the sufis had received orthodox religious training. Likewise, most ulama had sufi instruction and belonged to one or more orders. The leaders of the orders had many followers among the masses and enjoyed prestige as religious scholars as well. Their influence, then, was pervasive throughout the

---

[44.] Mottahedeh, *Loyalty and Leadership in Early Islamic Society*, 147.

[45.] *Ibid.*

[46.] McMahon and Ramsay, *Report on the Tribes of Dir, Swat, and Bajaour*, 20-21.

various strata of the population, including the ulama. Without specific offices in the religious structure, the sufi leaders (*pirs*) derived their power from the number of followers (*morids*) they attracted, their piety, their knowledge, and their ability to mobilize the masses. The absolute loyalty of a *morid* to the order allowed the leaders of orders to easily activate their followers.[47] The influence of the orders was prominent in Afghan society to the extent that almost every individual, including many high government officials, members of the royal family, and even rulers themselves, was the *morid* of a *pir*.

The most important orders in Afghanistan were the Qaderiyya, the Naqshbandiyya, the Chestiyya, and the Sahrawardiyya. In terms of number of adherents, the first two were probably the largest orders in Afghanistan.

Leaders of the Qaderiyya Order

The Qaderiyya order was established in northern Afghanistan during the thirteenth century. Adherents of the Qaderiyya order were concentrated in eastern and southern Afghanistan, Turkistan, Herat, and among the Dorranis. In the early nineteenth century, Sheikh Sa`d-Allah Gailani, a descendant of the order's founder, `Abd al-Qader Gailani (d. 1166), established headquarters in Siyawashan, south of Herat. Sheikh Sa`d-Allah belonged to the Jondiyya Baghdadiyya branch of the Qaderiyya order and was the first member of the Gailani family to settle in Afghanistan. Sayyid Hasan Affandi Gailani, known as the Naqib Saheb of Charbagh, also a descendant of `Abd al-Qader Gailani, came to Afghanistan from Baghdad in the early 1900s. He and his brothers, who had their seat in Baghdad, had many followers in Muslim countries.

Qaderiyya sheikhs and their disciples in the southern and eastern parts of Afghanistan played significant roles as power brokers, instigators of *jehad*, and mobilizers of the masses. Their influence was based on their noble ancestry, their reputation for scholarship and piety, and their large following. Many were also connected by family ties to powerful tribal leaders, who relied on them for advice. They exerted power by means of a network that linked them, on the one hand, to the order, and on the other, to an important *madrasa* and/or shrine. Through subordinate *mollas*, usually their disciples, these Qaderiyya sheikhs wielded extensive power, especially with the people of their region. As independent scholars with *madrasas*, they trained a great number of local *mollas*. Some of them were also custodians of important shrines and closely tied by tribal origin to the people. (See Table 4)

---

[47] A *morid* is admonished not to render an oath of allegiance to a *sheikh* as his spiritual guide unless he is absolutely certain of his strong affection toward the *sheikh*, because once he becomes a *morid* of a *sheikh*, he has committed himself to total adherence. The *morbid* must obey the *sheikh*'s orders under all circumstances and without hesitancy, even if they seem ill-advised to him. Al-Mojaddedi, *Rahnoma-I-Tariq*, 104, 106.

Leaders of the Naqshbandiyya Order

The leaders belonging to the Mojaddedi branch of the Naqshbandiyya order played a significant cultural and political role in Afghanistan. The Afghan historian 'Abd al-Hai Habibi provides the following information about this priestly family:

> During the time of the Sadduzai emperors and in the later periods, the Mojaddedi family provided celebrated spiritual leaders, talented poets, and scholars. They were responsible for the spread of the Naqshbandiyya order throughout Central Asia, from Khorasan to Sirhind, Transoxiana, and the Chinese border. They inspired a type of Islamic culture which was unique to the region of Khorasan and which was based on both sufism and *shari'at*.[48]

Mohammad Fazl-Allah, the author of *'Omdat al-Moqamat*, the most reliable source for the history of the Mojaddedi Naqshbandis, traces the origin of this family to a man named Shahab al-Din Farrokhshah, a descendant of 'Omar, the second caliph, who settled in Afghanistan in the time of the Ghaznavids and was buried in the valley of Farokhshah in Panjshir, north of Kabul. Imam Rafi'al-Din, a lineal descendant of this man, went from Kabul to Sirhind.[49] One of his offspring, Sheikh Ahmad Mojaddad Alf al-Sani (the son of Mawlana 'Abd al-Ahad) was born in Sirhind. He was guided in the Naqshbandiyya order by Khwaja Mohammad Baqi Kabuli (1012/1663) and was known as a great scholar and spiritual leader in Afghanistan and India.[50]

According to the author of *'Omdat al-Moqamat*, the main precept of the Naqshbandi order was adherence to the *shari'at*. The *sheikhs* of the Naqshbandi considered the slightest deviation from the *shari'at* a consequential anomaly. They brought the order into full harmony with the *shari'at* and advocated the principle of commanding good and forbidding evil and *jehad* in the way of God.[51] Each leader of the Mojaddedi branch of the Naqshbandi order was well versed in the *shari'at* and was venerated both as an *'alem* and an *'aref* (one who knows the divine secrets). Unlike the esoteric sufis who led an ascetic life, the Naqshbandis discouraged celibacy and withdrawal from active life. This may account for their active involvement in social and political affairs. By showing reverence for other orders, the Mojaddedi leaders earned respect from and commanded influence among other sufi adherents as well.

Shah Faqir-Allah was probably the first Mojaddedi to reside in Qandahar. Although he later (1737) moved to Shekarpur in Sind, he had a great deal of influence with the royal court in Qandahar and wrote religious advice to Ahmad

---

[48.] Habibi, *Tarikh-i-Mokhtasar-i-Afghanistan*, 2: 137.
[49.] Fazl-Allah, *'Omdat al-Maqamat*, 99-102.
[50.] *Ibid.*, 153-156.
[51.] *Ibid.*, 275.

Shah Abdali and his vizier, Shah Wali Khan.[52] The Mojaddedis who later resided in Qandahar were descendants of Shah Gholam Mohammad Fazl-Allah (d. 1822). His grandson, whose name was also Mohammad Fazl-Allah, was a prominent religious figure in the time of Timur Shah and the author of the `Omdat al-Moqamat.

Other branches of Mojaddedies settled in Botkhak, Herat, Charbagh Safa of Jalalabad, and Kabul. As we shall see, the Kabuli branch, also known as the Hazrats of Shurbazar (a district in Kabul) were important in Afghan politics during the 1920s.

The Hazrats of Shurbazar were the offspring of Shah `Abd al-Baqi (d. 1870). `Abd al-Baqi's son Seddiq, his grandson Fazl-i-Qayyum, and the latter's sons Fazl Mohammad (also known as Shams al-Mashayikh), Fazl 'Omar (also known as Nur al-Mashayikh), and Mohammad Sadeq, as well as Shams al-Mashayikh's son Mian Jan, were among the most revered religious figures in Afghanistan. (See Table 2) At the beginning of the twentieth century, the influence of the Hazrats of Shurbazar reached its peak. They had many adherents among high government officials, court members, and even members of the royal family, and they commanded great respect among the tribes, particularly the Mangals and the Ghelzais.

Another branch of the Mojaddedis settled in Herat. The most prominent figures of this branch were the Hazrat sufi Islam Karrokhi, who came to Afghanistan from Bokhara during the last quarter of the nineteenth century and aided in defense of the city of Herat when it was attacked by Fath 'Ali Shah, the Qajar ruler of Persia. Next most important in this group was Hazrat Mohammad `Omar Jan who, with his sons Hazrat `Abd al-Baqi and Hazrat `Abd al-Karim, participated in the Maiwand War (1880) against the British. Later, representing the ulama of Herat, he traveled to Persia to persuade Ayyub Khan to return to Herat and lead the Herati forces against the British.

The Hazrats of Karrokh had great influence with the people of Herat and Maimana and were custodians of the sufi shrines in the area. Zia al-Ma`sum, known as the Hazrat Saheb of Charbagh (d. 1919), resided in Charbagh in Jalalabad and was an influential Mojaddedi in the early twentieth century. He was the spiritual guide of Amir Habib-Allah, Sardars Nasr-Allah, and 'Enayat-Allah "over all of whom he possessed considerable influence."[53]

THE ROLE OF RELIGIOUS LEADERS IN AFGHAN POLITICS, 1839-1880

As a result of continuing political instability, the influence of religious leaders increased steadily during the first three quarters of the nineteenth century. At Timur Shah's death in 1793, the Dorrani kingdom was engulfed in fratricidal strife among his twenty-six sons. Between 1800 and 1834, there were four

---

[52.] Khan, "The Naqshbandi Saints of Sind," 37.
[53.] Adamec, Who's Who of Afghanistan, 142.

changes of rulers, from Zaman Shah to Mahmud, from Mahmud to Shah Shoja`, from Shah Shoja` back to Mahmud, and then a shift of dynasty from Sadduzais to Barakzais (another branch of Dorrani Pashtuns). Wars of succession among Sadduzai princes and power struggles between Sadduzai and Mohammadzai (Barakzai) sardars offered religious leaders and tribal chiefs opportunities to assume greater power and influence. With the decentralization of the Sadduzai kingdom, the elaborate state-sponsored clerical hierarchy began to disintegrate, and independent clergy and sheikhs of the sufi orders gained increasing power.

Increasingly, religious leaders were called upon to legitimize political authority. During succession disputes, claimants to the throne frequently sought out influential religious leaders to support their claims and undermine their opponents. For example, the shift of power from the Sadduzai to the Mohammadzai dynasty was endorsed by Mir Hajji, the son of the famous Mir Wa`ez (Mir Ahmad), when the former crowned Dust Mohammad Khan in 1834 at the `Idqah Mosque in Kabul.[54] During the Second Anglo-Afghan War (1879-1880), Shams-i-Jahan, Amir Shir Ali's widow, solicited support from Molla Moshk-i-`Alam to place her exiled son, Ya`qub Khan, or grandson, Musa Jan, on the throne.[55]

The coronation ceremony (*dastar-bandi*) was usually performed by one or two religious leaders immediately following the accession of a new ruler in order to legitimize the new regime. It involved wrapping a white muslin turban around the head of the new ruler and reciting verses from the Qur`an, after which the conducting clergyman would give the amir a copy of the Qur`an, signifying the new amir's pledge to rule in accord with the teachings of the holy book. New rulers sought the most influential religious leader in the country to perform the ceremony, as the reputation of the clergyman performing the coronation ceremony revealed to some degree the existing level of political support for the new ruler. Zaman Shah, one of Timur Shah's sons and his first successor, postponed his ceremony rather than have it performed by lesser clergymen of the court, who were eager to do it. Instead, he went at night to the residence of Shah Saffi-Allah Mojaddedi, the most exalted spiritual leader in the country, to receive the ceremony.[56] Claimants continued to seek the support of high-ranking clergy until Amir `Abd al-Rahman gained the upper hand in 1880.

Clerical Resistance to Foreign Aggression

During the nineteenth century, Afghanistan became a major playing field in the "Great Game of Asia." Great Britain had established control over India in the eighteenth century. In 1779, Britain's sovereignty over the Indian subcontinent was recognized by the Treaty of Paris. During the first quarter of the nineteenth

---

[54.] Mohan Lal, *Life of the Amir Dost Mohammad Khan of Kabul*, 1:168-69; J. P. Ferrier, 203.
[55.] Hensman, *The Afghan War of 1879-80*, 264.
[56.] Fofalzai, *Dorrat al-Zaman fi Tarikh-i-Shah Zaman*, 22-23.

century, while the British consolidated their power in India, Czarist Russia expanded the territory under its control to the south by subjugating and annexing central Asian kingdoms and northern parts of Persia (the Caspian provinces and the towns of Darband and Baku). Russia's steady advances created anxiety in Great Britain for the safety of its Indian empire. Afghanistan's strategic location as the "gateway to India" made it a focal point of British diplomatic and military strategy for decades. British invasions of Afghan territory resulted in the First and Second Anglo-Afghan Wars.

As Mehdi Farrokh has pointed out, every segment and every ethnic group of Afghan society was involved in Afghanistan's armed resistance against the British invaders.[57] Particularly active in the First and Second Anglo-Afghan Wars, the clergy served as participants and as mobilizers and leaders of the masses. Resentment toward the foreign occupiers united diverse Afghan forces against the British, and religious leaders stood at the forefront of the opposition as defenders of Islam and advocates of *jehad*. The call to *jehad* became the most effective catalyst for the defense of Afghanistan's territorial integrity and traditional culture during the nineteenth and early twentieth centuries.

The First Anglo-Afghan War (1838-1842)

The origin of British involvement in Afghanistan can be traced to Russian expansion into northwest Persia during the 1820s. Ahmad Shah, the Qajar ruler of Persia, was encouraged by the Russians to compensate for losses in the northwest by seizing Herat, at the time ruled by Kamran, a grandson of Timur Shah Sadduzai. In 1837, the Russian-backed Persian army attacked and besieged Herat. The siege of the city aroused a general uprising against the Persians, and religious leaders raised the banner of *jehad* against them. Mawlawi `Abd al-Haqq, a leading clergyman in Herat, declared that fighting the Shi`ite invaders was the "great *jehad*" *(jehad-i-akbar)* and a religious duty of all citizens. The declaration was distributed in pamphlet form throughout the city and generated an immediate response. Thousands of citizens, wearing white shrouds and carrying banners, joined forces to defend the city against the invaders.[58] According to Ferrier,

> The Afghans distinguished themselves daily by the most daring attacks on the besiegers: sometimes a handful of horsemen would issue from the town, charge a whole corps of Persian infantry, and never retire without many prisoners or committing great slaughter; sometimes a detachment would fight till the death of the last man among them.[59]

[57.] Farrokh, *Tarikh-i-Siyasi-i-Afghanistan*, 32.

[58.] Kateb, *Seraj al-Tawarikh* 1:135; Ghobar, 406; Fofalzai, *Dorrat al-Zaman*, 116.

[59.] Ferrier, 235-236.

While the Persians were engaged in the siege of Herat, a Russian mission led by Captain Vicovitch arrived in Kabul to establish commercial relations with the Afghan ruler, Amir Dust Mohammad Khan, who had seized power from the Sadduzais in 1834.[60]

Great Britain perceived the attack on Herat by the Persians and the dispatch of a mission to Kabul as preludes to a Russian invasion of India through Afghanistan. The British responded by occupying Kharak, the Iranian island in the Persian Gulf, forcing the Persians to relinquish claims over Herat. The British further tried to extend their control northward in order to preempt further Russian maneuvers. The best way to prevent Russian influence in Afghanistan was to install a ruler in Kabul who was well disposed to British interests. In 1838, Lord Auckland, the British governor-general of India, entered into negotiations with Shah Shoja`, the deposed Sadduzai ruler of Afghanistan (1804-1809), then in exile in India, and with Maharajah Rangit Singh, the Sikh ruler of Panjab, who had steadily advanced into Sadduzai territory in northern India, to enlist their cooperation in a joint military venture against Amir Dust Mohammad Khan. A treaty signed in 1838 by the three parties promised Shah Shoja` the throne of Afghanistan on the condition that he accept permanent stationing of British troops in Kabul. Parts of Afghanistan, including areas that later came to be known as the North-West Frontier Province (of British India), were promised to Ranjit Singh. In 1839, the combined forces, known as the Army of the Indus, advanced toward Kabul, and on August 7, they reinstalled Shah Shoja` on the throne of Afghanistan with little resistance, forcing Amir Dust Mohammad Khan to flee to Bokhara.

Initially, the British invasion did not generate strong opposition, perhaps because it was simply viewed as aid to the deposed Sadduzai king in a dynastic power struggle. The situation remained calm until 1841, when William Mac-Naghten, the British representative in Kabul, took charge of government affairs, and it became apparent that the king was only a puppet. According to Ferrier, one of the main causes of unrest was dissemination of a Persian translation of the Bible by the British and overt British missionary activities in Afghanistan.[61]

Opposition to British occupation began in Kabul and spread quickly to the provinces, with mosques serving as communications centers. The ulama refused to read the Friday sermon (*khotba*) in the mosques in the name of Shah Shoja`, alleging they could do so only for an independent sovereign and that Shah Shoja` was not independent.[62] In the city of Ghazni, Sayyid Qasem, a local religious leader, led a challenge to British control that resulted in the death of Colonel Herring, an important British officer.[63] Afterward, Mir Masjedi raised

---

[60] By 1838, as the result of intense internal strife among Dorrani princes, large portions of Dorrani or Sadduzai territory, such as Punjab, Kashmir, and Moltan, had been lost to the Sikhs, and local leaders in northern Afghanistan were proclaiming independence.

[61] Ferrier, 334, not confirmed by other sources.

[62] *Ibid.*, 332.

[63] *Ibid*, 335.

the banner of *jehad* against the foreign occupiers in Kohistan, north of Kabul. Recognizing the gravity of the situation, Macnaghten imprisoned several leading clergy. Finally, on November 2, 1841, during the early morning prayer, Mir Wa`ez Hajji Ma`sum (also known as Hafezji) proclaimed *jehad* in the Pol-i-Kheshti Mosque in Kabul. Holy war was immediately proclaimed in other mosques.

The role of religious leaders was prominent throughout the war. Not only did they preach *jehad*, but they also carried banners and fought alongside the military forces. In addition, they traveled to villages to persuade the people not to sell food to the British.[64]

The uprising gained momentum with the return from Bokhara of Sardar Mohammad Akbar Khan, the exiled son of Amir Dust Mohammad, and ultimately resulted in the defeat of the British and the death of Shah Shoja`, who had become the target of public hatred because of his alliance with the British. MacNaghten and his assistant, Major Alexander Burns, were killed. British garrisons at Kabul, Ghazni, and Qandahar were at once beleaguered, and communication with India was virtually cut off. Major Pottinger, the remaining British officer, abruptly concluded an agreement to evacuate the country. In January 1842, 4,500 British troops left Kabul for Jalalabad. Only Dr. William Bryden, a medical officer, survived the continuous attacks on route through the passes. The first British invasion of Afghanistan had thus ended in disaster. In 1869, Talboys Wheeler, the assistant secretary of the British Foreign Department in India, wrote that British occupation of Afghanistan was an incident that excites "more painful feelings than any other episode in the history of British India, excepting perhaps the mutiny of 1857."[65]

Although the British retaliated by attacking and burning the grand bazaar of Kabul in September of that same year, they made no attempt to remain in Afghanistan and withdrew immediately to India. The negotiations that followed resulted in a peace settlement. British policy makers saw it in their interest to adopt a policy of noninterference (or "Masterly Inactivity").

As a result of the peace settlement with the British, Dust Mohammad Khan of the Barakzai tribe, who had initially gained power in 1834, returned to the Afghan throne. His reaccession to power (1842-1867) was made possible, in large part, by the leading role his son, Sardar Akbar Khan, had played in the *jehad*. Dust Mohammad Khan founded the Mohammadzai dynasty, which retained power in Afghanistan until the establishment of a republican government in 1973. Instead of the title "shah," Dust Mohammad Khan adopted "amir," a term with religious connotations given to him earlier by Mir Ma`sum, the Mir

---

[64] Key religious figures were Mir Hajji Ma`sum and Mir Darwish (both sons of Sayyid Ahmad, Mir Wa`ez of Kabul), Mir Masjedi, Mir Mahbub Kabuli, Mir Gained, and Molla Ahmad. Ghobar, 544-550.
[65] Wheeler, *Memorandum on Afghanistan Affairs from A.D. 1700*, 112.

Wa`ez of Kabul.[66]  The title signified his role as the commander of the faithful (*amir al-mo`menin*) and the leader of *jehad* (against Ranjit Singh at the time of the latter's initial encroachments on Afghan territory).[67] Conceived as a religious duty, commitment to *jehad* was now a prerequisite for political legitimacy.

Amir Dust Mohammad's greatest achievement was the creation of a unified country. To retain power, he carefully balanced his relations with his politically ambitious brothers and with Great Britain. As a result of his cautious dealings with the British, he experienced several clashes with religious leaders. The ulama openly criticized him for agreements made with the British in 1855 and 1857 that had resulted in the loss of Peshawar and other southern territories to British India.[68] He resisted their pressure to wage *jehad* against the British to recover Peshawar and to defend Indian Muslims during the Sepoy Mutiny (May 1857).[69] Nevertheless, he managed to retain legitimacy, partly because in domestic matters he followed the rules of the *shari`at* and exhibited great piety.

Emergence of Warrior Sheikhs along the Indo-Afghan Border

As a result of the occupation of Peshawar by the British and the failure of the Sepoy Mutiny of 1858 to restore Muslim rule in India, an anti-British movement began in the Pashtun tribal region along the Indo-Afghan border. The leader of the movement was a "priest magistrate" in Swat, Molla `Abd al-Ghafur, known as the Akhundzada Saheb of Swat (d. 1878).  As a Qaderiyya *sheikh*, who traced his spiritual authority through a chain of eight predecessors to `Abd al-Qader Gailani,[70] he commanded enormous influence among the tribes, whom he united under the banner of *jehad* against the British. With numerous religious warriors (*ghazi*s) behind him, Molla `Abd al-Gafur turned Swat, a region in the vicinity of Peshawar, into a base for holy war (*ghaza*) against the British. The British portrayed him as a powerful religious leader "occupied day and night plotting against us."[71] In 1863 the Akhundzada of Swat took an active part in Ambeyla campaign in support of Indian Muslim resistant groups, the so-called Hindustani Fanatics.[72] Thus, tribal politics mingled with anti-British activities became a

---

[66.] The ulama argued that "the religious wars fought under the name and flag of any other than a king cannot entitle the warriors to the rights and honors of martyrdom....In `Idgah [the grand mosque in Kabul], Mir Vaiz [Wa`ez], the head priest of Kabul, put a few blades of grass on the head of the Sardar and called him [*amir al-mo'menin*]." Mohan Lal, 1:168-169; F. M. Kateb, *Seraj al-Tawarikh*, 1:127.

[67.] Kateb, *Ibid*; Reshtiya, *Afghanistan dar Qarn-i-Nozda*, 63.

[68.] Gregorian, *The Emergence of Modern Afghanistan*, 83.

[69.] *Ibid*. In his diary, Amir `Abd al-Rahman expressed disappointment at Dust Mohammad Khan's failure to take advantage of this opportunity to recover Punjab from the British. Mir Munshi, *The Life of Abdur Rahman*, 1:69-70.

[70.] Interview with Sayyid `abd al-Qayyum, known as Pacha Saheb, one of the last *sheikh*s in the line of the Akhundzada of Swat, Peshawar, Sept., 1994 (See Table 3).

[71.] Raverty, *Notes on Afghanistan and Baluchistan*, 251, f.n.

[72.] McMahon and Ramsay, 22.

dominant force in the Pashtun tribal regions on both sides of the border, and as will be seen in the following chapters, affected Afghanistan's relations with British India for decades to come. Molla `Abd al-Ghafur's *madrasa* in Swat produced a number of warrior *sheikh*s, including such figures as Molla Najm al-Din (the Molla of Hadda), Molla Mahmud Akhundzada, Molla Wali Moham-mad (or Sapri Molla), Palam Molla, Sahebzada Musahi, Molla Hamz-Allah, Sayyid Akbar Aka Kheil, and Molla `Abd al-Wahab Manki, who continued Molla `Abd al-Ghafur's tradition of strong commitment to the cause of *jehad*.

The Second Anglo-Afghan War (1878-1880)

The second British invasion of Afghanistan was provoked by a steady advance of Czarist Russia into Central Asia in the 1860s and 70s. When Benjamin Dis-raeli came to power in Great Britain, British policy toward Afghanistan was redefined. The policy of "Masterly Inactivity" was abandoned in favor of what came to be known as the "Forward Policy," which consisted of moving forward into Afghan territory, gaining control, and creating a buffer state to protect In-dia. By this time the British had occupied Sind (in 1842) and Punjab (in 1849) and had positioned themselves closer to the Afghan border.

In 1878, a Russian diplomatic mission headed by General Stelietov arrived uninvited at the court of Amir Shir `Ali Khan (1867-1879), Dust Mohammad Khan's son and successor. Enraged at the Russian presence in Kabul, Lord Lytton, the viceroy of India, demanded that the amir promptly receive a compa-rable British legation in Kabul. Amir Shir `Ali Khan's refusal to accede imme-diately to the demand afforded the British an excuse to invade Afghanistan. In November 1878, British troops attacked Qandahar, Kurram, and Kabul. As they approached the capital, Shir `Ali Khan, who was mourning the sudden death of the crown prince, fled north, leaving in charge a weak and ailing son, Ya`qub Khan. Lacking the will and ability to resist, Ya`qub Khan signed the Treaty of Gandomak in May 1879, which imposed on the new amir a permanent British mission in Kabul and ceded the Kurram Valley and Khyber Pass to British India.

On September 3, 1879, a mutiny over pay in the Herati regiment in the capi-tal gave rise to a violent revolt in the city, which resulted in the death of Sir Louis Cavangnari and several other British officers stationed in Kabul. This incident precipitated another British expedition into Afghanistan under the command of General Frederick Roberts, whose troops entered Kabul on October 18. At that point, Amir Mohammad Ya`qub abdicated and agreed to exile in India.

In the absence of strong central leadership, the clergy once again became the major force in mobilizing the Afghan population against the British. In the early stages of the war, the influential Molla Khwaja Nazir rallied followers in Chara-sia, near Kabul, in a fierce battle[73] that included female villagers among the

---

[73.] Hensman, 85.

combatants.[74] Ulama in Ghazni began giving defiant sermons in the mosques, and the practice was quickly taken up in Kohistan and Kabul.

The most important leader of the Second Anglo-Afghan War was Molla Din Mohammad, known as Moshk-i-`Alam (1790-1886), referred to by Forbes as "Peter Hermit of Afghanistan."[75] Moshk-i-`Alam adhered to the Qaderiyya order and enjoyed great reverence for his highly acclaimed *madrasas* in Ander and Shilgahr (in Ghazni), which attracted many students from Logar, Ghazni, Wardak, Qalat-i-Ghelzai, Hotaki, and districts of Jalalabad. On December 2, Molla Moshk-i-`Alam declared *jehad* in Ghazni and then proceeded toward Kabul with General Mohammad Jan Logari, Molla `Abd al-Ghaffur Langari, Mir Bacha Kohistani, and Akhundzada Mir `Osman Tagawi. Despite his advanced age, Moshk-i-`Alam launched a vigorous campaign against the British.

In the name of Musa Jan, the crown prince, Moshk-i-`Alam, took command of Afghan forces in Kabul.[76] At midnight on December 23, the night before the holy day of `ashura, Moshk-i-`Alam ascended the Asmai heights and lit a beacon, signaling various forces to attack Shirpur. While the onslaught forced the British to retreat within the walls of their Shirpur cantonment,[77] General Roberts regained control of Kabul. Howard Hensman, who accompanied the British army as a special correspondent for the *Pioneer* (published in Alahabad, India) and the *Daily News* (published in London), wrote in his diary:

> nearly every fighting man in North-Eastern Afghanistan flocked to the banners consecrated by Moshk-i-`Alam; and if the success of the jihad had been a little longer-lived—say by the interception of our reinforcements—there would have been streams of men setting in for Cabul [Kabul] from Turkistan, Badakhshan, and the Shutargardan district.[78]

In February 1880, the *jehad* led by Molla Moshk-i-`Alam regained momentum and prevented General Donald Stewart from advancing into Kabul. "By July, Lord Lytton's views about occupying Afghanistan had undergone a complete *volte-face*. Now he could not withdraw from Afghanistan quickly enough."[79] Russia's change of attitude regarding Afghanistan provided a good reason for withdrawal. On February 14, 1869, Lord Clarendon, the British foreign secretary, received positive assurance from the Russian foreign minister Prince Gortschakoff that the Russian emperor considered Afghanistan outside the Rus-

---

[74.] Reshtiya, 275.

[75.] Forbes, *The Afghan Wars*, 224.

[76.] Kateb, *Seraj al-Tawarikh*, 2:628-9.

[77.] *Ibid.*, 358.

[78.] Hensman, 264.

[79.] Barthorp, *The North-West Frontier*, 85.

sian sphere of influence and that Russian officers would no longer be allowed to visit Afghanistan.[80]

While anxious to leave, the British stayed on, waiting for a sovereign to emerge who would be acceptable to the Afghans and with whom they could negotiate terms of a settlement. The arrival at this juncture of Sardar `Abd al-Rahman, a nephew of Amir Shir `Ali Khan from Bokhara, seemed to satisfy everyone.

[80.] IOR, L/P&S/10/125, 3082, A.165, confidential, 1907. These preliminary negotiations formed the basis of the Clarendon-Gortschakoff Agreement of 1872-73.

2

Relations Between the State and the Ulama, 1880-1919

> *The great drawbacks to progress in Afghanistan have been those men who, under the pretense of religion, have taught things which were entirely contrary to the teachings of Mohammad, and that, being the false leaders of the religion, the sooner they are got rid of, the better.*
>
> —Amir `Abd al-Rahman[1]

> *Rise up for prosperity (haiy `ali al-fallah), O, noble Afghan nation! You must protect your dignity and your national honor. You must protect the independence of your government. Afghans, who have become known the world over for their bravery, pride and strong belief in Islam, must not accept the control or protection of a foreign non-Muslim nation.*
>
> —Mahmud Tarzi[2]

When Sardar `Abd al-Rahman came upon the scene during the Second Anglo-Afghan War, support for *jehad* was at its peak among the masses. `Abd al-Rahman used the mass sentiment for *jehad* for his personal political ends by sending messages to the leading chiefs of Turkistan, Kohistan, and Kabul, declaring his intent to expel the British. By this time, negotiations over succession to the Afghan throne had broken down. Neither of the most eligible candidates, Amir Mohammad Ya`qub and Sardar Mohammad Ayyub, the two sons of Amir Shir `Ali, was acceptable to all groups. The people of Herat, Qandahar, and Farah favored Sardar Mohammad Ayyub, while a *jerga* of 189 members, including Molla Moshk-i-`Alam, was held in Ghazni to support the deposed Amir Mohammad Ya`qub. Moreover, the people of Kabul, Kohdaman, and Logar disapproved of both candidates.[3] By July, Moshk-i-`Alam, who supported suc-

---

[1] Mir Munshi, 2:251.
[2] *Seraj al-Akhbar*, vol. 5, no. 10, 16 *Jady* 1294/January 7, 1916.
[3] Ghobar, 632.

cession in Amir Shir `Ali's line, had softened his position, and although his feelings toward the British did not change, he agreed to accept their choice as ruler of Afghanistan from among the claimants.  In his war diary, Howard Hensman wrote: "The old Molla, Moshk-i-`Alam, had, it is true, written to say he would accept the ruler whom we favored, but it was not expected that secessions from the Jacobin party would follow so rapidly."[4]

Jubilant crowds greeted Sardar `Abd al-Rahman as he entered Kabul's main gate, and on July 20, 1880, he was proclaimed king in Charikar, north of Kabul.[5] He immediately entered into negotiations with the British, who were anxious to evacuate.

The popular religious fervor that `Abd al-Rahman had used to his personal advantage was soon turned against him. Although negotiations with Britain's Lepel Griffin resulted in the complete withdrawal of British troops, the price extracted by the British was control over Afghanistan's foreign policy.[6] In July 1880, Griffin, then foreign secretary to the government of India, sent a letter to the amir declaring that "since the British government admits no right of interference by foreign powers in Afghanistan...it is plain that Your Highness can have no political relations with any foreign power except with the British government."[7] However, `Abd al-Rahman never formally accepted the terms of the agreement[8] because of the vulnerability of being caught between two aggressive imperial powers and his uncertainty about how his own position fit into British demands. West Ridgway, the British commissioner in Baluchistan, explained that the amir's friendly attitute toward the British resulted from practical considerations: "I do not believe that the Amir dislikes us much less than the Russians, but he is shrewd enough to see that the independence of Afghanistan is threatened more by the Russians than by us, and for this reason is loyal to us."[9] However, the amir's willingness to forfeit Afghanistan's autonomy caused religious leaders to question his commitment to independence. They accused him of acceding to British demands in order to save the throne for himself, a sacrifice of Afghanistan's independence for personal gain.[10] In contrast, Sardar Mohammad Ayyub's continuing resistance to the British in Herat and Qandahar, combined

---

[4.] Hensman, 435.

[5.] *Ibid.*, 640.

[6.] Ludwig Adamec, *Afghanistan, 1900-1923: A Diplomatic History*, 14-15.

[7.] IOR, L/P&S/10/125, 3082, A 165, 1907.

[8.] A report compiled by the political department of the India Office affirms "that there is no record of any formal acceptance by Amir `Abd al-Rahman of the terms set forth in Mr. Griffin's letter of July 1880." *Ibid.* The amir did, however, assured the British that "if I have the friendship of a great government like yours, how can I communicate with another power without advice from and consultation with you?" *Ibid.*

[9.] BACSOA, 21.

[10.] Ghobar, 641. In his autobiography, `Abd al-Rahman felt compelled to respond to the allegations of apostasy leveled against him by the clergy because of his alleged friendly ties with the British. Mir Munshi, *The Life of Abdur Rahman, Amir of Afghanistan*, 1:225.

with his decisive victory on the Maiwand front (near Qandahar) in 1880, increased his popularity with religious leaders, particularly with the influential Mojaddedis of Herat and Qandahar and with Molla Moshk-i-`Alam.

Many influential religious figures, such as Moshk-i-`Alam and some Kohistani and Qandahari religious leaders, such as the Mollas Amir Mohammad, `Abd al-Rahim, and `Abd al-Ahad, began to oppose Amir `Abd al-Rahman.[11]   In 1883, Moshk-i-`Alam led a disturbance against the amir in Zormat and Katawaz, urging the Waziris to resist his rule.     In fact, Molla Moshk-i-`Alam fought against `Abd al-Rahman until his death in 1886.  His son, Molla `Abd al-Karim, encouraged antigovernment activity among the Ghelzais.[12] In addition, Akhundzada `Abd al-Ghaffur (not to be confused with the Akhundzada of Swat), who was related to Molla Moshk-i-`Alam by marriage, rose up against the government in Charasia, near Kabul.

Sahebzada `Ata Mohammad, the spiritual leader of the Ghelzai and Dorrani tribes, was also a staunch opponent of Amir `Abd al-Rahman.[13] In Shinwar, the Molla of Hadda aroused the Shinwaris against the amir by accusing him of friendly relations with the British and of bringing Europeans into Afghanistan.[14] Molla `Abd al-Karim, who had played a prominent role in the Ghelzai Rebellion of 1886-1887, proclaimed the amir "the worshipper of himself and the friend of an alien Government."[15]

Despite considerable opposition among the ulama, Amir `Abd al-Rahman succeeded in consolidating his rule in Afghanistan.  He crushed separatist movements and destroyed or banished suspect Barakzai *sardar*s, tribal *khan*s, and potential claimants to the throne.  The British attributed `Abd al-Rahman's success partly to his own sagacity and partly to the "liberal support of arms and money granted to him by Indian government,"[16] which enabled him to build a strong army. To counter opposition from religious groups, he developed a threefold policy: 1) use of force, 2) ostentatious piety, and 3) control of religious endowments (*awqaf*) to make the clergy financially dependent on the state.[17]

[11.] Ghobar, 651.

[12.] Government of India, Foreign Office, *Biographical Accounts of Chiefs, Sardars, and Others of Afghanistan*, confidential, 145.

[13.] *Ibid.*, 51.

[14.] Hasan Kakar, *Government and Society in Afghanistan,* 164-165.

[15.] BACSOA, 7; Adamec, *Historical and Political Who's Who of Afghanistan*, 98.

[16.] BACSOA, 17.

[17.] In his autobiography, which was translated and edited by his secretary, Sultan Ahmad Mir Munshi, the amir wrote: "all the land and property, as well as money, which used to support the Mullahs, is transferred to the Government treasury, and monthly fixed salaries are paid out of the treasury to the persons employed in religious services...by adopting this system the Muslim ecclesiastical law, and its administration, are vested in the hands of the Crown; and they hold their offices under the sole privilege of the Crown. They are therefore bound, willing or unwilling, to obey the Crown, which stops all divergences and innovations, substituting for these general unity." Mir Munshi, *The Life of Amir Abdur Rahman*, 1: 205.

Once Amir `Abd al-Rahman had defeated his rival cousins, Sardar Ayyub Khan in Qandahar and Herat and Sardar Eshaq Khan in Balkh, he set about tightening control over the clergy. In 1882, he executed Mohammad `Omar Mojaddedi and his son, `Abd al-Baqi, who had supported Ayyub Khan, and he forced Mojaddedi's other sons into exile.[18] Akhund `Abd al-Rahim Kakar, another influential leader who had proclaimed the amir an infidel, was executed along with several other *molla*s who had taken sanctuary (*bast*) in the Khirqah-i-Sharif, the shrine in Qandahar that contains a robe of the Prophet.[19] Molla Abubakr of Ghazni and his family were imprisoned in Kabul,[20] and the allowances of Moshk-i-`Alam and his son were discontinued as early as 1881. In addition, the amir levied a tax of 15,000 rupees on Moshk-i-`Alam's land and "demanded seven years arrears at the above rate from his son [`Abd al-Karim]."[21]

`Abd al-Rahman's attitude of contempt toward some ulama is revealed in his autobiography:

> Many of these priests taught as Islamic religion strange doctrines which were never in the teachings of Mahomed [Mohammad], yet which have been the cause of downfall of all Islamic nations in every country. They taught that people were never to do any work, but only to live off others, and to fight against each other. Of course it is only natural that every one of these self-made kings should have levied separate taxes on their subjects, so the first thing I had to do was to put an end to these numberless robbers, thieves, false prophets, and trumpery kings. I must confess that it was not a very easy task, and it took fifteen years of fighting before they finally submitted to my rule or left the country, either by being exiled or by departing into the next world.[22]

Leaders of the sufi orders, particularly the Naqshbandiyya sheikhs, who had supported Eshaq Khan and Ayyub Khan against `Abd al-Rahman, also came under attack. While praising Sheikh Baha al-Din Naqshband, the founder of the order, as a sacred man and a hardworking potter, `Abd al-Rahman claimed that the sheikh's followers were false. Their principle reason for seeking disciples, he wrote, "was to extort money from them, that they themselves might lead a lazy life. They forget that it is entirely against the teachings, as well as against the practice of our Holy Prophet, who used to work hard himself."[23]

To confound religious pretexts for opposing his rule, Amir `Abd al-Rahman practiced strict orthodoxy. He placed himself imperiously at the head of a theocratic government and out maneuvered the ulama by claiming that "kings stand

---

[18.] Adamec, *Historical and Political Who's Who of Afghanistan*, 201-202.

[19.] Ghobar, 659.

[20.] *BACSOA*, 22.

[21.] *Ibid.*, 6.

[22.] Mir Munshi, *The Life of Abdur Rahman*, 1:218.

[23.] *Ibid.*, 1:265.

to their countries as vice-regents of God....[T]hey exercise the right of fortune or misfortune—of life and death—over those who are placed under his [*sic*] rule."[24] Indeed, `Abd al-Rahman was the first ruler in Afghanistan to promote the divine right of kings.[25] He even assumed the title *Zia al-Mellat Wa-al-Din* (Light of the Nation and the Faith) and claimed that as God's vice-regent on earth, it was his duty to implement divine law. Under his direction a number of pamphlets were printed, enjoining the faithful to the proper observation of the rules of the Qur'an and the teachings of the Prophet. The implicit purpose of the pamphlets, however, was to provide religious justification for his policies. The tracts emphasized "obedience to kings, paying of taxes, and steadiness in battle."[26]

To strengthen his image as an orthodox religious man, `Abd al-Rahman hired subservient clergymen to implement the *shari`at* while acting in compliance with his own policies. He increased the power of the *qazis*, who enforced law and order and sanctioned his policies. He also increased the number of *qazis* and offered them positions as administrators of the *shari`at* and overseers of the state's machinery in the capital and certain provinces.[27] Although the right of the *qazis* to make discretionary decisions remained intact, they were required to act in compliance with a set of unified procedures provided by the government in the *Asas al-Qozat* (basic guideines for *qazis*). The *qazis* became a significant element of the secondary elite, those who found religious justification for the amir's administrative policies. They sustained the link between *din* (religion) and the *dawlat* (the state). Along with other religious functionaries, the *qazis* were appointed directly by the central government after passing a special test before a board of examiners.

`Abd al-Rahman curbed the power of religious groups further by depriving them of their traditional sources of income. He brought the administration of religious endowments (*awqaf*) under direct governmental control. He imposed the first property tax on religious holdings and discontinued allowances to the heads of sufi orders for the maintenance of sufi headquarters (*khaneqahs*).[28] By making the ulama dependent on the government for their livelihood, he was able to subjugate most of them to the authority of the state.

In 1893, the amir was forced to sign what came to be known as the Durand Agreement, by which parts of the Pashtun tribal area were divided into British and Afghan spheres of influence. The demarcation of the Durand Line reinforced hostility toward the British and strengthened the political position of the clergy in eastern Afghanistan. Akhundzada `Abd al-Ghafur, who commanded great influence in the vicinity of the Khyber Pass, issued a dictum to the effect

---

[24] *Ibid.*, 15.
[25] Kakar, *Government and Society in Afghanistan*, 8.
[26] Ashraf Ghani, "Islam and State-building in a Tribal Society: Afghanistan 1880-1901," 279.
[27] Kakar, 35.
[28] Ghobar, 647; Kakar, 152.

that *jehad* against the British was a religious duty incumbent on all citizens.[29] The geographical location of Swat on the frontier between Afghanistan and British India facilitated the transformation of the sufi order into a promoter of holy war. Molla `Abd al-Ghafur's influential *khalifa*s, such as Molla Najm al-Din (known as the Molla of Hadda), Molla Hajji Akbar, Molla Faiz-Allah, Molla `Abd al-Wahab Manki, and Molla Hamz-Allah, were active in spreading the gospel of *jehad* throughout the region. Another leading figure involved in anti-British agitations was Molla Sa`id-Allah, known as Molla Mastan.

Amir `Abd al-Rahman tried to repress the activities of the tribal clergy by transferring to the state the authority to declare *jehad*. To justify the usurpation, he ordered books written asserting that no one but the caliph, amir, or sultan was authorized to declare *jehad*.[30] At the same time the amir enhanced his image as a pious amir or sultan, possessing religious and secular powers—the imamate and the amirate. Heresy, even contact with "infidels," was severely punished. Attempts were also made to enforce Hanafi doctrine on the Shi`a population. In the name of Hanafi orthodoxy, the amir prosecuted leading clergymen whose influence posed a threat to central authority. Molla Najm al-Din of Hadda, the celebrated disciple of the Akhundzada of Swat, was arrested and "arraigned before a tribunal of mollas on a charge of disseminating Wahhabism,"[31] a movement led by Sayyid Ahmad of Bareilly (1786-1831) in India.

Amir `Abd al-Rahman enhanced his image as a Muslim ruler mostly as a result of his successful campaign in Kafaristan (1895-1896) and the mass conversion of its people to Islam.[32] He skillfully turned the object of *jehad* toward the conquest of this isolated region in the northeast, whose inhabitants had retained their local creed for centuries. Leading tribal clergymen, including the Molla of Hadda, the amir's staunch adversary, felt obliged to join the campaign. Upon the conversion of the Kafari people to Islam, Kafaristan was given the name Nuristan (the land of light). The amir celebrated his conquest by assuming the title of *Zia al-Mellat Wa-al-Din* (Light of the Nation and the Faith).

Establishment of Hadda as an Important Religious Center

While `Abd al-Rahman had significantly reduced the political influence of the ulama in Afghanistan by the end of the nineteenth century, he did not greatly reduce their influence as social and religious leaders. Clergy-backed skirmishes and sporadic warfare against the British continued along the frontier. Holy war

---

[29.] Qureshi, 162. The Akhundzada of Swat claimed spiritual leadership through a chain of predecessors (*selsela*), mainly Sheikh Junaid of Peshawar and Sheikh Ahmad of Delhi, to Sayyid `Abd al-Qader Gailani. Interview with Sayyid `Abd al Qayyum (Padshah Saheb), the last sheikh in the line of the successors of Akhundzada of Swat, Peshawar, September 23, 1994.

[30.] Kakar, 125.

[31.] *BACSOA*, 148.

[32.] Kafaristan, land of the infidels (*kafar*s), is presently known as Nuristan.

(*ghaza*) became the dominant feature of tribal polity in eastern and southeastern Afghanistan.

After the death of Molla `Abd al-Ghafur, Hadda, seven miles south of Jalalabad, became the center of anti-British activities. Hadda rose to prominence as a religious center mostly because of the famous *madrasa*, sufi headquarters, and almshouse (*langer*) founded by the celebrated Molla Najm al-Din of Hadda. According to British archival sources, the Molla of Hadda had more than 100,000 followers and was the most powerful molla of Afghanistan at the end of the nineteenth century.[33] As the most capable student of the famous Akhundzada of Swat, Molla Najm al-Din commanded great reverence among the Pashtun tribes on both sides of the border. After his death his numerous disciples (*khalifa*s) exerted the same influence through a network that linked them with a large number of subordinate disciples among various tribes. Hadda's location in the heart of the tribal region enabled it to serve as sufi headquarters, a place for religious instruction and social welfare and a meeting place where the disciples gathered periodically to discuss important religious issues. The disciples of the Molla of Hadda were among the most influential clergyman of the first quarter of the nineteenth century in Afghanistan. (See Table 4)

Although the clergy had begun to revitalize their power in the tribal region, they did not pose a challenge to `Abd al-Rahman's absolute power. The amir continued to rule with an iron hand until his death in 1901. By then he had created a united Afghanistan and a strong central government with an effective administration. Lord Curzon, who visited `Abd al-Rahman in 1894 in Kabul, described him as

> at once a patriot and a monster, a great man and almost a fiend, [who] laboured hard and unceasingly for the good of his country....He welded the Afghan tribes into a unity which they had never previously enjoyed, and he paved the way for [Afghanistan's] complete independence.[34]

NEW POLITICIZATION OF THE ULAMA UNDER AMIR HABIB-ALLAH, 1901-1919

During the reign of Seraj al-Mellat Wa Din Amir Habib-Allah (1901-1919), son and successor of `Abd al-Rahman, the ulama gradually reasserted themselves as a political force. Factors that permitted their resurgence were 1) royal patronage, 2) a relaxation of central governmental control, and 3) the rise of nationalism and pan-Islamism.

Unlike his father, Habib-Allah revered the ulama and the *pir*s. He granted them land and allowances and he frequented the shrines.[35] Even more impor-

---

[33] *BACSOA*, 147, See also Adamec, *Who's Who of Afghanistan*, 207.

[34] Curzon (Marquess of Kedleston), *Tales of Travel*, 67.

[35] Fofalzai, *Timur Shah Dorrani*, 1:307.

tant, he relaxed the state's control over religious institutions and practices, and the ulama gradually regained their influence. Although still appointed by the government, they reacquired full jurisdiction as judges, imams, instructors, and custodians of shrines (*motawallis*). The leaders of the *tariqas* regained prominence. Members of the royal family, including the king himself, became aspirants of one or several *pirs*.

Habib-Allah also granted amnesty to families forced into exile by 'Abd al-Rahman, including important priestly families like the Mojaddedis of Herat, exiled for twenty years in Persia. It was also during Habib-Allah's reign that the Sayyid Hasan Affandi Gailani (brother of the Naqib of Baghdad, head of the Qaderiyya order) came to Afghanistan.   Habib-Allah granted him a princely pension, land, and a residence in Charbagh, near Jalalabad, and treated him with the utmost respect.[36] The Mojaddedis of Kabul, also known as the Hazrats of Shurbazar, regained their former position as highly revered spiritual leaders and went on to play an important political role in the twentieth century.

The revival of the ulama's influence was closely tied to renewed interest in *jehad* in Afghanistan during the first two decades of the twentieth century. Developments in and outside the country provoked even stronger anti-British sentiment and widespread support for *jehad*, especially after Turkey entered the Great War against the Allies. At the beginning, Habib-Allah encouraged *jehad* in order to strengthen his hand against the British. When Turkey entered the Great War against the Allies, who included Afghanistan's enemy, Great Britain, support for *jehad* was pervasive in Afghanistan. Given the traditional role of the ulama in *jehad*, as public eagerness for *jehad* grew, so did the ulama's influence and involvement in politics. By the end of World War I, the entire Afghan nation was ready to wage holy war against the British. As early advocates of war, the ulama were again at the forefront of Afghan politics.

Ironically, Habib-Allah had first suggested the possibility of *jehad* against the Russians, not against the British, when negotiating with the latter in 1904. The British were pressing him to accept an Anglo-Afghan military alliance ostensibly to protect Afghanistan from possible attack by Russia. Habib-Allah insisted that Afghanistan could follow Japan's lead in resisting Russian encroachment. All he needed from the British was financial assistance. He argued he would, if necessary, enlist the Persians and Central Asian Muslims in a pan-Islamic *jehad* against Russia.[37]

Three years later in 1907, a diplomatic conference was held in St. Petersburg to define spheres of British and Russian influence in Afghanistan, Persia, and Central Asia. After several months of negotiation, an agreement reached on August 31, 1907, stipulated equal commercial rights for both powers and demarcated a sphere of political influence for each. Afghanistan was declared to be outside Russia's sphere of interest, and Britain assumed political influence

---

[36.] Adamec, *Historical and Political Who's Who of Afghanistan,* 230;   May Schinazi, *Afghanistan at the Beginning of the Twentieth Century,* 117.
[37.] NAI, Jan. 1905, tel. 73k, Dec. 23, 1904.

there in exchange for an agreement not to annex or occupy any part for Afghanistan and not to engage in any military action there that might threaten Russia. Russia was only to engage in commercial and nonpolitical relations with Afghanistan.[38]

The Anglo-Russian convention had far-reaching repercussions in the Afghan court. The amir and members of the State Council (*Majles-i-Shura-i-Khas*) expressed their displeasure publicly.[39] Habib-Allah called a national assembly (*jerga*), which included prominent religious leaders. After consulting the tribal leaders and the ulama, the amir and the State Council concluded that *jehad* against the British was inevitable.

Reluctant to see fighting begin, Habib-Allah hoped that by threatening holy war in the tribal zone, he could force the government of India to withdraw its acceptance of the agreement devised at the convention. He established contact with Molla Pawinda (a disciple of the Akhundzada of Swat), who exerted great influence among Mas'ud and Waziri tribes on the British side of the Durand Line and offered him ammunition, men and money. As efforts were made to enlist men for the *jehad*, several leading ulama, headed by the Padshah of Islampur, a celebrated disciple of the Molla of Hadda, preached *jehad* in the Eastern Province. Enthusiasm for *jehad* swept across the country, and volunteer tribal warriors flocked into Kabul from every direction. The Padshah of Islampur raised a large tribal army in Konar, near Jalalabad, to be led to the frontier by Shaghasi 'Abd al-Qoddus Khan E'temad al-Dawla. Molla Pawindah, Molla Hamz-Allah, Lala Pir, and several others engaged in stirring up tribes across the frontier. The anti-British sentiments aroused by the call for *jehad* were so intense that Habib-Allah and Nasr-Allah Khan Na'eb al-Saltana, the Amir's younger brother, feared the situation would get out of hand. To avoid an outbreak of fighting, they blocked the E'temad al-Dawla from joining the troops in Konar, a decision that offended both the Padshah-i-Islampur and the E'temad al-Dawla. Infuriated by this order, the fervid anti-British prime minister resigned his post and wrote to the amir and his brother that in the future he would "never have anything to do with them or the business of the state."[40]

Anti-British sentiment continued to escalate. It appeared as though the entire Islamic world was in danger of being partitioned by the Europeans. As Arnold Kepple writes, "These fears received daily confirmation in the rumors of proposed railway construction across Persia, and the discussions about respective spheres of influence that [were] carried on in a cool proprietary tone in the newspapers."[41] In 1908 and 1909, the ulama of the Eastern Province joined in calling for *jehad* against the British. The leading clergy involved in anti-British agitation included the Padshah of Islampur, the Sufi of Baikitut, Sayyid La'l Shah (Molla Lalapir), the Hazrat Saheb of Chaharbagh, and the Akhundzada of

---

[38.] Adamec, *Afghanistan 1900-1923*, 70.
[39.] NAI/FPD, Secret File, July 1908, Nos. 276-278.
[40.] NAI/FPD, Secret File, July 1908, nos. 276-278, 46.
[41.] Kepple, *Gun-Running and the Indian North-West Frontier*, 78.

Tagaw, all disciples of Molla Najm al-Din of Hadda.[42] (See Table 4) In 1909, Molla Najm al-Din issued a religious decree (*fatwa*) urging the people to join in a holy war against the British. His call for *jehad* aroused excitement in Kabul, Logar, Kohistan, and the southern provinces.[43] Another *fatwa* issued by Ak-hundzada Mussahi, a disciple of the Akhundzada of Swat and the *pir* of Amir Habib-Allah and Prince Nasr-Allah, produced a similar effect.[44]

The primary instigator of anti-British agitation was Nasr-Allah Khan Na'eb al-Saltana, the amir's younger brother. A profoundly pious Muslim and the commander of the Afghan army, he advocated Islamic perspectives in domestic and foreign policy, a predilection that made him popular among the ulama. Assisted by Mawlawi `Abd al-Razeq (See Table 5), the influential chaplain of the royal household (*molla-bashi* or *molla-i-hozur*), "the central wire-puller of all transborder priestly fanaticism,"[45] the prince had established connections with virtually all the religious leaders in Afghanistan and across the border in the North-West Frontier Province of British India. Through a network of loyal *molla*s, the Na'eb al-Saltana promoted a nationalism based on Islam. British authorities viewed him as the main force behind anti-British riots in the North-West Frontier and as the man who had united the various factions of the clergy under the banner of Islamic patriotism.[46] According to Arnold Keppel, the Na'eb al-Saltana was also involved in smuggling some 30,000 rifles from the Persian Gulf through India in 1907. These rifles, brought to Qandahar via a network of *molla*s, were to be used to stir up the frontier tribes against the British.[47] In 1906, the Na'eb al-Saltana appointed Molla Sayyid La`l Shah as his agent to work in Khost among the Mangals, Waziris, and Mashuds.[48] On July 14, Lord Hardinge, the British viceroy of India, complained to the amir,

> I regret to have to inform you that during the past three months a se-
> ries of numerous raids have been committed into British territory,
> which I am informed are the results of efforts on the part of Mollah
> Pawindah to stir not only the Khost outlaws but the tribesmen of Wa-
> ziristan to commit outrages against the Government. Mollah Pawin-
> dah is said to have paid recent visits to Kabul and to be using YM's
> name in his appeals to the tribesmen to commit mischief.[49]

[42.] *Ibid.*, 25-26.
[43.] Ghobar, 740.
[44.] *Ibid.*
[45.] Government of India, serial no. 88 (secret), *Who's Who in Afghanistan*, 1914, 11.
[46.] Keppel, 72-73.
[47.] *Ibid.*, 52.
[48.] Adamec, *Historical and Political Who's Who of Afghanistan*, 181.
[49.] From HE the Viceroy to HM Amir of Afghanistan, IOR, L/P&S/14/6, Kharita no. 11, Simla, July 14, 1913.

The viceroy added that letters bearing the seals of Molla Pawidah and Na'eb al-Saltana were found in the possession of those captured.[50]

Despite being offended by the resolutions of the Anglo-Russian Convention, the amir, now inclined to avoid hostility with the British, gave in to the viceroy's pressures. He took repressive measures to stop the skirmishes instigated by the clergy near the frontier, and he dismissed and reprimanded Mawlawi `Abd al-Razeq, Na'eb al-Saltana's protégé, and Nazir Safar, the chief steward and seal holder, who had collaborated with Mawlawi `Abd al-Razeq. Several leaders of the disturbance in the frontier area were arrested and brought to Kabul for trial.

The amir's change of attitude toward the British turned the ulama and the anti-British elements in the court against him. Habib-Allah Khan's relations with the ulama had, in fact, started to deteriorate earlier in 1906, when, despite strong opposition by the Na'eb al-Saltana and several high-profile religious leaders, such as the Sultan of Islampur, he had accepted the viceroy's invitation to visit India. Clerical opposition to the amir's visit surfaced in the Eastern Province in response to rumors that he had become a Freemason. In its March 13, 1907, issue, the Indian newspaper *Pioneer* reported,

> A heavily attended meeting of mollas recently took place in the Laghman district not far from Jalalabad, at which inflammatory speeches were made, and the Amir was publicly accused of having changed his religion by becoming a Free-Masson [*sic*]. Some of the most bigoted mollas went so far as to say that he was unfit to remain their ruler. When news of the meeting reached Sardar [`Enayat-Allah] Khan, who was then at Jalalabad, he summoned about twenty mollas to him and attempted to reason with them.[51]

The amir responded vehemently to the charges. Upon his return, he executed four *molla*s.[52]

The Ulama and Liberal Nationalism

During the reign of Amir Habib-Allah, the concepts of Afghan nationhood and Afghan nationality began to take shape. Despite the country's isolation from the outside world, new ideas began to infiltrate as a result of the return of families who had been exiled by Amir `Abd al-Rahman and through the presence of Indian Muslim and Turkish teachers and technicians. Western-inspired nationalism and pan-Islamism added a new dimension to Afghanistan's struggle against British imperialism.

At the beginning of his reign, Amir Habib-Allah gave the impression of being a progressive, energetic ruler. He granted amnesty to exiled families, increased the power of the State Council, abolished torture in prisons, and pro-

---

[50.] *Ibid.*
[51.] NAI, Foreign Secret File, nos. 23-32, Feb. 1907.
[52.] Adamec, *Afghanistan, 1900-1923,* 67.

moted modern education by establishing new schools, a printing house (*Matba`a-i-`Enayat*), and a bureau of translation (*Dar al-Tarjoma*). As time passed, however, he became more authoritarian and, like his father, began to claim "divine rights." According to Ghobar, he often stated publicly that the ruler was God's vice-regent (*na'eb*) on earth and that his command was, in fact, the command granted by God.[53] The regime published a book heavy with quotations from the Qur'an, the *hadith*, and medieval Muslim writers that stressed that a Muslim state could not survive without the sultan or *padeshah*, who, as the shadow of God (*zell-Allah*) and a shepherd (*ra`i*), was the nourisher, guide, and protector of his subjects (*ra`iyyat*). Submission to authority (*eta`at-i-ulu al-'amr*, which, based on Qur'anic verse iv:62, meant the ruler), was pronounced the religious duty of every Muslim. The books emphasized that the ruler was responsible for maintaining order and providing safety and justice, according to the *shari`at*. In fulfilling those duties, the ruler was answerable only to God.[54]

Against this autocracy, a group of students and teachers, including some liberal ulama, formed the Secret National Party (*Hezb-i-Serr-i-Melli*), also known as the Constitutionalists (Mashruta Khwahan). Their aim, as their name implied, was to bring to an end the autocratic regime of Amir Habib-Allah and to establish a constitutional government. The head of the Mashrutah Khwahan was Mawlawi Mohammad Sarwar Wasef, an eminent religious scholar from Qandahar.[55] Mawlawi Wasef and his close collaborator, Mir Mohammad Qasem, espoused progressive ideas and advocated legislative reform.[56] Wasef wrote to Amir Habib-Allah, admonishing him to adopt constitutional government for the good of the nation. In many countries, he wrote,

> people have urged their government to form a system of government which would be in accord with people's will. In some countries, enlightened rulers have taken the initiative themselves. Since [Seraj al-Mellat wa al-Din] is a progressive and informed ruler,....it is hoped that he too will establish laws which would abolish arbitrary practices.[57]

Among other liberal ulama who advocated change were Mawlawi `Abd al-Ra'uf Qandahari (the son of Mawlawi `Abd al-Rahim Alikozai, executed by Amir `Abd al-Rahman) and his two sons, Mawlawis `Abd al-Wase` Qandahari and `Abd al-Rabb. Mawlawi `Abd al-Rauf was head of the Madrasa-i-Shahi and the chief `alem in the royal court. A document in the Afghan National Archives reveals that a group of ulama of the Madrasa-i-Chubfrushi in Kabul and other ulama, including Mawlawi `Abd al-Ra'uf, wrote a letter to Amir Habib-Allah

---

[53] Ghobar, 711.

[54] M. Taj al-Din Afghani, *Tohfat al-Amir fi Bayan-i-Soluk wa al-Tadbir* (The Gift of Amir on Assertion of Manners and Politics,) chaps. 1-5.

[55] Habibi, *Jonbesh-i-Mashrutiyyat dar Afghanistan*, 36.

[56] *Ibid.*, 37.

[57] *Ibid.*, 40.

requesting establishment of a biweekly paper in Kabul. E'temad al-Dawla submitted the request to the amir and received his approval.[58] The first issue of the paper appeared on January 11, 1906, under the editorship of Mawlawi 'Abd al-Ra'uf, and a poem in that issue called the amir's attention to progress made by other nations.[59]

In the winter of 1909, the amir became aware of a plot by the Hezb-i-Serr-i-Melli against his regime and ordered police action. Members of the Hezb were arrested. Some were sentenced to death and others to various terms of imprisonment. Among those arrested were several liberal ulama: Mawlawi Wasef, Molla Mohammad Sarwar Alekozai, Qazi 'Abd al-Ahad Solaimakhail, Molla Mohammad Akbar Akhundzadah, Mawlawi Gholam Mohai al-Din, Sahebzadah 'Abd-Allah Mojaddedi, Molla Menhaj al-Din, and Mawlawi 'Abd al-Wase' Qandahari, son of Mawlawi 'Abd al-Ra'uf.[60] That year, Mawlawi Wasef was executed with several other suspects on a charge of conspiring against the monarch. Moments before his execution, he slipped to a friend a piece of paper on which he had written a verse affirming that sacrifice was necessary in order to achieve liberal goals.[61]

The events of 1909 turned Amir Habib-Allah against the liberal groups. Since the *mashruta* movement had begun in the newly established Habibiyya College, the amir's interest in expanding the opportunity for education waned quickly. He refocused his energy on modernizing the court and spent the rest of his time on new hobbies—hunting and photography.

World War I and Pan-Islamism

The reign of Amir Habib-Allah coincided with the epoch of Islamic nationalism and pan-Islamism. The Turko-Italian War in 1911 and the Balkan Wars during the next two years generated a sense of solidarity in the Islamic world. Sultan 'Abd al-Hamid II's revival of the office of the caliphate in Turkey and the Young Turks' campaign in the name of the caliphate to promote pan-Islamism in India and Central Asia had already generated strong popular support for that office throughout the region, including Afghanistan.

A group of Afghan nationalists, headed by Mahmud Tarzi, editor of the Afghan newspaper *Seraj al-Akhbar*, set about reconciling tenets of Islam and nationalism. Publication of *Seraj al-Akhbar* marked a watershed in the development of political consciousness in Afghanistan. The paper took the lead in promoting support for Ottoman Turkey and for pan-Islamism. The Ottoman Sultan

---

[58.] *Ibid.*, 26; Ahang, 72-73.

[59.] Habibi, *Jonbesh-i-Mashrutiyyat dar Afghanistan*, 42-46.

[60.] Ghobar, 718-719.

[61.] *"tark-i-mal o tark-i-jan o tark sar dar rah-i-mashruta awwal manzel ast"* (Sacrificing material belongings and life is the first step toward establishment of constitutionalism.) Habibi, *Jonbesh-i-Mashrutiyyat Dar Afghanistan*, 38; Ghobar, 718. These words became the motto of liberals in subsequent years.

declared Turkey's entry into the Great War and called for an Islamic *jehad* against the Allies in defense of the caliphate (*khilafat*).

The Afghan ulama and Afghan nationalists responded enthusiastically to the Ottoman Sultan's call for *jehad*, not only because Turkey was the seat of the caliphate and all Sunni Muslims felt responsible for its defense, but also because an alliance with other Islamic forces against the Allies could strengthen Afghanistan's demand for complete independence from Great Britain. News of the *jehad* spread quickly among the people by pilgrims returning from Mecca with leaflets seeking support for Turkey and by secret Turkish envoys in the tribal areas on both the Afghan and British sides of the Durand Line. The influential tribal *molla*, the Hajji of Turanqzai, on the British side of the North-West border, awaited only the amir's lead to begin activities there.[62] *Seraj al-Akhbar* expressed deep sympathy for Ottoman Turkey and called India the abode of war (*dar al-harb*). Copies of this issue were distributed on the subcontinent and were read avidly.[63] The Indian newspapers *Al-Helal* and *Comrade*, edited by Mawlana Mohammad `Ali and `Abd al-Kalam Azad, also printed stirring articles in favor of Turkey. Their common sympathy for Turkey reinforced ties between Indian Muslims and the Afghan ulama and nationalists.

In 1915, a joint Turko-German mission, headed by Oscar Niedermyer, arrived in Kabul with a message from the German emperor and chancellor that encouraged the amir to join the *jehad* in favor of Turkey and asked him to allow troops of the Central Powers to pass through Afghanistan to India. The mission included several Turks and two Indian revolutionaries, Barakat-Allah and Mahandra Pratap, who later formed a provisional government in Kabul. At about the same time, Mawlana Mahmud Husain, a professor at Deoband College and one of the principal instigators of the Khilafat Movement in India, sent a disci-

---

[62.] Qureshi, *Ulema in Politics*, 224.

[63.] *Ibid.* On December 14 the viceroy wrote to Amir Habib-Allah: "It has been brought to my notice that a newspaper called the Siraj ul-Akhbar' [*sic*] which is published in Kabul contains a great deal of inaccurate and offensive matter in regard to the present war in Europe, which cannot but create a false impression in the minds of its readers as to the progress of that war and as to the motives of the British Government. I am well aware that this newspaper is in no way an official mouth-piece of your Majesty's Government, that it in no way represents the feelings of the Government of His Majesty, the King Emperor. But I consider it most undesirable that this paper should be disseminated at the present time in India, both because of inaccuracy and the offensive character of the articles it publishes, and because it is likely to produce, in the minds of the ignorant people, the idea that these articles reflect the feelings of Your Majesty's Government and that the relations between Your Majesty and myself are not as truly cordial as I am glad to know they really are. You may be sure that I have not the slightest desire to interfere in any of the internal affairs of Afghanistan, but I would suggest to Your Majesty as a friend, the desirability of taking steps, either to suppress this paper or to alter the present tone." IOR, L/P&S/14/6, Kharita no. 29-POA, Delhi, Dec. 14, 1914, from HE Viceroy to HM Amir of Afghanistan.

ple, Mawlana `Obaid-Allah Sindhi, to promote *jehad* in Afghanistan.[64] He also encouraged the Molla of Turangzai, his long associate, to raise the standard of *jehad* in the tribal area. The news of the arrival of the Turko-German mission electrified the entire frontier region.

Although some influential members of the Afghan court, such as Sardar Nasr-Allah and the E`temad al-Dawla, favored an alliance with Turkey, Habib-Allah remained firm in his belief that it was not in Afghanistan's best interest to enter the war. The amir hoped that by remaining neutral, he could later bargain effectively with the British for Afghanistan's unconditional independence. He believed that Afghanistan would lose in any escalation of hostility with Great Britain, and therefore rejected the overtures of the Turko-German Mission.[65]

Habib-Allah's resistance to entering the war and his unwavering policy of "Cautious Alliance" intensified the resentment of religious groups. Simultaneously, he offended the nationalists, who wanted complete independence from Britain and direct diplomatic and cultural relations with the rest of the world.

Religious leaders in the frontier zone, mostly disciples of the Molla of Hadda, encouraged raids on British territory. On April 18, 1915, the Molla of Chaknawur brought a significant tribal force to the vicinity of Peshawar, the border city between Afghanistan and British India, and crossed into British territory. In May, Lord Hardinge, viceroy and governor-general of India, informed the amir of the hostile ferment among the Mohmand tribes that had been instigated by the Chaknawur Molla in the vicinity of Peshawar, and the viceroy asked the amir to punish the persons who had incited hostilities.[66] But by the late summer the Molla of Chaknawur again tried actively to gain the cooperation of the Sufi of Baiktut and Nazian Molla, also disciples of the Molla of Hadda, to promote *jehad* among the Afridi tribe.[67] Meanwhile, the Molla of Turangzai, Sandakai Molla, and Babri Molla were engaged in agitating *jehad* among the Mohmand tribesmen.[68] Plans for a combined attack on the British border were thwarted by the outbreak of cholera in August,[69] but anti-British activities started again in September. The viceroy wrote to Amir Habib-Allah that "Mir Saheb Jan Padeshah, a Molla of Islampur, in Your Majesty's territories, has moved into Mohmand country with a considerable following, for the purpose of creating

---

[64] Qureshi, 246-247.

[65] On March 3, 1915, the viceroy wrote to Amir Habib-Allah: "I am delighted to have proof that in spite of such influences as may be at work in your territories Your Majesty is steadily pursuing the policy of neutrality which throughout you have declared to the King Emperor's Government. I have had evidence of your Majesty's wise influence in the temperate preaching of mollahs on the frontier and in the improved tone of the Siraj-ul-Akhbar [*sic*] newspaper." IOR, L/P&S/14/6, Kharita no. 6, POA, Mar. 3, 1915, from HE Viceroy and Gov. G. to HM Amir of Afghanistan.

[66] IOR, London, L/P&S/14/6, Kharita no. 10, PO-A, Simla, May 10, 1915, from HE the Viceroy to HM Amir Habib-Allah.

[67] IOR, L/P&S/10/544, P 3352, Sept. 15, 1915.

[68] *Ibid.*, P3845, 1915, P3258, 1915.

[69] *Ibid.*, P3553, Aug. 29, 1915.

trouble on that border."[70] The amir tried to dissuade the independent frontier tribes from supporting the *khilafat* cause. He sought the cooperation of a noted Nangarhari religious leader, Molla `Abd al-Hamid, to control anti-British ferment on the frontier.[71]

Ultimately, Habib-Allah convened a *jerga* consisting of 540 representatives in Kabul to discuss the request of the Turko-German Mission. According to Ghobar, his real purpose was to keep all potential sources of anti-British agitation under his surveillance in Kabul.[72] Among those invited were leading supporters of *jehad*, including the Padshah of Islampur, Molla Mohammad Mossahi, the Akhundzadah of Tagaw, the Mian of Buru, the Mian of Hessarak, the Ostad of Hadda, the Molla of Chaknawur, and members of the Mojaddedi family.[73]

At about this time, Habib-Allah printed a leaflet that extolled the medieval doctrine of obedience to authority (*eta`at-i-ulu al-'amr*) and warned that *jehad* could not be waged without the order of the ruler.[74] Copies were distributed in the mosques and at military headquarters throughout the country. In the meantime, Habib-Allah gave British authorities his promise of continued neutrality "so long as the internal interests of Afghanistan are not exposed to danger."[75]

The Turko-German mission left in May 1916, a few months after Habib-Allah's public announcement of Afghanistan's neutrality in January of that year. The amir's refusal of the Ottoman sultan's request disconcerted the nationalists and the ulama. Shortly after the departure of the mission, the British agent in Kabul reported that leaflets denouncing Amir Habib-Allah as the friend and servant of the British government and inciting the people to rebel against the orders of the amir were circulating in the major mosques in Kabul.[76] Later in June, the Padshah of Islampur announced at his daughter's funeral that the "amir would never break his faith with the British unless coerced by overwhelming force."[77]

A significant development at this time was the establishment of the Mojahedin coloney in Chamarkand in Bajaur close to the Indo-Afghan border. The Mojahedin were followers of Sayyid Ahmad Shah Bareilly, a disciple of Shah `Abd al-`Aziz of Delhi, who harbored the idea of establishing an Islamic state in the North-West Frontier, free of control of infidel Englishmen. In the last months of 1915, a group of Mojahedin, headed by Mawlawi `Abd al-Karim of Kanauj and Mawlawi Mohammad Bashir of Chiniyanwali Mosque at Lahore, founded a small colony in Chamarkand and settled around the mosque of the

---

[70] *Ibid.*, L/P&S/14/6, tel. no. S.994, Sept. 28, 1915.
[71] Ghobar, 739.
[72] *Ibid.*
[73] *Ibid.*
[74] *Ibid.*; *Seraj al-Akhbar*, Kabul, vi, no. 15, April 14, 1916.
[75] Adamec, *Afghanistan, 1900-1923*, 92.
[76] IOR, L/P&S/10/202, P2805, 1916.
[77] *Ibid.* Letter from George Roos-Keppel to the secretary of state for India, n. 4B N, June 17, 1916.

Molla of Hadda. Shortly afterward about a hundred Indians from Kabul and a hundred from Samasta joined the new settlers.[78] Under the patronage of Na'eb al-Saltana, Sardar Nasr-Allah, the Hajji of Turangzai, Mir Saheb Jan Padshah of Islampur, and Babri Molla, and by receiving monetary support from the Afghan government and contributions from important people in Kabul, the Chamarkand colony flourished.[79] By mid-1926, it had become an important center of anti-British activities, where the interests of the ulama, the Afghan nationalists, Indian-Muslim activists, and Turkish pan-Islamists converged.

In August 1916, the government of India discovered an anti-British conspiracy, known as "Silk Letter Case," connecting Kabul with anti-British elements in India. The Mojahedin of Chamarkand, termed "Hindustani Fanatics," were believed to have an integral part in the plot. At the same time, Roos-Keppel, the British commissioner in Baluchistan, was informed that the Afghan government was openly subsidizing the Mojahedin of Chamarkand.[80] These new developments resulted in increased pressure by British authorities for Habib-Allah to bring anti-British activities in the frontier area under control.

Even as the amir attempted to keep Afghanistan out of the war, preparations for mobilization continued openly and secretly. Pro-*khilafat* and anti-British sentiments were fueled further by a British-inspired Arab revolt in Hejaz against the Turks. On July 16, 1916, Mahmud Tarzi published another stirring article in *Seraj al-Akhbar* in which he labeled the Sharif of Mecca a traitor.[81] In Qandahar, a large group of *molla*s held a conference with the governor and asserted that the siege of the holy cities by the British had made *jehad* unavoidable. Despite his strong sympathy for the Turks, Na'eb al-Saltana, Sardar Nasr-Allah did not act openly against his brother but was involved covertly in anti-British agitation among the tribes. Near the end of 1917, when the amir came to suspect his brother's involvement in anti-British tribal revolts on the British side of the border, he prevented him from conducting further frontier tribal affairs.[82]

Outside the capital, public opinion was unanimously pro-war. Some religious leaders were independently in contact with pro-*khilafat* elements in India. In 1918, the Padshah Saheb of Islampur received a party of Indian Khilafatists in Islampur.[83]

In February 1919, when frustration over the amir's "cautious policy" had risen to a critical level, Habib-Allah was shot and killed in his camp on a hunting trip in the Eastern Province. A note prepared by the Political Department of the India Office on May 17, 1919, reads in part:

---

[78] Lal Baha, 102.
[79] *Ibid.*, 102.
[80] *Ibid.*, 105, 107.
[81] *Seraj al-Akhbar*, vi., no. 22, July 16, 1916.
[82] Adamec, *Afghanistan, 1900-1923*, 92.
[83] Government of India, "Who is Who of Afghanistan," 1920, 151.

The fidelity of the late ruler to the British connection is well known, and has formed the subject of eulogy in both Houses of Parliament. He had a difficult hand to play in the war, and he played it with consummate skill and success. He had to resist the pressure, not only of the German and Turkish agents who found their way to his capital, but of a large "KDD" element among his own people (his brother Nasrallah Khan being the leading spirit) who constantly urged him to assume the role of a "King of Islam" and declare war on the enemies of Khalif [*sic*].... How far the unpopularity of his war policy may have been among the causes of his assassination, it is difficult to say.[84]

[84.] "The Afghan Situation," NAI/FPD, India Office, A 177, May 17, 1919.

3

THE STATE AND THE ULAMA, 1919-1923
King Aman-Allah, Hero of Independence and Champion of Pan-Islamism

I put on the crown of the Islamic Kingdom of Afghanistan in the name of internal and external independence and freedom of Afghanistan....I, in this sacred name, accept the ruling of this country. I will also accept the sacred scripture of God and the sayings of the Prophet as my guide in all that I do.

King Aman-Allah[1]

In 1919, Aman-Allah Khan, Amir Habib-Allah's third son, emerged as the hero of Afghanistan's quest for independence and as a leader of Islam inside and outside his country. His call for independence in the name of Islam and his subsequent victory in the War of Independence gained him the support of the ulama, who would otherwise have challenged his authority and supported Na'eb al-Saltana to succeed Amir Habib-Allah to the throne. Within a few months of his coup, Aman-Allah had succeeded in uniting all powerful forces in Afghanistan under his leadership, and there followed three years of close cooperation between the state and the clergy. By exploiting the issue of Amir Habib-Allah's assassination and by channeling together nationalist and religious fervor, Aman-Allah was able to garner widespread popular and religious support—and ultimate legitimacy—in the contest for the throne between him and his uncle, Na'eb al-Saltana.

---

[1] NAI, FPD, A-177, "The Afghan Situation," May 17, 1919; Fofalzai, *Dar al- Qaza' dar Afghanistan,* 440.

THE RISE OF AFGHAN NATIONALISM

Aman-Allah's political views took shape during a turbulent period of growth in national self-awareness in Afghanistan following the Russo-British Convention of 1907. Muslim revivalism, Asian nationalism (inspired by Japan's victory over Russia in 1905), and events of World War I all affected the rise of Afghan nationalism.

The first political movement of the twentieth century in Afghanistan was aimed at removing the autocratic regime of Amir Habib-Allah in order to establish a constitutional government (*hokomat-i-mashruti*).[2] This constitutional movement was successfully suppressed by Habib-Allah before it became a major political force; however, it was the source of other national liberal movements. Despite its small membership, the Constitutionalist Party (*mashruta-khwahan*) exercised great political influence in Afghanistan for years to come.

Although the regime prevailed, it was faced with the emergence of a new political organization, the Young Afghans (*jawanan-i-afghan* or *Akhwan-i-Afghan*), whose primary objectives were unconditional independence (*esteqlal-i-kamel*) from Great Britain and progress (*taraqi*), meaning essentially, modernization. The Young Afghans consisted primarily of educated men, writers, journalists, and a number of Habib-Allah's pages (*gholam-bachas*), who had been recruited from provincial gentry in the time of Amir `Abd al-Rahman. The court pages held key positions in the administration and exerted considerable influence as a result of close relations with members of the court and family ties to powerful provincial leaders. According to `Abd al-Haiy Habibi, some of the most influential pages (*gholam-bachagan-i-khas*), headed by Mohammad Wali Darwazi of the nobility of Badakhshan, were closely associated with Prince Aman-Allah and his mother `Olya Hazrat[3] and were thus in the inner circle of court politics. In addition to these civil servants, some army officers and liberal members of the royal family, such as Prince Aman-Allah, also known as the `Ain al-Dawla (Eye of the State), were attracted to the political ideas of the Young Afghans. Because of the personal influence of certain of its members, the Young Afghan movement survived the regime of Amir Habib-Allah and came to play an important role in Afghan politics.[4] Although small in number and loosely structured, the Young Afghans evolved into a political force to be reckoned with between 1912 and 1919.

The ulama and the Young Afghans shared a commitment to complete independence for Afghanistan. They differed, however, in the way they perceived foreign control. To the Young Afghans, British control meant domination of Afghanistan by a foreign political power, which the Young Afghans felt was injurious to national pride and an obstacle to Afghanistan's access to the outside

---

[2] For more details about this movement, see Ghobar, 717-720, and Habibi, *Jonbesh-i-Mashrutiyyat dar Afghanistan*, 172-220.

[3] Habibi, *ibid.*, 82-83.

[4] For a list of members, see Habibi, *ibid.*, 181-220.

world and to progress in general. The ulama, on the other hand, saw British control as domination by non-Muslims and feared long-term consequences for the Islamic social and political order. However, because Afghan nationalism at the beginning of twentieth century was inspired by Muslim revivalist movements, there were several points of common interest between the moderate faction of the Young Afghans and the more liberal and politically active ulama. It was not until the introduction of Western-inspired social reforms by King Aman-Allah in the 1920s that significant conflict arose between the two groups.

The leading figure among the nationalists was Mahmud Tarzi, a widely traveled and prolific writer, who in 1912 became the chief editor of *Seraj al-Akhbar* (*Torch of News*), named after Seraj al-Mellat wa al-Din Amir Habib-Allah. Born to a leading family of the royal clan, Tarzi was privately educated at home by eminent scholars, among whom was his own father, Gholam Mohammad Tarzi, a distinguished poet. In the time of King ʿAbd al-Rahman, Tarzi's family was forced into exile to India and later to Ottoman Turkey. While in exile, Mahmud Tarzi came into contact with Young Turk writers. During a visit to Istanbul in 1896, he met Jamal al-Din Afghani, his idol from early boyhood. "The sage," he wrote, "had been a part of my daily recitations from the time I started to read and write."[5] Seven months of close association with Afghani in Istanbul had a profound effect on Tarzi. He later described this seven-month companionship with Afghani as "equivalent to seventy years of travel."[6]

During his career as editor of *Seraj al-Akhbar*, Tarzi championed pan-Islamism, nationalism, and modernization along Western lines. His articles in *Seraj al-Akhbar* brought to his readers modern European learning in history, philosophy, ethics, and religion. Although a staunch critic of European imperialism, he acknowledged the strength of the West, which he believed derived from the West's practical application of ideas.

While advocating positive action in defense of Islam, Tarzi complained bitterly about the pathetic condition of Muslims. He claimed that contemporary Islam was characterized by disunity, ignorance, weakness, and a lack of self-confidence. In his view, the backwardness of Muslims was due not to any inherent defect in Islam, but to the unreceptiveness of many Muslims to its teachings. Muslims, he argued, had the potential to unite for progress. To make this point, he noted repeatedly the pioneering role of Muslims in the arts and sciences (*fonun wa ʿolum*), reminding his readers that it was from the cultural centers of the Muslim world that science and philosophy had penetrated pre-Renaissance Europe.[7] At the end of a series of articles titled "What Are the Obstacles to the Progress of Muslims?" (*aya maneʿ-i-taraqi-i-mosalmanan chist*), he blamed the decline of Islam as a worldwide political and cultural force on a

---

[5.] Tarzi, "*Tarjoma-i-Ahwal-i-Sayyid Jamal al-Din Afghani*," *Seraj al-Akhbar,* vol. 6, no. 5, 21 *Mizan* 1295/Oct. 14, 1916.

[6.] Quoted in Rawan-Farhadi, *Maqalat-i-Mahmud Tarzi dar Seraj al-Akhbar-i-Afghania, 1290-1297 h/sh*, 15.

[7.] Schinasi, 194.

lack of proper understanding of the Qur'an. The Qur'an, he asserted, combined spiritual knowledge with knowledge of things temporal and provided guidelines for success in this world and the next. When Muslims properly understood the Qur'an, he maintained, they spread to the world not only the message of the Holy Book, but also literacy and the arts and sciences. The decline of the Muslims began, he argued, when they stopped using the Qur'an as their guide in affairs of the world and applied its teachings only to matters of the hereafter.[8]

Tarzi blamed the ulama for the general lack of knowledge about the Qur'an. Unlike their predecessors, who had been agents of pre-Renaissance literary and scientific achievements, the ulama of later periods, according to Tarzi, had become too rigid about peripheral issues (*foru*`), paying insufficient attention to the main principles (*osul*). Their failure to guide believers, Tarzi argued further, had led to widespread ignorance and to the acceptance of ideas and practices alien to Islam. Folk practices and superstitions (*kharafat*) had replaced rational religion (*din-i-`aqli*), and Muslims had gradually lost their confidence, sense of unity, vigor, vitality, and leadership role in science and culture.[9]

In his articles, Tarzi championed Asian revivalism and pan-Islamism. In his multivolume Persian translation of a history of the Russo-Japanese War (*jang-i-rus wa japan*), originally written by the chief of staff of the Turkish army, he intended to show how a small but determined Asian nation was able to defeat a great power and revitalize itself in the act of confronting the West. He believed that Muslims could prosper again if the ulama, who guided the masses, understood the spirit of Islam.

The new prosperity would, however, require royal guidance. In the absence of an effective ecclesiastical organization, Tarzi hoped a benevolent and enlightened monarch would assume the role of religious reformer and reinterpret Islam to meet contemporary needs. In this hope, he initially applauded the benevolent policies of Amir Habib-Allah, attempting by flattery to draw the amir's attention to his responsibilities and to neutralize reactionary forces in the royal court.[10] Sometimes, however, his zeal exceeded caution. Once he explicitly condemned autocracy, alleging it was non-Islamic and criticizing a certain group of ulama for promoting belief in the divine right of kings. He wrote,

> The God-loving, truthful ulama and *sheikh*s, who guided the people in the true path, have long been extinct [and replaced by impostors]. Parading in the cloaks of their great predecessors, these impostors sacrificed truthfulness and justice for personal gain and exalted

---

[8] *Seraj al-Akhbar*, vol. 6, no. 21, 16 *Jawza* 1296/June 6, 1917.

[9] *"Aya mane`-i-taraqi-i-mosolmanan chist?* (What Are the Obstacles to the Progress of Muslims?)," *Seraj al-Akhbar*, vol. 6, nos. 14-21, 5 *Hut* 1295—16 *Jawza* 1296/Feb. 23—June 6, 1917.

[10] Nawid, "Political Advocacy in Modern Afghan Poetry," 8.

earthly Muslim rulers to supernatural beings, glorifying them and granting them questionable rights.[11]

In his articles, Tarzi also dealt with Western concepts of government, statehood, and nationality, explaining them in a framework of Muslim ethical values. His political views were best expressed in a series of articles titled "Religion," "State," "Fatherland," and "Nation" (*din, dawlat, waten, mellat*), which appeared in the column "Ethics" (*akhlaqiyyat*). He explained that these four elements were interrelated, that one could not exist without the others, and that ruler and ruled had equal responsibility to defend the fatherland and protect Islam.

Tarzi believed that a benevolent ruler concerned primarily with the people's welfare could win the loyalty of the masses and educate them to share effectively in government and social development. It was, he wrote, the responsibility of the state to maintain a harmonious social balance through legislation and administration.[12] He understood clearly that change could only be achieved at the state and local levels with the cooperation of the ulama.

He viewed Islam as a binding force that could unite Muslims against Western imperialism. In his article "If Muslims Unite (*agar mosolmanan mottahed shawand*)," he focused on the ulama members' leading roles in society as jurists, teachers, and preachers in the mosques, and he appealed to them to use their influence to enlighten the masses and to unite various ethnic and tribal groups under the banner of Islam.[13]

Islamic unity (*ettehad-i-eslami*) was, in Tarzi's view, a prerequisite for national unification. He hoped to see an Afghan Islamic identity that would transcend tribal, ethnic, regional, and sectarian loyalties and unite the nation in development. He urged the *Shi`as* and the *Sunnis* to put aside their differences in order to save Islam. In its July 21, 1917, issue, *Seraj al-Akhbar* printed an article titled "Long Live Unity" that lauded the coalition of the *Shi`as* and *Sunnis* in the Caucasus and prayed for similar cooperation between these sects in other parts of the Muslim world.

Toward the end of his journalistic career, Tarzi gradually abandoned his laudatory tone in his references to Amir Habib-Allah. The Islamic nationalism aroused by the Great War gave him the opportunity to take a more assertive stand. *Seraj al-Akhbar* moved in a new direction, attempting to channel public sentiment in defense of the fatherland. In contrast to Habib-Allah's neutrality during the war, Tarzi advocated Islamic unity and support for Ottoman Turkey, while also championing Afghan nationalism. By the end of the war, he was the driving force behind Afghan nationalism, and his articles criticizing Habib-Allah's neutrality became increasingly strident. When ulama in the Eastern

---

[11.] *Seraj al-Akhbar*, vol. 6, no. 21, 16 *Jawza* 1296/June 6, 1917, 9.

[12.] *"Din, dawlat, watan, mellat* (Religion, State, Fatherland, Nation)," *Seraj al-Akhbar*, vol. 4, nos. 20-24, 27 *Jawza*—10 *Asad* 1294/June 17—Aug. 1, 1916.

[13.] *Seraj al-Akhbar*, vol. 5, 16 *Hut* 1294/Mar. 6, 1916.

Province instigated tribal skirmishes against the British in 1916, *Seraj al-Akhbar* called for complete independence—internal and external.

Amir Habib-Allah tolerated Tarzi's inflammatory writings as long as they did not actually threaten the peace. Cautious in his dealings with the British, Habib-Allah hoped to settle the question of independence through diplomatic bargaining and peaceful negotiations, not combat. For some time in his negotiations with the British, he referred to Tarzi's articles as evidence of strong anti-British sentiment in Afghanistan. However, as editorials in *Seraj al-Akhbar* became increasingly provocative, Habib-Allah tightened control over the newspaper. He was outraged when, on January 7, 1916, an article appeared under the title "Rise Up for Prosperity (*haiy `ali al-falah*)," appropriating the second phrase of the call for daily prayer and advocating a national uprising against the British. Tarzi decried the Muslims' indifference to the war, endorsed the ulama's call for *jehad*, made a passionate appeal to Afghan pride, and called upon the nation to rise up against the British.

> Muslim advocates are preaching the gospel, singing songs of truth, loudly appealing to Muslims everywhere to wake up, to be alert, but who is listening? Who is paying any attention? Who understands? Who moves? Who? Where? When?...We should be singing our own song, playing our own music, and leading our own cara-van....*Seraj al-Akhbar* is a Muslim newspaper...and solely Afghan. The songs it sings and the music it plays amplify the attitude of the Afghan and the dignity (*moqamat-i-`olwiyat*) and honor (*sharafat*) of the Afghan nation.[14]

Following poignant remarks about Afghan pride and the bravery of the Afghans during the First and Second Anglo-Afghan Wars, he concluded:

> Rise up for prosperity (*haiy `ali al-fallah*), O, noble Afghan nation! You must protect your dignity and your national honor. You must protect the independence of your government. Afghans, who have become known the world over for their bravery, pride and strong be-lief in Islam, must not accept the control or protection of a foreign non-Muslim nation.[15]

Habib-Allah censored the article and reprimanded Tarzi for having called the faithful to arms at an inappropriate time, and he fined him 26,000 rupees.[16] However, Prince Aman-Allah secretly paid the fine the same day in order to save Tarzi from further punishment.[17] Two years later, Habib-Allah alleged a

---

[14.] *Ibid.*, vol. 5, no. 10, 16 *Jadyi* 1294/Jan. 7, 1916, censored article.

[15.] *Ibid.*

[16.] A. H. Habibi, "*Yak waraq-i-gomshoda-i-tarikh* (A Lost Page of History)," *Masawat*, Kabul, 7 *Qaws* 1346/Nov. 29, 1967.

[17.] *Ibid.*

connection between *Seraj al-Akhbar* and a plot on his life, and he shut the newspaper down.

By this time, Tarzi had accomplished his primary objectives. He had established a philosophical base for reform and had developed a nationalist ideology based in Islam. His emphasis on pan-Islamism and Asian nationalism had attracted many supporters from abroad, particularly among Indian and Central Asian Muslims. In addition, Tarzi's unpublished satiric works were being circulated underground among the Young Turks,[18] and it was partly through the influence of *Seraj al-Akhbar* that Kabul became the center of many pan-Islamic activities during and after the war.

TARZI, PRINCE AMAN-ALLAH, AND THE NATIONALISTS

Tarzi's views and ideas had a profound impact on the rising generation of Afghan intellectuals—mostly young liberal court members, schoolteachers, and writers. Among the most enthusiastic of Tarzi's admirers was Prince Aman-Allah, whose marriage in 1916 to Tarzi's daughter, Soraya, brought him into close contact with Tarzi and his circle. It was mainly as a result of the influence of his father-in-law that Aman-Allah developed a zeal for freedom from Western imperialism for Afghans in particular and for Asians in general.[19] In accord with Tarzi's views, Aman-Allah keenly supported the position that Afghanistan should enter World War I against the British and the Allied powers.

In 1918, following an attempt on Amir Habib-Allah's life, a number of Young Afghans were arrested. A report prepared at that time by the Mostawfi al-Mamalek included the names of Prince Aman-Allah and 'Olya Hazrat among those involved in the conspiracy. Although spared severe punishment as a result of intervention by Na'eb al-Saltana, the amir's brother and Aman-Allah's uncle, Aman-Allah and his mother fell out of favor with Amir Habib-Allah following the assassination attempt.

Frustrated with Amir Habib-Allah's foreign and domestic policies, the nationalists wanted drastic changes in the orientation of the state. To them the young, energetic Prince Aman-Allah seemed well suited to lead the nation. He had shown great sympathy toward liberal causes, had a passionate desire for independence from foreign control, and had a reputation as a benevolent prince and defender of the oppressed.[20]

[18.] Stewart, 9; Habibi, *Jonbesh-i-Mashrutiyyat dar Afghanistan*, 170.

[19.] As a young boy, Aman-Allah was educated by well- known Afghan scholars and Muslim Indian and Turkish teachers. He was also instructed by 'Abd al-Quddus E'temad al-Dawlah, who took a keen interest in the young prince, apparently hoping to forge a political alliance with 'Olya Hazrat, Seraj al-Khawatin, Aman-Allah's mother and Amir Habib-Allah's powerful wife.

[20.] Ghani, 92-93.

AMAN-ALLAH'S SUCCESSION TO THE THRONE

Following the assassination of Amir Habib-Allah on February 19, 1919, there was a brief period of strife between two ideologically opposed political factions. Proponents of orthodoxy were led by Na'eb al-Saltana, Sardar Nasr-Allah, and nationalist reformers were led by `Ain al-Dawla Aman-Allah Khan. Both groups had opposed Habib-Allah's pro-British inclinations during the Great War and shared the view that Afghanistan should go to war to assert its independence. They diverged primarily in their interpretations of the way to apply Islamic principles to domestic policy. The proponents of orthodoxy rejected innovation. The modernist nationalist reformers, mostly Tarzi's followers, hoped for a new social order and nurtured the idea of a modern nation-state, also based on Islamic principles.

By strict primogeniture, the first in the line of succession was Sardar `Enayat-Allah Mo`in al-Saltana, Amir Habib-Allah's eldest son. It was, however, expected that Nasr-Allah Khan, the Na'eb al-Saltana, would succeed Habib-Allah because Amir `Abd al-Rahman had desired it this way, and Habib-Allah had agreed to this arrangement. Sardar Aman-Allah `Ain al-Dawla ranked fourth after his second elder brother, Sardar Hayat-Allah, the `Azz al-Dawla.

The day after Amir Habib-Allah's assassination in the Eastern Province, several prominent religious leaders long allied with Na'eb al-Saltana issued a *fatwa* declaring that the amir,

> being a martyr (*shahid*) must, according to custom, be buried at once in the clothes he had on at the time of his death without waiting for any elaborate ceremonies, and that his body could only be committed to the earth by his elected successor.[21]

The religious leaders intended the *fatwa* to facilitate an immediate transfer of power to Na'eb al-Saltana, Sardar Nasr-Allah, who was with his brother in the Eastern Province. Sardar `Enayt-Allah, the eldest son, who was also with the amir in Jalalabad at the time of the assassination, waved his claim to the throne in favor of his uncle, Na'eb al-Saltana, Sardar Nasr-Allah. `Azz al-Dawla Hayat-Allah Khan, the second son, and high-echelon officials present joined Sardar `Enayat-Allah Khan in declaring an oath of allegiance to Na'eb al-Saltana.[22] According to Hafez Saif-Allah, the British envoy present at the scene, the ceremony (*dastar-bandi*) was performed by prominent religious leaders of the Eastern Province, including Sayyid Hasan Gailani, the Naqib of Baghdad, and Mir Ma`sum, the Hazrat of Charbagh, with Sayyid Jan, the Padshah of Islampur, officiating.[23] Na'eb al-Saltana's accession to the throne in Jalalabad was chal-

---

[21.] Letter from G. Roose-Kepple to D. Bray dated Mar. 5, 1919, NAI, FPD, June 19, 1919, no. 89.

[22.] NAI, Simla Records 1, Government of India, FPD, June 1919, no. 158.

[23.] *Ibid.*

lenged at once in Kabul by `Ain al-Dawla Aman-Allah Khan, who was acting as vice-regent in his father's absence. Upon hearing the news of the amir's death, Aman-Allah seized control of the army and the arsenal in Kabul and pronounced Na'eb al-Saltana a traitor and murderer of his father. The grounds alleged for Aman-Allah's accusations were the hasty and improper burial of the amir, and lack of concerted action to apprehend the assassin.[24]

On February 21, Aman-Allah held a court session (*darbar*) and announced that he would not render allegiance to a criminal and that his two older brothers had forfeited their right to the throne by accepting Na'eb al-Saltana's usurpation. He declared further that he would not allow the assassination of his father to go unpunished, and he stated that his father, as a Muslim ruler, was also father of the nation. He vowed to pursue the offender and the instigators of the crime and bring them to justice.[25] By demanding retribution for the murder of the amir, Aman-Allah won the support of the army officers and the nobility loyal to Habib-Allah.[26]

The news of the surrender of high army officers to Aman-Allah in the capital and his promise to increase army pay incited troops in Jalalabad to mutiny against Na'eb al-Saltana.[27] Despite pledges of support from influential religious leaders in Jalalabad, Nasr-Allah announced his abdication on February 28, claiming he wanted to avoid civil war and bloodshed in Afghanistan.[28] British observers, who were watching closely, drew different conclusions. George Roos-Keppel, chief commissioner in the North West Frontier, believed that with the help of the important religious leaders, who were all on his side, Nasr-Allah could have raised a tribal army sufficiently strong to defeat the government

---

[24] "*Saltanat Amir Aman-Allah Khan* (The Reign of Amir Aman-Allah Khan)," *Aman-i-Afghan*, vol. 1, no. 1, 22 *Hamal* 1298/Apr. 12, 1919.

[25] *Ibid.* Muslim criminal law gives the slain person's next of kin the right to retaliate or redeem the murderer once his guilt has been proven in a court of law. The Pashtun code of honor (*pashtunwali*), governed by complex tribal blood relationships, gives even greater weight to the concept of retribution (*badal*). An unavenged murder, according to the *pashtunwali*, is considered an ignominy. The closest member of the victim's family is expected to reciprocate the offence. The proverb "a legitimate son will not overlook his father's murder (*az sar-i-khun-i-padar farzand saleh nagzarad*)" suggests the significance of the custom of retaliation in Afghan culture. Aman-Allah used this appeal to this time-honored custom as a political move to discredit his uncle and older brothers as unworthy heirs to the throne.

[26] *Ibid.*

[27] Maconachie, 12.

[28] Na'eb al-Saltana's letter of abdication, dated 25 *Jamadi al-Awwal* 1337/Feb. 28, 1919, is printed in *Aman-i-Afghan*, vol. 1, no. 2, 22 *Sawr* 1298/May 12, 1919. According to the British envoy in Kabul, the Padshah of Islampur tried his best, without success, to persuade Nasr-Allah not to abdicate, promising a force of fifty thousand in support of Nasr-Allah if it came to a battle between him and his nephew. NAI, FPD, No. A-177, "Diary of the British Agent in Kabul," Feb. 28, 1919.

troops if he had had a large sum of money with him in Jalalabad and the time to organize his resources.[29]

Richard Maconachie concluded later that Na'eb al-Saltana's defeat was an inevitable outcome of the rising tide of nationalism:

> It is reasonable to find in the success of Amanullah not merely the reward of superior tactics, but also an illustration of the broad fact already noticed that the impulse behind recent movements in the East is nationalist rather than religious in character, and that when the two forces come into conflict the advantage lies with nationalism....Mullahs are still keen on Nasrullah, but it is toward Aman-Allah that the army and people have turned.[30]

Aman-Allah acceded to the throne the same day Nasr-Allah announced his abdication. He was formally crowned by distinguished religious leaders in Kabul. Hazrat Fazl Mohammad Mojaddedi (later Shams al-Mashayikh) and Akhundzada Hamid-Allah, known as the Molla of Tagaw, performed the ceremony (*dastar-bandi*) at the `Idgah Mosque in Kabul. The new king took the traditional oath, promising to rule according to the sacred law, the *shari`at*.

Whether by design or accident, the primary goal of the Young Afghans was realized. The cantankerous, autocratic amir was removed and replaced by a young, energetic son, committed to Afghanistan's independence and modernization. The triumph of the liberals was fully realized with the appointment of Mahmud Tarzi as minister of foreign affairs, the release of political prisoners, including leading members of the underground Constitutionalist Party (*mashruta-khwahan*), and the appointment of liberals to the newly established legislative council and to key administrative positions.

Despite the endorsement of religious leaders in Kabul, the tribal ulama of the Eastern Province, long allied with Nasr-Allah, began sporadic incursions against the Kabul regime. Their misgivings regarding the new regime were confirmed when a tribunal in Kabul sentenced Nasr-Allah to life imprisonment as "the alleged originator and main instigator of Amir Habib-Allah's murder."[31] Questionable acts that had eased Nasr-Allah's accession to the throne provided the pretext for the condemnation. However, the probable reason for his imprisonment was to remove him as a threat to the new regime.[32]

---

[29] NAI, Simla Records 1, Government of India, FPD, June 1919, no. 158 and no. 640-R, Peshawar, Mar. 5, 1919.

[30] Maconachie, 12.

[31] Fraser-Tytler, *Afghanistan: A Study of Political Development in Central Asia*, 195; Adamec, *Afghanistan 1900-1923: A Diplomatic History*, 109.

[32] There was at least one attempt by Na'eb al-Saltana's supporters on the new king's life. That attempt was made by the son of Nazir Safar, the correspondence secretary (*amin al-ettela`at*) under Habib-Allah, who had assisted Nasr-Allah in anti-British activities. Nazir Safar also had relations with the tribal clergymen who supported Nasr-Allah.

In Bajawar in the Eastern Province, the powerful Molla of Chaknawur imposed a tribal levy (*lashkar*) to support Nasr-Allah.   Hajji `Abd al-Razeq, the head *molla* (*molla-bashi*), Nasr-Allah's most trusted follower, fled to Swat to join the Molla of Turangzai and the Molla Babri against the regime. Sporadic opposition surfaced elsewhere in the Eastern Province, and the government responded by issuing orders for the arrest of many *molla*s in the vicinity of Jalalabad neighborhood.[33]   The two most prominent were Qazi Baba Morad, the head Qazi of Kabul who was also a member of the State Council, and Molla `Abd al-Razeq, who was the rector of Madrasa-i-Shahi and head of the  Religious Advisory Council (*hai`at-i-mizan wa tahqiq*).[34]   This early clerical opposition to the regime was, however, soon overshadowed by the outbreak of the War of Independence, also known as the Third Anglo-Afghan War.

THE WAR OF INDEPENDENCE AND THE MOBILIZATION OF THE ULAMA

Aman-Allah's proclamation of the War of Independence in April 1919 and his subsequent call for a holy war (*jehad*) dramatically altered the attitude of religious groups toward the regime. These actions effectively won Aman-Allah the support of the ulama and political legitimacy for the early years of his reign. By declaring war and proclaiming *jehad* when his dynastic right was still in question, Aman-Allah was able to draw the allegiance of religious groups away from his uncle.

Before his assassination, Habib-Allah had begun negotiating the issue of Afghanistan's independence from the British. On February 2, 1919, he wrote to the viceroy requesting that Afghanistan be represented in the Paris Conference. In the letter, he also demanded a document from the British recognizing Afghanistan's unconditional independence. Apparently, he expected Afghanistan's neutrality during the war to be rewarded with independence, but the British government was unwilling to make concessions on this matter. On the same day that Habib-Allah was assassinated, the secretary of state for India, Edwin Montagu, drafted a letter affirming that Afghanistan would remain under British

---

A minor officer in charge of guarding Habib-Allah's tent the night of the assassination was tried and executed for the murder. The trial and its outcome did not, however, satisfy the public. Rather, it was seen as a staged hearing to protect the identity of the real murderer. Rumor focused on Shoja al-Dawla, later Afghan minister in London, the superintendent of the amir's camp (*farrash-bashi hozur*), as the prime suspect and on `Olya Hazrat and Aman-Allah, who had fallen out of favor with the amir, as instigators of the assassination. See Mir M. S. Farhang, *Afghanistan dar Panj Qarn-i-Akhir*, ii, 477-478, and Habibi, *Jonbesh-i-Mashrutiyyat dar Afghanistan*, 200-203.

Nasr-Allah died in prison in 1920, widely believed to have been poisoned by order of the king. Ghobar, however, rejects this theory. See Ghobar, 750.

[33.] NAI, FPD, June 1919, no. 89.

[34.] Adamec, *Who's Who of Afghanistan*, 107.

protection. However, as a result of the assassination, the note was never sent to Kabul.[35]

The creation of a Ministry of Foreign Affairs (*nezarat-i-khareja*) immediately following Aman-Allah's accession to the throne revealed his likely intent to declare Afghanistan's independence. On March 3, 1919, Aman-Allah wrote a letter to Lord Chelmsford, viceroy and governor-general of India, in which he expressed the wishes of his people to conclude a treaty of friendship with the British as a free nation.[36] Unwilling to await the British response, Aman-Allah unilaterally declared Afghanistan's complete independence, evidently willing to face an adverse British reaction.

The tragic incident at Jallianwalabagh on April 13, 1919,* provided Aman-Allah a pretext for action. The day that hundreds of Indians were killed or wounded by order of a British officer at Jallianwalabagh, he convened a *darbar* in Kabul and declared that it was time for Afghanistan to take up arms against the British and reclaim its independence. A *jehad*, he said, had become necessary for the good of Islam and the country. Quoting from the Qur'an (3:103), he urged his people to "hold together, not to scatter, but to catch fast the rope of God."[37] He also made preparations for war with the British, planning simultaneous attacks on three fronts: at Khyber under Commander in Chief Saleh Mohammad, at Khost under Sepahsalar Nader Khan and Spin Boldak, and at Quetta under 'Abd al Qoddus Khan, the E'temad al-Dawla.

The sacralization of military action as holy war was highly successful. Ascribing religious significance to military operations against the British was something of a tradition in Afghanistan. Holy war was the first order of priority for the ulama, who saw their historic role as guardians of Afghanistan against the British. Opposing the regime during a holy war would link them to the infidel party and amount to rejection of a pillar of Islamic obligation. Indeed, the official proclamation of *jehad* tapped a deep feeling among the clergy. The ulama who had defended Nasr-Allah's right to the throne on religious grounds were now compelled to recognize Aman-Allah as the legitimate ruler of Afghanistan and to support him against the British. Accordingly, all of the prominent religious leaders of the country joined in support of the new regime within a month of the declaration of *jehad*. The Padshah of Islampur, a powerful ally of Nasr-Allah, came voluntarily to Kabul to declare his allegiance to Aman-Allah.[38] In June 1919, the Molla of Chaknawur and Molla Payinda (the Ostad of

---

[35] Stewart, 28.

[36] For the text of the letter, see Adamec, *Afghanistan's Foreign Affairs*, 110.

*On April 13, 1919, the British army in India, headed by Brigadier General Reginald Dyer, opened fire on a crowd gathered for a celebration at Jallianwalabagh in Amritsar, a city in Punjab, leaving 379 dead and 1,200 wounded. This incident created great bitterness in India.

[37] Royal Proclamation of *Jehad*, no title, n.d., distributed in Dakka and the Peshawar area; "The Afghan Situation," May 17, 1919, NAI, FPD, A-177.

[38] Adamec, *Who's Who of Afghanistan*, 193.

Hadda), both zealous supporters of Nasr-Allah, joined the Afghan forces in Dacca, an outpost near Jalalabad, with their followers. Mawlawi `Abd al-Razeq, Molla Lalapir, the Hajji of Turangzai, and the Hazrat of Botkhak, along with other ardent supporters of Nasr-Allah, all joined the government in opposition to Britain.

Most of the ulama actively participated in the War of Independence, and it was in the war effort that they exerted most influence over the masses. Fazl Mohammad Mojaddedi (later Shams al-Mashayikh) and his brother, Fazl `Omar (later Nur al-Mashayikh); Mawlawi `Abd al-Wase` Qandahari; Mawlawi Fazl al-Haqq; Akhundzada Mossahi; Molla Utmanzai; Molla Mohammad Jan Khan; Molla `Abd al-Rahman Baiktuti; and Molla `Abd al-Hamid Alekozai, the *mota-walli* of the Shrine of Khirqa-i-Sharif in Qandahar, were among the prominent religious leaders who served at the front.[39]

In one sense, the declaration of war against the British was in response to a long-standing demand of the ulama, particularly the tribal ulama of the Eastern Province and their counterparts on the British side of the Durand line. Hajji `Abd al-Razeq (also referred to as Mawlawi and Molla), who was the head molla (*molla-bashi*) and who had considerable influence with the tribal clergy on both sides of the frontier, acted as a liaison between the Afghan government and tribal leaders on the British side. He had initially gone to Swat and Bajawur to join his close friends and collaborators, the Hajji of Turangzai and Molla Babri, to raise tribal levies to support Nasr-Allah. Subsequently, the government issued warrants for his arrest. Realizing that Molla `Abd al-Razeq could be a great asset during the war, Aman-Allah reversed his earlier decision and instructed the molla to stay in Bajawur. "A loyal servant of the state and an eminent religious scholar such as your holiness," Aman-Allah wrote, "will be needed there to attend to matters of great importance to the state and religion."[40] Surmising from the order that plans for a major offensive against the British were in the offing, Molla `Abd al-Razeq changed his attitude toward the new regime. By the time war was officially declared, he was active in the region, making contacts with tribal leaders. He held *jerga*s in Swat, Dir, Chitral, and Bajawur, which served to build a tribal coalition against the British.[41]

Shortly after the proclamation of *jehad*, some forty thousand fighting men were gathered under the leadership of Molla Babri, the Hajji of Turangzai, the Sarkani Molla, and the Padshah of Islampur. (See Table 4) Konar, Jalalabad, and Bajawur came under the command of Mawlawi Mohammad Ebrahim of Kamma, also known as Mawlawi Kamawi. Meanwhile, Pashtu and Urdu translations of the proclamation of *jehad* were distributed across the border in Peshawar and Rawalpindi.[42]

---

[39] Ghobar, 763-764; Fofalzai, *Negahi ba Tarikh-i-Esterdad-i-Esteqlal-i-Afghanistan*, 32.
[40] Royal Decree (*farman*), dated Jamad-i-Thani 29, 1337/Apr. 2, 1919, cited in M. Wali Zalmai, *Mojahed Afghan*, 36-38.
[41] *Ibid.*, 43-44.
[42] *Ibid.*, 74-76, 81.

The Molla of Chaknawur imposed a tribal levy (*lashkar*) in Mohmand, and, following Saleh Mohammad Khan's defeat in Dakka, continued the fight against the British in Mohmand Dara. He was able to persuade the local population, which was suffering from food shortages, to continue to fight by obtaining food from neighboring villages.[43]

Sheikh Fazl `Omar Mojaddedi (Nur al-Mashayikh) accompanied the government troops in the Southern Province (Samt-i-Jonubi or Paktia). In a speech delivered in the Friday mosque in Zormat, he announced the intention of the king to obtain Afghanistan's complete freedom from "the fraudulent English colonizers, no matter how great the sacrifice." He explained that although Afghanistan was and always had been an independent country, the British, after their defeat in the Maiwand War, had deceitfully imposed on the former amirs conditions that resulted in the loss of Afghanistan's external independence. He emphasized that Islam did not concede to servitude (*reqiyyat*) and urged the citizens to respond positively to the king's call for *jehad* to secure Afghanistan's complete independence. "We will obtain our freedom," he declared, "by sacrificing ourselves, our belongings, our children and our families. What will be more rewarding than to die as a martyr (*shahid*) or to live as one who has struggled in the way of God *(mojahed)* and to gain glory in this world and the next?"[44]

It was as a result of the active cooperation of the powerful tribal ulama, such as the Molla of Chaknawur, Mawlawi Fazl al-Rabbi, the Akhundzada of Tirah, and Padshah Gol (the son of Hajji of Turangzai) in rallying the Afridi, Waziri, Jaji, Mahsud (Mas`ud), and Mohmand tribes to battle that Sepahsalar Nader Khan was able to claim victory at Thal in Waziristan. Although the British interpreted the outcome of the battle differently, the confrontation at Thal had a decisive effect on the peace negotiations that followed.

On July 20, an Afghan mission headed by Shagasi `Ali Ahmad Khan met Sir Hamilton Grant in Rawalpindi to discuss terms of peace. The negotiations resulted in a treaty signed at Rawalpindi on August 8, 1919, in which Great Britain recognized Afghanistan as a fully sovereign state. The ensuing discussions between Mahmud Tarzi and Sir Henry Dobbs during the Mussoorie Conference (April 17-July 24) in 1920 concentrated on issues relating to the Pashtun tribes along the Durand Line and the establishment of diplomatic relations between the two countries. The negotiations in Mussoorie did not reach a conclusive agreement. Discussions resumed upon the arrival of the Dobbs mission in Kabul in January 1921 and continued late into the year. The Anglo-Afghan Treaty signed in Kabul on November 22, 1921, guaranteed Afghanistan's internal and external independence and provided for the exchange of diplomatic representation between Kabul and London, a provision earlier opposed by Lord Curzon, then

---

[43.] A letter from Molla `Abd al-Razeq reveals that the government later excused these villages from paying taxes that year because they had provided grain to the inhabitants of Mohmand Dara at the request of the Molla of Chaknawur. Chaknawri Letters, no. 1.

[44.] Fofalzai, *Negahi ba Tarikh-i-Esterdad-i-Esteqlal*, 71.

minister of foreign affairs for Great Britain.[45]   On March 6, 1922, Sir Francis Humphrys arrived to take up the post of the first British minister in Kabul.

DEFENDER OF ISLAM

In his quest for legitimacy, Aman-Allah adhered to Islamic values. Following the *jehad* and the War of Independence, he performed other acts of religious zeal to enhance his image as a defender of Islam, and he espoused religious ideals with enthusiasm, despite his strong commitment to reform. At the same time, the press stressed the religious duties of the ruler and the religious functions of the state by featuring stories with Islamic themes such as faith (*iman*), God-given success (*tawfiq*), and that which is good and proper (*maslehat*) for the nation. By delivering passionate speeches and personally leading the prayer in the mosques, the king himself used Friday prayers to stimulate a high level of religious devotion. The media depicted him as the nation's father (*padar-i-mellat*), who extolled the traditional values of Afghans and whose judgment should be obeyed by his children with no objection. *Aman-i-Afghan*, a semiofficial newspaper created shortly after Aman-Allah's accession to replace *Seraj al-Akhbar*, commended the king's "inspirational Friday sermons (*khotba*s) dealing with philosophy and various important aspects of Islam. These *khotba*s, which conform to the needs of the time, provide an illustrious model for the mosque preachers."[46]

For the first three years of his reign, Aman-Allah's relations with the ulama were cordial and often friendly. Although British sources refer consistently to his apathy toward religious groups, other sources indicate that he cultivated excellent personal relations with eminent religious leaders in Kabul long before ascending the throne. According to `Ali Ahmad, Aman-Allah had won over celebrated religious leaders such as Sheikh Fazl Mohammad, the Hazrat of Shurbazar and the patriarch of the Mojaddedis of Kabul, and Shah `Abd al-`Azim, known as the Shah Saheb of Qal`a-i-Qazi, both of whom commanded great reverence in Kabul.[47] Aman-Allah visited Shah `Abd al-`Azim frequently and received from him the appellation `Adel al-Dawla (the Justice of the State) for his concern for the people's welfare. As a devoted adherent of the Shah Saheb, the young prince had been at the death bed of Shah `Abd al-`Azim and had participated in the ritual of preparing his body for burial.[48] As a result of these

---

[45.] For details of the war and the subsequent negotiations with the British, see Adamec, *Afghanistan, 1900-1922*, 109-142; and Ghobar, 756-784.

[46.] *Aman-i-Afghan*, 22 *Saur* 1303/Apr. 2, 1923.

[47.] `Ali Ahmad, "Fall of Amanullah," 1-2. Shah `Abd al-`Azim was a *sayyid* from Foshanj in Qandahar (not to be confused with Foshanj in Herat) who adhered to the Qadriyya order. He resided in Qal`a-i-Qazi, near Kabul.

[48.] Interview with Sayyid Taj al-Din, Oakland, California, Dec. 28, 1988. Sayyid Taj al-Din's father was the usher of the palace. He accompanied Aman-Allah during these visits. Aman-Allah's genuine reverence for the Shah of Qal`a-i-Qazi was confirmed by his last wish, to be buried next to the grave of this holy man.

earlier contacts, the religious leadership in Kabul, led by the Hazrat of Shurba-zar, supported Aman-Allah's succession to the throne. Farhang claims that the support of this segment of the high clergymen was an important factor in estab-lishing Aman-Allah's legitimacy as Habib-Allah's successor.[49]

Following his accession to the throne, Aman-Allah remained favorably dis-posed to religious leaders. He granted the Hazrats of Shurbazar land and appel-lations of priestly distinction—Shams al-Mashayikh (Sun of the Sheikhs) to Fazl Mohammad Mojaddedi and Nur al-Mashayikh (Light of the Sheikhs) to his younger brother, Fazl `Omar Mojaddedi. According to Shah Agha Mojaddedi, author of *Habib-Allah Khadem-i-Din-i-Rasul-Allah*, Aman-Allah treated the Hazrats of Shurbazar with utmost respect, often soliciting their advice and ac-cepting their intercession.[50] The influence of the two Hazrats was so great that even the powerful E'temad al-Dawla requested their help in his relations with the king.[51]

Aman-Allah showed similar respect for religious leaders in the Eastern Province and on the British side of the border. He granted them robes of honor and monetary rewards for their activities during the war. He also treated the Padshah of Islampur with great respect. He appointed the latter's son, Babujan, governor of Konar, and he sent his car to bring the Padshah to a meeting in Jalalabad.[52] He also drove two miles from the capital to meet the Molla of Chaknawur to thank him for his services during the war.[53] Then in the fall of 1919, he received the Molla of Chaknawur with ceremonial pomp in Kabul.

No evidence attests more eloquently to Aman-Allah's great regard for spiri-tual leaders early in his reign than a letter to Shah `Abd al-Khair, who, at the time, lived in India.

> Seated on the throne of learning and knowledge and spiritual guid-ance of the Muslims, commander of the world, Shah `Abd-al Khair, may you be preserved. The sincerity and friendship which I have cherished for a long time toward that spiritual leader are daily on the increase.
>
> Now the agitation of the mind and spiritual attraction have induced me to trouble that chief of the learned and spiritual King with this sincere epistle to make haste to beg the prayer of that blessed guide.
>
> Although I consider your holiness disdainful of worldly ornaments, particularly the use of articles made of gold, yet I venture to send your holiness a watch and compass (for finding the direction of Mecca) by the way of unity of Islam, and as a way of my yielding un-feigned obedience toward that great spiritual King. It is the only sin-cere desire of this faithful disciple that whenever your holiness hap-

---

[49]. Farhang, vol. 1, part 2, 498.

[50]. Shah Agha Mojaddedi, *Amir Habib-Allah Khadem-i-Din-i-Rasul-Allah*, 14.

[51]. Letter of E'temad al-Dawla to Shams al-Mashayikh (Fazl Mohammad Mojaddedi), quoted in Ghobar, *Afghanistan dar Massir-i-Tarikh*, 802-803.

[52]. IOR, P/L&S/10, 813 P3933, no. 15, Apr. 12, 1919.

[53]. *Ibid.*, P8332, 1919 no. 43, Nov. 1, 1919.

pens to look at the watch for determining the time of the five prayers, your holiness may remember this faithful disciple and pray for him.
Your friend and faithful disciple, Amir Aman-Allah.[54]

ALLIANCE OF THE STATE AND CLERGY TO
REUNITE PASHTUN LAND

Recovery and reunification of Pashtun land was another issue of common interest to the nationalists and the ulama. Apart from the relation of this issue to kinship, the reunification of Pashtun land and the recovery of the occupied territories had other importance for the ulama. Since the mid-nineteenth century, when Peshawar was lost to the Sikhs and then to the British, the ulama had been adamant in their demand for its recovery, mainly because Peshawar was an important religious center, where some highly acclaimed ulama had received their religious training. With the enforcement of the Durand Line, resentment against the British grew stronger, resulting in decades of clergy-backed skirmishes along the border.

The question of reunification of the Pashtuns became an important foreign policy issue immediately after the War of Independence. Having proven himself a man of courage and action, qualities much admired by the Pashtuns, Aman-Allah won the support of the clergy and powerful tribes of the Eastern Province. Shortly after the conclusion of the peace treaty at Rawalpindi, a mission of the frontier tribes (*wafd-i-aqwam-i-sarhadi*), composed of delegates of Hezb-al-Allah (a Pashtun political organization formed by the Hajji of Turangzai and Molla `Abd al-`Aziz Utmanzai), the Mojahedin of Chamarkand, and representatives of the Mohmand, Shinwar, Bajawar, and Salarzai tribes from the British side of the Durand Line petitioned to be protected by the Afghan government in repayment for services they had rendered during the war. The petition bore the signature of several tribal ulama, including Mawlawis Bashir, Ebrahim of Kama, Molla Miagul of Swat, Molla Fazl Akbar, Padshah Gol (the son of the Molla of Turangzai), and several others.[55]   Another letter signed by delegates of the tribes, including several clergymen, contained an oath of allegiance by the tribes to the Afghan king and a request to be governed in all domestic and foreign matters by the Afghan government, because these tribes considered themselves an integral part of Afghanistan in terms of religion, language, and ethnicity.[56] Obviously, the regime could not settle the question of reunification without another major confrontation with the British. The option chosen was to encourage anti-British uprisings in the area by means of covert moral and financial support and to link Pashtun insurgence with the broader issue of pan-Islamism. At a time when negotiations for a permanent peace settlement were under way in Mussoorie, agitations at the border could give Afghanistan leverage in bargain-

---

[54.] Quoted in Stewart, 45.
[55.] For the text of the letter, see Zalmai, 79-82.
[56.] For the text of the letter, see *ibid.*, 82.

ing with the British. After the conclusion of the Rawalpindi Peace Treaty, Colonel Shah Dawla, the commander of a cavalry regiment in Khost, remained in Wana in Waziristan and raised tribal levies to garrison abandoned British posts. In January 1920, he was joined by Molla ʽAbd al-Razeq, the adamantly anti-British molla. With the financial support and blessing of the regime and help from Molla Hamz-Allah and Molla Fazl al-Din Pawinda of the Masʽud tribe, Molla ʽAbd-al-Razeq made Waziristan the center of anti-British operations.[57]

By this time, the Chamarkand Mojahedin Colony on the frontier had become an important political center, bringing together revolutionaries from India, nationalists from Afghanistan, Young Turks, anti-Bristish ulama, and sufi *sheikhs*, all intent on overthrowing British rule in India. Sepahsalar Nader Khan, who had gained popularity among the tribes during the war, was dispatched to Jalalabad to promote greater solidarity between tribes on the Afghan and British sides of the frontier. Nader Khan established the newspaper *Ettehad-i-Mashriqi* (Eastern Unity) in Jalalabad and assisted in funding publication of *Al-Mojahed* in Chamarkand. Both newspapers were vehemently anti-British and pan-Islamic and largely meant for consumption in the North-West Frontier Province.

On January 31, the Sepahsalar held a *jerga* at the tomb of Akhundzada Molla Najm al-Din, the well-known Molla of Hadda. The *jerga* included some five thousand tribal delegates from both sides of the border. White banners with clasped hands, as a symbol of unity, were distributed among the delegates, with the intention of establishing loose suzerainty by Afghanistan over the Pashtuns on the British side of the Durand Line. The tribes had tenaciously maintained their communal identity despite their partition by the Durand Line, and when from time to time tribal leaders from the British side participated of their own initiative or by invitation from the Afghan government in *jerga*s held in Kabul and Jalalabad, the government of India had never objected. This time, however, the tribesmen's audience with the king in Kabul and later their participation in the *jerga* at Hadda was met with a strong protest from the viceroy.[58] The Afghan government argued that the tribes had for decades participated in the *jerga*s and had come to Kabul, which they considered the seat of Islam, and had received allowances and rewards for visiting their Muslim king. Their visit this time, according to the Afghan government, was not different from previous calls.[59] The British, however, adamantly refused to accept any Afghan right to delve in the affairs of the tribes within the British boundary. During the Mussoorie Conference, Sir Henry Dobbs, the secretary of state for India, once again objected to the Hadda *jerga* and to other instances of this practice and was able to extract an agreement from Tarzi, the Afghan foreign minister, "to ensure that the frontier tribes, being tranquil, shall not take antagonistic steps against the

---

[57.] *Ibid.*, 100-148.
[58.] Maconachie, 239.
[59.] Letter of King Aman-Allah to the viceroy, Feb. 10, 1920, kharita 14, quoted in Maconachie, 239.

subjects of her friend."[60] The right of visitation by tribes within British jurisdiction was later discussed with Humphrys, the British minister in Kabul. The king told Humphrys that if the tribesmen came to visit him, he would not refuse to see them, but promised that he would not send for them.[61]

Despite these agreements, covert Afghan assistance to anti-British operations in Waziristan continued. Shah Mahmud, Nader Khan's younger brother and the civil and military high official in the Southern Province (*Samt-i-Jonubi*), was commissioned to provide financial assistance to operations in Waziristan.[62] In 1922, Molla `Abd al-Razeq, who had by then assumed the title of president of the mojahedin (*rais al-mojahedin*), openly assailed the British and sent inflammatory messages calling for a Muslim uprising against them. An open letter bearing his seal and signature, addressed to "officers and material helpers of the British government," warned, "you should believe that I will never stay my efforts for your destruction and by the grace of God will succeed in my mission."[63]

In another message dated February 5, 1922, Mawlawi `Abd al-Razeq enjoined all followers of Islam in India, particularly those employed by the government, to rise up against the British:

> You are all aware of the state of the *Khalifat al-Muslimin*, that he is under British surveillance in Constantinople....Do you know who is called *Khalifat al-Muslimin*? According to the *shari`at*, in every age there should be a *khalifa*...[whose] obedience and help is the duty of every Muslim. Any Muslim who turns his head from obedience to the *khalifa* gets out of the circle of Islam....You must be aware of this law, that if the *Khalifat al-Muslimin* is besieged by a powerful enemy the strength of whose opposition the *khalifa* does not possess and cannot save the Islamic territories without the expeditious help of the Muslims of the world, it is incumbent upon them to help him by all means and fight against the enemies of Islam.[64]

Mawlawi `Abd al-Razeq's communication, along with copies of correspondence proving the involvement of Afghan officials in activities in Waziristan, was sent to Humphrys, the British minister in Kabul.[65] Persistent British protests forced the regime to comply with British demands for the removal of Molla `Abd al-Razeq from Waziristan. In a telegram dated April 19, 1922, Humphrys reported to the viceroy that Tarzi had assured him he would recall Mawlawi `Abd al-Razeq and had promised...that most drastic measures would be taken, under per-

---

[60] Maconachie, 240.

[61] Telegram no. 204, Kabul, Dec. 28, 1922, *ibid*.

[62] Royal Decree (*farman*), dated 22 *Mizan* 1299/Oct. 14, 1920. For the text, see *ibid.*, 168-169.

[63] For the English translation of this letter, see IOR, L/P&S/1019, P 1789, 1922, Apr. 2, 1922.

[64] IOR, L/P&S/10/1019, P 1789, Feb. 10, 1922.

[65] *Ibid.*, P 2754, 1922, June 14, 1922.

sonal direction of the king, to prevent attacks on the British side of the border."[66] A few days later, the viceroy informed the secretary of state for India that `Abd al-Razeq had left for Kabul and advised him that "it might be politic for you to thank Tarzi for his prompt and effective action."[67]

Anti-British activities in the tribal area diminished as a result of the removal from Waziristan of Mawlawi `Abd al-Razeq, but did not die out entirely. The government continued to rely on the tribes and support them against the British, and some of the most influential religious leaders of the tribal area, such as the Hajji of Turangzai, remained strong allies of King Aman-Allah to the end.

ALLIANCE OF THE STATE AND THE ULAMA IN SUPPORT OF PAN-ISLAMISM

Afghanistan's victory over the British coincided with the rise of strong anti-British sentiment throughout the Muslim world and with the rise of pan-Islamism as a political force.[*] Popular consciousness of Islamic unity and brotherhood were raised in Afghanistan during the war largely through the provocative articles of Mahmud Tarzi in the *Seraj al-Akhbar*. Muslim publications in India, such as *Al-Helal, Zamindar, Comrade, Hamdard,* and, particularly, the Persian-language paper *Habl al-Matin,* published in Calcutta, also contributed to the spread of pan-Islamic sentiment in Afghanistan.

Common interests had drawn Indian Muslims, Afghan nationalists, and pan-Islamists together against the British from the outbreak of World War I. The main channel of communication between Indian Muslim leaders and Afghan politicians was the ulama. Tribal *molla*s on both sides of the Durand Line, particularly the faction of the high ulama who had received training in religious schools in India, were in close contact with Indian Muslim leaders. As a result, certain ulama in Afghanistan came to play an important role in Afghan politics in conjunction with the *khilafat* movement in India.

The Hajji of Turangzai and his close friend and collaborator, Molla `Abd al-Razeq, were particularly important agents of communication between Afghan and Indian ulama. As a disciple of the Molla of Hadda, the Hajji of Turangzai had connections with virtually all influential clergymen in Afghanistan. He maintained similar relations with the ulama of Deoband as a result of personal relations with Sheikh al-Hind Mawlana Mahmud al-Hasan, the rector (*sadr-i-modarres*) of Deoband College in India. Molla `Abd al-Razeq also had long-standing relations with Indian ulama. As a student of the famous Indian religious scholar Mawlana Rashid Ahmad Ganguhi, "a member of the innermost

---

[66.] IOR, L/P&S/10/1019, P 166, Apr. 21, 1922.

[67.] *Ibid.*, P 1753/1922, telegram from the viceroy to the secretary of state for India, Apr. 27, 1922.

[*]Pan-Islamism as a political movement was initiated by Jamal-al-Din al-Afghani. Young Turk intellectuals, such as Nimek Kamal and `Ali Suavi, gave it a militant dimension in an effort to protect the Ottoman Empire from disintegration.

circle of the ulama who guided the policies of Deoband,"[68] `Abd al-Razeq was connected to the politics of Deoband, which at the time were stridently anti-British.

Shortly after the arrival of the Turko-German Mission in Afghanistan, Sheikh al-Hind Mawlana Mahmud al-Hasan sent Mawlawi `Obaid-Allah Sindhi, a highly learned religious scholar, to Kabul to promote the cause of Turkish and Indian Muslims. In the same year, a number of other Indian religious scholars, among them Mawlawis Barakat-Allah; `Abd al-Rabb; and Mohammad Bashir, the son of the preacher of the Chanwala Mosque in Lahore, also came to Kabul and received employment from the government. Mawlawi `Obaid-Allah was appointed director of public instruction and Mawlawi Barakat-Allah became a newswriter for Na'eb al-Saltana, and, at the same time, did editorial work for *Seraj al-Akhbar*.[69]

With the arrival of these clergymen, the influence of Deoband politics in Kabul became pronounced. By virtue of close contacts with members of the royal family and with important men in the Afghan government, Indian revolutionaries gained the support of high Afghan officials and established themselves as an ancillary political force in Kabul. There, they played an important role in establishing communications among Muslim leaders of India, Central Asia, and Turkey. In September 1916, Mawlawis `Obaid-Allah, Barakat-Allah, and Mahendra Pratap, a revolutionary from the United Province of India, formed the Provisional Government of India in Exile at Kabul with the consent of Nasr-Allah Khan, the Na'eb al-Saltana. During early meetings held at the house of Hajji `Abd al-Razeq, the intercessor between the revolutionaries and the crown, it was decided that the Provisional Government would be presided over by an Afghan prince, such as Prince Aman-Allah, who would later be succeeded by Mawlawi `Obaid-Allah Sindhi as president of the Provisional Government in Exile.[70]

These early close relations with Indian revolutionaries explain, in part, Aman-Allah's keen interest in the cause of the nationalist movement in India from the time of his accession to the throne. Another motive was, of course, a desire to obtain the support of Indian political activists for the cause of Afghan independence. Aman-Allah's proclamation of war against the British in April 1919, which was distributed in pamphlet form in Jalalabad and in Peshawar, made several references to the British army's brutal treatment of the crowd at Jawalalanpur, declaring that "the Indians were justified in rising up against the British."[71] Mawlawi `Obaid-Allah Sindhi, who was connected to Indian Muslim leaders and the Mojahedin of Chamarkand, made an effort to enlist the cooperation of Indian Muslims by sending the following message to the British side of

---

[68] Qureshi, 223.

[69] Habibi, *Jonbesh-i-Mashrutiyyat dar Afghanistan*, 131.

[70] *Ibid.*, 137.

[71] Royal Proclamation of *Jehad*, no title, n.d., distributed in Dakka and the Peshawar area.

the border: "The Provisional Government has entered into a compact with the invading forces. Hence you should not destroy your real interest by fighting against them, but kill the English in every possible way."[72] Mawlawi `Abd al-Bashir, editor of the newspaper *Al-Mojahed* in Chamarkand, printed inflammatory messages in support of the Afghans. He was the agent of Hajji `Abd al-Razeq and played an important role in stirring up the Mahsuds (Mas`uds) against the British.[73]

King Aman-Allah's inflammatory messages were distributed among the *molla*s by the Afghan agent in Peshawar and were read avidly in the Qessa Khwani bazaar and Mohabat Khan Mosque in Peshawar, where the *molla*s openly declared *jehad* in support of King Aman-Allah.[74] The excitement caused by Aman-Allah's declaration prompted the British to ban political gatherings in Peshawar and to close the twelve gates of the city to prevent further contact with Kabul.[75]

The dream of independence, dear to Indian nationalists, first became a reality in Afghanistan when the British were forced to accede full independence to Afghanistan. As a result of this victory over the British, Aman-Allah gained great popularity in India.

Aman-Allah's Support of the Khilafat Movement

The victory of the Allies in 1918 and their intention to eliminate the very name of the "Sick Man of Europe," as Ottoman Turkey was then called, created great concern among pan-Islamists, particularly among Indian Muslim leaders. In November 1918, Indian Muslim activists organized the Khilafat Conference in Bombay, demanding that "full justice be done to the falling Muslim regime in Turkey."[76]

Shortly after the War of Independence, Aman-Allah became involved in the question of the caliphate, showing his support for the cause of Turkey and the related *khilafat* movement in India. In February 1920, he requested that the viceroy in India accept an Afghan deputation to the king-emperor on the question of the caliphate.[77] The issue of the caliphate was brought up once again in April during the conference in Mussoorie in India. During the opening session of negotiations, Mahmud Tarzi demanded to know the attitude of the British government on the question of the caliphate and the situation in Hejaz:

[72.] Manifesto signed by `Obaid-Allah, found at Thal in Warzistan, cited in Maconachie, 15.
[73.] "Afghanistan, Evaluation of British Legation." IOR, L/PO/5/30 (i) [N 874/97].
[74.] `Abd al-Haiy, *Afghanistan awe Sarhad*, 331-332.
[75.] *Ibid.*, 332.
[76.] Yusufi, 4.
[77.] Maconachie, 33.

In view of intense religious feeling which has been aroused in Afghanistan and the neighboring Mohammadan countries, it was of the utmost importance that the British government should declare a policy with regard to the *khilafat* and the Holy Places of Islam.[78]

The British representative assured Tarzi that the situation in Hejaz had improved, with Mecca and Medina being entirely independent under the sharif, but asserted that "no modification in the Turkish peace terms could be made out of regard for Afghan sentiments."[79] Despite this negative response from the British, Tarzi, a dedicated pan-Islamist, took full advantage of his visit to establish close ties with the leaders of the *khilafat* movement in India and to assure them privately that "one of the aims of the Afghan war [was] to secure a just peace for Turkey, and [that] the Afghan king would lay down his life for the sake of preserving the sanctity of [the] *khilafat*."[80]

The Treaty of Sevres in 1920, aimed, among other things, at dismembering the Ottoman Empire, outraged Afghan and Indian Muslim leaders. The Afghan government started fund-raising projects in Kabul to support Mostafa Kamal's military actions in Turkey and to support the *khilafat* movement in India, which looked to the Afghan monarch for leadership. *Ettehad-i-Mashriqi* of Jalalabad wrote that if the question of the caliphate were not settled according to Islamic law, the holy palaces of Islam came under non-Muslim control, and the integrity of the Ottoman Empire were injured, it would not be possible for the Muslims of India to be loyal to the British government.[81] In a similar vein, *Aman-i-Afghan* of Kabul printed a provocative article titled "Islam, Moments of Life and Death" in support of the caliphate.[82]

On March 7, 1920, Mahatma Gandhi's manifesto on the caliphate was printed, urging noncooperation if the demands of Muslims with this regard were not met.[83] In the summer of 1920, Mawlana Mohmud Hasan, who had been released from a long confinement in Malta, mobilized the Deoband ulama in support of the *khilafat* movement.[84] The news of the Hindu-Muslim coalition in India and the activities of Mawlana Mahmud Hasan, known as Sheikh al-Hind, were followed enthusiastically in Afghanistan. At the memorial service held in Kabul following the death of Mawlana Mahmud Hasan (November 30, 1920), King Aman-Allah personally attended the ceremony and publicly announced, "Sheikh al-Hind started a movement; I will, God willing, take it to a successful conclusion."[85]

---

[78] Maconachie, 37.

[79] *Ibid.*

[80] Quoted in Adamec, *Afghanistan, 1900-1923: A Diplomatic History*, 153; Qureshi, 260.

[81] *Ettehad-i-Mashriqi*, vol. 1, no. 5, 23 *Hut* 1298/Mar. 13, 1920.

[82] *Aman-i-Afghan*, vol. 1, no. 1, 22 *Hamal* 1298/Apr. 12, 1919.

[83] *Collected Works of Mahatma Gandhi*, 73-76, cited in Richard Gordon, 451.

[84] Minault, *The Kilafat Movement*, 103.

[85] NAI, FPD, confidential, nos. 31-32, no. 132; Qureshi, 261.

The Afghan regime's support of Indian Muslims went beyond verbal pronouncements. In the early months of 1920, a group of Indian Muslim religious leaders, in their outrage over the Treaty of Sevres, declared that British India was "the abode of war" (*dar al-harb*) because the British government had thwarted Islam by dismantling the Ottoman Empire. They began admonishing Indian Muslims to migrate to Muslim countries. The *fatwas* issued by Mawlawis Kalam Azad and `Abd al-Bari of Firangi Mahal Lucknow made migration (*hejrat*) a sacred duty of all Muslims. At about the same time, in remarks on the anniversary of the death of his father, King Aman-Allah encouraged the *hejrat* movement by offering asylum to thousands who were contemplating leaving India.[86]

The regime's patronage of the *hejrat* movement was met with enthusiasm by the ulama. The Hajji of Turangzai provided accommodations in Waziristan for some 20,000 *mohajerin*, who were on their way to settle in Afghanistan. The religious leaders in Kabul pronounced the *hejrat* movement comparable to the flight of the Prophet from Mecca to Medina and declared that it was the king's religious duty to meet and welcome the immigrants (*mohajerin*) in person. In compliance with the suggestion of the ulama, the king drove several miles outside the capital to meet the caravan of immigrants in Bagram, north of Kabul.[87]

The Afghan government provided the *mohajerin* assistance ranging from financial aid to settlement facilities. A camp was established near Jabal al-Seraj to the north of Kabul for the rehabilitation of the immigrants. In the same year, regulations regarding the settlement of Indian immigrants (*nezam-nama-i-mohajerin-i-hindi*) specified their rights as settlers.

The regime continued to follow events in India with keen interest. British archival materials reveal that during the Mussoorie Conference close relations were established between the Afghan delegates and the leaders of the *khilafat* movement in India and that later the Afghan envoy at Simla corresponded with Shawkat `Ali.[88] The anti-British Hindu-Muslim coalition in India had already favorably disposed Afghans to Indian Hindus. For his part, Aman-Allah strongly supported the participation of Indian Muslims in the effort to topple British imperialism in India and took advantage of the opportunity to promote equal rights for Hindus in Afghanistan, which was essential to his nation-building policy of equality for all. He reduced the poll tax (*jazya*) by half and gave Hindus permission to attend military school and join the Afghan army, buy property, and rebuild Hindu temples that had been destroyed. Taxes from the Hindus were reduced to an amount equal to that paid by Muslims. Moreover, Aman-Allah announced that Hindus should occupy seats in the State Council. Divan Naranjan Das, an important member of the Hindu community in Kabul, was made a member of the Afghan delegation in negotiations with the British at

---

[86] Chief commissioner of NWFP to private secretary to viceroy, telegram, Apr. 29, 1920, *Chemsford Collection*, vol. xxiv.

[87] IOR, L/P&S/10/813, P7025, 1920, no. 23, Aug. 5, 1920.

[88] IOR, L/P&S/961, 897K, P427, Jan. 9, 1922.

the Mussoorie Conference, a gesture that made a great impression on the Hindus of India. The statutory requirement that Hindus wear an orange-colored turban to distinguish them from Muslims was abolished. Aman-Allah also issued a proclamation prohibiting the killing of cows in Afghanistan. The reason given in the proclamation for this prohibition was that Hindus had promised to support the Muslim cause. There was little Muslim opposition to these measures at the time, given greater pan-Islamic interests and feelings of sympathy for Hindus.

Aman-Allah's promotion of pan-Islamic goals and his heroic challenge to British imperialism made him the "Islamic King par excellence." The renowned Indian Muslim poet-philosopher Mohammad Eqbal dedicated his famous poem, "*Payam-i-Mashreq*" ("Message of the East") to Aman-Allah. Another Muslim poet, Vahid Dastgardi, an Iranian, praised Aman-Allah in his "*Chekama-i-Ettehad-i-Eslami*" (a poem in praise of Islamic unity) as the champion of Islamic solidarity.[89]

Aman-Allah's popularity outside Afghanistan prompted some pan-Islamic activists to propose that he be declared *khalifat al-Moslemin*, given the decline of the caliphate in Turkey and Aman-Allah's status as the only independent Muslim ruler. The idea of elevating the Afghan ruler to the position of caliph, if the office were abolished in Turkey, had been considered among Muslims for a long time. During the reign of Amir Habib-Allah, the British expressed concern that the amir of Afghanistan "might lay claim to the Caliphate."[90]

Among the most enthusiastic supporters of the idea of King Aman-Allah's election as caliph were the Afghan ulama and the Afghan prime minister, Sardar 'Abd al-Qoddus E'temad al-Dawla. As the position of the Ottoman sultan became progressively uncertain, observers began to speculate that the king of Afghanistan might be elected caliph. Reportedly, the Baku Congress of 1920 discussed separating the sultanate from the caliphate and "decided to offer the latter to the [Afghan] Amir."[91] E'temad al-Dawla, the Afghan prime minister, had already raised the question with Henry Dobbs. In May, Dobbs telegrammed from Mussoorie that Tarzi was also openly advocating that the way should be paved for recognition of King Aman-Allah as caliph, "since he [Tarzi] considers Turkey past praying for."[92] In November 1920, Jamal Pasha, one of the leaders of the Committee of Union and Progress,* arrived in Kabul with a special mission to make Kabul the center of pan-Islamic activities by recommending Aman-Allah as a candidate for the office of caliph. The idea received the immediate approval of the high clergy in Kabul. The British intelligence bureau in the North-West Frontier Province reported private meetings between Jamal Pa-

---

[89] Gregorian, 236.
[90] Maconachie, 261.
[91] *Ibid.*
[92] *Ibid.*
*The Committee of Union and Progress was a Turkish nationalist reform organization whose members were in control of the Ottoman government until the outbreak of World War I.

sha and Shams al-Mashayikh.[93] The Molla of Tagaw and Shams al-Mashayikh immediately began testing public opinion regarding the idea.[94] A few days later, after the arrival of Jamal Pasha, the Hazrat Saheb of Shurbazar (Shams al-Mashayikh), publicly declared in the Masjid-i-Jame`, the major congregational mosque in Kabul, that "the Amir, being the sole independent [Muslim] ruler left, [is] now head of Islam, and...the Musalman world should salute him as the *Khalifa*."[95] While leading the congregational prayer that day, Mawlawi `Obaid-Allah, head of the Indian revolutionaries in Kabul, endorsed the pronouncement made by Sham al-Mashayikh.[96] The amir, however, publicly declared that the issue of caliphate concerned all Muslims and should be decided by the community of Muslims as a whole and that he had no intention of taking such a great responsibility upon himself.[97] He also refused the proposal presented by the leading clergy in Kabul during the Friday prayer on December 3, 1920, that he assume active leadership of the *khilafat* movement with assistance from Turkish and Indian Muslims, who were, reportedly, ready to support him.[98]

Despite Aman-Allah's public statement that he had no interest in the office of caliph, the British became increasingly concerned about the possibility of Afghan and Indian nationalists forming a coalition against them. The government of India communicated its concern to the secretary of state for India in London, emphasizing, "we can no longer afford to neglect the possibility of [the] Amir being elected....It is unnecessary for us to point out [the] grave situation for India which [the] Amir's election might bring about."[99] The *Literary Digest* of London commented, "enemies of Britain among her Indian subjects, who seek separation from her, would welcome an invasion by the Afghans, it is charged, believing it would indirectly help the cause of Mr. Gandhi and his adherents."[100] At the same time, the Indian paper *Amrita Bazar Patrika* wrote that Mr. Gandhi did not believe in the possibility of an Afghan invasion but "evidently" thought "that a little flirting with Muslim sentiment would do no harm."[101]

On the other hand, the prospect of an Afghan attack on India alarmed other Hindu activists. They feared that an Afghan invasion would induce a massive national uprising against the British and, if successful, would once again establish the "Muslim-Raj at Delhi."[102] The *Madras Mail* berated Gandhi as a traitor

---

[93.] "North-West Frontier Intelligence Diaries, 1919-1920," IOR, L/P&S/10/813, PA 743, no. 50, Dec. 16, 1920.
[94.] *Ibid.*
[95.] Maconachie, 261; Adamec, *Afghanistan's Foreign Affairs to the Mid-Twentieth Century*, 79; Stewart, 135.
[96.] Maconachie, 61.
[97.] *Ibid.* PA 268, no. 4, Dec. 9, 1920.
[98.] *Ibid.*
[99.] *Ibid.*
[100.] "If the Afghans Invaded India?" *Literary Digest*, vol. 89, July 16, 1921, 16.
[101.] *Ibid.*
[102.] *Ibid.*, 17.

and asserted that "by sitting idly by, Mr. Gandhi will be helping an invading enemy to conquer the country."[103]

The question of the caliphate continued to be among the most important foreign policy issues during the first three years of King Aman-Allah's reign. On March 1, 1921, a treaty of defensive alliance was signed in Moscow between the Angora (Ankara) government and Afghanistan, in which the latter recognized Turkey as the "model to be followed" (*moqtada-beha*), a term used to acknowledge the Islamic caliphate as the highest religious authority. The Turkish newspaper *Hakimmiet-i-Mellie* hailed the treaty as "the blessed clauses which bind together governments of [the] East united in faith and interest."[104] Likewise, the Muslim Indian newspaper the *Islamic News* editorialized, "The highest and most stupendous possibility which this alliance contains and which we prayfully anticipate is that of a Mid-Asian League of Nations. We only await a word from Persia and this dream will become a reality."[105]

Aman-Allah's Support of Central Asian Muslims

The regime's pan-Islamic policies were not limited to support of Turkey and the caliphate. As early as the autumn of 1919, the Afghan government had gone to the defense of Central Asian Muslims who were threatened by steady Bolshevik advances. Aman-Allah provided arms and ammunition to the leaders of the Basmachi, the freedom fighters resisting the Bolsheviks.

Interest in Central Asian affairs was stimulated by Turkish pan-Islamic activists such as Kazim Beig (a member of the Turko-German mission), Jamal Pasha, and Enver Pasha. During his stay in Kabul, Jamal Pasha helped to reorganize the Afghan army with the intent of advancing pan-Islamic goals. In the following year, Enver Pasha, former Turkish war minister and the main instigator of pro-*khilafat* and pan-Islamic movements during the war, traveled to Central Asia via Moscow. He was sent by the Soviets to promote interest in Bolshevism, but instead declared himself amir and led the Basmachis against the Bolsheviks in the hope of restoring independence to Bokhara and uniting Central Asian Muslims into a confederation of Muslim states. The arrival of Jamal Pasha in Afghanistan and the activities of Enver Pasha in Central Asia aroused excitement in Kabul. The Afghan government monitored with keen interest the activities of the Central Asian Muslims under the leadership of Enver Pasha. Sepahsalar Nader Khan was sent to Qataghan (a province near Bokhara) to keep an eye on developments on the other side of the border and to send men and munitions secretly to Enver Pasha.[106]

[103.] *Ibid.*

[104.] *Hakimiet-i-Millie* (Angora, Turkey), Apr. 25, 1921, quoted in IOR, L/P&S/10/958, P2478.

[105.] *Islamic News*, May 12, 1921.

[106.] For details of King Aman-Allah's involvement in Central Asian affairs see Adamec, *Afghanistan's Foreign Affairs*, 66-71.

Once again, the call to *jehad* created excitement among the ulama. Many crossed the border to join in the holy war. One such was Mawlawi 'Abd al-Haiy Panjshiri, a distinguished Deobandi *'alem* who, for his dedication to *jehad,* received from Enver Pasha the title of Sheikh al-Islam. Meanwhile two prominent ulama from Herat, Mir of Gazargah, custodian of the shrine of Khwaja `Abd-Allah Ansari, and Hazrat Saheb of Karrokh, were dispatched by order of the king to Turkistan to assure people there of Afghanistan's sympathy and support.[107] The link between the ulama and Central Asian activists were Mawlawi Barakat-Allah and his close collaborator, Mawlawi `Abd al-Razeq.

In August 1921, the State Council ratified the treaty of friendship between Afghanistan and Soviet Russia. The king claimed that the treaty would put the Afghan government in a better position to protect the rights of Central Asian Muslims.[108] Article 8 of the treaty did indeed stipulate recognition of the independence of Khiva and Bokhara from Russia. In May, Bokhara had fallen to the Young Bokharans supported by Bolshevik forces. Despite protests and diplomatic pressure from Soviet Russia, Aman-Allah gave refuge to Sayyid Mir 'Alam Khan, the amir of Bokhara, and continued to support former Bokharans against Bolshevik forces. At the same time, the Afghan government insisted on British formal recognition of the independence of Khiva and Bokhara and requested military assistance for Bokharan forces via Afghanistan.[109]

While pan-Islamism appealed mostly to the masses as a religious concept, it was used by political leaders in the Muslim world to promote their political ambitions. Aman-Allah saw in pan-Islamism an opportunity to expand Afghanistan's anticolonial victories.

Pan-Islamism, as Gregorian states, was a vehicle through which Afghanistan could be allied with other Muslim states and thus enhance its power and influence among nations.[110] The ultimate goal for Aman-Allah appears to have been formation of a confederation of Central Asian states under his leadership as caliph or spiritual ruler of Muslims in Central Asia. In 1921, Henry Dobbs reported that "the amir's real motive in contemplating a closer treaty with ourselves based on exclusion of Russian influence is [a] desire for almost immediate expansion in the north."[111]

Dobbs warned Aman-Allah of the possible negative outcome of such ambition and advised him that tampering in the affairs of Central Asian nations might provoke an aggressive response from the Soviets against Afghanistan.[112] Sepahsalar Nader Khan, who was in charge of monitoring Central Asian activi-

---

[107] General Staff, "Summary of Events in Afghanistan from August 8-June 12, 1919," NAI, FPD, Frontier B, Confidential, no. 31.

[108] Adamec, *Afghanistan, 1900-1923,* 140.

[109] Adamec, *Afghanistan's Foreign Affairs to the Mid-Twentieth Century,* 70.

[110] Gregorian, 236-237.

[111] "Comments on the Final Reports of Sir Henry Dobbs on His Mission to Kabul," NAI, FPD, File no. 2, 1922.

[112] *Ibid.*

ties from Qataghan, also communicated to Aman-Allah negative consequences for Afghanistan that could result from the uprising in Central Asia. In a hand-written memo addressed to the king, Nader Khan speculated on several possible favorable and not so favorable outcomes that the Basmachi insurrection in Central Asia could have for Afghanistan: 1) restoration of the ex-amir of Bokhara to his throne and unification with Afghanistan or acceptance of Afghan suzerainty, 2) internal independence for both Farghana and Bokhara with Afghanistan controlling their foreign policies, 3) unification of both principalities with Afghanistan, and 4) the strengthening of pan-Turanism under the tutelage of the Turks, resulting in the establishment of a strong, united Turkic kingdom under Enver Pasha and the establishment of relations with British India through Pamir and Chitral. If the latter were to happen, Nader Khan presumed it would be impossible to prevent the Uzbeks of Afghanistan from joining the movement.[113] It was probably the fear of the emergence of a powerful Turkic confederation in the north that prompted the regime to moderate and redefine its policy toward Central Asia.

Whatever his motives, Aman-Allah's actions with regard to several pan-Islamic issues greatly affected his relations with the Afghan ulama. His support of the *khilafat* and Basmachi movements certainly enhanced these relations. Other actions that promoted shared pan-Islamic goals contributed further to good relations with the ulama. As Gregorian states, the Afghan ulama who had been trained in Deoband and "were both militantly pan-Islamic and anti-British, joined the modernist nationalists in support of Amanullah's pan-Islamic policies."[114]

By 1922, King Aman-Allah had not only consolidated his position as the legitimate ruler of Afghanistan, but had earned from the ulama the titles of Ghazi (one who fights for the defense of Islam) and Saif al-Mellat-i wa al-Din (the Sword of the Nation and the Religion).[115] He was hailed as a hero and as the defender of Islam, both inside and outside Afghanistan.

[113.] AWSW Document Collection. For the full Persian text see Appendix J (1).

[114.] Gregorian, 237.

[115.] Fofalzai, *Dar al-Qaza' dar Afghanistan*, 441.

4

REFORM AND REBELLION
Resistance to Change, 1924

Since the days I was `Ain al-Dawla, my aims and aspirations have been concentrated on one single issue—the tranquility and prosperity of the Afghan nation. But it was necessary to find a guideline. What could lead the nation toward progress and prosperity? In answer to this question I found no better way than the shari`at. Accordingly, I appealed to the Divine ordinances. Following the example of leaders of Islam, I enacted a set of nezam-nama [regulations] as a guideline, because the only way to free the oppressed is through the rule of law. I am hopeful that government officials and individual Afghans will observe its provisions.

King Aman-Allah[1]

Your forefathers, who were the rulers of Afghanistan, did not invade our country as you have done....[W]e protested against the action of your government in issuing the nezam-nama, which is contrary to the shari`at.

Molla `Abd-Allah[2]

At the height of his popularity, King Aman-Allah inaugurated a massive program of reform that continued to affect life in Afghanistan many years after his abdication. The king's ten-year reign, commonly referred to as the Amaniyya or Amani era (*dowra-i-amaniyya*), was marked by his great enthusiasm for change. His ambitious nation-building program, launched in two stages—in 1923 and 1928—embodied intensive social and political reforms that challenged the authority of traditional rural local elites, the tribal *khan*s and the *molla*s.

---

[1] King Aman-Allah's address to the nation on the occasion of `Id-i-Fetr, *Ershad-i-Neswan*, Kabul, vol. 1, no. 12, *Hut* 1302/Mar. 1923.
[2] Reply of the rebel forces to King Aman-Allah, IOR, L/P&S/1081, P4397, no. 38, Oct. 9, 1924.

Discontent over the Amani reforms resulted in militant opposition to the government in 1924 in Khost, a locality in southeastern Afghanistan. Spearheaded by lower-ranking *mollas*, the rebellion quickly spread to surrounding areas, threatening the legitimacy of the regime. Although the Afghan clergy did not respond as a unitary force during the rebellion, the uprising of 1924 marked the first manifestation of the clergy's dissatisfaction with the Amani regime and the beginning of a breach between the state and the ulama.

THE REFORM MOVEMENT

Sporadic reform efforts had been attempted in Afghanistan in the mid-nineteenth century. The most important nineteenth-century advocate of reform was Sayyid Jamal al-Din Al-Afghani (1838-97), the famous Muslim thinker, who preached Islamic rejuvenation, pan-Islamic solidarity, and resistance to European domination. Afghani had served as consultant to the Afghan Amir Mohammad A`zam (1867-68), to whom he had presented his ideas for reform before proceeding to India in 1886. The outbreak of conflict between Amir Mohammad A`zam and his half brother, Shir `Ali Khan, halted enactment of Afghani's reform program. Nevertheless, Amir Shir `Ali, who succeeded A`zam Khan, attempted to implement some of Afghani's ideas, in particular, administrative reforms, reorganization of the Afghan army, introduction of lithographic printing, and the establishment of a military and a civilian school that offered courses in English. Shir `Ali also inaugurated the first regular postal service between Kabul and Peshawar; reformed the tax system; established a newspaper, *Sham al-Nahar*, to disseminate progressive ideas among educated Afghans; and created a council composed of thirteen members to advise him on matters of state. However, with the eruption of the Second Anglo-Afghan War, the state machinery, together with most of these innovations, was demolished, and anarchy prevailed until `Abd al-Rahman seized power in 1880.

`Abd al-Rahman's great achievement was the establishment of a strong central government with a strong army and an effective bureaucracy. He built an arms factory (*mashin-khana*) and founded a school to train court pages (*gholam-bachagan*) to become civil servants, but his rule was based largely on repression. As Kakar points out, `Abd al-Rahman's closed-door policy, tight control of printed materials, and prohibitions against citizens having any contact with outsiders effectively prevented advances in the field of education.[3] According to Gregorian, `Abd al-Rahman was well aware of the benefits that modern European science and technology could offer Afghanistan. However, his constant fear of European imperialism and his belief that "the great safety of Afghanistan lies in its natural impregnable position" made him resistant to change brought in by outside influences.[4]

[3.] Kakar, 161-162.
[4.] Gregorian, 152-153.

Amir Habib-Allah, `Abd al-Rahman's successor, ended Afghanistan's intellectual isolation and opened the country to new ideas, principally by founding Habibiyya College and a military school, both of which employed foreign Muslim teachers. Habibiyya College soon became the nucleus of a constitutionalist movement (*mashruta-khwahan*), whose main objective was the establishment of constitutional rule by means of a legislative assembly (*majes-i-mashwara*) and free elections. The constitutionalists vowed to struggle for Afghanistan's unconditional independence and pledged allegiance to the principles of Islam and the Qur'anic axiom "to enjoin good and forbid evil" (*al amr-i bi al-ma`ruf wa `an al-nahy-i min al-monkar*). Among their other objectives were the establishment of diplomatic and commercial relations with other nations, unification of the diverse ethnic groups of Afghanistan, expansion of public schools, creation of news media to inform the people, and promotion of science and modern technology (*madaniyyat-i-jadid*).[5]

Although the initial activities of the constitutionalists were suppressed, nationalism and liberal ideas were promoted in *Seraj al-Akhbar* under the editorship of Mahmud Tarzi and spread quickly among Afghan intellectuals. It was Tarzi who laid the ideological foundation for reform by arguing that progress (*taraqi*) was necessary in order to protect Afghanistan's Islamic identity and assure its independence from colonizing European powers. With regard to religion, Tarzi expressed broad-minded views, emphasizing the rational nature of Islam. In a number of articles, he attempted to impress upon the ulama that Islam was in perfect accord with nature, reason, progress, and enlightenment. In addition, he attempted to persuade the ulama to take an active role in awakening the masses.[6]

Members of the nobility who had returned to Afghanistan after years of exile in India, where they had been introduced to technological developments, were also important agents of reform. Some now held important positions in the royal court. The most influential of these individuals were members of the Yahya-Khail family. Three senior members of the family—Sardars Mohammad Yosuf, Mohammad Asef, and Mohammad Solaimam—known as elite associates or privy advisors to the king (*mosahebin-i-khas*), and four junior family members—Mohammad Nader, Mohammad Hashem, Shah Mahmud, and Shah Wali—each of whom held an important position in the army, exerted a great deal of influence in the court of Amir Habib-Allah.

Habib-Allah's visit to India in 1906 was another impetus for change. Inspired by India's progress along Western lines, he introduced a modest reform program in Afghanistan that included the creation of textile and power factories; the construction of new roads and modern buildings in Kabul, Jalalabad, and Paghman; improvements to the postal system and to public health; expansion of trade; and the establishment of a printing house (*matba`ai-i `enayat*) and a

---

[5.] Habibi, *Jonbesh-i-Mashrutiyyat dar Afghanistan*, 87-88.
[6.] For more about Tarzi's arguments to the ulama on the issue of change, see Nawid, "The Feminine and Feminism in Tarzi's Work," 360-361.

translation bureau (*dar al-tarjoma*). He also founded a teacher-training college (*dar al-mo`alimin*) and Habibiyya College, both of which were staffed principally by Indian Muslims and Turks. It was partly through the influence of revolutionary Indian Muslim teachers, such as Dr. `Abd al-Ghani, and Turkish pan-Islamists, hired to help with development projects,[7] that new political ideas were introduced to people of education and to some government-employed clergymen in Kabul.

Early in 1911, in an article that appeared in the British-Indian newspaper the *Pioneer*, a reporter characterized the court of Habib-Allah as divided into two camps—those who supported moderate reforms and those who opposed any reforms of Western origin. The article listed several supporters of reform, including Ishek Aqasi `Ali Ahmad Khan, Sardar Solaiman Khan of the Yahya-Khail family, and other courtiers who had returned from exile following Habib-Allah's declaration of amnesty for all families. According to the *Pioneer* article, the formerly exiled members of the court, who also possessed greater education, were the major advocates of reform. The more conservative court members, identified in the *Pioneer* article as Ishek Aqasi Sardar `Abd al-Qoddus Khan (E`temad al-Dawla), Sepahsalar Amir Mohammad Khan, Mustawfi al-Mamalik Mohammad Hosain Khan, and some older Mohammadzai Sardars and older military officials, favored making improvements in military technology but opposed other reforms—even the construction of railroads and telephone lines. According to the reporter, those members opposed to reforms other than military technology were afraid that an influx of Western engineers would jeopardize Afghanistan's internal independence. The ulama reportedly shared the opinion of the latter group and were preaching against all reforms. The *Pioneer* reporter concluded, "The amir, who is a progressive ruler, will achieve his progressive objectives only if he succeeds in bringing the clergy under full control."[8]

Tarzi actually attempted to use the *Pioneer* article to garner support for development from the antireform elements in the court and among the ulama. In an editorial titled "Correction of Wrong Impressions (*tashih-i-afkar*)," he defended the ulama and maintained that contrary to the report in the *Pioneer*, the ulama of Afghanistan were fully aware of the exigencies of the modern world, as were court officials and the nobility (*ashraf*), and that they all supported His Majesty in his effort to lead Afghanistan forward. The Afghan ulama, he coun-

---

[7.] Dr. `Abd al-Ghani, his brother Najaf `Ali (one of Aman-Allah's private tutors), and twelve other Indians taught at Habibiyya College. The military school (Maktab-i-Harbiyya) was run by a Turkish officer. Munir `Ezzat Baig, a Turkish doctor who was in charge of the hospital in Kabul, was said to have been a favorite of the amir and to have served as a link between him and Constantinople. Munir `Ezzat Baig is also credited with having done a lot to promote pan-Islamism in Afghanistan. Adamec, 1975, 203.

[8.] The *Pioneer* article is quoted extensively in *Seraj al-Akhbar*, vol. 1, no. 10, 1 *Hut* 1290/Feb. 20, 1911.

tered, were not against civilization (*tahzib*) and were in favor of progress (taraqi.)[9]

The educational reforms of Habib-Allah were, in fact, endorsed by a majority of the ulama in the capital, partly because Habibiyya College continued to emphasize Islamic studies and because the majority of the teachers were recruited from among the Afghan ulama. Other reforms and development projects were, for the most part, outside the concerns of the ulama and, therefore, did not arouse clerical opposition. The amir's modest program for Westernization in the social realm, confined to procedural etiquette and the adoption of Western dress in the royal court, created some resentment in religious circles,[10] but not enough to evoke open clerical protest.

DRAFTING THE CONSTITUTION AND LEGAL CODES

Aman-Allah directed his attention to reform soon after securing international recognition of Afghanistan's independence. In an address to the nation during the Muslim festival of `Id-i-Fetr of 1923, he declared his intention to enact regulations to lead the nation forward and improve the condition of all Afghans. Shortly thereafter, he introduced regulations known as the *nezam-nama* (from the Arabic word *nezam*, meaning order), a term current in the Middle East following the *Tanzimat* period in nineteenth-century Turkey. The new regulations were intended to bring greater order to the administration of government, to regulate social relationships, to promote human dignity, to ensure equality before the law without regard to ethnic origin or distinctions of class, and to promote the general welfare and tranquility. In addition, Aman-Allah intended these regulations to provide a foundation for modern education and economic development.

In Islam, God is theoretically the legislator. Rulers exist to enforce divine mandates. In practice, however, Islamic rulers gradually assumed the right to supplement the *shari`at*, with secular ordinances known as `orf, in the form of edicts (*farman*s), judicial verdicts authorized by the ulama (*fatawa*, plural of *fetwa*), and decrees (*ahkam*). Such regulations existed from the time of the 'Abbasids, and Muslim thinkers rationalized their enactment by Muslim rulers. Both Al-Mawardi and Ibn Khaldun distinguished between the immutable laws of Islam and state regulations, the latter being subject to change as circumstances required. Ibn Khaldun argued further that state laws (*qawanin*, plural of *qanun*) were necessary for the governance of the state (*molk*).[11]

Afghan rulers, like other Muslim rulers, issued decrees, edicts, and regulations, sometimes collected into *fatwa*s. One such collection, the *Fatawa-i-Ahmad Shahi*, compiled during the reign of Ahmad Shah Dorrani (1747-1773), existed in the Pashtu Tolana Library in Kabul. Amir Shir `Ali issued regulations

---

[9.] *Ibid.*
[10.] Abdul Ghani, *A Review of the Political Situation in Central Asia,* 79-81.
[11.] Rosenthal, 19.

concerning military conscription, blood feud, and taxation.[12] Regulations promulgated by `Abd al-Rahman reorganized the state and the administration of justice. Sultan Mohammad Mir Munshi, `Abd al Rahman's chief secretary, grouped Afghanistan's laws during `Abd al-Rahman's reign into two categories—those set forth in the *shari`at*, which are compulsory and unchangeable, and state regulations and laws of custom, which "are always modified by the amir, to suit the condition of people and to keep pace with the progress of the country. While the religious law declares the rule, the amir believes that he has the right to define how that rule is to be applied."[13]

During the reign of Amir Habib-Allah, state regulations came to be called *nezam-nama*s, and the public became more aware of secular law (*qanun*) than they had been under previous rulers.[14] Among Habib-Allah's *nezam-nama*s were the law of education (*nezam-nama-i-ma`aref*), the law of wedding ceremonies (*nezam-nama-i-`arusi*), the law of customs duties (*nezam-nama-i-dak-khanaha*), the law of travel documents (*nezam-nama-i-rahdari*), and the official attire code (*nezam-nama-i-albasa*).[15] In addition, the ulama of the Bureau of Assessments and Research (*mahfel-i-mizan wa tahqiqat*)[16] were commissioned to assemble the *Seraj al-Ahkam* into detailed and comprehensive volumes.[17] These volumes, based on authoritative Hanafi lawbooks, were an attempt by the Afghan ulama to produce a Hanafi version of the *Majalla*, a codified book of laws compiled between 1869 and 1876 in Ottoman Turkey during the *Tanzimat* period, when legislative reform was undertaken in response to pressures from Western powers.[18]

Independence and reform were at the core of the political ideology of Aman-Allah and the Afghan nationalists. After independence, the Afghan intelligentsia also gradually shifted their orientation from a religious to a political perspective, and Aman-Allah began to lay the groundwork for social, political, legal, and economic reforms. Some state regulations and selections from the *shari`at* had

---

[12.] Mir Monshi, 80.

[13.] *Ibid.*, 127.

[14.] *Qanun* refers to order, security, efficiency, protection of the rights of people, the regulation of government departments, obedience to the king, industrial and agricultural progress, the increase of industry and commerce, and all the things which can be seen as necessary....The *shari`at* does not forbid these things. *Seraj al-Akhbar*, vol. 3, no. 1, 25 *Sonbola* 1292/Sept. 17, 1913, 2-3.

[15.] The text of some of these laws appears in various issues of *Seraj al-Akhbar*.

[16.] *Mahfel-i-Mizan wa Tahqiqat* was established in 1902 in Kabul under the direct supervision of Amir Habib-Allah and Na`eb al-Saltana Nasr-Allah Khan and consisted of nine ulama. Fofalzai, *Dar al-Qaza dar Afghanistan*, 413.

[17.] According to Fofalzai, the compilation of *Seraj al-Ahkam* begun in the time of Amir `Abd al-Rahman but was completed in the time of Amir Habib-Allah. Among the main authors of this work were Hajji `Abd al-Razeq, the *molla-bashi*, and `Abd al-Rahman Baiktuti. Fofalzai, *Dar al-qaza dar Afghanistan*, 406-407.

[18.] For more information about the *Majalla*, see Berkes, *The Development of Secularism in Turkey*, 168-169.

been codified before Aman-Allah's reign, but Aman-Allah surpassed his predecessors in the number of state regulations he created. Moreover, he promulgated state regulations with the intent of propelling change.

Although complying with the *shari`at*, Aman-Allah's reforms had a Western flavor.[19] They reflected the ideas of late nineteenth- and early twentieth-century Muslim reformers, whose main concern was to defend Islam against military, cultural, and technological challenges of the West. According to these reformers, Islam had to be fortified from within and revitalized as a social, political, and cultural force in order to withstand attack from the West. In the late nineteenth century, Sayyid Jamal a-Din Afghani; Sheikh Mohammad `Abduh of Egypt and his successor, Rashid Rida; and the Lebanese Sobhi Mahmasani advocated a new interpretation of religious law "to loosen the grip of rigid and all-inclusive finality that had characterized orthodox jurisprudence since the third century of Islam."[20] Afghani and `Abduh emphasized the role of reason in the interpretation of religious law. They argued that instead of relying on interpretations of medieval jurists, Muslims should understand that the essence of Islam is implicit in the Qur`an and should use the principle of legal reasoning (*maslehat*)—what is good for society—as the guiding principle in lawmaking. These theories greatly influenced reform movements in Egypt and Ottoman Turkey.

The Turkish experience with legal reform became a model for Aman-Allah. Like Afghanistan, Ottoman Turkey was a Sunni Muslim state, ruled by adherents of the Hanafite school of the *shari`at*. Most important, Ottoman Turkey was the seat of the caliphate, and Aman-Allah assumed that changes inspired by Turkey would be readily accepted by the Sunni ulama in Afghanistan. Turkey's influence in Afghanistan was evident as early as the time of Amir `Abd al-Rahman.[21] In the time of King Habib-Allah, the influence of Ottoman Turkey increased with the arrival of Turkish teachers, doctors, technicians, and military advisors in Kabul. After the War of Independence, the influence of Turkey increased partly as a result of Mahmud Tarzi's affiliation with the Turks and partly as a result of the activities of Turkish pan-Islamic activists, such as the famous Jamal Pasha. Several Turkish military officers also served in Afghanistan and assisted with the reorganization of the Afghan army and the drafting of military and administrative codes. They included Badri Baig, Ziya Baig, General Fakhr al-Din Pasha, General Kazem Pasha, and Zawad Baig.

[19.] In an article titled "What Is Law and Who Is the Legislator? (*qanun chist wa waze`-i-an kist?*)" that appeared in the semiofficial *Aman-i-Afghan* newspaper, the laws were classified into two categories—those relating to the soul (*ruh*), which are the divinely inspired rules of the *shari`at*, and those relating to the physical being (*jesm*), which are man-made laws (*qawanini-i-madani wa siyasi*)—which determine legal rights and limits and are enacted by knowledgeable national leaders in response to exigencies of the time. *Aman-i-Afghan, Jawza* 13, 1299/June 3, 1920.

[20.] Kerr, *Islamic Reform*, 55.

[21.] An example of Turkish influence was the establishment of the corps of court pages (*gholam-bacha*), which was inspired by the Ottoman janissary system.

Aman-Allah's regime based new state regulations on principles of the Hanafi Sunni school and claimed that its main objectives were to preserve Islamic practices and revive the glory and prestige of Islam through economic development and strength.[22] In a royal decree published in the introductory chapter of the new codified criminal law (*Tamassok al-Qozat*), Aman-Allah declared that through new rules and a new order based on the *shari`at*, the government would be able to reinstitute Islamic justice (*`adalat*), which had lost much of its power due to inconsistent legal procedures and the fact that Afghan judges did not have sufficient command of Arabic.[23]

Early in 1919, the Religious Council for Religious Sciences (*shura-i-`olum*) and the Legislative Council (*mahfel-i-qanun*) were set up to study Hanafi jurisprudence and the codified Turkish laws. The councils consisted of government-appointed ulama of the High Religious Committee (*Hai`at-i-Tamiz)*, mostly headed by two scholars from Qandahar—Mawlawis `Abd al-Wase` and Mohammad Ebrahim Barakzai, the minister of justice. They also included a group of writers belonging to the Young Afghan Party, including the radical liberal `Abd al-Rahman Ludin; a number of Mohammadzai Sardars; and Badri Baig, the former Istanbul police chief who had come to Kabul as a member of Jamal Pasha's mission. The same council later undertook the codification of the *nezam-nama*s.

In February 1923, the Fundamental Law (*nezam-nama-i-asasi-i-dawlat-i-`aliyya-i-afghanistan*) was promulgated.[24] The law, which consisted of seventy-three articles and nine sections, was the first document of its kind in Afghanistan. The sections addressed the duties and prerogatives of the king, individual rights, the duties of ministers, the duties of government officials, the functions of the state council (*shura-i-dawlat*) and advisory committees (*majales-i-mashwara)*, the organization of the courts (*mahakem*) and the designation of their duties, financial affairs, regulations regarding the administration of the provinces, and miscellaneous topics.

The text began by declaring Afghanistan's complete internal and external independence and territorial integrity. Article 2 proclaimed Islam the official religion of the state; however, reference to Sunni Hanafism was deliberately omitted, probably to avoid turning the Shi`a population against the cause of nationalism. The second chapter of the Constitution constituted the Afghan bill of individual rights. Article 8 declared that all people residing in Afghanistan were Afghan citizens, regardless of religion or creed. Article 10 abolished slavery in Afghanistan, and Articles 9 and 10 provided that no individual could be arrested

---

[22] See Aman-Allah's message to the *Jerga* of Hadda, *Ettehad-i-Mashriqi*, Jalalabad, vol. 1, no. 1, *Jamadi al-Thani*, 2, 1338 (1298 solar Hejra), 2. See also Aman-Allah's speech on the occasion of the `Id-i-uzha of 1303 (1924) in *Ruydad-i-Loya Jerga-i-dar al-Saltana-i-Paghman, 1303*, 14-20.

[23] *Tamassok al-Qozat al-Amaniyya*, 2-3.

[24] The *Loya-Jerga* of Jalalabad, consisting of 872 members from the Mohmand, Bajawur, and Afridi tribes, ratified the first draft of the Constitution.

or punished, except as provided in the law. Article 16 recognized the equality of all citizens before the law. Articles 19 and 20 guaranteed the security of personal property, and Article 22 discontinued confiscation and forced labor. Article 24 prohibited all types of torture.

Equality before the law and the guarantee of individual rights were granted in response to the demands of the liberals. Aman-Allah was to show the world that Afghanistan was willing to match guarantees accorded in other progressive states. However, the *Mashruta-Khwahan*'s most basic demand, constitutional limits on the power of the monarch, was not realized. In fact, the Constitution weighted power overwhelmingly in the monarch's favor.

Article 25 declared the king head of the government. The role of the monarch remained dominant. Article 16 declared him the supreme judge, and Article 7 named him commander-in-chief of the army. Article 7 also invested him with the authority to promulgate and sanction laws, to appoint and dismiss the prime minister (*sadr-i-a'zam*) and other ministers, to grant pardons and reduce legal punishments, to declare war, and to conclude peace. At the same time, the Constitution provided for limited representative government. Article 29 established a State Council (*shura-i-dawlat*) at the seat of government and Advisory Councils (*majales-i-mashwara*) in the provinces, which were composed of equal numbers of elected and appointed members. These prerogatives were granted to the king under the umbrella of the *shari'at*, which considers the *uli al-amr* responsible for conducting the affairs of society.

The Constitution emphasized the religious underpinnings of the state and the role of the *shari'at*. Article 5 identified the monarch as servant and protector of the religion of Islam. Article 4 recognized his sovereignty, and royal succession provided he commit fully to government under Islamic law. Before the drafting of the Constitution, certain members of the nobility in the court had voiced opposition to introducing a constitutional monarchy. According to Ghobar, E'temad al-Dawla, Aman-Allah's first prime minister, argued that constitutional government was an antireligious innovation. Early in 1920, E'temad al-Dawla attempted to enlist religious leaders in Kabul and Qandahar to oppose the proposed change to a constitutional monarchy.[25] He succeeded in eliciting the following manifesto from a group of ulama in Qandahar:

> Rationally and legally there is only one type of government, the *khilafat-imamat*, which is essential for the enforcement of divine law, *qanun-i-asmani*, and the implementation of the political order ordained by the Almighty. Whatever good or bad [may affect] the human race is determined by this type of authority. The remainder, be it political or natural, constitutional or republican, Bolshevik or Menshevik, whose foundation is not based on divine judgment and which does not consider universal justice for the external and internal well-

---

[25.] Letter dated 26 *Saratan* 1299/July 17, 1920, from E'temad al-Dawla to Shams al-Mashayikh and Nur al-Mashayikh, quoted in Ghobar, 802-803.

being of individuals in this world and the next, but in the name of rectitude instructs corruption and in the guise of civilization encourages hatred and terror, is hereby rejected on the authority of the *shari'at* and by simple reason.[26]

Whether this early clerical opposition to the establishment of a constitutional monarchy was an expression of genuine concern on the part of conservative ulama in Qandahar or was staged by the prime minister to protect monarchical prerogatives is hard to determine.

In May 1923, the Fundamental Administrative Law (*nezam-nama-i-tashkilat-i-asasi*) established a basic administrative structure with a clear hierarchy and rules regulating governmental functions. Executive authority was vested in a Council of Ministers, which consisted of the ministers of war, foreign affairs, interior, justice, finance, education, and commerce, and the independent presidency of health, each of whom was directly responsible to the king.

A State Council was created to advise the king and to formulate, amend, and sanction new regulations. The State Council had two kinds of rule-making authority: 1) issuing decrees relating to its advisory opinions, and 2) issuing directives in times of emergency.

Between 1919 and 1928, the State Council passed some 140 codes and statutes that incorporated aspects of Aman-Allah's reforms. Although the Constitution was ratified in 1923, most of its subordinate regulations (*nezam-nama*s) appeared much earlier.[27] These regulations laid the foundation for ambitious administrative, legal, financial, and social reforms. Administrative functions were better organized and centralized. A new tax law was introduced, and the legal system was unified. Social reforms included the abolition of slavery; expansion of the educational system, including formal education for women and reformation of mosque schools; the imposition of universal conscription; and attempts to curtail polygamy, child marriage, and Pashtun customs relating to the treatment of women. Family matters were defined by a uniform written code of statutory laws.[*]

THE EFFECT OF REFORM ON THE RURAL-TRIBAL POPULATION: ORIGINS OF THE KHOST REBELLION

The Impact of Tax Reforms

After the War of Independence the government was badly pressed for finances. The expenses of the war depleted the reserve Amir Habib-Allah had accumu-

---

[26.] Ghobar, 804.

[27.] Summaries of the *nezam-nama*s appear in Poullada and Rawan-Farhadi. See Poullada, 66-91 and Rawan-Farhadi, "*Jonbesh-i-Qanungozari dar Afghanistan*," 8-34. A list of these laws also appears in Appendix B.

[*]The reforms of the Amani period are set forth in detail in Poullada's work. I will deal here only with the reforms that had a direct bearing on the rebellion of 1924.

lated in the Kabul treasury. The British owed the late amir money through a program of subsidy, but they refused to pay it until the Afghan leadership accepted their terms for peace, which Aman-Allah in turn refused to do. Army pay was greatly in arrears, and the pay raise granted by Aman-Allah at the time of his accession placed an additional burden on the state treasury. In addition, the government was committed to large capital expenditures on public works. The need for revenue was therefore imperative.

In its first year, the new regime attempted to resolve the financial crisis through legislation. The king also set an example by reducing his personal and household expenses. In line with his example, government allowances to members of the Mohammadzai royal clan, which had been established in the time of King `Abd al-Rahman, were reduced or stopped entirely, as were pensions to religious dignitaries granted in the time of King Habib-Allah. Lands belonging to the crown in various provinces were put up for sale, and orders were issued for the immediate collection of all arrears in revenue, some of which were as much as five years overdue in Khost.[28]

Tax reform was undertaken to generate revenue desperately needed to implement new projects. In 1920, the Tax Law (nezam-nama-i-maliyya) put in place an effective tax-collecting procedure controlled by the central government. The new law eliminated in-kind tax payments (jensi) in favor of cash tax payments (naqdi). This law also put in place the first increase in land revenue since the time of Amir Shir `Ali Khan.[29]

The new law stressed the role of taxes within the practice of Islam. The opening chapter of the law quoted the Qur'an verse, "Obey God and Obey the Prophet and those amongst you who are in position of command...," and added that the paying of taxes is a religious duty (zakat) incumbent upon Muslims. According to the law, the Prophet and the four "Rightly Guided Caliphs" also collected taxes for the purpose of jehad and the defense of Islamic territory.

Early in 1919, the government increased the land tax, import and export duties, and taxes on grazing rights (maliyya-i-mawashi) and introduced Afghanistan's first income tax, maliyat bar `ayedat. At the same time, internal tariffs and certain taxes deemed arbitrary by the new regime were abolished,[30] and taxes owed in arrears (baqiyyat) were forgiven by the Arrears Exemption Law (nezam-nama-i-mohasebat-i-baqiyya). In areas like Qandahar, Qataghan, and Badakhshan, where tax payments were greatly in arrears, citizens gladly accepted an increase in current taxes for relief from their past-due obligations.[31] But even more revenue was needed to construct a new road between Kabul and Jalalabad, expand education, extend telephone and telegraph lines, and build a new capital in Dar al-Aman and a winter capital in Laghman. (The budget for

---

[28.] General Staff Branch, "Summary of Events in Afghanistan between August 8, 1919 and June 12, 1920." NAI, FPD, Frontier B, confidential, nos. 31-32, 1920, 16.
[29.] Afghan Government. Afghanistan dar Penjah Sal-i-Akhir, 59.
[30.] Eshtehar (Kabul), no. 13, 15 Hut 1299/Mar. 6, 1920.
[31.] IOR, L/P&S/10/1081, P950, 1924, no. 5, Jan. 31, 1924.

the construction of Dar al-Aman was 10 million rupees [the Afghan currency of the time], 30 percent of the state's total revenue for one year.[32]) Another great expense was the maintenance of diplomatic legations, now established in several Asian and European capitals. But the most important and costly commitment was education.

In 1923, Aman-Allah cut military expenditures and levied new taxes to support education. In addition, import and export duties were collected in cash on the spot, the export of all gold and silver was strictly prohibited, and orders were issued for all revenue to be collected in currency only, instead of partly in kind, as had been done formerly.

Not surprisingly, the increased land, livestock, and customs taxes brought about discontent. In addition, high Afghan military officials, who already resented the influence Aman-Allah had given to the Turks in the Afghan military, were indignant about decreased funding for the military. Their dissatisfaction gave rise to a level of unrest that threatened to weaken the king's military base and make the regime more vulnerable to rebellion.

In the spring of 1923, a poll tax (*maliyya-i-sarana*) was levied on all males in the Kabul district.[33] Later that year, interest was imposed on past-due taxes.[34] In addition, the government began collecting a new education tax (*maliyya-i-ma`aref*) and soliciting voluntary contributions (*e`ana*) to expand education. The government-controlled press printed the names of contributors. One newspaper reported that the poor inhabitants of Khost, whose daily diet consisted of maize, had contributed 75,000 rupees,[35] and in May 1923, *Aman-i-Afghan* reported that the civil servants of Qandahar had donated one month of their salaries to support Afghan students in Europe.

A major reason for popular resentment against the new taxes was corruption among the officials collecting taxes. The assessment of land revenue gave unprecedented powers of interrogation and intimidation to officials in charge. Reports of corruption proliferated. New collection procedures ended the *qarya-dari* system, under which the village head (*qarya-dar*) had collected taxes in his village. Instead, appointed salaried employees of the central government performed the task. Ironically, the change was intended to eradicate bribery. In fact, the new tax-collecting machinery, with its huge staff, provided even more opportunities for graft.[36]

[32.] IOR, L/P&S/10/961, no. 2, Jan. 1923.

[33.] IOR/LP&S/10/961, no. 12, P2023, May 22, 1923.

[34.] *Ibid.*

[35.] Ghobar, 790.

[36.] Ali Ahmad, "The Fall of Amanullah," 22. Embezzlement and corruption were denounced frequently in the pages of *Setara-i-Afghan* of Jabal al-Seraj in Kohistan. Earlier in December 1920, the government appointed a supervisory commission to explain tax laws to taxpayers, report on corruption, and recommend measures for ensuring proper conduct. Members of the commission included Mawlawi Abd al-Rahman Baiktuti, the revered Grand Qazi of Kabul. The commission, whose mandate was specified in the Tax Collection Inspection Law (*nezam-nama-i-taftish-i-maliyya*) failed in its mission, as did

In addition, far too many resources were spent on projects that contributed insignificantly, if at all, to economic growth. Hence, the reforms brought no immediate benefits to the rural population, where tax increases were most burdensome. In an effort to satisfy the immediate needs of the rural population, land reform was introduced. For the first time ever in Afghanistan, state land (*amwal-i-khalesa* or *amwal-i-sarkari*) was sold at a low price to farmers, giving rise to a class of "peasant proprietors."[37] However, according both to Ghobar and to Grotzbakh, only landowners with large holdings benefitted from the reform.[38] According to Poullada, the new system monetarized the economy, with taxes being collected in cash rather than in kind, permanently affecting the economic picture of Afghanistan.[39] According to Grotzbach, "a switch to the collection of tax entirely in cash favored large landownership,"[40] though large landowners represented a small percentage of the landowning population.[41] Unappreciative of the long-term objectives of the regime, rural taxpayers were initially confused and suspicious. Tax increases plus changes in tax collection procedures, combined with rampant corruption, generated general resentment toward the reforms. Given this general level of resentment, when a rebellion broke out in Khost the population in the surrounding areas was predisposed to sympathize with the rebels.

Objection to tax reform was not the declared reason for the Khost Rebellion, mainly because the Khost Rebellion was led by the clergy, who based their opposition to the regime's reforms on religious grounds and who had no religious basis for opposing tax increases—the *shari`at* permits a ruler to issue new taxes according to the needs of the time. Tax reform was, however, at the root of general discontent in Qandahar. Taxes fell heavily on landowners, who were mostly leaders of the powerful Barakzai tribe, the very group most discontent with the military reforms. In October 1924, the British military attaché in Kabul reported that the Barakzais of Qandahar, who had always sent men and military support to the central government in times of trouble since the reign of Amir `Abd al-Rahman, had refused to send a single man to defend the regime during the Khost Rebellion, claiming that the introduction of new taxes and reforms had reduced them to poverty and turned their people against the amir.[42] At the

---

Aman-Allah's other efforts to fight corruption. According to a report prepared in January 1923, government officials were being spied upon from all sides, and "if the amir himself is not sitting on their doorstep in disguise, he is listening on the telephone to one of their subordinates relating the day's progress in the bribery market....None the less, bribery appears to flourish still." IOR, L/P&S/10/1081, P1311, no. 5, Feb. 1, 1923. Many sources indicate that the problem of corruption proved intractable throughout the 1920s.

[37.] Poullada, *Reform and Rebellion*, 135.

[38.] Ghobar, 791; Grotzbach quoted in Beattie, 139.

[39.] Poullada, *Reform and Rebellion*, 133.

[40.] Grotzbach quoted in Beattie, 139.

[41.] *Ibid.*

[42.] IOR, L/P&S/10/1120, no. 123, Oct. 1, 1924.

Loya-Jerga of Paghman in 1924, the Qandahar representatives vociferously opposed tax increases.[43]

Resentment, mostly over new taxes, was heightened by the introduction of social reforms that interjected government into private matters, such as the conduct of marriages, funerals, and business transactions. By encouraging the adoption of new social habits, the government had intended to revitalize the nation and thus had promulgated statutes to outlaw, among other things, the wearing of traditional shoes (*paizar*) and the use and production of opium, snuff, Indian hemp (*chars*), and tobacco.[44] Although it is difficult to assess the extent to which the new regulations were implemented, the speedy advance and broad scope of the rebellion suggest that the frustrations and bitterness brought on by the threat of these changes disposed the rural populous to support rebellious forces.

The Impact of Reforms on Tribal Autonomy

The Pashtun tribes were the group most greatly affected by the reforms. They were menaced both by the imposition of universal conscription and the abrogation of practices of the Pashtun tribal code of honor (*pashtunwali*) in favor of new regulations.

The Conscription and Identity Card Act of 1923 (*nezam-nama-i-tazkera-i-nofus*), which made military service compulsory and universal, was the most unpopular new government policy. Military conscription was not new, but the manner in which the new law was to be implemented threatened tribal autonomy and traditional life. The law stipulated that only the registration or identity card (*tazkera*) would be accepted in courts of law. Citizens were thereby forced to obtain the *tazkera* when registering for conscription and then, consequently, accept government regulation of their private lives or risk loss of other rights. For example, marriages had to be officially registered with an identity card number to be legal. By means of the *tazkera*, the regime intended to enforce the new family law and thereby control polygamy and child marriage. A popular phrase, "register for *tazkera* and accept death" (*tazkera begir wa bemir*), reveals the depth of resentment against the *nezam-nama*. A target of that resentment, a bookseller in Jalalabad who carried copies of the *nezam-nama*, was nicknamed *Nezami* in ridicule.[45]

[43.] *Ruydad-i-Gozareshat-i-Loya-jerga-i-1303*, 236. During this period, the Qandaharis adopted the word *gham*, meaning sorrow or worry, for taxation. In 1925, the king asked them to discontinue the use of the word. He argued that paying taxes (*maliyya*) was the same as giving alms (*zakat*) and that religious duty required they contribute willingly to the state treasury (*bait al-mal*). See *Taftish-i-Welayat-i-Qandahar*, 114-115.

[44.] These statutes were mentioned in *Aman-i-Afghan*, 19 *Jawza* 1302/May 1, 1923; see also, IOR, L/P&S/10/961, no. 25, Aug. 1923.

[45.] Interview with Musa Shafiq, Qargha, Aug. 15, 1976.

During the War of Independence the government had relied heavily on tribal levies mobilized by religious leaders. Those Pashtuns in the frontier region who had proven their military skills in the three Anglo-Afghan wars considered themselves natural warriors and resented having to send their sons to Kabul for training. The efforts of Jamal Pasha, who was Turkish, to reorganize the Afghan army according to Western standards also offended them. Given their recent victories over the British, the tribesmen regarded themselves as better warriors than the Turks. In addition, the tribal chiefs (*khans*), who had formerly controlled military recruitment, resented the loss of special privileges related to those duties.

Since the time of Amir 'Abd al-Rahman, military recruitment had been based on a system known as "one of eight" (*hasht-nafari* or *wandi*), whereby one man was selected for military duty from a group of eight, with the rest being made responsible for the expenses of his family during his time in service.[46] The ulama, members of the royal family, and government officials were exempted from military service. The most common method of recruitment was *qawmi*, whereby every tribe or subtribe furnished a quota of men to the central government, a procedure that reinforced regional and tribal autonomy. The tribe was then responsible for support of the recruit's family during his service. Under the new conscription law, tribal aid was discontinued, and the government was unable to support both the soldiers and their families. In fact, the ration money and grain (*ghala*) paid to the soldiers were not adequate for their needs, and their families received none.[47]

Another source of resentment was the creation of an exemption fee (*qimat-i-'awazi*), with which a man could purchase release from military service.[48] The 'awazi benefitted the rich and contradicted the ideal of universal conscription. The possibility of exemption also encouraged corruption by creating another opportunity for bribery.

Because of its kinship with the royal clan, the Barakzai tribe in Qandahar supplied men for the Royal Cavalry (*Resala-i-Shahi*) and was exempt from general conscription.[49] Since the time of the Mangal uprising (1912-1913) during the reign of Habib-Allah, the Mangal, Zadran, and Ahmadzai tribes had also been exempted from conscription.[50] The new conscription laws denied these and all other exemptions and privileges formerly granted to the ulama and the royal family. Not surprisingly, antigovernment revolts in 1924 were concentrated in the regions populated predominantly by the four tribes that were most threatened by conscription reform.

Under the old system, the power of tribal leaders to select military recruits reinforced regional and tribal authority. Aman-Allah's goal of a government-

---

[46] *Aman-i-Afghan*, 16 *Dalw* 1302/Feb. 7, 1923.

[47] 'Ali Ahmad, 10; Maconachie, P337, 155.

[48] *Nezam-nama-i-Tazkera-i-Nofus wa Osul-i-Pasport wa Qanun-i-Tabe'yiat*, Article 26.

[49] Kakar, 79; *Seraj al-Tawarikh*, 1217.

[50] Ghobar, 713.

controlled, unified system countermanded the tribal code (*pashtunwali*) by which a man's identity and honor were defined in relation to his tribe. The increased control afforded the state by a Western-style standing army greatly threatened tribal leaders, who felt little loyalty to the central government. Their main motive in the revolt of 1924 was to curtail loss of their authority to the central regime.

For centuries, tribal life in the region had been controlled by tribal codes of honor. In cases of injury, sexual assault, violation of property rights, and homocide, tribal rules took precedence over the *shari'at*, and disputes were settled by *jerga*s. Punishment was based on customs defined by Pashtun concepts of bravery (*mailanai*), manliness, and honor. A murder was a stain on the slain man's family and usually resulted in an avenged murder (*badal*). Pashtuns seldom subscribed to the Qur'anic principle of forgiveness as an alternative to avenged murder.[51]

Pashtuns exacted punishment according to tribal rules rather than to the religious judge's (*qazi*'s) interpretation of the *shari`at*. The *pashtunwali* held the clan, not the individual alone, responsible for a misdeed, so a felony committed by an individual usually developed into conflict that affected all members of the clan or tribe. Pashtun tribes feared that the state would destroy the *pashtunwali* and, with it, tribal autonomy by enforcing the new criminal law (*Tamassok al-Qozat*), which relied heavily on the *shari`at* and ignored Pashtun customary practices, and by enforcing the new penal code, which was fashioned after Turkish and European codes.

Women and their treatment were very important in the social and legal framework of the tribe. As the highest symbol of family honor, women were a major focus of tribal and intertribal conflicts. They could also be used to achieve a peace settlement, inasmuch as the stain of blood could be removed by comparable loss or by an arbitral marriage whereby the family or tribe of the culprit provided one or several brides to the family of the victim without paying bridal money or wedding expenses.[52] This practice was also applied in the case of rape and physical assault. Although originally a Pashtun custom, it had become a widespread practice, referred to derogatorily in Persian as *bad-dadan* (given in marriage in shame). The Marriage Law of 1923 abolished this custom and the tradition that forced a widow to marry a close relative of her husband, condemning both practices as degrading to women and contrary to the teachings of the Qur'an.[53]

[51.] "Forgive even when angry" (Qur'an 42:37); "Let evil be rewarded by evil. But he who forgives and seeks reconciliation shall be rewarded by God" (Qur'an 42:40).

[52.] Pazhwak, "Ta`amolat-i-Hoquqiyya wa jaza 'iya-i-Melli," 350.

[53.] Marriage Law, Articles 9 and 10.

The Kohat and Landi Kotal Incidents

The relationship between the state and the tribes deteriorated further as a result of two incidents in the tribal area on the Indian frontier. On April 14, 1923, the wife of an English officer of the Border Regiment was murdered and her daughter abducted in Kohat on the British side of the border by `Ajab Gol, an Afridi tribesman from the independent tribal zone (*sarhad-i-azad*), who then took refuge in Afghan territory. A few days later, two Englishmen were killed in Landi Kotal in the Khyber region by two Sango Khail Shinwaris as an act of revenge for relatives killed by the British in Peshawar in 1909. These two incidents developed into a political crisis between Afghanistan and British India in 1923. The British demanded the arrest and prosecution of the criminals and asked the Afghan government to put a final stop to such outrages.[54]

The incidents created a predicament for the Afghan government. As a newly independent state, anxious to establish diplomatic relations with other countries, Afghanistan needed to demonstrate an ability to deal expeditiously with such incidents. At the same time, it was imperative that Afghanistan maintain good relations with the frontier tribes along the Durand Line, as they constituted the chief defensive shield against invasion from the southeast. Previous Afghan rulers had, in fact, been very careful to secure the goodwill and support of the tribes along the border in case of future conflict with India. Having proved their loyalty and strategic value to Afghanistan during the War of Independence, the tribes expected the government to demonstrate loyalty to them in return.

The two murder cases afforded the British, who were greatly offended by the Afghan government's support of anti-British uprisings in Waziristan and in India, an extraordinary opportunity to undermine the regime's relations with the Pashtuns. According to Maconachie, "The arrest and trial of Afghan subjects who had committed crimes in India would have been a departure from all precedent in Afghanistan. Amir Habib-Allah, even when in receipt of subsidy, had never gone so far."[55] The timing could not have been more opportune for the British. The incidents occurred just when public opinion against Aman-Allah's regime was on the rise as a result of general discontent over new laws and regulations.

The dilemma generated heated debate in the cabinet and resulted in dissension between Nader Khan, the minister of war and frontier expert, and Moham-

---

[54.] In response, on August 15, *Aman-i-Afghan* printed extensive coverage of the incident in Kohat, claiming that a British major accompanied by British troops had insulted `Ajab's wife and attempted to carry her off. Enraged by the insults, `Ajab had resolved to achieve revenge by carrying off the British major's wife. He failed, however, because the woman was very fat. Instead, he carried off the major's daughter. The newspaper asserted, moreover, that the Afghan government was not responsible for the incident, because the perpetrators were not residents of Afghanistan. *Aman-i-Afghan, Asad* 22 1302/Aug. 15, 1923.

[55.] Maconachie, P249, 102.

mad Wali Khan, "the man of international affairs," who, after returning from his mission to introduce Afghanistan to Europe, had replaced Mahmud Tarzi as foreign minister. Mohammad Wali Khan was careful to deal with the problem in a diplomatic manner in an effort to avoid embarrassment to Afghanistan, which was on the verge of concluding treaty relations with European countries. Sepahsalar Nader Khan, on the other hand, "saw in compliance with the British demands the tip of the wedge which would in time shatter Afghan influence among the frontier tribes."[56] He adamantly opposed making concessions to the British.

At this juncture, the king approached several religious leaders, among them the Hajji of Turangzai, the Padshah of Islampur, and the Molla of Chaknawur, who were influential among the frontier tribes, to assist in solving the problem. The Molla of Chaknawur and the Hajji of Turangzai were reported to have proposed inciting anti-British agitation in the Independent Territory in order to deter the British from pursuing the murder cases further.[57] The proposal of these clergymen appears not to have been endorsed. After several months of attempting to evade the issue, the Afghan government finally apprehended and detained the offenders in Jalalabad. Later in August, before a trial date had been set, the offenders escaped from prison and sought shelter with the Hajji of Turangzai and the Molla of Chaknawur.[58] Their escape was likely facilitated by the government, which was eager to avoid further problems with the tribes.

For their part, the British increased pressure on the Afghan government by refusing to allow arms purchased from France to be transported to Afghanistan via India. In a memorandum to the Afghan foreign minister dated September 19, Humphrys, the British minister in Kabul, laid down the following conditions for transit of the arms: arrest and genuine trial proceedings against the Landi Kotal murderers, banishment of `Ajab Gol and his party to a place far from the Indian border, and complete cessation of anti-British intrigue in Waziristan.[59]

In November 1923, Nader Khan who, according to Maconachie, was "the main obstacle to compliance with the British demand," was relieved of responsibility for frontier affairs and was replaced by Mohammad Wali Khan,[60] and the government yielded to diplomatic pressures to arrest the members of the Landi Kotal gang and deport them to Turkistan.[61] Ardali and Dawud Shah, the two Sango Khail Shinwaris who killed the two Englishmen, were to be captured and surrendered to the British, but on January 21, 1924, Ardali and one Afghan soldier were killed in the attempt to capture the two suspects, and Dawud Shah escaped.

[56.] Maconachie, P261, 113.
[57.] IOR, L/P&S/1081, P2311, no. 19, May 24, 1923.
[58.] IOR, L/P&S/1081, P3813, no. 33, Sept. 5, 1923.
[59.] Maconachie, P249, 103.
[60.] Maconachie, P282, 124.
[61.] Maconachie, 115.

The crisis passed in March 1924, when the British released the arms confiscated in Bombay.[62] However, the regime's capitulation to British demands, which resulted in the death of Ardali, had serious consequences for the regime's relations with the tribes. The Pashtuns were infuriated with the king, because he had failed to protect three Pashtun Muslims from a non-Muslim, foreign enemy. Moreover, he had betrayed the time-honored Pashtun custom, which obliges a man to protect those who seek refuge in his territory even if the fugitive is his own great enemy.[63] According to `Abd al-Haiy, the author of *Afghanistan awe Sarhad (Afghanistan and Frontier)*, Humphrys was well aware of the axioms of the *pashtunwali* and knew that failure to offer protection to the offenders would expose the king to charges of cowardice and treason and jeopardize his credibility among the Ghelzai tribes,[64] who were distinguished by the great number of their descent and the geographic expanse of their affinal network.

Official British correspondence reveals British satisfaction at the outcome of the Kohat and Landi Kotal incidents. On January 24, 1924, in its weekly report, the intelligence bureau in the North-West Frontier Province wrote that "the killing of Ardali is a most satisfactory event from every point of view."[65] Official British reports of tribal displeasure toward the amir and his officials greatly increased toward the end of January 1924, several weeks before the outbreak of the Khost Rebellion. On January 31, the North-West Frontier Province intelligence bureau reported that after the Friday prayer at Pish Bulak (in Jalalabad) a tribal leader "got up and publicly declaimed his wish that God might destroy such Islam as the Afghan government represented and might prosper *kofr* [infidelity] if Islam was what they had recently been experiencing in Afghanistan."[66] On that same day, Humphrys reported to London, "in regard to actions taken against Kohat and Landi Kotal murderers, the amir is finding it difficult to save face with the Mullas."[67] Curiously, on the same day, the British Consul in Jalalabad wrote,

> Deportation of `Ajab and his party of males and females to Turkestan, and the murder of Ardali are matters which have greatly shattered the reputation of the Amir....If the element of apprehension from the Amir as a ruler were eliminated, there was no doubt that a

---

[62.] On March 19, 1924, Humphrys informed the foreign minister of the release of arms. Maconachie, P258, 111.

[63.] The importance of this principle is illustrated in the name of a Pashtun tribe, the Khogiani (pig protector). According to legend, one of their ancestors protected a wild pig, an animal greatly disdained in Muslim culture, against its attackers, simply because the animal had taken refuge in the man's domain.

[64.] `Abd al-Haiy, *Afghanistan awe Sarhad*, 363.

[65.] IOR, L/P&S/1081, P832, no. 4, Jan. 24, 1924.

[66.] *Ibid.*, P950, 1924, no. 5, Jan. 31, 1924.

[67.] Tel. no. 30, Kabul, April 2, 1924 quoted in Machonachie, P264, 115.

fitwa of *kufr* (excommunication) would have been passed against him.[68]

In February, the British intelligence officer in the North-West Frontier Province reported in his weekly diary that "the Afghan frontier is no longer a home away from home for the tribal desperado....These events have been a serious blow to Afghan prestige among the independent tribes."[69] In fact, when Aman-Allah went in person to Jalalabad to discuss the matter with the Sango Khail Shinwaris and the Mohmands, they reportedly declined the invitation to visit with him because of their displeasure over the killing of Ardali.[70] According to Adamec, the government's acquiescence to the British had by this time angered the tribesmen sufficiently to the point of their considering rebellion.[71]

The Anglo-Afghan crisis had another dire consequence. It resulted in the deterioration of relations between the amir and his most capable general, Sepahsalar Nader Khan. At the outbreak of the Khost Rebellion, Mohammad Wali Khan replaced Nader Khan as minister of war, and Nader Khan was appointed ambassador to Paris. The reason for these changes seems to have been growing suspicion on the part of the amir of Nader Khan's great influence with the tribes and his possible fomenting of rebellion. Coincidentally, the British intelligence office in the North-West Frontier Province considered Nader Khan's dismissal from tribal affairs "of great significance and to be likely to result in decreased intrigue."[72] Whether Nader Khan was involved in a conspiracy with the tribes against the regime is not clear. It is, however, certain that he was upset about the cuts in the military and the influence of Turkish military officers over Aman-Allah. He was also adamantly opposed to the rapid introduction of wide-ranging reforms. In a private interview with Humphrys on April 4, 1924, Nader Khan criticized Aman-Allah for cutting the military, pushing reforms precipitously, and promulgating the Constitution (the *nezam-nama*) without first persuading the public of the need for the changes. The government, he complained, had invited the consultation of dozens of foreign experts but had not developed an operative plan. As a result of these policies, orthodox ulama and their followers in rural Afghanistan were in revolt "and the power of the state was scarcely able to cope successfully with the disorders which had arisen."[73]

[68.] Telegram 564, Mar. 15, 1924, from the viceroy to the secretary of state, quoted *ibid.*, P264, 115.

[69.] IOR, L/P&S/10/1081, P1054, no. 6, Feb. 7, 1924.

[70.] *Ibid.*, P1297, 1924, no. 8, Feb. 21, 1924, and P950, 1924, no. 5, Jan. 31, 1924.

[71.] Adamec, *Afghanistan 1900-1923*, 94.

[72.] L/P&S/10/1081, P4847, no. 23, Nov. 1923.

[73.] Kabul dispatch no. 52, Apr. 4, 1924, Maconachie, P281, 123.

The Impact of Reforms on Tribal and Rural Clergy

Religion is often a catalyst for social and political revolt. In Afghanistan, the opposition to Amani reforms was first articulated in Islamic terms, with religious leaders at the forefront of the opposition. Rebellion spread widely, spurred on by provocative messages circulated through local mosques by the lower-ranking rural clergy, the *molla*s. In contrast, the majority of the influential tribal religious leaders remained neutral, and high ulama in the capital even supported the regime during the rebellion. It was not until the *Loya-Jerga* was convened in 1924 that high ulama voiced opposition to the reforms, and when they did, their methods were quite different from those of their counterparts in the countryside.

The village *molla*s, mostly lower-ranking clergy, constituted the largest segment of the religious establishment. They identified in general with the rural tribal population, and they interpreted the reforms as an attempt by the government to diminish the social force of Islam. Their opposition to the reforms was substantive, as many of the regime's new regulations encroached upon their prerogatives. Their function in the tribal order of the rural population encompassed a variety of duties, ranging from leading daily prayers and running mosque schools, to attending to legal matters and acting as arbiters of local disputes. Given their prominence in the local order, regulatory changes were likely to threaten their role. The threat was greatest in the tribal regions where "[t]he local tribesman equates his Pashtun lineage to Islam. To him they are inextricably bound and interrelated."[74]   Indeed, the *molla*'s function in tribal areas was prescribed by the *pashtunwali*. Changes in the tribal way of life would mean changes in the mollas' role and influence.

There was yet another reason for the resistance of the lower-ranking mollas to the reforms of 1923. Unlike the higher ulama in the capital and the influential tribal religious leaders (the sufi *sheikhs*), who supported the regime in promoting pan-Islamism, the lower clergy concerned themselves almost exclusively with village affairs and knew little of international affairs. Uninformed about modernist Muslim thinking and pan-Islamism, local clergymen were offended by what they perceived as breaches of Islamic orthodoxy and interference in their realm of authority.

Threatening to the lower-ranking mollas was the government's intervention in religious schools (*madrasa*) and other institutions. In 1923, the ministries of education and justice drew up a curriculum for training *qazi*s, and uniform training for *qazi*s became compulsory. To supplement the *Maktab-i-`Olum-i-Sharqiyya* (School for the Study of Eastern Sciences), founded in 1921 to train *qazi*s, *imam*, and instructors of the *madrasa*s, in 1923 Aman-Allah founded *Maktab-i-Qozat* (School for Judges), a special training school for the *qazi*s that was designed to integrate reform into the religious structure. The program of study maintained traditional patterns but offered modern studies. The textbooks in the curriculum included the following: *Fosul-i-Akbari, Kafiyya, Sharh-i-*

[74.] Ahmad, "Emergent Trends in Moslem Tribal Society," 86.

Molla, Kanz, Sharh-i-Waqayya, Hedayya, the translated Qur'an, *Osul-i-Shahi, Nur al-Anwar, Seraji,* theology (*`aqayyid*), Islamic history, the history of Afghanistan, geography, mathematics, *Akhlaq-i-Mohseni, Tamassok al-Qozat,* Fundamental Law (*Nezam-nama-i-Asasi*), and General Penal Code (*Nezam-nama-i-Jaza-i-`Omumi*).[75] The first students graduated in 1923 and were appointed to judicial courts, replacing *qazi*s trained in older schools.[76] Future *qazi*s and other religious functionaries, it was announced, would be selected only from among graduates of these two new schools.[77] Simultaneously, a secular board of examiners was formed to check the credentials of *qazi*s before their appointment to the courts.[78] These procedures, which undermined the traditional selection mechanisms of the religious establishment, offended the *qazi*s, and their distrust of the regime continued to mount.

The lower-ranking ulama feared that changes in education would disrupt the traditional way of life. The most threatening trends were 1) the expansion of the curriculum of state-controlled Islamic studies, 2) the increasing number of Western teachers in the country's educational system and, 3) the expansion of secular education.

Although secular education had been introduced into Afghanistan by Amir Habib-Allah, most instructors until this time had continued to be chosen from among the ulama, and traditional religious schools had remained the only system of education outside the capital. So the changes instituted by Habib-Allah did not significantly reduce the ulama's influence in education.

King Aman-Allah widened the scope of modern education. He maintained religion as a basic part of education, but placed the teachers and curricula outside the control of the ulama. In 1923, the government expanded its authority to include mosque schools, which until that time had been the exclusive domain of the *molla*s. In the fall of 1923, an administrative regulation mandated use of these schools to spread literacy in remote villages.[79] Supported by the local community, the curricula of these schools were adapted to meet state standards. The schools taught only religious studies, reading, and writing. In the absence of textbooks, teachers were allowed to use religious texts and classical literature; for example, *Qa`eda-i-Baghdadi, Panj Ketab, Mahmud-Nama,* Golistan, *Bostan, Akhlaq-i-Mohseni,* and *Anwar-i-Sohaili.* Local offices of the Ministry of Education taught local *molla*s new teaching methods for two and a half hours in the summer and three hours in the winter. In addition, new courses were added, and

---

[75] *Eslah,* Khanabad, Afghanistan, vol. 1, no. 48, in Ahang, 163.

[76] *Aman-i-Afghan,* 12 *Saratan* 1302/July 4, 1923.

[77] *Ibid.,* 14 *Saratan* 1299/July 5, 1920.

[78] *Nezam-nama-i-Tashkilat-i-Asasi,* Fundamental Administration Law, 1300/1921, Articles 34-36.

[79] See, *Nezam-nama-i-Makateb-i-Khanagi* (Regulations Pertaining to Private or Mosque Schools), 1302/1923.

the program of study was to be evaluated periodically by a board of examiners appointed by the central government.[80]

In 1923, Aman-Allah set about implementing many of his ideas. He organized official publicity to popularize the conscription law and general education, including public shools for girls. An example of this publicity appeared in *Ettehad-i-Mashriqi*, in the form of an appeal for education and conscription endorsed by an influential *sheikh*, the Molla of Sarkani.[81]

Social and political change were happening rapidly throughout the country. The establishment of language schools (*makateb-i-alsana*) in 1923 was a significant development, inasmuch as it placed these sources of secondary education in the hands of European directors and teachers. Plans included the creation of language schools in the provinces.[82] In the Amaniyya and Amani schools, French and German were the media of instruction for subjects designed to prepare Afghan youth for more advanced studies in the sciences and technology in the West. A group of boys was sent straightaway to study in Europe.

A large number of foreign technicians, doctors, and businessmen arrived in Kabul between 1919 and 1923 to assist in the effort to bring about change. With increased diplomatic relations throughout the world, Afghans initiated many contacts with the West. European influence on cultural and social life had begun in the time of Amir Habib-Allah. Now Western influence intensified. The *molla*s feared the growing influence of foreigners on the Islamic belief system and way of life, not only within the educational system but also in Afghan society. They were concerned that the minds of Afghan youths would be polluted with non-Islamic ideas from the West. Foreign influence was perceived as part of a conspiracy by non-Muslim Europeans and atheistic Soviets to thwart Islam.

The *molla*s based their arguments on theological grounds and questioned the validity of the *nezam-nama*s. Unfortunately, documents relating to the rebellion are too few to reveal nuances of the protests or the line of argument expressed by the *molla*s during the rebellion. Afghan press reports reflect the view of the government, and Afghan historians have generally ignored the causes of the rebellion, presuming it was instigated by the British. It is the reports of the debates among the higher ulama during the *Loya-Jerga* of 1924 and the coverage in the Anglo-Indian press that reveal the main points of clerical opposition. The *molla*s objected to provisions of the Constitution, the Marriage Law, and the Penal Codes that they believed contravened the *shari`at*. A major cause of opposition was the first clause of the Constitution, which assured individual freedom with no mention of the constraints decreed by the *shari`at*. The Marriage Law, along with female education and provisions of the Penal Codes, provided the ideological basis for the *molla*s to resist change.

[80.] *Ibid.*

[81.] On January 13, 1923, *Ettehad-i-Mashriqi* published an appeal for support of education endorsed by Sarkani Molla and signed by a number of notables in Konar. IOR, L/P&S/10/1081, P1054, no. 6, Feb. 7, 1924.

[82.] *Aman-i-Afghan*, 14 `Aqrab 1302/Nov. 9, 1923.

Aman-Allah's most controversial reforms related to the emancipation of women. Resentment over reforms relating to the status of women was the most powerful weapon of the opposition in its fight against other reforms. The family is the basis of Islamic social structure and features prominently in Pashtun customary practices. The changes Aman-Allah initiated in family law were considered his most outrageous innovations and were doomed to failure because they too harshly defied tradition. The new Marriage Law was widely perceived as an attempt to weaken the traditional family structure defined in the Qur'an. It was also interpreted by many in the clergy as an attempt to weaken Islam as a social force.

The first code to deal with marriage issues and the status of women in general was the Marriage Code of 1920 (1299). The code was published in pamphlet form with the title "Law Concerning the Conduct of Weddings, Marriages and Circumcisions *(Nezam-nama-i-`Arusi, Nekah wa Khatnasuri)*." In subsequent years, this *nezam-nama* was amended and revised several times.[83] The Marriage Law was purportedly based on the principles of Hanafi law. It opened with the following paragraph:

> Since most of the cases brought before the courts are related to the problems of child marriage, extravagant marriage expenses, and the mistreatment of women, the following provisions are issued in order to remove some of the causes of discord, disunity, and suppression, and to reaffirm the equal rights of women provided by the sacred *shari`at* and by the principles of Hanafi law.[84]

The first Marriage Code of 1920 dealt with child marriage, bridal price, and extravagant weddings.

In 1923, a more exhaustive marriage law with twenty-four articles was enacted. Article 1 of the new code discouraged polygamy by quoting from the Qur`an: "[M]arry of the women, who seem good to you, two or three or four; and if ye fear that ye cannot do justice, then only one."[85] On the authority of this verse, the law prohibited polygamy if there were fear of injustice toward any of the wives. The would-be husband was required to produce two witnesses in court to testify to his ability to do justice to both the present and future wife. Only after the sworn confirmation of an attesting authority (*mossadeq*, an honest Muslim male) could the would-be husband obtain the court's permission to marry an additional wife. Polygamous marriages without court approval were declared invalid, and violators were sentenced to two years' imprisonment or a fine of 2,000 rupees.

The code of 1923 also required that marriages be registered by the state. Registration of any marriage in which the bride had not reached puberty was

---

[83.] Three different versions are dated 1920, 1922, and 1924. There may be more.

[368.] *Nezam-nama-i-`Arusi, Nekah wa Khatnasuri*, opening chapter.

[85.] Qur'an 4:3.

forbidden by Articles 5 and 6, and the dowry, previously determined by tribal or family status, was set at 30 rupees for all citizens by Article 15. Article 15 also prohibited all types of monetary gifts traditionally received by the bride's father—*shir-baha* (milk money), *toyana* (wedding expenses), and *walwar* (bridal money).

Restraints on the practice of polygamy and the elimination of child marriage were among the most objectionable provisions of the Marriage Law. Both were sensitive issues to pious Muslims because polygamy is permitted in the Qur'an, and because the Prophet married one of his wives, `Ayisha, when she was very young. Partly because of these provisions against polygamy and child marriage, the Afghan Marriage Law was one of the most progressive in the Muslim world. In fact, the Soviets used it as a model in the predominantly Muslim Central Asian states under their control.[86]

The requirement that marriages be registered with the state reduced further the authority of the *molla*s, although they were still permitted to conduct marriages. Such interference in the realm of religious law was deemed by the ulama as innovation (*bed`at*), a type of heresy.

The *molla*s also took issue with the opening of public schools for female students in the capital. The first girls' school (*maktab-i-masturat*) was opened in 1920.[87] As with all the reforms, women's education was justified with religious arguments in the press and in speeches of government officials. Articles by Mahmud Tarzi in 1913 in the *Seraj al-Akhbar* advocating education for women had provoked a heated debate between Tarzi and Qazi Mohammad Rafiq, a prominent clergyman in the capital.[88] Tarzi's compelling arguments had, in the end, forced the clergyman to admit in writing that education for women was permitted in Islam.[89] Debates of this kind continued in the newly established government-sponsored press in the capital and in the provinces.

In 1921, Queen Soraya published a statement in which she enumerated examples of religious texts that favored education for women.[90] Publication of the statement forestalled confrontation on the topic with conservative religious elements. At about this time, a weekly women's magazine, the *Ershad-i-Neswan*, was founded by Asma Rasmiya, wife of Mahmud Tarzi, with Tarzi's niece, Ruh Afza, as editor. In 1923, the government organized a propaganda campaign throughout Afghanistan to generate popular support for female education and the conscription law.

[86.] Massell, *The Surrogate Proletariat*, 219.

[87.] The few students were daughters of the royal family, court members, and other high officials.

[88.] *Seraj al-Akhbar*, vol. 3, no. 10, 8 *Dalw* 1292/Jan. 28, 1913.

[89.] *Ibid.*

[90.] A full translation of the statement appears in Appendix C.

The rebel *molla*s maintained the puritanical view that women should not be seen outside their homes,[91] and considered the introduction of public schools for girls an assault on the principle of seclusion of women (*hejab,* or *parda*). Articles in the press praising female education (*ma`aref-i-neswan*) were interpreted by the rebel *molla*s as a prelude to an official scheme to forcibly remove girls to Kabul, as a counterpart to conscription for boys.

Opposition focused on the legal reforms, which involved the bureaucratization of the legal and judiciary systems, translation and codification of Islamic criminal law, and promulgation of a penal code based on Islamic principles but modeled after European codes. The intent of the government in creating a unified judiciary system was twofold—to curb the autonomy of the *qazi* and eradicate corruption. Similarly, the government intended to force the Pashtun tribes to obey the central government by formulating a new Criminal Law that ignored many customary practices of the *pashtunwali.*

The new Criminal Law (*Tamassok al-Qozat*)[92] was compiled by Mawlawi `Abd al-Wase` Qandahari in 1920 and approved by members of the High Religious Council (*Hai'at-i-Tamiz*), who declared that it conformed with the *shari`at.* Like the Ottoman Turkish criminal law (*Al-Majalla*), it was based on selected provisions of Hanafi law rather than on the prevailing Hanafi view on every issue. Each provision was derived from some well-known Hanafi lawbook such as the *Hedayya, Fath al-Qadir, Nahaya, Al-Tahawi, Fatawa-i-`Alamgiri, Fatawa-i-Qazi Khan, Al-Badi`, Mohit al-Sarrakhsi, Jame` al-Romuz,* and *Al Seraj al-Wahaj.* The two books of the first volume dealt with rights (*hoquq*) and punishment (*jaza*). There were three types of rights: the rights of God (*hoquq-Allah*), the rights of the individual (*hoquq al-`abd*), and the rights of society (*hoquq al-nas*). There were also three types of punishment: those predetermined by God (*hodud,* plural of *hadd,* meaning literary limitations), the retaliations for homicide (*qesas,* plural of *qesa*), and the less severe punishments not prescribed in the Qur'an (*ta`zirat,* plural of *ta`zir*).

The *hodud* were legal punishments predetermined by God (*`oqubat-i-moqaddara*) for five major crimes: adultery, wine drinking, accusing a virtuous woman of illicit sex (*qazaf*), theft, and highway robbery. The *qesas* were retaliations prescribed for deliberate homicide. The power to determine *ta`zirat* punishments was vested in the king, who was also responsible, under Article 6, for the proper execution of the *hodud* punishments. The distinction between *hodud* and *ta`zir* punishments in Article 13 was taken from the famous Hanafi lawbook *Khazanat al-Rawiyya,* which states "A *hadd* is a predetermined punishment ordained by God (*moqaddara*). A *ta`zir* is an undetermined punishment

---

[91.] Amir Dust Mohammad, Amir Habib-Allah, and even Amir Aman-Allah himself (in the first year of his reign) had strictly forbidden women to appear in public.

[92.] *Tamassok,* meaning "grasp," is derived from a saying of the Prophet: "O' community of believers, I have left you something that if you grasp it firmly and rely on it, you will never lose the way to progress in this world and the next—God's Qur'an and my example of behavior." *Tamassok al-Qozat,* title page.

(*ghair-i-moqadara*) and is decreed by the Sultan." In the application of the rule of *ta`zir*, the *Tamassok al-Qozat* left great discretion to the ruler, as the *uli al-amr* and fountainhead of order, to protect the public interest (*maslehat*) and maintain public order (*nezam-i-molk*). Toward that end, the General Penal Code (*Nezam-nama-i-Jaza-i-`Omumi*) and the Military Penal Code (*Nezam-nama-i-Jaza-i-`Askari*) were promulgated in 1923.

The Penal Code, modeled on Turkish and French legislation, did not abrogate precepts of the *shari`at*. Rather, it imposed *ta`zir* as an administrative measure to assure public safety and uniform court procedures. Previously discretionary punishments (*ta`zirat*) were now prescribed for acts of corruption (*fesad*), ranging from breaches of the internal and external security of the state to cases of rape, molestation, gambling, and medical malpractice. A large portion of the Penal Code was devoted to punishments for corruption and abuse of authority by judges and civil servants. In Article 2, the code distinguished felonies (*janh*), gross misdemeanors (*jenayat*), and villainy (*qabahat*), and designated corresponding punishments: punishment for committing a felony (*ta'dibiyya*), retribution for gross misdemeanors (*tarhibiyya*), and corrective punishment for villainy (*takdiriyya*). The punishments ranged from the death penalty (*e`dam*) to imprisonment (*habs*) and fines (*jaza-i-naqdi*). The code designated Islamic punishments for usury, theft, apostasy, and drinking. Traditional Islamic practices, such as flogging and public exposure of the criminal (*tashhir*), were adopted for activities forbidden in the *shari`at*, such as gambling, drinking, giving false witness, and perjury (Articles 180-181).

Although Islamic teachings relating to crimes and punishments were incorporated into the *nezam-nama*s, the very act of translating and codifying the *shari`at* offended the *molla*s. The use only of selected provisions of Hanafi law was also offensive to them. Although the Penal Code was conceived theoretically as supplemental to the *shari`at*, in practice the Penal Code often prevailed. This bias often changed the outcome of cases because the main thrust of the Penal Code was to safeguard public policy, whereas the *shari`at* emphasized individual rights.[93] One unpopular provision was the establishment of fines (*jarima-i-naqdi*). According to the more puritanical ulama, fines were contrary to Hanafi law.

The core issue in the dispute over the Criminal Law, however, was a provision vesting the power to determine discretionary punishments (*ta`zirat*) in the state. According to the ulama, each crime was a unique case for which *ta`zir* punishment could not be predetermined. Rather, a *qazi* should examine the time, location, type, and circumstances of the individual crime and apply precepts of the *shari`at* and his personal judgment. Under the new regulations, the *qazi*s stood to lose their autonomy and their monopoly of the legal profession, prerogatives they had enjoyed for centuries. Not even Amir `Abd al-Rahman, who greatly restricted the authority of the ulama in the late nineteenth century,

---

[93.] Musa Shafiq, 1976.

had dared to limit these prerogatives. Now the new Criminal Law, the *Tamassok al-Qozat*, threatened to restrict both.

The ulama saw the formulation and codification of the *shari`at* into legal regulations as a sign of the government's intent to secularize the law. That the *shari`at* is basically concerned with the rights of the individual rather than the rights of society explains in part the negative attitude of the orthodox clergy toward the law of the state.

Another premise questioned by the *mollas* was the clause in the Fundamental Law that declared all citizens equal before the law, regardless of creed. The *mollas* were also irritated by the measures of tolerance granted to the Hindus by the constitution because in the *shari`at* a clear distinction is made between the rights of Muslims and non-Muslim subjects. Although new taxes were being levied, the king reduced the poll tax (*jazya*) on the Hindus, a religious minority in Afghanistan, by one-half and lifted the requirement that Hindus wear a yellow turban to distinguish themselves from Muslims. Aman-Allah also gave Hindus the right to attend the military school, join the Afghan army, buy property, and rebuild the Hindu temples that had been destroyed. Taxes on Hindus were reduced to an amount equal to that levied on Muslims. In addition, Aman-Allah announced that Hindus should occupy seats on the State's Council.

Many Muslim Afghans, and especially the *mollas*, were offended by the new rights extended to the Hindus. During a visit in March 1923 to Lalpura, a locality in the Jalalabad district, Aman-Allah met with the leader of the Hindu community and announced the reduction of the poll tax on Hindus. He also ordered that a Hindu school that had been destroyed by order of the Molla of Chaknawur for being constructed at the site of an old mosque be rebuilt at a different location at the government's expense.[94] The *mollas* and people of Lalpura were reportedly incensed by this demonstration of tolerance toward the Hindus.[95]

Although well intentioned, the reforms initiated by Aman-Allah were not well received. Opposition to them began to surface in the fall of 1923. Government attempts to enforce conscription in Zamindawar, Posht-i-Rud, and Katawaz in southern Afghanistan provoked an uproar that continued until the beginning of November.[96] During the government operation in Zamindawar, a Nurzai battalion in Qandahar mutinied over delays in pay.[97] In the city of Qandahar, opposition to conscription resulted in repeated clashes between the Qandaharis and government forces. On November 27 and again on December 11, 1923, shops closed in Qandahar, and protestors took refuge in the shrine of the Kherqa-i-Sharif and refused to leave until the government promised to postpone conscription. The official in charge of enforcing the law fled to India, fearing

---

[94] IOR, L/P&S/10/1081, P1603, secret, no. 12, Mar. 22, 1923.
[95] *Ibid.*
[96] IOR, "Summary of Events in Afghanistan," July 15, 1923, to June 30, 1924.
[97] *Ibid.*

for his life.[98] Similar outbreaks occurred in the Eastern Province, where the Solaiman Khail, Ghelzais, and Khugianis also protested conscription.[99]

Initially, the revolts were sporadic, with no leader to give the insurgents cohesion. The real challenge then came from the rural clergy, who began to infuse the revolts with passionate Islamic rhetoric. Early in October 1923, a group of *molla*s in Jabal al-Seraj protested the appointment of Western teachers.[100] The government arrested several of the most outspoken *molla*s,[101] but they were later released as the result of the intervention of the highly revered Molla of Taqaw.[102] By the end of 1923, the *molla*s in Qandahar were deeply involved in the anti-government movement. The British agent in Qandahar reported that the Hazrat of Deh-i-Khwaja, an influential local *molla*, "had become prominent as the leader of opposition in the city of Qandahar."[103]

THE OUTBREAK OF THE KHOST REBELLION

As opposition to conscription continued in Qandahar, a more intense rebellion broke out in Khost, a region in the Southern Province. In March 1924, a group of *molla*s in Khost took a hostile view of the new regulations as inconsistent with the *shari`at*.  The chief instigators were Molla `Abd-Allah, known as Molla-i-Lang; the lame molla, Qazi `Abd-Allah Jan; an ex-*qazi* of the Southern Province; and Molla `Abd al-Rashid. Lacking the charisma and lineage of the influential tribal religious leaders, Molla `Abd-Allah was an Islamic ideologue, who used his knowledge of the *shari`at* to couch tribal grievances in religious terms. The conflict began when a Mangal tribesman contested the marriage of another tribesman, claiming that the bride had been betrothed to him in childhood. The local official, Amir al-Din, interceded on behalf of the newlywed couple and with the bride's consent denied the claim of the plaintiff on the basis of provisions of the new Marriage Law, which prohibited forced marriages and marital arrangements before the age of puberty. Molla `Abd-Allah, who had been deprived by legal reforms of his authority to settle local disputes, protested the decision, accusing the local official of acting against the *shari`at* and asking him to reverse his decision. Amir al-Din's refusal to consider the request provided Molla `Abd-Allah a pretext with which to arouse the Mangal tribe to rebel against the government.[104] Resorting to Islamic rhetoric, he succeeded in a short time in consolidating various tribes in support of his cause.

[98.] IOR, L/P&S/10/961, no. 2, Jan. 3, 1924.

[99.] *Ibid.*, no. 84.

[100.] *Ibid.*, no. 22, Nov. 2, 1923.

[101.] *Ibid.*

[102.] *Ibid.*, P3907, no. 23, Sept. 1923.

[103.] IOR, L/P&S/10/961, no. 48, Apr. 7, 1924.

[104.] Kateb, *Tazakkor al-Enqelab*, 3.

With the collaboration of Malik Boland Khan, a Zadran tribal leader, `Abd-Allah and other *molla*s raised the banner of opposition in the name of Islam against the reforms and instigated a militant revolt:

> With the new code in one hand and the Koran in the other, they called the tribes to choose between the word of God and that of man, and adjured them to resist demands, the acceptance of which would reduce their sons to slavery in the Afghan army and their daughters to the degrading influence of Western education.[105]

The tribal *molla*s, who had effectively stoked anti-British emotions in the past, now aroused tribal and religious fervor against the reforms. Their call for the defense of the *shari`at* gave disgruntled parties the impetus needed to coalesce. General dissatisfaction suddenly burgeoned into a holy war. The *nezam-nama*s, viewed as government-created substitutes for the *shari`at*, were the immediate target of opposition. The rebel *molla*s allegedly declared that the reforms were inspired by the Soviets, a new foreign enemy, and were aimed at destroying Islam.[106]

At first the government did not take the uprising seriously. By the end of March, however, governmental authorities had begun to appreciate the gravity of the situation. On April 26, *Aman-i-Afghan* reported that the Mangals in Khost were proving troublesome as a result of propaganda being spread by treacherous elements and foreign enemies of the country. The newspaper added that the rebel *molla*s were influenced by the propaganda, because they were unable to provide sound religious reasons for opposing the *nezam-nama*s and were unwilling to discuss them logically with the ulama of the capital. The newspapers stressed that the *nezam-nama*s had been compiled and sanctioned by the most learned ulama of the capital and were in full conformity with the *shari`at*, of which the government was the guardian.[107] Subsequent articles in *Aman-i-Afghan* elaborated the theme that the Khost *molla*s were not adequately informed about Islam and that the new laws had been endorsed by the high ulama, experts in religious law.

At the same time, the regime attempted to placate the tribes by clearing up misgivings about the Landi Kotal incidents. A slightly earlier article in the newspaper, titled "Afghanistan and Its Northern and Southern Neighbors," had attempted to correct misunderstandings about the government's policy toward Pashtun tribes living in the independent tribal zone, known as Yaghistan, along the Durand Line. The article argued that strong ethnic, linguistic, and religious bonds existed between Afghanistan and the frontier tribes (*aqwam-i-sarhad*) and that these tribes would never abide British rule nor desist from acts of vengeance against the British. According to *Aman-i-Agfhan*, these tribes considered Af-

---

[105.] L/P&S/10/161., no. 84, July 3, 1924.

[106.] *Daily Express*, May 1, 1924.

[107.] *Aman-i-Afghan*, vol. 5, no. 1, 6, *Sawr* 1303/May 26, 1924.

ghanistan their home and trusted the Afghan government in times of conflict with the British. This bond, the article continued, was well illustrated in the case of `Ajab Khan, whom the British had failed to capture. In compliance with His Majesty's order, `Ajab Khan and his family had agreed to exile in Turkistan, away from British territory. The article concluded that Afghanistan wished to have friendly relations with Great Britain but at the same time desired for the tribes prosperity, tranquility, and safety from foreign threat.[108] However, the message the government may have hoped to communicate in the press, only reached small numbers of readers in the urban centers. In the countryside, the *molla*s, as spiritual leaders of the masses, effectively controlled what was communicated to the people.

By the middle of April, the whole Southern Province was involved in the insurrection. As resistance increased, the government attempted a peaceful settlement by sending a delegation made up of the minister of justice, Mawlawi Mohammad Ebrahim; the Grand Qazi of Kabul, `Abd al-Rahman Baiktuti; and several highly respected ulama to persuade the rebel *molla*s that the reforms did not conflict with the teachings of Islam.[109] The mission included a group of small female students who were to demonstrate their knowledge of Islam to the tribesmen and thus deter suspicions about the purpose of the women's schools.[110]

Meanwhile, the Afghan legation in London objected to what it regarded as exaggerated reports about the situation in Khost. It contended the protest of the *molla*s was a sign of political awakening and an expression of freedom of thought and speech encouraged by the new political climate in Afghanistan. The disturbance in Khost, according to the Afghan mission, was nothing more than a meeting of a group of ulama in Khost who were critical of certain aspects of the reforms. Two of their spokesmen had met with ulama of the capital and discussed their views. The ulama of the capital "expressed themselves as unanimously of the opinion that the new laws were absolutely consistent with the injunctions of Islam."[111] Similar interpretations were articulated in the government-sponsored press at home.

Contrary to the government's optimistic official stance, the negotiations proved futile. The rebel *molla*s not only refused to accept the high ulama's reasoning, but also accused them of having sold their souls to the government. If

---

[108.] *Ibid.*, no. 2, 23, *Sawr* 1303/May 13, 1924.

[109.] Ghobar, 807; Poullada, *Reform and Rebellion*, 122; Maconachie, P300, 134; IOR, L/P&S/10/961, no. 48, Apr. 7, 1924. According to Fazl Ghani Mojaddedi, during negotiations with members of the mission Molla 'Abd-Allah won over Nur al-Mashayikh to his cause. In contrast Shams al-Mashayikh adamantly opposed Molla 'Abd-Allah's plan to dethrone Aman-Allah, eventhough he agreed with Molla 'Abd-Allah that certain aspects of the reforms were not in line with the *shari'at* and therefore had to be revoked or altered, he was adamantly opposed to Molla 'Abd-Allah's plan to dethrone the king. Fazl Ghani Mojaddedi, *Saltanat-i-A 'lahazrat Aman-Allah Khan*, 240.

[110.] I am grateful to Tahera Sorkhabi, a member of the female student group that was part of the conciliatory mission, for this information. Interview, Kabul, Aug. 1976.

[111.] *Morning Post*, May 24, 1924.

the ulama of the capital were true believers, the rebels argued, they would also be fighting against the regime.

The Khost *mollas'* antireform slogans were well received in the areas surrounding Khost. Far from resolving the problem for the government, the negotiations with the rebel leaders gave them a broader forum in which to proclaim their grievances. Moreover, the rebel *mollas* used this time of negotiation to consolidate their forces and establish contact with neighboring tribes. Within a short period of time, the rebellion in Khost attracted sympathy and support from discontented parties throughout the Southern and Eastern Provinces.

The weakness of governmental jurisdictions at the local and provincial levels contributed to the rapid spread of the rebellion. The dislocation of local government caused by the sudden introduction of the new administrative code (*nezam-nama-i-tashkilat-i-asasi*) and the reduction in troops in the provinces as a result of military cuts had left local authorities incapable of dealing with eruptions of violence.

Toward the end of May, hostilities resumed. When it became obvious that mediation was futile, the government intensified efforts to suppress the rebellion by force. The first major clash between government troops and rebel forces occurred on June 2 at Tira Pass, between the Logar Valley, not far from Kabul, and at Zormat, in the Southern Province. The government troops were defeated. A few days later, the *Qet`a-i-Namuna*, a regiment trained by Jamal Pasha, defeated the rebels and reopened communications between Kabul and Gardiz. However, in May the rebel forces regained the upper hand. The zeal of the Khost *mollas* drew together discontented elements in the rural areas and generated more support among the tribes. During the first half of July, rebellion spread in Katawaz and Ghazni, and gradually the Ahmadzai, Solaiman Khail, 'Isa Khail, Sultan Khail, and Eshaq Khail tribes became involved.[112]

In all of these areas, local *mollas* led the antigovernment uprisings. In Wardak, Molla `Abd al-Ahad and Molla Sobhan compounded the attacks of the aroused population by plundering the government treasury.[113] On May 1, 1924, the *Daily Express* reported that the rebellion was a fanatical Islamic revolt inspired by *mollas* against "certain democratic reforms" instituted by the Afghan govenment with the objective of curtailing the power of the clergy and of the local chiefs. However, according to the *Daily Express*, the *mollas* claimed the reforms were instigated by the Soviets.[114]

The threat to the government increased with the spread of a rumor, perhaps by enemies of the regime, that Aman-Allah had become a Qadiyani heretic.[115] The rumor apparently started in Waziristan, whence it spread to surrounding areas. The king was alleged to have said that the teachings of all prophets, in-

---

[112] Maconachie, P300, 135; Adamec, 1974, 88; IOR, L/P&S/10/961, no. 124, Oct. 2, 1924.
[113] Ghobar, 808.
[114] *Daily Express*, May 1, 1924.
[115] IOR, L/P&S/10/961, PD, case no. 17306, 1924.

cluding Mohammad, were "inapplicable to the present age" and that the *nezam-namas* were designed to meet the requirements of the age of science and technology.[116] These allegations had dire consequences for the crown, as they raised religious questions about the legitimacy of the ruler. The regime suspected that propaganda against the *nezam-namas* had been spread from India—that *mollas* of Mangal and Gardiz, in consultation with disaffected ulama in Kabul, had submitted copies of the *nezam-namas* to the *Jami`at al-`Ulama-i-Hind* in Delhi and had asked their opinion as to whether the new regulations contradicted the *shari`at.* In fact, the Afghan foreign minister wrote to the Afghan ambassador in Delhi and to the Afghan trade agent in Peshawar to find out if representations from *mollas* of Gardiz and Mangal had been received in their localities.[117]

With the approach of the religious Feast of Sacrifice on July 13, the rebel forces dispersed to their homes. During the period of military inactivity, Sardar Mohammad Wali and certain high ulama of the capital attempted anew to negotiate a settlement with Molla `Abd-Allah, the principal rebel leader. Again, the negotiations broke down, and no agreement was reached.

Matters took a new turn with the arrival in the area of rebellion of `Abd al-Karim, a slave-born son of Amir Ya'qub Khan (who ruled for five months in 1879), the son and successor of Amir Shir 'Ali Khan, who was forced into exile in India in 1879. `Abd al-Karim left India surreptitiously to lead the rebel forces in Khost. He filled the rebels' need for a leader at a moment when they were somewhat discouraged by their defeat in Altimar. According to his own testimony, recorded by British authorities after his arrest, he was informed about the rebellion in Khost when escaping from India. With help from two Zadran tribal *khans*, he managed to cross the border into Afghanistan and take advantage of an opportunity to regain the throne his father had lost. After his arrival in Afghanistan, influential leaders in Khost, mostly Zadrans and Mangals, rendered allegiance (*bai`at*) to him.[118] By then, Khost and parts of Ghazni and Zurmat were already in revolt.

[116.] *Ibid.* no. 84, July 3, 1924.
[117.] IOR, L/P&S/10/1081, supplement to Intelligence Bureau Diary, no. 28, July 24, 1924.
[118.] Enclosure, India Foreign Secretary, letter no. 9, Feb. 5, 1925, IOR, L/P&S/1/1112, P529.

5

RELATIONS BETWEEN THE STATE AND THE CLERGY, 1924-1927

The sacred religion of Islam has made the designation of imam incumbent upon us as a Muslim nation and has determined that all matters, commands and prohibitions be conducted in accordance with the shari`at of the Prophet Mohammad (may peace be upon him) under the direct administration of the uli al-'mr, the king, [whose authority must be obeyed] in accordance with God's command, "obey God, obey the Prophet and those in authority among you."

Ulama delegates[1]

During the years 1924 to 1925 the state increased its traditional religious activity, and the high ulama occupied significant positions of leadership in national politics. The regime's efforts to modernize the Afghan legal system, improve the status of women, and reduce parochial doctrines offensive to religious minorities came under attack from the ulama in the Grand General Assembly (*Loya-Jerga*) of July 1924. In response to a peasant-tribal revolt instigated by village *molla*s, the religious leadership presented itself as arbiter between the state and the rebel forces. In addition, the high-ranking ulama exploited the situation by publicly expressing concern about issues they had been hesitant to bring up earlier. Aman-Allah's acquiescence to the ulama's demands reflected the state's perception of the rebellion's importance. Concessions made in the *jerga*, although successful in securing the regime's religious image at the time of rebellion, proved a major setback to Aman-Allah's program of modernization.

As the threat of rebellion passed, the regime gradually returned to its earlier position. Despite the high ulama's demonstration of support for the crown, the king's attitude toward the ulama underwent a drastic change after the rebellion.

---

[1]. *Ruydad-i-Gozareshat-i-Loya-Jerga*, 408.

105

He realized that the rigid outlook of the ulama posed a formidable barrier to his modernization program. By 1927, the state and the high ulama reached a break in matters of public policy.

THE *LOYA-JERGA* OF 1924

On July 16, 1924, at the height of the rebellion, a *loya-jerga* brought together, in Paghman, Aman-Allah's summer capital, 1,054 delegates representing religious, tribal, and landowning interests. The assembly's official purpose was to "raise the edifice of the state upon the Islamic system of consultation (*mashwarat*) and to make it possible for the nation to express views on all vital concerns of the state pertaining to the national weal."[2]   However, Aman-Allah's covert reason for calling the *jerga* was to obtain the consent of the ulama to his policies and thereby intimidate the rebel *mollas*.

Islam was at the heart of the ideological debates, both among the ulama and between the ulama and the monarch, who personally presided over all sessions of the *jerga*. Religious fervor revived by the Khost Rebellion permeated the *jerga* debates. The king selected the first day of the Feast of Sacrifice (*'Id-i-Ozha*), when Muslims traditionally lay down their differences, to open the *jerga*. He preceded the opening by delivering a series of speeches in the 'Idgah Mosque and personally conducting sermon prayers (*khotba*).

Aman-Allah's fiery speech inaugurating the *jerga* decried the backwardness of Muslims, in general, and of Afghan Muslims, in particular. His selectively chosen phrases from the Qur'an invoked the theme of Islamic unity and brotherhood. He quoted from the Muslim Indian poet-philosopher Mohammad Eqbal a line suggesting that the backwardness of Muslims resulted from their misunderstanding of their religion and not from Islam itself, noting that Islam is adaptable to all times and conditions. He appealed to the people to discard animosity toward each other, to unite as brothers under the banner of Islam, and to send their sons to school so that education and modern technology could enable the nation to withstand foreign domination and preserve its Islamic character.

The president of the State Council reminded the delegates of the *Loya-Jerga* of the doctrine of submission to the authority of the ruler (*eta`at-i-uli al-amr*) and of the importance of council (*mashwarat*) by quoting the Qur'anic verse, "And those who answer the call of their Lord and establish worship, and those affairs are decided by council among themselves" (Qur'an XLII:38). He cited other verses of the Qur'an, pointing out that the *shari`at* has granted the ruler the right to make legal decisions in consultation with the ulama, and he explained how that principle related to the king's decisions of the preceding five years. The king had been guided, he added, by the ulama of the High Religious Council (*Hai'at-i-Tamiz*).[3]

---

[2] *Aman-i-Afghan*, 11 *Jawza* 1303/May 31, 1924.
[3] *Ruydad-i-Gozareshat-i-Loya-Jerga*, 54-56.

To Aman-Allah's disappointment, the ulama did not submit to his views, and instead demanded nullification of all state legislation that they believed conflicted with the tenets of Hanafi Islam. These debates of the 1924 *Loya-Jerga* were the first public expression of the high-ranking clergy's opposition to Aman-Allah's reforms.

The protests of the high-ranking clergy fell into three broad categories. First, the ulama of the High Religious Council had justified legal and social reforms with the principle of limited interpretation (*ejtehad-i-moqayyad*), permitting a jurist under appropriate circumstances to reinterpret the law within certain limits.[4] The puritanical Deoband-trained ulama and some other members of the ulama elite, who had supported the regime earlier, were offended by the *nezam-nama*s that did not fit within the framework of Hanafi doctrine. Now that they had begun to express their dissatisfaction, they would not back down.

Second, most of the high ulama who had earlier supported the regime's policies were surprised by the rapid pace of change and the government's growing control over religious institutions, which could in time affect their own positions. The high clergy who acted as judges (*qazi*s) felt threatened by the bureaucratization of the legal system.[5]

Third, the rebel *molla*s had aroused the ulama's attention to important religious issues and had raised questions about the ulama's piety because they had not addressed these issues.

The ulama participating in the *jerga* were more circumspect than the rural clergy. In order to win the monarch over to their position, the ulama participating in the *jerga* exalted the monarch for his great achievements and his defense of the *shari`at* and Islam. Their only goal, the participants insisted, was to remove the bases of rebel *molla*s' opposition. They shifted blame from the government to the ulama of the High Religious Council, who, they argued, had relied on obscure rules (*rawayat-i-za`ifa*), misleading the king and his State Council.[6] Still, the ulama went on to argue vehemently against the reforms, partly to establish their own scholarly reputations and partly to satisfy their puritanical philosophies, turning the *jerga* into an arena for recondite debate. The ulama's condemnation of the members of the *Hai'at-i-Tamiz* arose partly from longstanding competition between the ulama trained in Afghanistan, in particular, graduates of the Madrasa-i-Shahi, who filled most important religious positions in the capital, including membership in the *Hai'at-i-Tamiz*, and the Deoband-trained ulama.[7] (See Table 5)

Domestic issues that aroused controversy included the Criminal Law (*Tamassok al-Qozat*) and its counterpart, the Penal Code, as well as the Funda-

---

[4] Musa Shafiq, 1976.

[5] *Ibid.*

[6] *Ruydad-i-Gozareshat-i-Loya-Jerga*, 112-113.

[7] I am grateful to `Aziz al-Din Fofalzai for this information, which I obtained from him in an interview in June 1976.

mental Law, the Marriage Law, the Commercial Law, female education, conscription, and taxation.

Mawlawi Ebrahim Kamawi, a prominent Deobandi scholar, proposed that the criminal codes be reviewed first. Thereupon, the other ulama who had not been involved in formulating the codes rose from their seats and, in one voice, requested that the Penal Code be brought into full conformity with provisions of Hanafi jurisprudence (*feqh*) and that a new criminal code be compiled in the form of *fatwa*, or legal decrees composed by the ulama, to replace the unpopular *Tamassok al-Qozat*. Their outspoken demands reflected the ulama's preoccupation with legal reforms.

Changes advocated by the ulama in the *jerga* included restoration of the right of the *qazi*s to pass judgment in cases requiring less severe punishment not prescribed in the Qur'an (*ta`zirat*). They argued that determination of the punishment prior to commission of the crime was against the *shari`at*, under which the amount and type of punishment vary according to such factors as time and place of occurrence.[8] The ulama maintained unanimously that fixed prison sentences were inappropriate; the *shari`at* requires imprisonment only until the criminal sincerely repents and reforms.[9] They also demanded that religious judges (*qazi*s) and religious officials (*mofti*s) be present in the civil courts (*mahakem-i-ma'murin*).[10] Monetary punishments for certain crimes (*ta`zirat bi al-mal*), sanctioned by Imam Abu Yosuf,[*] were declared to be contrary to the prevailing Hanafi doctrine.

The controversy among representatives of the clergy and the ulama of the *Hai'at-i-Tamiz* centered around technical details, seemingly trivial but capable of changing the outcome of Aman-Allah's legal reforms. For example, the ulama as a group opposed Article 2 of the Constitution, demanding that the official religion of the state be named specifically. They also universally protested translation of the *shari`at* into Persian. The Molla of Chaknawur protested that the *feqh* literature loses its sanctity for the layman when translated.[11] A religious scholar from the frontier area claimed that a false rumor associating the Afghan government with the Qadiyani sect had found credence among the tribes and urged that this rumor be refuted by defining the state's official creed to be Sunni Hanafi Islam.[12] The king's explanation for not specifiying an official state religion—his desire not to offend the large Shi`a population of Afghanistan or to estrange the friendly neighboring country Iran—had little impact; the ulama prevailed.

[8.] *Ruydad-i-Gozareshat-i-Loya-Jerga-i-Paghman*, 318.

[9.] *Ibid.*, 314.

[10.] *Ibid.*, 321.

[*]Abu Yosuf Ya`qub bin Ebrahim Ansari (732-785), a disciple of Abu Hanifa, was a famous theologian who served as a judge in the court of the `Abbasid caliph, Harun al-Rashid.

[11.] *Ibid.*, 116.

[12.] *Ibid.*, 151.

The Constitution had not distinguished between Muslim and non-Muslim subjects, another matter of concern to the ulama. The protesting ulama contended that the failure to make the distinction violated the tenets of Islam and created a danger for the Islamic state. Even Mawlawi `Abd al-Wase` Qandahari, one of the original authors of the Constitution, opposed Article 2, claiming it had been inserted in his absence.[13] Once again, the ulama prevailed.

The ulama then demanded redefinition of the term freedom (*azadi*) as used in Article 9. Mawlawi Ebrahim Kamawi stated that the word *azadi* could be construed to mean religious freedom or freedom to engage in activities contrary to the Islamic moral code.[14] The king responded to Mawlawi Kamawi's comment in a long speech in which he explained the meaning of "individual freedom," enumerating the atrocities of previous regimes and expressing disappointment that the ulama, professed guardians of Islamic justice, had remained silent then and were now objecting to measures promoting social justice.

The delegates responded enthusiastically to Aman-Allah's moving speech.[15] In a rare moment, the nonclerical members of the *jerga*, showing strong support for the king's democratic policies, dominated the ulama. Most outspoken among them were delegates of the Hazara tribes, an oppressed ethnic group in central Afghanistan. Moved by these delegates' enthusiastic demonstration of support for the king's democratic policies, Mawlawis `Abd al-Bashir and `Abd al-Hosain, who belonged to the liberal faction of the ulama, took the stand and expressed gratitude for the king's outstanding service to the country and his benevolent attitude toward the nation. Mawlawi `Abd al-Hosain pointed out that in the West people have had to fight for freedom against oppressive political regimes, whereas in Afghanistan the king was voluntarily giving up power for the benefit of the nation. He reminded *jerga* members that the king of Afghanistan was the only ruler who had of his own initiative limited his power to conform with the tenets of the sacred law.[16] At the end of the debate, the *jerga* added a line to Article 9 that acknowledged both viewpoints present: "Afghan subjects are bound by the religious rite and political institutions of Afghanistan."[17]

Discussion of the laws relating to polygamy and child marriage was extensive. These issues produced unreconcilable hostility between Aman-Allah and one of the most powerful ulama of Afghanistan, Nur al-Mashayikh Fazl `Omar Mojaddedi. The king tried to allay opposition by enumerating the social problems associated with child marriage and polygamy. He declared that the intent of the Marriage Law was to minimize such problems and remove a major source of discord and disunity, to defend the rights of Afghan women according to the teachings of the Holy Book, and to urge Muslims to comply with the Qur'anic

---

[13] *Ibid.*, 125-126.
[14] *Ibid.*, 136.
[15] *Ibid.*, 136-140.
[16] *Ibid.*, 155-158.
[17] Poullada, 291.

principle of justice (`adalat).` He quoted the Qur'an on the topic of polygamy, stating that Muslim men have accepted the first half of the verse, "marry one, two, three or four", but have ignored the second part which says, "and if you fear that you cannot do justice, then [marry] only one...."[18] Mawlawis `Abd al-Rashid and Mohammad Hosain, members of the Hai'at-i-Tamiz, once again backed the king, reciting from the Qur'an and quoting a saying of the Prophet (hadith) favorable to women.

Mawlawi Mohammad Bashir, a member of the High Religious Council, replied that polygamy was permitted in Islam to provide for women whose husbands had died in war, not for the physical gratification of men. His statements in support of the new law elicited a storm of protest from his colleagues, who objected primarily to the provision concerning the attesting authority (mosaddeq). They argued that God permits a man to marry four wives and that nowhere in the Qur'an, hadith, or feqh literature is a man required to obtain authorization from a court or a witness, affirming his ability to treat his wives equally. According to Mawlawi Fazl al-Rabbi, the Qur'an addresses husbands directly on these matters, and temporal authorities (uli al-'amr) have no right to interfere. He added that one could not predict a man's behavior and that only after marriage could it be ascertained whether he could treat his wives equally.[19] Also venting objection to the Marriage Law, Shams al-Mashayikh urged that the clause of the law assessing monetary fines for second, third, and fourth wives be removed.[20] After many hours of discussion, the restriction on polygamy was eliminated. The jerga participants suggested, however, that the law clarify the measures for protection of women who are treated badly by their husbands, in order to permit the government to punish the husbands.[21]

The provision of the Marriage Law that pertained to child marriage (nekah-i-saghira) generated the most heated controversy. The majority of the ulama, including Nur al-Mashayikh, maintained that the Prophet's marriage to `Ayisha, a minor, set the precedent for the faithful. An opposing measure, they argued, would countermand a practice established by the Prophet (sonnat).[22] Nur al-Mashayikh heatedly attacked the king's argument against child marriage, which he described as a provision of grave importance in the feqh literature. He declared, as well, that abolition of child marriage was an act against the practice of the Prophet (sonnat), tantamount to apostasy. According to one source, Nur al-Mashayikh advised the king to repent for his opposition to the sonnat and his doubt of the Prophet's ability to treat his wives equally.[23] However, neither the official report of the jerga nor any other publication recorded this advice.

[18.] Ruydad-i-Gozareshat-i-Loya-Jerga, 167-169.

[19.] Ibid., 172.

[20.] Ibid., 73.

[21.] Ibid., 335.

[22.] Ibid., 183-186.

[23.] Emruz, (Lahore), May 1, 1978; Tardid-i-Shayi'at Batela-i-Shah-i-Makhlu', 16-17.

The discussion in the *jerga* resulted in a decisive victory for the conservative ulama. The lengthy debate over child marriage made Qandahari, the head of *Hai'at-i-Tamiz*, the target of ridicule by his colleagues, and his failure to gain support for his arguments led to loss of prestige for him as an `alem`. He was even contradicted by Qazi `Abd al-Rashid, a close collaborator in the formulation of the *nezam-nama*s. The liberal ulama, fearing other possible repercussions, remained silent, hoping to conceal their part in the formulation of the *nezam-nama*s.[24] In the end, the orthodox ulama gained control, and ulama who had previously supported the reforms joined the opposition.

Every topic discussed underwent religious scrutiny, and the ulama imposed their stamp on every issue. Even Aman-Allah finally conceded that he had been misled by the *Hai'at-i-Tamiz*, and he turned his anger on Mawlawi `Abd al-Wase`, its president, whom he blamed for the provisions of the *nezam-nama*s that conflicted with the *shari`at*.[25] Shortly after the *jerga*, the Mawlawi was arrested for breach of his duties as an `alem`.[26]

By the end of the *jerga*, Aman-Allah had capitulated to most of the ulama's objections. The *jerga* subjected all government legislation to the approval of a committee of seven religious scholars chosen by them, thus giving them a de facto veto in all political matters. Mawlawis `Abd al-Haiy Panjshiri, Mohammad Ebrahim Kamawi, Mir `Abd al-Baqi, Goldast Qataghani, Mohammad Rafiq, Fazl al-Rabbi, and `Abd al-Khaliq Sorkhrudi, mostly Deoband-trained ulama, were designated to serve on the committee to review all governmental regulations and bring them into line with Hanafi law.

A new criminal code, titled the Amani Decrees (*Fatawa-i-Amaniyya*) and based exclusively on Hanafi law, was to be formulated to replace the unpopular Criminal Law (*Tamassok al-Qozat*). Upon the recommendation of the Molla of Chaknawur, the *jerga* instructed that the new criminal code be written in Arabic, to affirm its sanctity, and supplemented with Persian and Pashtu translations. Compilation of the new code was assigned to the newly formed committee. Shortly after the *jerga* of 1924, the *Fatawa-i-Amaniyya* was compiled under the authorship of Mawlawi Ebrahim Kamawi, `Abd al-Wase` Qandahari's chief critic.[27]

The *jerga* declared that all business transactions must be conducted according to provisions of the *shari`at*. They also decided that the directive on the back of identity cards (*tazkera*) stipulating that without the "*tazkera*, the evidence of witnesses, transactions of divorce..., sales and purchases, and the solemnization of marriages are invalid" was not in accord with the *shari`at* and should be removed. In addition, the right to determine *ta`zirat* punishments was returned to

---

[24.] *Ruydad-i-Gozareshat-i-Loya-Jerga*, 185-186.

[25.] *Ibid.*, 187.

[26.] IOR, L/P&S/1120, MADK, nos. 106-107, Sept. 1 and 8, 1924; also interviews with Fofalzai in Kabul, 1976, and with Musa Shafiq in Qargha, 1976.

[27.] According to Musa Shafiq, Mawlawi Ebrahim's son, the unpublished manuscript was still in existence in the Royal Palace library in 1976. Interview with Musa Shafiq.

the *qazis*, and *qazis* and *moftis* were henceforth to be included as jurors in trials of government officials in the civil court (*mahkama-i-ma'murin*).

In the field of education, the *jerga* delegates recommended expansion of religious schools in the capital and in the provinces. They also agreed that students could learn Western languages after they had completed their religious education, so long as such study did not challenge their religious tenets. The education of girls was restricted to religious studies conducted only in their homes. The provisions of the Marriage Law imposing conditions on second, third, and fourth marriages were removed, as were restrictions on child marriage.

Article 2 of the Fundamental Law was revised to read: "Islam is the official religion of Afghanistan, and Hanafism is the state's formal religious rite. Hindus and Jews in Afghanistan are protected by the law, provided they pay the poll-tax (*jazya*) and adopt distinctive signs and do not disturb public morale and tranquility." Article 9 was revised to read: "All Afghan citizens enjoy freedom subject to strict observance of religious duties as imposed by the *shari`at* and the state penal codes."

The ulama also recommended the formation of the Association of the Ulama of Afghanistan (*Jam`iyyat-i-`Ulama-i-Afghanistan*), whose members were to be recruited from among religious scholars in the country, and the establishment of religious supervisory units (*ehtesab*) in districts of each city to enjoin the good and forbid evil (*al-amr bi al-ma`ruf wa al-nahy `an al-monkar*) and to supervise the conduct of religious functionaries in the mosques.[28]

In return for acceding to the ulama's demand for a totally Islamic system, Aman-Allah was able to restore his image and legitimacy as a righteous ruler at a time when rebel forces were gaining strength. On the whole, the ulama of the *jerga* presented themselves as well-wishers of the king, willing to cooperate with the government. They praised Aman-Allah's religious conviction and deep concern for the welfare of the nation. They also praised the king's democratic outlook and behavior and begged him to accept two titles as symbols of their appreciation for his devotion to Islam and the nation: Sovereign and Victorious Commander of the Faithful (*Al-Ghazi Amir al-Mo'menin Tolwak*) and Sword of the Nation and the Faith (*Saif al-Mellat-i-wa al-Din*). Aman-Allah politely declined the titles, maintaining that "for him, the God-granted title of *ghazi* was enough."[29]

The events of 1924 confirmed the clergy's role as power brokers and guardians of the traditional Islamic order. These events also marked the triumph of the conservative ulama over the liberal ulama represented by Qandahari. The *jerga*'s debates and most of its resolutions revealed a gap of centuries between the conservative ulama and the reformists, who were seeking new interpretations

---

[28.] For the full text of the resolutions of the jerga, *see Ruydad-i-Gozareshat-i-Loya-Jerga*, 302-335. For an English translation, see NAI, FPD, 283-F, 1929; IOL, L/P&S/10/1120, MADK, no. 106, Sept. 1, 1924.

[29.] NAI, FPD 283-F, 1929; *Ruydad-i-Gozareshat-i-Loya-Jerga*, 407-408, 413.

of Islamic law. The reformist Islam espoused by the regime was simply not acceptable to the majority of the ulama of Afghanistan, who adhered to the age-old practice of unquestionable acceptance of the interpretations of the law (*taqlid*) by the nineth-century Hanafi theorists.

ALLIANCE OF THE STATE AND CLERGY TO SUPPRESS THE REBELLION

Having defeated those aspects of the reforms that conflicted with their interests, members of the high clergy were willing to sanction such unpopular reforms as conscription and tax increases. Most important, they gave the regime a *fatwa* against the rebel clergy. It read in part,

> We ulama of the *Loya-Jerga* have corrected the few infirm provisions that had been included in the *nezam-nama*s through the approval of the ulama advising the king and have brought them into line with Hanafi law....We *ulama, sadat*, and *mashayikh*, on behalf of the participants of the *jerga*, declare that whoever either by personal choice or encouragement of others would rise up against the State, the *ulu al-'amr* has the right by authority of the *shari`at* to impose any type of punitive measure which he feels appropriate. We, the ulama, *sadat*, and *mashayikh* and delegates are ready to sacrifice our lives to suppress the traitors who have left their black imprints on the proud history of the Afghan nation.[30]

Following the *Loya-Jerga*, religious leaders continued to publicly support the king. During the congregational prayer on August 1, the Molla of Chaknawur delivered a Friday sermon (*khotba*), eulogizing the king for having agreed to the ulama's recommendations. He declared that the *nezam-nama*s were now being brought into full conformity with the *shari`at* and even phrases in the codes about which there could be a shred of doubt had been obliterated.[31]

The high clergy justified their renewed support of the regime with Aman-Allah's willingness to establish what they judged to be a legitimate religious foundation for Afghan society. Once the legitimacy of the regime was established by its commitment to the *shari`at*, the ulama were obliged by Sunni practice to obey the ruler and prevent any movement that could result in anarchy. (See Chapter 1.) As a result, the high-ranking ulama were caught in a dilemma. By issuing a *fatwa* supporting the regime, they effectively imposed the death penalty on their lower-ranking colleagues. To resolve the dilemma, several leading members of the high clergy, including the Molla of Chaknawur, the Ostad of Hadda, the Mir of Gazargah of Herat, and Sayyid Aqa-i-Khaksar, submitted a petition to the king on behalf of the ulama of the *Loya-Jerga* in which they requested that His Majesty forgive the rebel *molla*s' past sins and offered

---

[30] *Ruydad-i-Gozareshat-i-Loya-Jerga*, 347-348.
[31] IOR, L/P&S/10/1120, P3655, no. 98, Aug. 11, 1924.

their services as mediators between the state and the rebel *molla*s to resolve the conflict through negotiation.[32]

By then, however, the rebellion had expanded. At the end of July, a mixed force of Jaji, Mangal, Zadran, and Ahmadzais cut communications between Kabul and Gardiz and advanced into the southern end of the Logar Valley. On August 2, after killing the local official and annihilating the government forces, the rebel forces occupied Altimur (Tira) Pass in Logar and reached Hesarak, eight miles from the capital. Meanwhile, a local rebellion broke out in Logar, and some of the Ahmadzai Ghelzais joined the rebels. By the end of August, all Ghelzai tribes had joined the rebellion. The main rebel forces consisted of Solaiman Khail Ghelzais, under the personal command of `Abd al-Karim, whose pledge to govern the country with the assistance of a council of forty ulama had gained him acceptance as amir in the Southern Province. Molla `Abd-Allah was appointed `Abd al-Karim's major advisor and grand *qazi* and Molla `Abd al-Rashid Sahaki was appointed grand *mofti*.[33]

The news of the rebels' victories threw Kabul into a panic; several quarters of the city began preparing to defend themselves. A proclamation was issued calling older classes of ex-soldiers into service. In mid-August, Hajji `Abd al-Razeq and a number of other ulama from Kabul accompanied Shah Wali Khan to enlist the support of tribes bordering disaffected areas.[34] However, when the rebels' victory seemed imminent, most of the rebel fighters, who had captured considerable booty in Logar, deserted and went back to their homes. `Abd al-Karim stated later, "this victory rather proved to me a source of ruin in that almost all my soldiers left hurriedly for their homes with the loot."[35] Faced now with defeat, Molla `Abd-Allah called for a truce.

While preparing to protect the people and property along the dissidents' route toward the capital, the government tried again to avoid further bloodshed by means of negotiations. Although, during the *jerga* discussions, the king had expressed his determination to put down the rebellion by force,[36] he was now willing to negotiate with the rebel leaders through the high ulama. On September 1, the British military attaché in Kabul reported, "on the whole the royal intentions are benevolent and recently certain important officials who have been given full powers have been dispatched to Samt-i-Jonubi [the Southern Province] to inform the people of the benevolent intentions of His Majesty."[37] A leaflet containing the following message was distributed among the tribes:

---

[32] *Ibid.*, 378-379.

[33] Diary of the Military Attaché in Kabul, IOR, L/P&S/10/1120, P411, no. 111, Sept. 15, 1924.

[34] From Humphrys to the secretary of state for foreign affairs in India, telegram, Aug. 12, 1924, IOR, L/P&S/10/1112, P3342, Aug. 18, 1924.

[35] Statement of Abdul Karim Khan, *ibid.*

[36] *Ibid.*, 378-390.

[37] IOR, L/P&S/10/1120, P3570, Sept. 1, 1924, no. 106.

> On religious grounds and owing to the lack of material means, you
> are not able to fight against the government. For instance, on the re-
> ligious side all the [ulama] of the *shari`at* of the Prophet have exam-
> ined and have drawn up and will continue to draw up the Fundamen-
> tal Code of the State. Thanks be to God that religious law exists
> throughout the country and no one can have the slightest belief these
> actions of yours are due to religious motives. Indeed, all of the ulama
> of the country have declared your actions as ignorant and rebellious.
> In worldly matters, also, you can never be successful because under
> the *shariah* of the Prophet (peace be on him) all the ulama and the
> whole of the nation have ordained that to kill you is legal and that
> these ignorant actions of yours justify the government in taking arms
> against you.[38]

On September 6, a mission of some thirty ulama, including Shams al-Mashayikh
and his brother Nur al-Mashayikh (the Hazrat of Shurbazar), Hajji `Abd al-
Razeq, the Ostad of Hadda, the Molla of Chaknawur, and the Akhundzada of
Tagaw, who had just returned from the *hajj,* proceeded to Logar under the leadership of Sardar `Osman Khan, a noted theologian, to take part in negotiations
with the rebel leaders. Meanwhile, E`temad al-Dawla, Sardar `Ali Ahmad Khan
(the governor of Kabul), and several other high officials were dispatched to reason with the rebels. Negotiations once again proved futile.

Molla `Abd-Allah used the truce as a stratagem to gain time. The regime's
attempts to produce a settlement through mediation by religious leaders only
boosted the rebels' morale. Molla `Abd-Allah interpreted the king's efforts to
negotiate as a sign of weakness and as repentance under pressure. He maintained that prior to the king's "repentance," `Abd al-Karim Khan, a man of royal
descent, was proclaimed amir of Afghanistan and that no one could challenge
the propriety of his election according to the *shari`at*.[39] The dissident leaders
insisted on the king's abdication,[40] declaiming him as an iconoclast whose policies had caused dissention and bloodshed in the country. In response to the
king's proclamation, the rebel *molla*s blamed the government for having caused
bloodshed among Muslims, and they made derogatory statements about the high
ulama of the capital and the spiritual leaders who had collaborated with the regime:

> We are aware that this rebellion is against [the *shari`at*], but we are
> not in fault on account of the misconduct of your officials and ulama
> in your pay, who misrepresented to you to gain their own ends and
> compelled you to issue laws against the *shariah*....You say the laws
> you issued are not against the *shariah* and were issued by ulama. We
> beg to say that these ulama did so under the pressure of the govern-

---

[38.] Diary of the Military Attaché in Kabul, *ibid.* no. 106, Sept. 1, 1924.

[39.] Statement of Abdul Karim Khan, issued after his arrest. IOR, L/P&S/10/1112, P529,
1925, confidential.

[40.] *Ibid.* P4220, Sept. 22, 1924, no. 115.

ment or to get money from you. It is these very scholars who were called to Kabul lately to a conference which decided to amend the laws which they had first thought were in conformity with the *shariah*. If they had been true to their religion they would have stuck to their first opinion....You say that the spiritual leaders have decided that we are infidels and liable to be beheaded in accordance with the *shariah*. We beg to ask how can any reliance be placed on such spiritual leaders when they change their tune at every turn.[41]

Even the execution of a Qadiyani missionary, which happened during the rebellion in response to allegations that the king was a supporter of the Qadiyani creed, did not change the attitude of the truculent Molla `Abd-Allah and collaborating *molla*s toward the king. They continued their accusations, but, this time, because of the enthusiastic support of the regime by the Shi`a Hazara tribes, they accused the king of being a Shi`a sympathizer.[42]

Continued tribal opposition to the regime seems to have been, at least partly, provoked by the *Loya-Jerga*'s failure to address issues important to the tribes. One such issue was compulsory military service, a major cause of insurrection, which, far from being settled to the tribes' satisfaction, was endorsed by the high ulama in the *jerga*. The only major change made in the conscription bill was the reduction of the exemption fees, with the alternative of producing a substitute.[43]

The *molla*s continued opposition to the *nezam-nama*s prompted varying protests. Different dissident groups had different reasons to protest government policies, but all of them included conscription reform. In addition, according to `Abd al-Karim, among the major complaints of the dissidents against the amir was that he had published a book, called *tazkera*, which was believed to have "defied established tenets of Islam."[44] Other complaints against the king protested the abolition of the the veil (*hejab*) and the opening of an orphanage, presumably, to recruit boys for military training. In addition, the amir was accused of abrogating fifteen parts of the Holy Qur'an and encouraging liquor consumption in the country.[45]

When all efforts for a peaceful settlement failed, Aman-Allah resolved to crush the rebellion by force. The arrival at the end of August of Junker airplanes, strengthened the military position of the government, despite the lack of trained pilots. Toward the end of summer, government troops engaged the rebels on four fronts: Gardiz, under the command of Mohammad Wali Khan, the minister of war; Jalalabad, under `Ali Ahmad Khan, the governor of Kabul; Ghazni, under the direction of the deputy war minister, `Abd al-`Aziz Khan; and Wardak, under the combined leadership of E`temad al-Dawla, Sardar Shah

---

[41.] English translation of rebel molla's manifest provided by Frontier Intelligence Bureau, 1923-24, FIBD, IOR, L/P&S/10/1081, P4397, no. 38, Oct. 9, 1924.
[42.] FIBD, IOR, L/P&S/10/1081, P114, no. 11, Dec. 1924.
[43.] *Ruydad-i-Gozareshat-i-Loya-Jerga*, 322-323.
[44.] Statement of Abdul Karim.
[45.] *Ibid.*

Wali, Spahsalar Gholam Nabi Charkhi, and General `Abd al-Wakil Nuristani. Involvement of such prominent figures in the war demonstrated the seriousness of the government's intent to terminate the rebellion.

While beginning to implement strong military action against the rebels, the regime simultaneously proceeded with efforts to disparage the rebel leaders as traitors who served British interests in Afghanistan. The fact that the claimant to the throne had come from British India to spearhead the rebellion worked to the regime's benefit by providing the opportunity to invoke nationalist Islamic sentiment against the rebels.   In August, when the pretender's identity became known in Kabul, the government wasted no time alerting the people to the suspicion that, once again, the British were meddling in Afghanistan's internal affairs. By broadcasting this presumption about `Abd al-Karim's arrival, the government was able to divert the public's attention from discord over reform to unification for the nation's defense against an outsider.

The press began alluding to British involvement in the rebellion. *Aman-i-Afghan* insinuated that Great Britain was the enemy behind the scenes.[46] *Haqiqat* of Kabul, *Ettehad-i-Mashriqi* of Jalalabad, and *Tolu`-i-Afghan* of Qandahar followed suit.  They portrayed `Abd al-Karim as a British instrument, a man who had come from the land of infidelity and had been swayed by the enemy's interests since childhood. Questioning British motives in generously supporting Afghan refugees of royal descent in India, *Aman-i-Afghan* wrote, "the Europeans act with so much foresight that we orientals don't understand the mysteries of [their actions] until their actual objects eventually come to light....There are many events before us the consequence of which we understand only when we find ourselves face to face with trouble."[47]   In the same vein, *Haqiqat* questioned the source of `Abd al-Karim's financial support and made disparaging observations about his patrons, presumably the British.[48]

Curiously, the British themselves were anxious to know the source of military and financial support to `Abd al-Karim. It was generally suspected in India that the Bolsheviks were providing money to the rebels.[49]   The North-West Frontier Province Intelligence Bureau agent wrote in his weekly diary,

> I believe that other agencies have also endeavored to obtain evidence in proof of this theory but, as far as I know, no proof has yet been secured. If this is the case it is only fair to say that the Bolsheviks have not been able to finance Abdul Karim [*sic*] regularly. The pretender certainly arrived in Khost with a fair amount of money....The Bolsheviks would hardly have supplied him with funds prior to his escape

---

[46.] *Aman-i-Afghan*, 17 *Sonbola* 1303/Sept. 6, 1924.
[47.] *Aman-i-Afghan*, Nov. 22, 1924; FIBD, IOR, L/P&S/10/1081, P137, no. 46, Dec. 18, 1924.
[48.] FIBD, *ibid.*, P4757, no. 41, Nov. 6, 1924.
[49.] FIBD, 1923-24, ibid., P4397, no. 38, Oct. 9, 1924.

from India and had they done so, they might reasonably have continued it with greater ease in Khost.[50]

The Afghan government was equally frustrated at not finding evidence to prove
that the British were behind `Abd al-Karim. On his return to Kabul from a mis-
sion in France, Mahmud Tarzi told the British chief officer in Peshawar that
despite inordinate efforts, the Afghan government had found no evidence to
show British support of `Abd al-Karim's activities. The officiating foreign min-
ister in Kabul, Shir Ahmad Khan, shared this opinion, and, in an interview with
Maconachie, who was acting at the time as the British *chargé d'affaires* in Kabul
in Humphrys' absence, he admitted that the Afghan government had no proof of
British involvement in the rebellion. Shir Ahmad Khan also showed Maconachie a leaflet written in Pashtu, which had been issued by the chief commissioner of the North-West Frontier Province in India and which offered a reward
for the arrest of `Abd al-Karim. Shir Ahmad Khan then told Maconachie that the
king "was greatly impressed by this fresh evidence of British good faith."[51]

Shir Ahmad Khan confessed to Maconachie that the Afghan government was
using anti-British propaganda to extract a *fatwa* of *jehad* from the ulama against
`Abd al-Karim and Molla `Abd-Allah, explaining that the necessity to undermine `Abd al-Karim "outweighed everything else, and the best chance of suc-
cess in this direction lay in making it known that he was acting as the tool of the
unbelievers."[52] Shir Ahmad Khan assured Maconachie that at a later date the
Afghan government would announce that further investigations had proven that
the British had no involvement in the rebellion.[53]

Despite evidence to the contrary, Afghan historians have been unanimous in
their belief that the British instigated the Khost Rebellion. The Soviet press also
harbored this suspicion. However, other than citing the arrival of `Abd al-Karim
from India, which was presumed to have been arranged by the British, neither
has ever provided corroboration to support the presumption. Whether the British or, for that matter, any other foreign power was involved in the Khost Rebellion is difficult to determine. It is, however, certain that `Abd al-Karim's
arrival in the Southern Province in the midst of the rebellion caused the British
government great embarrassment, and it is hardly likely the British would have
created such chagrin for themselves. In December 1926, Denys Bray, foreign
secretary to the government of India, wrote of British policy regarding the
tribes: "when the Khost rebellion looked ugly and Abdul Karim had put us in the

---

[50.] *Ibid.*
[51.] *Ibid.*
[52.] Notes from an interview between Shir Ahmad Khan, officiating foreign minister, and
the British chargé d'affaires in Kabul, Sept. 17, 1924, IOR, L/P&S/10/1112, P4221, no.
116, Kabul, Sept. 27, 1924.
[53.] *Ibid.*

wrong by joining the rebels, we were anxious to do nothing which would put a spoke in the amir's wheel."[54]

The anti-British propaganda, carefully orchestrated by the government-controlled press, was highly successful in turning public opinion against the rebels. On August 12, the British *chargé d'affaires* in Kabul sent a telegram to India stating that 'Abd al-Karim's "adventure is subject of much comment in Kabul and is openly attributed to British intrigue.[55]

The ulama, whose fear was fueled by the memory of past British involvement in Afghanistan, were now determined to fight against the rebel *mollas*. By then it had became obvious that the rebel *mollas* were referring to the *shari'at* indiscriminately to justify their actions against the government. Their rejection of the resolutions of the *Loya-Jerga*, to which Aman-Allah had acceded, belied their frequent invocation of the *shari'at* and their professed motives. Between July and December 1924, the ulama issued several *fatwas* condemning the rebel *mollas*' uprising against the government. On September 3, 1924, *Haqiqat* of Kabul reported that the *imam* of the Congregation Mosque in Kabul "read out a proclamation of holy war and urged his congregation...to show no mercy to the rebels."[56] *Tolu'-i-Afghan* of Qandahar printed a decree of *jehad* issued in Kabul by 180 ulama.[57] Meanwhile, several influential religious leaders, including the Padshah of Islampur, the Hajji of Turangzai and his son Padshah Gol, and the Molla of Chaknawur declared their support of the government. Reports from Peshawar asserted that the Molla of Chaknawur had personally accompanied the government forces "with a view to exerting favorable influence."[58] Similarly, a call from the Padshah of Islampur and Molla Sayyid Akbar 'Akka Khail brought together a large number of Afridi fighting men in Jalalabad to support the government troops. The ceremonial arrival of the Afridis, bearing black standards with the Afghan coat of arms and names of the tribe with verses from the Qur'an, signified the excitement generated by the proclamations of *jehad*. Emissaries from the northern provinces were sent at the same time to enlist the Khugianis, the Mohmands, the Shinwaris, the Waziris, and the Hazaras for a combined offensive on Khost.

The intense anti-British feeling generated by the government's portrayal of 'Abd al-Karim's arrival was the main factor in rallying forces to end the Khost Rebellion. The legitimacy of the Amani regime was once again linked with *jehad* and, for the second time, Aman-Allah was able to fortify his government by appealing to nationalist Islamic sentiment.

---

[54] NAI, Simla Records, FPD, File 240-F, 1926, secret, no. 23.

[55] IOR, L/P&S/10/1112, P3352, Aug. 12, 1924.

[56] IOR, L/P&S/10/1120, MADK, no. 107, Sept. 8, 1924.

[57] *Tolu'-i-Afghan*, *Sonbola* 18, 1303/Sept. 7, 1924. British archival reports confirm this story. See IOR, L/P&S/10/1120, P4111, no. 111, Sept. 15, 1924; IOR, L/P&S/10/961, no. 124, Oct. 1924.

[58] Reuters, quoted in *Morning Post*, Aug. 28, 1924, and in *Manchester Guardian*, Aug. 28, 1924.

Despite the successful advance of the rebels in the Logar Valley in October, which once again threatened the capital, in November government troops forced the rebels out of their headquarters in Logar and Gardiz. Molla `Abd-Allah and his followers, who were now reduced to the Zadran and Solaiman Khail tribes, continued their fight until the end of December, but the rebellion had lost much of its force and major surrenders had been negotiated. Finally, on December 22, the leaders of the Zadran tribe came to Kabul to negotiate a settlement.

On January 30, 1925, Molla `Abd-Allah was arrested during an unsuccessful attempt to take refuge in the Mohmand country across the border with India. Before his arrest, the Molla apparently tried to make a deal with the government by proposing that in return for safe conduct he would expose the entire story of the rebellion and reveal the names of certain influential ulama in Kabul and high officials in the government who were involved in the plot.[59] Whether the government took him seriously and tried to extract from him the names of people who allegedly worked behind the scenes against the king is not clear. A few days after Molla `Abd-Allah's surrender, British authorities arrested `Abd al-Karim in Lahore, where he had fled from Afghanistan. Mahmud Tarzi's demand for his extradition was refused by the British on the grounds that the Afghan government had refused a similar request from them in the case of Rajab, the Landi Kotal murderer.[60] `Abd al-Karim was, however, removed far from Afghanistan's borders to Burma, where he committed suicide two years later.

On May 25, 1925, sixty leading rebels, charged with disturbing the peace and collaboration with foreign enemies, were led to Siah Sang heights in Kabul and shot by a firing squad in the presence of enormous crowds. Among the people executed were Akhundzada Molla `Abd-Allah, his three sons, and his son-in-law, Molla `Abd al-Rashid Sahaki, who had proclaimed himself the "Idol Breaker" (bot-shekan), in reference to his earlier clandestine act of breaking Nader Khan's bust at the monument of independence.[61] Moments before his execution, Molla `Abd al-Rashid harangued the crowd and denounced the amir and his officials as infidels (kafers).

The Anti-Qadiyani Campaign

From the time of the jerga through the suppression of the rebellion, the government was careful not to jeopardize its improved relations with the ulama. To strengthen his ties with the ulama, Aman-Allah mounted a campaign against Qadiyanism, a religious movement that began in India in the mid-nineteenth century.

During the Loya-Jerga, the ulama had shown intense anti-Qadiyani feelings. The Qadiyanis, also known as Ahmadiyyas, believed that their founder, Mirza

---

[59.] Telegram dated Jan. 3, 1925, Kabul, L/P&S/10/1112, P122.

[60.] Telegram from Kabul, dated Jan. 21, 1925, from Humphrys to the secretary of state for foreign affairs, India Office, ibid., P212.

[61.] Interview with Sayyid Taj al-Din, San Francisco, Jan. 1988.

Gholam Ahmad of Qadiyan, was a latter-day prophet. This belief contradicted the orthodox Islamic precept of the finality of prophethood (*khatam-i-nabuwwat*), which affirmed that the Prophet Mohammad was the last in the line of prophets (*khatam al-nabi'in*). The ulama considered Qadiyanism a heresy and believed Qadiyanis had no place in an Islamic state. Heresy had, in fact, never been tolerated in Afghanistan. Both Amir `Abd al-Rahman and his son, Amir Habib-Allah, had punished heretics harshly, executing several Qadiyani preachers who had entered Afghanistan. During the first years of King Aman-Allah's reign, some Qadiyani *molla*s had entered Afghanistan and remained. The government's tolerance or lack of awareness of their activities gave rise to a rumor that the king was a supporter of the Qadiyani movement, and that he had himself become a Qadiyani.

Shortly after the *Loya-Jerga* ended, the government confronted these rumors with a widely publicized campaign against heresy. Article 123 of the Penal Code established the death penalty for this offense. On September 6, 1924, Molla Ne'mat-Allah, a Qadiyani missionary, was executed, and some thirty other Qadiyanis were arrested. Later that month, two other Qadiyani *molla*s were stoned to death.

The detention and execution of Qadiyanis in Kabul were met with a hail of protest from Qadiyani communities in India and England. Afghanistan's violation of human rights was vehemently attacked in the *Times of London* (Feb. 13, 16, and 27, 1925). Although the secretary of Deoband College (Dar al-`Olum-i-Deoband) in India circulated leaflets challenging the Qadiyani doctrine and justifying the execution of Qadiyani *molla*s in Kabul,[62] the Indian press generally denounced the execution of Qadiyanis in Kabul. Early in March, the `Ali brothers, leaders of the *Khilafat* Committee, wrote to the king to inform him that the stoning of Qadiyanis had caused unpleasant repercussions in India.[63]

In response to these criticisms, the semiofficial newspaper *Aman-i-Afghan* published arguments against Qadiyanism to justify the execution of the Qadiyani *molla*s. On September 4, 1924, *Aman-i-Afghan* printed a response to foreign protests. The editorial reviewed the history of the Qadiyani movement, arguing that Qadiyanism was a political, rather than a religious, movement, designed to serve British colonial interests in India. As such, it had, according to the editorial, many enthusiastic supporters among the British and their allies. The writer emphasized that, as an independent country, Afghanistan was free to formulate its laws in accord with its traditions (`*adat*) and moral spirit (*ruh-i-akhlaqi*) and to conduct its affairs in its best interests. The writer argued further that Afghan law had never before allowed freedom of belief (*azadi-i-`aqida*), because the overwhelming majority of the Afghan population was orthodox Muslim. Any ideology that would offend prevailing beliefs would disturb the public. The term "freedom" in Article 9 of the Afghan Constitution, continued the writer, was applicable solely to Jews, Hindus, and followers of other creeds, whose

---

[62] IOR, L/P&S/10/1137, P1123 no. 7, Mar. 12, 1925.
[63] *Ibid.*, P1431, no. 9, Apr. 9, 1925.

systems of belief were entirely different from Islam and who had been accepted in Afghan society for centuries as separate religious minorities. The writer concluded that the Qadiyanis were wasting time and money appealing to the League of Nations and to the American and European governments for help, because no power had the right to interfere in the internal affairs of a free nation.[64] In the same issue, *Aman-i-Afghan* printed the text of two telegrams, one from *Jam`iyyat-i-`Ulama* of Delhi and one from the ulama of Deoband, both of which applauded the Afghan government's actions against Qadiyani heretics and congratulated the Afghan nation on having an orthodox and right-minded ruler.

It appears that *Aman-i-Afghan* was, in addition to responding to outside attacks, attempting to convince local readers that the provisions of the *shari`at* were being fully observed. The British minister in Kabul wrote later that the execution of the Qadiyanis was "Aman-Allah's response to the charges of heresy brought against him during the Khost rebellion. In quieter times this extreme penalty may not be exacted."[65]

The Execution Of Piperno

In the same year, religious measures were applied in the case of Dario Piperno, an Italian engineer who shot and killed an Afghan policeman on duty in July 1924. Following proceedings that extended over several months, when it was thought the matter was finally settled in accordance with religious law (namely, Article 98 of the *Fatawa-i-Amaniyya*, prepared shortly after the *Loya-Jerga*), Piperno was executed in 1925 on charges of first-degree murder (*qatl-i-`amdi*).[66]

The case of Piperno presented a very delicate situation for the regime. A Muslim had been murdered by a non-Muslim employee of a European government at a time when the regime was trying hard to improve relations with religious groups and when the general mood in the country was distinctly anti-foreign. On the one hand, the government had to satisfy the demands of religious groups for severe punishment. On the other hand, it was trying to secure Afghanistan's reputation as a progressive nation on the international scene. The case was further complicated by another sensitive issue—national pride. Aman-Allah needed to demonstrate that Afghanistan would not yield easily to outside pressure.

The Afghan government's unwillingness or failure to stay Piperno's execution created an acute state of tension between the Afghan and Italian govern-

---

[64.] "Qadiyaniha wa trafadaran-i-anha ba deqqat bekhwanand (Qadiyanis and Their Supporters Should Read Carefully)," *Aman-i-Afghan*, Sonbola 12, 1303/Sept. 4, 1924.
[65.] IOR, "Summary of Events in Afghanistan," 1924, case no. 17603, confidential.
[66.] Beck, "Das Afghanisch Strafgesetzbuch," 78. A full account of these proceedings appears in Ludwig Adamec, *Afghanistan's Foreign Affairs to the Mid-Twentieth Century*, 158-162; see also, Maconachie, 158-162. The discussion here is limited to the relevance of Piperno's case to Aman-Allah's dealings with the orthodox groups.

ments, exacerbated by high-handedness on both sides.[67] The diplomatic corps and foreign residents in Kabul became concerned for the safety and rights of foreigners in Afghanistan. The Western press expressed similar concerns, protesting that the outcome in Piperno's case was contrary to all civilized canons of law.[68] The main protest of the Western press was that Piperno's case was prejudiced by the Islamic law of evidence, which did not allow a non-Muslim to testify in court.[69] Western diplomats found the death penalty exacted by the Afghan courts unacceptable because, by European law, Piperno had committed manslaughter.[70] The fact that Piperno was executed even though the relatives of the murdered policeman had remitted their right of retribution made the case more incomprehensible to Western diplomats in Kabul. It appeared to them that the Afghan government had even denied Piperno the proper implementation of Islamic law.[71]

Piperno's execution developed into a serious international issue. The Italian government protested the case as a miscarriage of justice and asked the Afghan government to meet several Italians' demands for reparation.[72] However, Afghan authorities repudiated charges of inhumanity and maintained that Piperno had been tried and executed in accordance with Afghan law to which he had bound himself by contract: under Article 8 of the Constitution, all foreigners residing in Afghanistan are made subject to Afghan law. During a private interview with Humphrys, Aman-Allah vehemently protested the Italian demands and emphasized that he could do nothing that would in the slightest degree bring dishonor to his country.[73]

Piperno's execution had serious consequences for Afghanistan's foreign relations. Application of Islamic law in the case of a non-Muslim foreigner earned the government widespread international opprobrium, and the matter, along with the treatment of the Qadiyanis, was cited later by the British as a factor in opposing Afghanistan's admission to the League of Nations. The British argued, "because of its strong adherence to the principles of the Sharia [*sic*], it is unlikely that Afghanistan would cleave to the principles of the Covenant."[74] Afghan authorities were aware of the negative repercussions Piperno's execution

---

[67] Adamec, *Afghanistan's Foreign Affairs*, 103-104; May Schinasi, "Italie-Afghanistan, 1921-1941, part ii, De l'affaire Piperno a l'évacuation de 1929."

[68] Beck, 79.

[69] NAI, FPD, 621-F, 1925, d. 43.

[70] Beck, 78.

[71] *Ibid*. In a letter dated July 9, 1925, Humphrys wrote: "The Penal Code of September 1924...is said to be under revision, and is unintelligible....The obscurity of the language of the Code is due mainly to the circumstances in which it was drafted....As a concession to the rebels, the Amir was forced to repeal the Nizam-namah [*sic*] at the Loe Jirga [*sic*] held in September 1924. To take its place, the present code was drafted by five illiterate Mullahs....The result is an unintelligible compromise." Maconachie, 372.

[72] Schinasi, *ibid.*, 291.

[73] NAI, FPD, 621-F, 1925, no. 48.

[74] NAI, PSD, Memoranda, 1898-1938(2), 1928.

would have outside the country, and they believed that Great Britain was exploiting the Piperno case to suggest that Afghanistan was incapable of handling its foreign affairs.[75]

It was, in fact, over this issue mainly that Mahmud Tarzi offered his resignation as foreign minister. Although his resignation was not accepted, he refrained from much involvement in public activities. Tarzi was, reportedly, particularly offended at not being informed in advance of the final decision of the law courts in the Piperno case.[76]

ATTEMPTS BY THE REGIME TO REASSERT ITS POSITION

The conservative resurgence lasted for only a few months. During that time the government rallied the support of conservative elements and, with the help of cooperative ulama, suppressed the rebellion. As soon as the threat of further rebellion passed, Aman-Allah returned to the concessions he had granted under pressure and began to renege on them and force the ulama into the background. Although the government introduced no new reforms between 1925 and 1927, it returned to its earlier efforts to centralize political authority and the educational system and to advance women's rights. By 1926, the ulama were forced into retreat.

Aman-Allah began to appeal directly to the masses by conducting inspection tours in the provinces to persuade the public of the importance of his educational and administrative reforms and to establish closer ties between the government and the people. He took with him high government officials who were assigned to inspect various administrative units and report abuses.[77] At the same time, he reestablished close contact with the tribes. Specifically, he attended tribal *jergas*, visited influential *khans*, contributed generous endowments to tribal religious leaders, and paid for the renovation of the important tribal shrine at Hadda.

Revision of the Criminal Law Relating to the Rights of Foreigners

A few months after the Khost Rebellion was suppressed, Aman-Allah abandoned his policy of strict orthodoxy. His decision to amend the Criminal Law to protect the rights of foreigners in Afghanistan was a significant reversal of a concession made to the ulama at the *Loya-Jerga* of 1924. In 1926, another shooting of an Afghan by a European occurred. A German geographer named Strated Sauer shot and killed an Afghan while motorcycling between Peshawar and Kabul. According to Sauer, he did so in self-defense. The German minister in Kabul made an inept attempt to smuggle Sauer out of the country. The Af-

---

[75] Rawan-Farhadi, *Maqalat-i-Mahmud Tarzi dar Seraj Al-Akhbar*, 27.

[76] *Ibid.*

[77] A description of one such tour appears in *Taftish-i-Welayat-i-Qandahar (The Inspection of the Province of Qandahar)*, 1924.

ghan government was quick to charge the German minister with a gross breach of diplomatic faith.

According to British archival reports, the Afghan government made "an honest attempt to conduct the [Sauer] trial without partiality. Counsel for the defence, interpreters, [and] non-Muslim witnesses have been allowed and the public are admitted."[78] Sauer was sentenced to four years in prison but pardoned a few days later by the king "in consideration of the good motives that brought the accused to Afghanistan."[79] The British minister in Kabul reported that the Afghan government had agreed to conduct trials publicly, to hear defense evidence, to admit testimony of non-Muslims with the same standing as that of Muslims, to provide a competent interpreter, and to promptly give a copy of the judgment to the accused.[80] A request to the government by British, French, German, and Italian diplomats in Kabul to rescind application of the Islamic measure (*qesas*) in cases of murder involving foreigners was referred to the State Council for study. Shortly thereafter, Mahmud Tarzi, the Afghan foreign minister, assured the foreign representatives that *qesas* would be abrogated in such cases.[81]

Women's Rights

In social matters, the state also began to relax some of the restrictions of the *Loya-Jerga*. For example, the regime reasserted its position on women's rights and female education, areas that fell into its larger framework of social change and were considered essential for the overall development of the Afghan nation.

In 1912, Tarzi had taken initial steps in addressing women's issues and in challenging the traditional attitude toward women in Afghan society. He defined woman as the other half of man (*nim shaqa-i-digar-i-mard*), based on a saying of the Prophet that women are the other half of men and exactly like them (*enama al-nesa'e shaqayiqo al-rejal*) and argued that without the progress of this half of society, the other half could not develop fully.[82] Tarzi stressed that Islam was based on equality for all, men and women, and tried to inspire in women a sense of self-awareness, self-respect, and confidence in their ability for self-improvement and rational thinking. Emphasizing the important role women played in training their children, he suggested that education was even more important for women than it was for men.[83]

As I have mentioned elsewhere, Tarzi's articles provided the basis for the themes developed more fully in the 1920s on the education of women in Af-

---

78. "Summaries of Events in Afghanistan for the Periods 1st July 1925 to 30th June 1926," NAI, Government of India, FPD, nos. 32-37, 1926.
79. Adamec, *Afghanistan's Foreign Affairs*, 104.
80. Kabul, telegram 84, July 9, 1925, in Maconachie, P655, 372.
81. Humphrys, telegram 91, Kabul July 15, 1926, in Maconachie, P660, 374.
82. Gregorian, 172; Nawid, "The Feminine and Feminism in Tarzi's Work," 382.
83. Nawid, *ibid.*

ghanistan. His appeal to the women of the royal court to remove themselves from the restricted sphere of the harem and help reform social and political conditions was important as it encouraged royal women to take an active part in promoting women's issues in later years. The person affected most by Tarzi's ideas was his daughter, Queen Soraya, who became the moving force behind the movement to improve the status of women in the 1920s in Afghanistan. Her declaration of 1921 (Appendix C) provided strong arguments for female education and for giving women the opportunity to compete with men in various fields, including Islamic theology. This declaration laid the foundation for women's education in Afghanistan.

In 1926, in the face of the ulama' strong opposition to reforms relating to women, the royal couple pushed forward with plans for female education and improving the status of women in general. Even during the *jerga* debates, the king had complained vociferously about prejudicial male attitudes toward women. He had described women as the "oppressed, voiceless sector of the nation (*tabaqa-i-mazlum-i-bezaban-i-mellat*)," victims of the selfishness and brutality of men. To the ulama he had declared, "For God's sake, consider the rights of these [human beings], because God has made you responsible to look after them and protect their interests."[84]

After the suppression of the Khost Rebellion, the girls' schools in Kabul gradually reopened. In the beginning, female students were summoned to the royal palace to resume their studies under the queen's personal supervision in the form of private schooling (*maktab-i-khanagi.*)[85] As well as promoting women's education, the king pushed the issue of marital rights. In a speech given in Jalalabad on May 28, 1926, he encouraged his audience to follow the *shari`at* in this matter, arguing that in accordance with the Holy Law of Islam, widows should be permitted to remarry freely.[86]

On November 9, 1925, in an address to a large gathering at the shrine of Kherqa-i-Sharif in Qandahar, Aman-Allah explained the *nezam-nama*s and ended by talking about female education. Islam, he stressed, has always recommended education for both men and women, and it is through proper education that women can become aware of their religious responsibilities and raise educated children.[87]

By the end of 1925, girls' schools were officially reopened. The king and the queen paid personal visits to the schools to make the girls aware of their future responsibilities and to encourage them to see that they had equal natural capacity with men and thus prepare them to take an active part in public life. On July 7, 1926, the British military attaché in Kabul reported:

---

[84]. *Rudad-i-Gozareshat-i-Loya-Jerga*, 147.

[85]. Beck, 76.

[86]. IOR, L/P&S/10/1170, MADK, June 10, 1926.

[87]. *Taftish-i-Welayat-i-Qandahar*, 242.

His Majesty also paid a visit to the girls' school and told the girls to learn riding and other modern arts and that they should even take the opportunity, if offered, of taking a trip in an aeroplane as European women do. He considered that the purdah [veiling] system has been enforced to an absurd extent in Afghanistan, saying that it was an excellent system up to a certain limit and that the real purdah is that of the soul, and that purdah should not be allowed to interfere with the progress of the nation.[88]

A year later, during a speech opening Independence Day celebrations, Aman-Allah addressed the women of Kabul, pointing out their duties to the nation and their responsibilities as mothers of future generations of Afghans.[89] It was reported that "a considerable number of ladies of the capital participated in the ceremonial activities of Independence Day, slightly veiled,"[90] in contrast to the custom heretofore of being completely veiled.

THE WANE OF PAN-ISLAMISM

By 1926, pan-Islamism had lost much of its appeal as a religious and political force in the region. With the deaths in 1922 of two of its most active advocates, Enver Pasha and Jamal Pasha, pan-Islamic activities began to wane in Central Asia. With the fall of Bokhara in 1922, and the establishment of the republican states of Uzbekistan and Turkmenistan under Soviet rule in the fall of 1924, the Basmachi movement and pan-Islamism lost their force in Central Asia.

But the most important contributing factor to the decline of pan-Islamism was Kamal Ataturk's abolition of the caliphate in 1924. The news of the repudiation of the caliphate became known in Kabul early in March of that year, shortly before the outbreak of the Khost Rebellion, and created outrage among the ulama and other supporters of the caliphate in Afghanistan. In agreement with the ulama, the regime condemned Kamalist Turkey's treatment of the caliphate. In an article titled "The Abolition of the Caliphate and the Position of Muslims (*Elgha-i-Khilafat wa Mowqef-i-Moslemin*)," *Aman-i-Afghan* reported that Turkey eliminated the caliphate because of its inclination to imitate the European ideal that religion and administration are mutually opposed to each other and impossible to reconcile and in order not to give Westerners the opportunity to criticize the Turkish government for being subservient to religious obligations and religious law. The newspaper reported further that Sharif Hosain, Ghazi Amir Aman-Allah Khan, Sheikh Sanusi, and Amir `Abd al-Karim had been proposed as possible candidates for the office of caliphate but argued that since the election of a new caliph was a question of vital interest for all

---

[88.] IOR, L/PS/10/1176, MADK, no. 51, July 7, 1926.

[89.] *Ibid.*, no. 73, Aug. 2, 1927.

[90.] *Ibid.*, no. 74, Aug. 29, 1927.

Muslims, a caliphate conference should be held in a pure Islamic state, free from any type of foreign influence, to settle this matter.[91]

During the Khost Rebellion, Jamal Pasha's relationship to the new conscription law and Badri Beig's to the *nezam-nama* caused a wave of anti-Turkish sentiment. The Turks' abolition of the caliphate further intensified this ill feeling. According to a report prepared by the British legation in Kabul, the Fundamental Code and its counterparts were misinterpreted, but they were later "denounced as the work of a nation [namely, Turkey] which had deposed the caliph and turned its back to Islam."[92]

In the *Loya-Jerga*, the ulama were intensely aroused by the issue of the caliphate. The first session of the *jerga* was devoted almost entirely to this topic. The Treaty of Friendship with Turkey that was signed three years earlier in Moscow on March 1, 1921, was hotly debated. Influenced by the strong pro-caliphate sentiments at the time, Aman-Allah had accepted Article 3 of the Treaty by which Afghanistan recognized Turkey, seat of the caliphate, as a model to be followed (*moqtada-beha*). Now that the caliphate had been abolished by the Turks, Aman-Allah was anxious to remove this clause with the backing of the *Loya-Jerga*.

The discussions generated a storm of protest against Turkey and Mostafa Kamal. The orthodox groups, who viewed Kamal Ataturk as a traitor to the cause, had misgivings about the new government in Turkey. Several speakers, including Faiz Mohammad Khan, the minister of education, and `Abd al-`Aziz Khan, the ex-minister of the interior, demanded severance of political relations with Turkey.[93] The ulama agreed in the end for the regime to continue relations with Turkey but urged that Afghanistan, as the only other independent Muslim Sunni country, assume leadership on the issue of the caliphate.

The ulama suggested gathering religious scholars from all over the world to Kabul to address the topic. Outspoken advocates of such a conference were Mawlawis Mohammad Husain, Fazl al-Rabbi, Mohammad Bashir, and Padshah Gol Jan, the son of the Hajji of Turangzai, who were the most active supporters of the caliphate in Afghanistan and in the tribal area. They concluded that the king of Afghanistan, the sole independent Sunni ruler, was the most suitable leader to call such a meeting.[94]

But the king, who had until then ardently supported the *khilafat* movement, altered his position. Still acknowledging the caliphate as a symbol of solidarity among Muslims, he questioned its present role. "Naturally and rationally, the caliph should not interfere in the worldly matters of Muslims who are not under his rule. If he does, would the Iranian, Indian, Egyptian, Moroccan, Algerian, Afghan, Chinese, and other Muslims of the world obey his commands when they conflict with their national interests? No. Never! In my humble view, the

---

[91.] *Aman-i-Afghan*, 28 *Hut* 1302/Mar. 18, 1924.

[92.] Kabul Despatch 12, July 13, 1925, quoted by Maconachie, P357, 169.

[93.] *Roydad-i-Gozareshat-i-Loya-Jerga*, 70, 74-76.

[94.] *Ibid.*, 66, 90.

caliph serves no purpose in today's world except to create problems for himself and his country. If you should ask the Turks the reason for abolishing the caliphate, they will immediately give you the same answer."[95]

Several reasons can account for Aman-Allah's withdrawal of support for the caliphate. The primary reason was probably that he wanted to avoid conflict with two neighboring powers at a time when Afghanistan had critical internal problems. Afghanistan's support of the *khilafat* movement had already created anxiety among authorities in India and in the Soviet Union. Discussion of forming an Islamic confederacy, possibly with Aman-Allah as the caliph, was threatening to both the British and to the Soviets. British authorities in India viewed the possibility of Aman-Allah's election as caliph by leaders of the *khilafat* movement in India as imminent and feared such a step would present the "most immediate potential danger to India."[96]

The Soviets were equally alarmed by Aman-Allah's activities in Central Asia. On June 3, 1921, the Soviet minister in Kabul had expressed to Afghan authorities the Soviet Union's displeasure with the direction of events and had informed the Afghans that such developments would jeopardize peace in the region.[97] To allay Soviet suspicions, an official announcement in *Aman-i-Afghan* made on July 29, 1922, stated that "Afghanistan in no circumstances wishes to create trouble for her neighbors."[98] Afghans fighting under Enver Pasha's command in Central Asia were called back to Afghanistan twenty days later.[99]

Another reason for Aman-Allah's withdrawal of support for the caliphate, as was obvious from his statements in the *Loya-Jerga*, was his realization that local nationalism now overshadowed pro-caliphate sentiment in Turkey and part of the Arab world. He no doubt also recognized that even if the office of caliphate were to be restored, he was unlikely to be elected caliph, because he could not fulfill two traditional requirements of the office: control over the holy cities of Mecca and Medina and a claim to Quraish ancestry.

Although Aman-Allah agreed to call an Islamic conference in Kabul, his general position on the matter undoubtedly disturbed the ulama, particularly the Deobandies, who were fervent supporters of the caliphate. This disagreement most likely hardened resistance to the king's reforms in subsequent sessions of the *jerga*.

The abolition of the caliphate had a paralyzing effect on the *khilafat* movement in India. With the caliphate abolished by the Turks themselves, the *khilafat* agitators had no reason to continue their fight against the British on behalf of the caliph. The *hejrat* movement too had ended in failure and had left an after-

---

[95] *Ibid.*, 81-82.
[96] Adamec, *Afghanistan, 1900-1923*, 79.
[97] Letter from the Soviet Commissariat of Foreign Affairs to Its Minister in Kabul, June 3, 1921, in *Monasebat-i-Afghanistan wa Ettehad-i-Shurawi*, 21-22.
[98] Adamec, *Afghanistan's Foreign Affairs*, 71.
[99] *Ibid.*

math of bitterness. The only issue of controversy left for the *khilafat* activist was possession of the holy cities of Mecca and Medina (*haramain*) by King Hosain, a British puppet by general estimation. This argument lost ground also when Ibn Sa'ud was elected king of Hejaz on January 8, 1926. In June of that year, Ibn Sa'ud held a pan-Islamic conference attended by representatives from all the Sunni Muslim countries, including Afghanistan. The Afghan delegates were unhappy with the outcome. *Aman-i-Afghan* reported,

> Unfortunately the majority of the representatives were of the Najdi sect, and so the only solutions reached were those agreeable to the Najdis. This conference, if held regularly and attended by representative Muslims, should eventually be of value to the Muslim world.[100]

THE DECLINE OF ANTI-BRITISH ACTIVITIES ALONG THE BORDER

The decline of the *khilafat* movement in India also resulted in the decline of anti-British activities along the border. The British, now politically in a stronger position in India, were able to consolidate their power in Waziristan. The Afghan government tolerated the British move, realizing that the time was not right to intervene in matters relating to Waziristan. However, according to one British observer, "the Afghan politician...seems now to look forward to the time when, owing to the progressive weakening of the Central Government, communal tension will develop into civil war, and the Indian Moslem will look 'across the passes' to Afghanistan whence cometh his help against the Hindu. That would be the opportunity which the Amir thought had come in 1919."[101]

Another possible reason for withdrawing support from anti-British activities was the regime's suspicion of relations between the Bolsheviks and political activists in Kabul, particulary among Indian revolutionaries. Upon discovering various covert activities, the government had become wary of such relations and feared the spread of a network of international espionage into the country. In October 1922, Mawlawi 'Obaid-Allah Sindhi and other Indian revolutionaries, who had until then acted as contacts between Kabul and leaders of pan-Islamism outside Afghanistan, were expelled from Kabul when the government became aware that they were being financed by the Soviets. Suspicious of the services these revolutionaries might be providing the Soviets, the government declared their continued presence in Kabul undesirable.[102]

Hajji 'Abd al-Razeq, a fervent pro-*khilafat* and anti-British activist in the tribal region, was also being carefully watched in Kabul. The government had restricted his anti-British activities, mostly in response to repeated protests by the British but also because of its suspicion that the Hajji had established rela-

---

[100.] *Aman-i-Afghan*, 26 *Sonbola* 1305/Sept. 17, 1926.
[101.] Maconachie, P293, 130.
[102.] MADK, 33 (1), 1922, quoted in Maconachie, P227, 93.

tions with the Bolsheviks.[103] The regime's suspicions about the aged `Abd al-Razeq were not unfounded. It appears that his contempt for the British and his uncompromising devotion to the cause of Waziristan prompted him in 1925 to seek help secretly from the Soviets for his cause. Agabekev, the undercover agent who worked for OGPU, the Soviet intellegence organization, was at that time on duty in Afghanistan. He wrote in his diary about a meeting arranged by Suirts, the Soviet minister in Kabul, between him and the Molla-Bashi. Molla `Abd al-Razeq, whom he refers to as Sheikh al-Islam, told him in detail about the anti-British uprising in 1919 in Waziristan and about the major role he played in the insurrection with the encouragement of Jamal Pasha and the promise of arms from him, but explained that because the arms promised did not arrive, the operation in Waziristan came to nothing. At the end of the meeting, the Molla-Bashi expressed his desire to go back among the independent tribes to organize a partisan war against the British and requested the Soviet government assist him in this purpose by providing 100,000 rubles, five hundred rifles, and one hundred cartridges per rifle.[104]

> I promised the Sheik to refer the proposition to my superiors. Indeed, I reported without delay to Moscow. By the first mail the Ogpu replied accepting the proposition in general but declining to furnish rifles....We were then in the month of Ramadan. The Shiek was too old and feeble to last out so long a fast; he died.[105]

The British in India received with joy the news of `Abd al-Razeq's death. The North-West Frontier Province Intelligence Bureau reported,

> the death of Hajji Abdul Razaq is a welcome piece of news, and the Bolshevik Legation at Kabul will find it difficult to fill his place. The late Hajji had long been a thorn in the flesh of the Govenment of India, but had lately become even more dangerous in his role as the Chief Bolshevik agent in Kabul.[106]

The *Aman-i-Afghan* praised Molla-`Abd al-Razeq as Afghanistan's greatest religious scholar and as a stouthearted *mojahed*, and considered his death "a great and eternal loss."[107] Even outside Afghanistan he was considered a hero of the Islamic cause against the British. The Iranian newspaper, *Naw Bahar*, published in Mashhad, printed a eulogy praising Molla `Abd al-Razeq as the firm pillar (*rokn-i-rakin*) of Islamic unity and the major proponent of Irano-Afghan friendship.

[103.] This suspicion was expressed by the king in a private interview with Humphrys. See Maconachie, P223, 93.
[104.] Agabekev, *OGPU: The Russian Secret Terror*, 58-59.
[105.] *Ibid.*, 59.
[106.] Quoted in Lal Baha, 116.
[107.] *Aman-i-Afghan*, Kabul, *Hamal* 29, 1304/Apr 18, 1925.

The government's support of anti-British operations did not entirely stop after Molla `Abd al-Razeq's death. Aman-Allah continued to assist the *mojahedin* colony in Chamarkand through Mawlawi Bashir, the head of the colony and editor of the anti-British newspaper *Al-Mojahed,* which was now published in Pashtu instead of Persian. Mawlawi Bashir, who had a high clerical position in Kabul, remained in touch with the Bolsheviks, "possibly with full knowledge of Afghan authorities."[108]   He also maintained close contact with the Hajji of Turangzai, the well-known advocate of the Pashtun cause against the British. But by and large, Aman-Allah had given up his ambitions in the independent Pashtun tribal zone and was now anxious to normalize Afghan relations with Great Britain. He acceded to the repeated demands of the British to stop funding religious endowments and making monetary gifts (literally, purchase of the turban, *kharch-i-longi*) to the tribal *mollas* who lived on the British side of Durand Line.[109]   Meanwhile, Sepahsalar Gholam Nabi Charkhi, the civil and military governor of the Southern Province, assured the British minister in July that "nothing would be done on the Waziristan border that would jeopardize relations between our two contries."[110]

Aman-Allah was now anxious to maintain friendly relations with all countries in order to promote economic development projects at home. Nevertheless, he assured his admirers in the Muslim world of his continued support of their cause.[111]   Despite the strong anti-Turkish feelings that emerged during the rebellion and were expressed during the *Loya-Jerga* of 1924, Aman-Allah now strengthened diplomatic and political ties with Kamalist Turkey, doing just the opposite of what the ulama had wished. The years 1926 and 1927 witnessed a dramatic rise in Turkish influence in Kabul as evidenced by a large influx of Turkish advisors, educators, and administrative personnel.[112]   In the spring of 1926, Fakhri Pasha was replaced by Nabil Beig as Turkish minister. In a cordial speech, the new minister emphasized the marked increase in friendship between Kabul and Ankara.[113]   In subsequent years, Turks occupied various high positions in the State Council, the Ministry of Foreign Affairs, and the Ministry of Finance.[114]   The legal advisor to the Foreign Office was Javid Beig, a close associate of Mostafa Kamal and husband of the sister of Latifa Khanom, Kamal's divorced wife.[115]   Afghan religious leaders began to suspect that Aman-Allah was following the path of Ataturk, who had abolished the caliphate and secularized the Turkish state.

[108.] Lal Baha, 116.
[109.] NAI, Simla Records, FPD, File no. 240-F, 1926, Secret, no. 26.
[110.] *Ibid.,* no. 24.
[111.] Gregorian, 239.
[112.] Maconachie, 170.
[113.] IOR, L/LP&S/10/1170, MADK, no. 32, Apr. 28, 1926.
[114.] *Ibid.,* no. 36, Apr. 18, 1927.
[115.] *Ibid.,* no. 57, May 30, 1927.

Influential religious leaders in Kabul who had signed the *fatwas* of *jehad* against the rebel *mollas* now realized that they had weakened the position of the clergy. Shams al-Mashayikh and his brother Nur al-Mashayikh, and Mir Saheb of Qasab Kucha, another prominent religious leader in Kabul, who had previously remained aloof from politics, were reportedly offended by the mass execution of the *mollas* who had fought in the name of Islam. They also supported the opposition to Aman-Allah's stand against child marriage and polygamy.[116] The king's position on the status of women and his close ties to Kamalist Turkey also aroused grave misgivings among the ulama, although they did not express their opposition to these policies openly.

The Khost Rebellion and the *Loya-Jerga* of 1924 marked major turning points in relations between the state and the clergy. As a result of the events of 1924, Aman-Allah's attitude toward the ulama changed drastically. He become convinced that the clergy were a stumbling block in the way of progress and that they would dismiss any idea outside the scope of their traditional training. Some of these frustrations had emerged during the *jerga* debates, when, once or twice, he burst out in anger and accused the ulama of ignoring social realities in order to promote their own interests. During the debates over the Penal Code, he had stated angrily,

> You revered ulama and *sheikhs* present in this meeting tolerated all types of atrocities under the old regimes and submitted to their views....Why were you mute then? Why did you ignore the Qur'anic principle to enjoin good and forbid evil (*al-amr bi al-ma`ruf wa nahy `an al-monkar*)? Why did you not make them see what was right and what was wrong, and why have you now sharpened your tongues against me?[117]

In several instances he pointed out that his responsibility to the nation was greater than that of the ulama's and that he surpassed the clergy in his sincere efforts to promote Islam and improve conditions in Afghan society.[118]

Aman-Allah interpreted the ulama's protests against his reforms as a sign of ignorance (*jahl*). A year after the rebellion was suppressed, he erected a monument titled Knowledge and Ignorance (`*elm wa jahl*) as a symbol of his victory over the "ignorant *mollas*."

In 1925 and 1926, Aman-Allah began to reassert his authority over the ulama, taking repressive measures against some eminent members in their ranks. Mawlawi `Abd al-Rahman Baiktuti, the Grand Qazi of Kabul, was arrested for supposedly having taken a bribe to release Sauer, the accused German killer.[119] During his inspection tour in Jalalabad, Aman-Allah denounced the *mollas* for holding the Qur'an in one hand and the sword in the other, but he praised the

---

[116.] Fofalzai, Kabul, 1976.

[117.] *Gozareshat-i-Ruydad-i-Loya-Jerga*, 118.

[118.] *Ibid.*, 117, 121-122, 138, 388, 391.

[119.] Ghobar, Kabul, June 30, 1976.

Hajji of Turangzai and the Molla of Chaknawur as real *mojaheds*. Despite this expression of reverence toward the Molla of Chaknawur, he tried to curb that molla's freedom of action in the tribal areas, and, for a short time, Aman-Allah prevented him from leaving Jalalabad. Later, however, a royal decree issued in June 1926 permitted the sheikh to proceed to the *hajj* at the government's expense and promised him a yearly pension (*mostamari*) in return of his good services for the religion and benediction (*do`a-gu'i*) for the state.[120] The sheikh was instructed, however, to abandon the practice of touring different villages with a large following of religious students (*tollab*) to enjoin the good and forbid evil ( *al-amr bi al-ma`ruf wa al-nahy `an al-monkar*), because this responsibility had been transferred to government functionaries.[121]

The expulsion of Nur al-Mashayikh was significant among anticlerical policies. Aman-Allah had come to suspect involvement on the part of this sheikh in the Khost Rebellion.[122] Also, the latter's unyielding position on the issues of child marriage and polygamy and his public chastisement of the king on these points had annoyed Aman-Allah. According to one source, Nur al-Mashayikh left Afghanistan voluntarily as a protest against the king's policies.[123] However, Ghobar writes that the king forced Nur al-Mashayikh to leave and withheld further punishments only out of respect for the sheikh's elder brother, Shams al-Mashayikh.[124]

The expulsion of Nur al-Mashayikh increased his bitterness toward the regime, and he began to gather forces against Aman-Allah. These acts resulted in irreconcilable hostility between the king and the powerful, priestly Mojaddedi family. In 1926, the senior member of the Mojaddedi family, Shams al-Mashayikh, who was closely allied with the king, died. After his death the spiritual leadership of the Mojaddedi Naqshbandiyya went to Nur al-Mashayikh, now a firm enemy of the king. Residing in Dera-i-Esma`il Khan, on the northwestern border of India near Afghanistan, Nur al-Mashayikh organized antigovernment activities on both sides of the border.

By 1927, the forces that had allied the ulama with the government were gone. Some of the high-ranking ulama who had supported the government and the king himself during the rebellion were now bitter as a result of the regime's moves toward secularization. Although the ulama did not at that time publicly oppose the regime, by the end of 1927, some of its prominent members had become disenchanted with Aman-Allah.

The general situation in the country, however, remained calm, and the government made some progress in its efforts to make the population aware of the

---

[120.] Chaknawuri letters, Farman, no. 115, 8 Jawza 1305/June 4, 1926. See Appendix J (3) for the full text.
[121] Chaknawuri letters, Farman, no. 190 *Jawza* 15, 1905/June 5, 1926. See Appendix J (4) for the full text.
[122.] Ghobar, 808; NAI, FPD, no. 51-F, 1928; *Tarjoman-i-Sarhadi*, Feb. 2, 1928.
[123.] *Emruz* (Lahore), May 1, 1978.
[124.] Ghobar, 808.

long-term benefits of the reforms. In June 1926, the British Foreign Department in India reported that law and order had been reestablished in various provinces through a concentrated effort on the part of local governors and that the king's inspection tours in Qandahar and Jalalabad had had positive results. The report also mentioned the government's success in obtaining recruits for the army from areas such as Qandahar, the Eastern Province, and the Southern Province, which had earlier resisted conscription.[125]

---

[125] "Summaries of Events in Afghanistan for the Periods 1st July 1925 to 30th June 1926," NAI, Government of India, FPD, no. 32-37, 1926.

6

THE RETRENCHMENT OF THE HIGH CLERGY
Revolts against Secularization and the Emancipation of Women

I wish to organize a party to strengthen the national unity further, to help the progress of the country and to do away with absurd customs which are observed with the impression that these have been enjoined by the Faith. This party will be known as the Independence and Renewal Party (Ferqa-i-Esteqlal wa Tajaddod). The principles of our religion are the best as compared with other religions of the world. The things we have copied are absurdities and a disgrace to Islam.

King Aman-Allah[1]

Before the coming of Islam women were subject to their parents, husbands, and sons, but Islam gave them an equal status with men. If prevailing views regarding the veiling of women (hejab) remain unchanged, then there will be no possibilty of progess for any Muslim nation.

Queen Soraya[2]

The year 1928 began with great hopes for the future of Aman-Allah's reforms, but his plans ended in disaster. From November 1927 through June 1928, King Aman-Allah and Queen Soraya undertook a Grand Tour "to bring back to my country everything that is best in European civilization, and to show Europe that Afghanistan exists on the map."[3] The trip was the high point of the Amani era. The Western press campared King Aman-Allah to Peter the Great (1696-1725)

---

[1] Translation of the king's speech from *Aman-i-Afghan*, NAI, FPD, no.4-F (secret), 1928, no. 4274.

[2] Queen Soraya, *Aman-i-Afghan*, Asad 2, 1307/July 25, 1928.

[3] *The Literary Digest*, Feb. 4, 1928.

of Russia, who had undertaken a similar tour to familarize himself with modern European ways.[4]

The tour, which included visits to several European and Middle Eastern countries did enhance Afghanistan's international prestige. Fraser-Tytler noted that the royal couple's charm, dignity, and affability made a favorable impression in Europe.[5] In India and Egypt, the Afghan monarch was hailed as the defender of the East against Western imperialism. A small country, previously little known in the world, Afghanistan received much attention in the Western and Middle Eastern presses. Contacts made on the tour expanded Afghanistan's diplomatic, cultural, and commercial ties with the international community, and there was even talk of Afghanistan's entering the League of Nations. The triumphant tour also boosted Aman-Allah's popularity at home. "On the whole," wrote Humphrys, "a feeling of gratitude towards the king who had done so much to advertise the importance of Afghanistan abroad, was probably uppermost in the minds of the majority who welcomed him home."[6]

Despite its great success, the royal journey had several drawbacks. First, the king's long absence from the country gave rise to delinquency and excessive corruption in the administration. In turn, resentment over excessive administrative abuses by government officials was a major factor in the rapid spread of revolts in the fall of 1928. In addition, the opposition groups found ample opportunity during Aman-Allah's absence to strengthen their position against the government.

Aman-Allah's visit to Europe inspired him to introduce sweeping reforms in 1928. On his trip to the West, he became keenly aware of the backwardness of his country, and he returned to Afghanistan with a passionate desire to promote its development. This passion was expressed in one of his speeches: "Paris filled me with joy, Berlin astounded me, London caught my imagination, but it was the love of my homeland which ignited fire in me."[7] Aman-Allah's great urge to lead his country toward progress prompted him to embark on a radical reform program. Ronald Wild, the correspondent of the *Daily Mail* of London in Kabul, described King Aman-Allah's reform program as "the beginning of the greatest emancipation movement ever staged in the East".[8]

Official communications heralded the tenth anniversary of independence and the beginning of a new era, declaring that the first ten years of the Amani government had been concerned with establishing peace in the country, developing diplomatic relations with foreign powers, and gaining knowledge with which to

---

[4] *Ibid.*, May 5, 1928.

[5] Fraser-Tytler, 207.

[6] Confidential letter from Humphrys to Hederson, London, July 15, 1929, no. N3255/1/97, IOR/LPS/1285, 1929, P5464.

[7] Fofalzai, *Safarha-i-Ghazi Aman-Allah Shah*, 321.

[8] Wild, *Amanallah: Ex-King of Afghanistan*, 5.

chart the future development of Afghanistan and that it was now time to put new ideas into practice.[9]

This time, Aman-Allah was not willing to implement reforms slowly nor to wait for the endorsement of the clergy. Unlike his contemporary, Mostafa Kamal, who put the *shari`at* aside completely in his endeavors to modernize Turkey, Aman-Allah tried to change Afghan society by reforming the country's religious institutions. Rather than separate religion from politics, as Kamal did in Turkey, Aman-Allah set about to purge the practice of Islam in Afghanistan of folk ways, traditional taboos, and superstitions, which he claimed were espoused by ignorant and self-interested clergy.[10] Like his grandfather, Amir `Abd al-Rahman, Aman-Allah cracked down on the clergy's power. Whereas the anticlerical policy of `Abd al-Rahman aimed at strengthening the power of the state and the position of the monarchy, Aman-Allah's policy aimed at destroying the pervasive influence of the clergy in order to open the way for Afghanistan to progress along modern lines.

SECOND STAGE OF REFORMS

The *Loya-Jerga* of 1928

In late August 1928, Aman-Allah convened a *Loya-Jerga* of some 1000 members in Paghman. Before the *jerga* convened, the semiofficial press recommended that people elect men of moderate views as their representatives, rather than conservatives, who would cleave to old and backward customs, and extremists, who would suggest impracticable radical changes.[11] The king presented his new program, which included the formation of an Assembly (*Shura-i-Melli*), whose members were to be elected directly by constituents without the intervention of *molla*s and *khan*s. He also laid the groundwork for national banks, mineral development, improved postal and telegraph systems, and railway and road construction, and he expanded secondary education in the provinces. The national flag was changed from a black standard to a vertically striped black, red and green flag embellished with an emblem of sheaths of rye encircled by golden mountains over which soared the nation's star and the royal sun. The king announced that black was symbolic of Afghanistan's oppression by foreigners represented the past; red, the blood shed for independence; and green, Afghanistan's victory and hope for the future. The new flag signified the regime's move toward secularization. The appearance of the queen and the presense of several women representatives in the *Loya-Jerga* indicated a significant departure from tradition.

Some parts of the reform program built on earlier changes and were not surprising. Others, particularly those intended to promote secularization, were un-

---

[9.] MADK, no. 86, Sept. 17, 1928.
[10.] Report on the *Loya-Jerga* of 1928, NAI, FPD, File 163-F, nos. 1-8.
[11.] *Anis* (Kabul), July 27 and Aug. 5, 1928.

settling to the clergy and the faithful. Most disturbing were reforms pertaining to family law, the legal system, and women's issues. With regard to the latter, the *jerga* formulated a new code (*nezam-nama-i-neswan*) to deal with issues pertaining to women.

There is little information about the composition and activities of the *Loya-Jerga* of 1928. The limited records indicate that, in contrast to their behavior in the *jerga* of 1924, the ulama voiced little opposition. Either they were forced to acquiesce or the ulama most likely to oppose reforms were excluded from participation. The most extended debate about issues relating to the *shari`at* concerned the minimum age for marriage and the unveiling of women (*raf`-i-hejab*),[12] and the government's proposals on these topics were among the very few not passed.[13] In a later speech, King Aman-Allah commented,

> This year's *jerga* was better than the previous ones, as many useful matters were settled. It is all due to the fact that the representatives had been elected directly by the people and *sheikhs*, *mollas* and *khans* had nothing to do with them.[14]

Aman-Allah also succeeded in reversing the decisions of the *Loya-Jerga* of 1924 regarding monetary and *ta`zirat* punishments. The state regained the right to determine the type of *ta`zirat* and to reinstitute provisions of the penal code abrogated by the *Loya-Jerga* of 1924. Civil courts were also planned to function alongside *shari`at* courts. The *jerga* also passed a resolution requiring prospective mosque functionaries to take examinations before being allowed to undertake duties as teachers and preachers. The *jerga* also passed a bill banning the Indian ulama from entering Afghanistan.

Aman-Allah's victory in the *jerga* could have produced positive results for his government had he not insisted on more radical changes. After the grand tour, his popularity was so high that people were predisposed to accept his leadership. In June 1929, Humphrys wrote to London that had Aman-Allah confined himself to reforms that did not contravene tribal traditions and the religious practices of the people, and had he paid serious attention to the condition of the soldiers and the repression of corruption in government, he would have, no doubt, gained the country's support and left behind a name to rank among the greatest rulers.[15]

[12.] `Ali Ahmad, 18.

[13.] For details of Aman-Allah's reform proposals in the *Loya-Jerga*, see Adamec, *Afghanistan's Foreign Affairs*, 13; Stewart, 369-397.

[14.] Royal speech at the Estur Palace, *Aman-i-Afghan*, *Mizan* 14, 1307/Oct. 6, 1928.

[15.] Confidential letter no. N3255/1/97, P5464/1929, dated July 15, 1929, from Humphrys to A. Hederson, London.

Declarations at Estur Palace

In mid-October Aman-Allah moved with determination toward his goals. He had already packed the cabinet with young officers who were likely to support him in implementing change. Impatience and radicalism dominated his political mood, and flattery by high officials and foreign advisors encouraged this trend.[16] A series of four lectures at the compound of the Estur Palace (location of the Ministry of Foreign Affairs) set the tone for the government's new course of action. During these four lectures, Aman-Allah declared himself "revolutionary ruler" (*padshah-i-enqelabi*) and announced far-reaching reforms to include 1) compulsory wearing of European suits and hats in Kabul; 2) promotion of the visual and performing arts and expansion of music schools; 3) formation of a single political party, the Party of Independence and Reform (*Ferqa-i-Esteqlal wa Tajaddod*) to expedite political advancement; 4) abolition of premature marriages among students, setting a minimum age of eighteen for girls and twenty-two for boys; 5) changing the weekly holiday from Friday to Thursday, so that people could take care of private matters on Thursday and be free Friday to attend congregational prayer; 6) compulsory coeducation for boys and girls under age eleven, to save the cost of maintaining separate schools; 7) abolition of polygamy among government officials; 8) founding of a home economics school (*Maktab-i-Raziya*), a midwifery school, and a women's hospital; and 9) expansion of lycées, European language schools, in the provinces.[17] In addition, he proposed that new law courts be opened to operate in a similar fashion to judicial systems in other countries. He declared the present *qazis* unfit to hold their positions, and announced plans to open a suitable school for their training.

Mobilization of Women

In his speech in the *Loya-Jerga* of 1928, the king emphasized that no country could fully prosper as long as its women remained isolated behind the veil. The unveiled appearance of the queen and other female members of royalty in European cities during the Grand Tour was symbolic of the royal intention to remove the traditional segregation between the genders in Afghanistan. It was hoped that the great popularity that Queen Soraya had gained outside her country during the tour would pave the way for the removal of the veil and would inspire women to become visible in society. Queen Soraya was probably the first Muslim woman of royal rank to appear publicly unveiled in Europe and by doing so had captured the attention of the world. However, in her visits to Muslim coun-

---

[16.] Habibi, 1986, 165. During August and September the king and a group of close advisors drew up his new reform program. The king's closest advisors during this time included Ziya Homayun— an Iranian law specialist, whose extreme influence with the king had offended many high officials and court members—and the new Turkish ambassador, Hekmat Bay, who had free accessd as a private guest to the palace.

[17.] *Amani-i-Afghan*, joint issue, *Mizan*, 11, 14, 18, 1307/Oct. 3, 6, 10, 1928.

tries the queen had been persuaded to abide behind the veil. The Egyptian and Iranian governments were apprehensive about receiving the Afghan queen unveiled for fear of religious protest. In deference to King Fuad and Reza Shah's request, Soraya wore the veil in Egypt and in Iran.[18] The news of the queen's touring unveiled in Europe and the Iranian and Egyptian governments' protest to her unveiled visit traveled back to Kabul. Orthodox groups were perturbed by the queen's actions, and according to a report prepared by the British consul in Qandahar, rumors surrounding Soraya's appearance in Europe had created great anxiety among the Qandahari ulama.[19]

During October the campaign against female seclusion intensified. Upon their return from Europe, the queen and several female members of royalty discarded the traditional Afghan veil (*chadari*) and attended public ceremonies in modest Western clothes and hats with only a short tulle veil covering their faces.

The force behind the feminist movement, Queen Soraya held interviews with foreign reporters regarding the status of women in Islam and wrote several articles for the press in support of women's rights. She maintained that Islam was the only religion that gave women equal status with men and that *hejab* was not an Islamic practice, because in the early days of Islam, women accompanied men in the battlefield and did the same valuable work done by Western women today. Had *hejab* been an Islamic ordinance, she argued, there would have been a specific punishment ascribed for it in the *shari`at*.[20] In an article published in the *Aman-i-Afghan*, the queen provided strong arguments in favor of unveiling and education for women, claiming that veiling originated as a local practice but erroneously became a religious obligation in the minds of the common people. She explained that the reference to veiling in the Holy Qur'an points only to morals, and it is never mentioned as an injunction requiring punishment if disobeyed. According to religious law, a women is required to conceal from public view her body except for her face, her palms, and her feet, the same parts she must conceal and expose during daily prayers and pilgrimages to Mecca.

The article then went on to say that if the prevailing ideas about the seclusion of women (*hejab*) remained unchanged, there would be no hope for the progress of Muslim nations, as it is a proven fact that women are an important force in the development of civilization. Until the female population of the East, she wrote, receives appropriate education based on modern methods, it would be impossible for women to be of great use to society. Attacking the narrow-minded view of the ulama regarding the education of women she wrote,

> And they who, on account of their narrow-mindedness, say that women could get proper education even inside [their homes] have really misunderstood the meaning of education....For the benefit of Eastern people, I advise them to reject the common belief regarding

---

[18.] Wild, 101.

[19.] MADK, no. 38, May 7, 1928; Fraser-Tytler, 210.

[20.] Queen Soraya's interview with the press, printed in *Partap* (Lahore), Sept. 12, 1928.

> [the seclusion of women] and adopt what Islam actually prescribes for women, thereby regulating their own peculiar custom.[21]

The queen campaigned against the absolute veiling prevalent in Afghanistan, the all-enveloping *chadari* and *borqa`*. Instead women were encouraged to wear what came to be known as a school cloak (*chadari-maktabi*): a short cape and a long overskirt. The king announced that the discarding of the *chadari* was optional but that women who exposed themselves beyond the limits prescribed by the *shari`at* would be punished. This meant that during the performance of daily prayer, they should expose only those parts of the body permitted by law, that is, their faces, hands, and feet.

At the end of his lecture series at Estur Palace, the king announced that Islam does not require women to cover their faces, hands, and feet. A woman would be allowed to perform her five prayers with these parts exposed. At this point in the speech, Queen Soraya removed the transparent veil she had been wearing since returning from Europe, and several ladies present at the meeting followed her lead. After the royal couple had dramatically discarded the age-old tradition of veiling, the king announced the imminent departure of some twenty-four female students who had been selected to go abroad for higher education.

The king and queen held special meetings in the Arg and Delkosha palaces, during which they discussed girls' schools raising women's awareness of their social responsibilities. The goal of these schools, the monarchs explained, was to transform women into responsible, self-confident citizens. Even during their international tour, the royal couple had taken on the task of making Muslim women aware of their rights and their potential for progress. In India, Queen Soraya had advocated education for Muslim women.[22] For instance, in an interview with a reporter of *Habl al-Matin* of Calcutta, the queen had argued that Islam gives women more rights than any other religion and that the main impediment to the progress of Muslim women was misinterpretation of the teachings of Islam.[23] In the Soviet Union, the king pointed out to a Muslim delegation that "the conservative priests misinterpreted the teachings of Islam, particularly in regard to relations toward women."[24] He then asked Mofti Sadruddinov to explain to the Muslim population the proper teachings of Islam regarding women.[25]

Under the queen's leadership, female members of the royal family were assigned a crucial role in initiating and supervising all aspects of the emancipation campaign. During the *Loya-Jerga* of 1928, despite the ulama's opposition, the *jerga* members ratified the king's proposal for enactment of a *nezam-nama* to set

---

[21.] *Aman-i-Afghan*, 5 *Saratan* 1307/July 25, 1928, quoted in Stewart, 375-376.
[22.] Wild, 98-99.
[23.] *Aman-i-Afghan*, nos. 15 and 16 (joint issue), 29 *Sawr* and 2 *Jawza* 1307/May 19 and 23, 1928.
[24.] NAI, File 46-7, nos. 1-170, 1928.
[25.] *Ibid.*; Adamec, *Afghanistan's Foreign Affairs*, 126.

forth women's rights and responsibilities in society. The *jerga* also passed another proposal for establishment of the Society for the Protection of Women *(Anjoman-i-Hemayat-i-Neswan)*, which was formed shortly after the *jerga* by Princesses Kobra and Hajera, Aman-Allah's sisters, under the direct supervision of the queen. The immediate purpose of the *Anjoman* was to inspire women's self-respect, competence, and assertiveness; its long-term objective was to prepare women for future political activities. There was even talk of including women in the State Council.[26] Members also discussed the freedom of women from servitude in their houses. Women were asked to stand up for their rights and for equal status with men in their homes. High-echelon administrators and civil servants in general were called upon to set a personal example by emancipating the female members of their households. The queen assumed a very active role in these activities. On October 29, the British military attaché reported:

> The queen has put herself at the head of a female secret service department. The object of this new department is to disseminate propaganda in the country for the emancipation of women and to keep a watch on any reactionary movement among women....The queen, or in her absence her deputy, is presiding over a court in which cases concerned with divorce, wife beating, starvation, and similar matters affecting women are tried and decided.[27]

The king and queen's campaign against the veil upset the traditional elements in society. The royal couple had argued that tribal and rural women, the majority of the female population, already kept their faces uncovered both within and outside their homes, and that only urban women were required to cover themselves completely and to stay in their houses. The king encouraged only exposure of the face for urban women, a practice already common in certain parts of the Middle East such as Syria and permitted by the Shafi`i school of law. Even this compromise was too radical for the Afghan ulama, who adhered to the Hanafi view, espousing complete *hejab* with no exceptions.[28] They also objected to unveiling on the grounds that it symbolized Westernization in Kabul, where upperclass women already often dressed in the latest European dresses and hats.[29] Their faces were at the beginning covered only by a sheer veil hanging down from the hats, which in the eyes of the ulama was a fraudulent pretension to *hejab*.

[26.] Mott-Smith, "Behind the Purdah in Afghanistan," 16.

[27.] MADK, no. 104, Oct. 29, 1928.

[28.] Ne`mat-Allah Shahrani, 1976.

[29.] Mott-Smith, 14-15. Saif Azad, the editor of *Azadi-Sharq*, who had accompanied the king during the tour, was given permission to open a branch in Paghman to introduce the women's journal *Rahnoma-i-Banuwan* (*Ladies Guide*). Printed in Berlin, the journal's main objective was to introduce women to the latest European fashion.

Disparagement of the Ulama and Assaults on Popular Religious Practices

By 1928, the king had become convinced that the ulama were a major hindrance to reforms and that change would be impossible unless the clergy were stripped of their political and social power. He therefore accompanied his announcement of reforms with a crackdown on the religious establishment. Holding the ulama accountable for much of the popular antireform sentiment, he denounced them as corrupt, hypocritical, restrictive, and narrow-minded, and claimed that they had distorted the teachings of Islam and had "battened on the credulity of the poor classes."[30] Later, during the lectures at Estur Palace, he repeated such statements and "repudiated their influence on future policies of the state."[31] In his public speech at the compound of the Foreign Ministry (Estur Palace), the king spoke of various social defects, such as the "gross superstitions of the people and their unchivalrous attitude toward women and of the exaggerated powers of the fanatical priesthood,"[32] and he went on to announce the formation of the Party of Independence and Modernity (*Ferqa-i-Esteqlal wa Tajaddod*), whose main objective was to legitimize social reforms. Soon after the speeches at the Estur Palace, the party's platform was published. According to Article 3, one of the party's main objectives was to "remove from religion the superstitious and heretical beliefs which do not conform with Islam but have become a part of popular belief through old customs."[33]

Aman-Allah was actually using the arguments and terminology of the twentieth-century fundamentalist reformers, who claimed a return to the fundamental sources of Islam, the Qur'an and the *sonnat*. Emphasis on *tajdid* (renewal) by "revivalist reformers" such as Mohammad ibn `Abd al-Wahhab in the Arabian Peninsula and Sayyid Qotb in Egypt was tantamount to criticizing the traditionalist mode of Islam.[34] Like the Wahhabi and Muslim Brotherhood movements, Aman-Allah's efforts to purify Islam were both radical and revolutionary. Unlike the adherents of these movements, however, Aman-Allah perceived *tajdid* in nationalistic and modernist terms. The *tajaddod*'s second objective was to loosen judicial constraints and promulgate progressive regulations: "It is the aim of the Party to establish new laws that will meet popular needs, conform with the requirements of contemporary civilization, and ensure social, political, and economic [development]."[35]

The king made his trend toward secularization overt. During one speech the king told his audience, "I received an honorary degree of civil law from Oxford University. It was not unsuitable, as I have framed and organized the laws of

---

[30] Humphrys' report to the British foreign secretary, IOR, L/P&S/10/1289, P53, Part 6, 1928-29; 'Ali Ahmad, 18; Anis, *Bohran Wa Nejat*, 29.
[31] Humphrys' report to the foreign secretary, IOR, L/P&S/10/1289, P53, Part 6, 1928-29.
[32] *Ibid.*
[33] For a translation of the party platform, see Appendix D.
[34] Voll, 40.
[35] See Appendix D.

my own country."[36] *Aman-i-Afghan* printed a royal declaration that the present *qazi*s were unfit to act in the law courts, that the law courts would be modernized, and that new schools would open to train the *qazi*s in correct procedures and interrogation. The king added that the *nezam-nama*s would be amended.[37] Among his proposals to the *Loya-Jerga* were establishment of civil courts side by side with the *shari`at* courts and promulgation of a separate civil law to eliminate corruption within the judiciary by taking away the *qazi*s' right to determine *ta`zirat* punishments.[38]

The weekly *Anis* of Kabul (established May 5, 1927), under the editorship of Mohaiy al-Din Anis, a liberal, reflected this trend toward secularization. *Anis* argued that the ulama in Afghanistan were unfit for their work owing to their "lack of general education and ignorance of psychology."[39]

The ulama were divested of many traditional governmental functions. In the *Loya-Jerga,* Aman-Allah requested that all Deoband-trained ulama be banished from Afghanistan.[40] He maintained, giving examples, that the Deoband-trained ulama of Afghanistan, the same group that had so vociferously protested the *nezam-nama*s of the *Loya-Jerga* of 1924, were an instrument of foreign intrigue. His proposal that all Deoband-trained ulama be detained in one place and not permitted to travel without prior sanction by the government was clearly an effort to remove from the scene the most vocal group of ulama, those who had spoken out against his reforms. Meanwhile the regime launched a small indoctrination program. Government officials were appointed to promote reforms in the mosques, and training seminars were scheduled for mosque functionaries.

Along with the anticlergy campaign, Aman-Allah attacked the Sufi *pir*s and *morshed*s. He maintained that Sufi orders were represented by false, self-interested *pir*s and had no place in the contemporary Muslim world. During the grand tour he had spoken openly against the *pir-morid* system and had blamed imposter *sheikh*s for creating disorder by traveling from country to country in search of followers. These *sheikh*s, he claimed, had caused confusion in the Indo-Afghan frontier area by their frequent visits to various villages on both sides of the border in pursuit of followers (*morid*s).[41] The king's main target was Nur al-Mashayikh, who resided at the time in Dera Esma`il Khan (in the vicinity of the Khybar on the British side) and commanded tremendous influence among the Ghelzai tribes. Nur al-Mashayikh also had many followers in the army and

---

[36.] Sept. 30, 1928, quoted in MADK, no. 94, Oct. 4, 1928.

[37.] *Aman-i-Afghan,* 11 *Mizan* 1307/Oct. 3, 1928.

[38.] MADK, nos. 84 and 86, Sept. 10 and 17, 1928; NAI, FPD, 523-F, no. 1.

[39.] *Anis,* 19 *Sawr* 1307/Sept. 10, 1928, quoted in MADK, no. 49, May 1928.

[40.] Ali Ahmad, 19; MADK, no. 84, Sept. 10, 1928; *Aman-i-Afghan* (supplement) 11 and 12 *Sonbola* 1307/Sept. 2 and 3, 1928.

[41.] He cautioned his audience against pseudo *sheikh*s by reciting the following line: "*ay basa eblis adam roy hast pas ba har dasti nabayad dad dast* (There are money devils in the guise of pious men./ Hence one should not hasten to hold any extended hand.)" See Fofalzai, *Safarha-i-Ghazi Aman-Allah Shah,* 20.

even among high-ranking administrators. During his lecture at Estur Palace Aman-Allah stated:

> Everyone calls himself a *pir* these days. There are many devils in the form of men; hence you should not give your hand into the hand of everyone. It is very difficult to find a [genuine] *pir*. You should first come to me to ask that you wish to become the *morid* of such and such a *pir*, and I will tell you all about him.[42]

Meanwhile the government brought the administration of religious endowments, *awqaf*, under its control and discontinued monetary grants to religious learders. On September 3, 1928, the British military attache reported that several influential tribal religious leaders, including the Molla of Chaknawur, the Hajji of Turangzai, and the Ostad of Hadda, had come to Kabul to greet the king on his return from Europe. Not only did the king refuse to see these dignitaries, he sent them a message telling them if they were found touring the villages and accepting money from their parishioners, it would not go well for them. As might be imagined, the party of *molla*s returned home very disappointed.[43] The earlier friendship between these dignitaries and Aman-Allah was never rekindled.

High government officials and army officers were asked to dissociate themselves from the leaders of the Sufi orders. "Military regulations," Aman-Allah stated, "forbid the men in the army from joining political parties. There is no difference between joining a party and becoming the *morid* of a *pir*. The *pir*s have also strange differences among them. If a man becomes the follower of one *pir* and the other the follower of another *pir*, friction will be created in the army."[44]

Following these announcements, the president of the municipality of Kabul was authorized to summon the *molla*s and the *mo`azen*s of the mosques in Kabul and instruct them about the role they should play in edifying the masses along modern lines.

GENERAL RESPONSE TO REFORMS

Dissention among the Political Elite and the Opposition from Liberals

The unity of purpose and close cooperation that existed at the beginning of the Amani period between the king and his most trusted officials, Sardar Mahmud Tarzi, Sepahsalar Mohammad Nader, and General Mohammad Wali, gradually declined. The major source of dissent was over policy decisions. Although political leaders generally agreed that Afghanistan should move forward toward modernization, there existed from the very beginning a conflict of opinion on

---

[42] *Aman-i-Afghan*, 14 *Mizan* 1307/ Oct. 6, 1928.
[43] MADK, n. 83, Sept. 3, 1928.
[44] *Ibid.*

the strategy for modernization. The king himself pushed for a comprehensive reform program, encompassing changes in all aspects of social and cultural life, the economy, law, education, communications, health, arts, sports, and so on. Among the serious critics of this comprehensive approach was Sepahsalar Nader Khan, who favored a selective approach and recommended adoption of modern technology and science, which he perceived as beneficial to economic growth, but who opposed social and cultural reforms. Mahmud Tarzi, the idealogue of the reform movement, did not separate social issues from other aspects of modernity. He was, however, opposed to the king's radical approach of introducing too many reforms very fast. Mohammad Wali, who served as the regent in the king's absence, expounded the ideas of the Young Afghans, whose main objective was to change the political structure and minimize the power of the Pashtun Mohammadzai ruling class in the government.

Personal disagreements among Mahmud Tarzi, General Nader, and General Mohammad Wali further exacerbated high-level dissention over the king's policies. Division in the cabinet, in the words of Schinasie, resulted in the interruption of the careers of Tarzi and Nader Khan in the early years of the Amani period, depriving the state of two outstanding statesmen.[45] The relationship between Tarzi and General Nader Khan had soured mainly over the involvement of Turkish officers in the Afghan military. Prompted by Tarzi, the zealous advocate of close ties with Turkey, Aman-Allah had agreed to give the task of the reorganization of the Afghan army to Turkish officers Jamal Pasha and Ziya Baig. Sepahsalar Nader Khan, who was under the impression that he was in charge of this task himself, was offended by this decision and blamed Tarzi for the growing influence of the Turks in the Afghan army.[46] The Landi Kotal and Kohat incidents brought the conflict to a head. Tarzi and General Mohammad Wali, who replaced Tarzi temporarily as foreign minister in 1922, insisted that if the problem were not handled properly at the first outburst of an international problem, the British would have a chance to show failure on the part of Afghanistan to honor treaty agreements and to question Afghanistan's ability to conduct its own foreign affairs. Sepahsalar Nader Khan, on the other hand, believed that compliance with British demands would inflame the tribes and cause irreparable damage to the government's relations with the Pashtun tribes along the border. A heated discussion over this and other policies prompted the Sepahsalar to resign in November 1923 from his post as minister of war. In July 1924, he left Afghanistan to act as the Afghan minister to Paris. Officially, Nader Khan was transferred to Paris to receive medical treatment in Europe and to acquire knowledge about French military technology. In reality, he was removed from the scene because Aman-Allah, through the influence of certain court members, suspected that Nader Khan would incite the tribes against him.

[45.] Schinasie, "Italie-Afghanistan, 1919-1941," iii, *AION* (Naples), vol. 52, no. 2, 1992, 128.
[46.] *Ibid.*, 130.

In 1926, a rift emerged between the king and Sepahsalar Mohammad Nader over a family matter when Princess Nur al-Seraj, Aman-Allah's sister, who had been betrothed to Nader Khan's younger brother (Mohammad Hashem) was urged to break the engagement and marry her cousin, Hasan Jan. Because the union had been initiated by the king himself, the Sepahsalar and his family took offense. On November 20, Nader Khan resigned from his post as Afghan minister to Paris and retired to the south of France, where his younger brothers, Mohammad Hashem (Afghan minister in Moscow) and Shah Wali Khan, joined him. An attempt by Mahmud Tarzi to reconcile the king and Nader Khan proved futile.[47]

With the death of `Abd al-Qoddus Khan E`temad al-Dawla in the early months of 1928, the king lost a strong ally and an adroit negotiator, who had been instrumental in procuring the support of the high clergy in Kabul during the early years of his reign. Although nominally still the prime minister, E`temad al-Dawla retired from public activity several years before his death due of his advanced age. Mahmud Tarzi also gradually withdrew from taking an active part in state affairs. A few months after Sepahsalar Mohammad Nader's departure to Europe in July 1924, Tarzi, who had been displeased with the king over the handling of Piperno's case, presented his resignation, which was not accepted. Although he remained nominally in his post as foreign minister until 1928, he refused to take an active part in state matters and retired almost entirely to private life. His withdrawal from politics was largely due to disagreements with the king on issues related to the modernization strategy.

In 1927, Tarzi, who was in Switzerland, learned about the king's intention to embark on a grand tour of Europe. Tarzi immediately sent a letter to Aman-Allah and tried to dissuade him by arguing that touring for several months, aside from being a burdensome cost for taxpayers, would have negative political consequences for the regime because of the king's long absence from the country.[48] Aman-Allah disregarded Tarzi's suggestions and instead ordered him to join the royal entourage in Cairo. In Rome, Tarzi once again took the liberty to advise the king to shorten his visit and reconsider radical development plans. Realizing that his suggestions had no effect, the bitter foreign minister left on January 15, 1928, for Caux near Montreux in Switzerland on account of poor health and excused himself from escorting the royal couple for the rest of their journey.[49]

An important political meeting took place in Italy. During the king's visit to Naples, Sepahsalar Nader Khan, accompanied by his brothers Shah Wali Khan and Hashem Khan, came to greet Aman-Allah. During this meeting, Nader Khan expressed his views on state matters and advised the king that the existing sociopolitical structure and cultural ethos of Afghanistan did not allow hasty, radical changes.[50] Failing to impress his views upon the king, Sepahsalar re-

---

[47] *Ibid.*
[48] Schinasie, "Siradj al-Akhbar: l'Opinion Afghane et la Russie," 1992, 129.
[49] *Ibid.*
[50] Interview with `Aziz Naim, Nadir Khan's grandson, London, Summer 1991.

turned to the south of France and refused to participate in ceremonial functions. He later refused the king's order to return to Afghanistan.[51]

Conflict in the cabinet affected the strength and cohesion of the political leadership. By 1928, dissention among government officials had gone from bad to worse. Attempts to get a cabinet together to work under the newly appointed prime minister, Shir Ahmad Khan, proved to be impossible, as no high-ranking administrator was willing to work under him. A quarrel between Mohammad Wali Khan, the war minister, and Mahmud Tarzi in November prompted the former to submit his resignation. The king summoned the two officials and reconciled them.[52] However, he finally accepted their repeated requests to resign from their posts on the pretext of poor health.[53] Tarzi was replaced by the dynamic but hotheaded radical Gholam Seddiq of the influential Charkhi family, and Mohammad Wali Khan was replaced as minister of war by `Abd al-`Aziz Khan.

Divided by personal ambitions and ethnic and personal rivalries, the administrators, in general, became the most formidable obstacle to the implementation of the king's progressive ideas. Many were even corrupt and disloyal. The few who remained dedicated to Aman-Allah were arrogant, quarrelsome, and unpopular with other officials.

Educated groups, a very small segment of the Afghan population, generally viewed Aman-Allah as an enlightened and progressive ruler, a benevolent monarch who believed in freedom and equality and considered himself *khadem-i-mellat*, "servant of the nation," whose duty was to arouse his people to political consciousness and to lead them in progress. In the eyes of the liberals (members of *Jawanan-i-Afghan*), however, his reign contained many elements of traditional absolutism with no separation of power. Governmental functions were concentrated in the hands of the monarch, and the executive branch was independent of judicial review. In their view, Aman-Allah's regime was distinct from earlier regimes in terms of the sophistication of its legislative, administrative, and judicial techniques, but not in the matter of power.

After the Khost rebellion, the liberal groups began to show signs of disagreement with the regime's policies. Some liberals affiliated with the regime felt that the king had overstepped his authority and had opened the way toward dictatorship. The execution of Molla `Abd-Allah and other rebel leaders without trial had offended not only the religious establishment in Kabul but had also perturbed the liberals, who were now concerned about the increasingly autocratic practices of the monarchy. `Abd al-Hadi Dawi, a moderate liberal, and the then-minister of finance, was reported to have presumed on the basis of his close relationship with the king to warn him that it was imprudent to punish the rebel *molla*s without a fair trial and a guilty verdict from a religious court, only to be reminded by the king that he was "the grandson of Amir `Abd al-

---

[51] Schinasie, *ibid.*, 130.

[52] IOR, L/P&S/10/1137, no. 23, Nov. 20, 1928.

[53] *Aman-i-Afghan*, 12 `Aqrab 1307/ Nov. 3, 1928.

Rahman."[54] In the fall of 1925, the British military attaché in Kabul reported "that several anonymous letters were sent to the king demanding constitutional government."[55] Feeling uneasy about these demands, the king called for a special meeting of the State Council, which, according to the military attaché, failed to arrive at any decision on the subject.[56]

After touring Europe, the king increased his control over policy even more. During the *Loya-Jerga* of 1928, he proposed an amendment to the Constitution to establish parliamentary government, but in practice the authority of the monarchy remained intact. Liberal groups became apprehensive about the consequences of his autocratic rule.[57] During one of the sessions of the *Loya-Jerga*, Mohaiy al-Din Arti, also a member of the radical wing of Jawanan-i-Afghan, and `Abd al-Rahman Ludin spoke out against the king's monopoly of power. Arti stated that government officials were only concerned with their own positions and showed no respect for the opinion of others or for the cause of progress. He pointed out corruption at the level of high officials, arguing that every effort for development would be annulled as long as the highest echelon of administrators was protected by the umbrella of monarchy.[58]

At first the king welcomed free discussions of the country's problems and agreed to form a responsible cabinet under Shir Ahmad Khan, former president of the State Council. Later, however, on account of persistent disputes among high officials, he announced that no one else was as strongly committed to progress as he and that he must, therefore, provisionally "take the burden of the work that should devolve on the premier on his own shoulders."[59] From the audience, Ludin pointed out to the king the discrepancy between his role as revolutionary ruler and the outdated power structure of his government.[60]

As the election law of the National Assembly was being formulated, the liberal intelligentsia began to create a nucleus for political opposition.[61] Two political associations were formed. The first association was the moderate liberal group *Mashruta-Khwahan* led by Mir Sayyid Qasem, a former editor of *Aman-i-Afghan*, and by `Abd al-Hadi Dawi, a close associate of Tarzi, who had been imprisoned by Amir Habib-Allah along with several other suspects after an assassination attempt on the amir's life. Dawi had been released from prison shortly after King Aman-Allah's accession to the throne and had been appointed to important positions, such as Afghan minister to London and later as minister of finance. This association grew from a social club that met at the Café Wali (named after Mohammad Wali, the regent) in Kabul with the objective of estab-

---

54. Habibi, *Gonbesh-i Mashrutiyyat dar Afghanistan*, 226.
55. *MADK, 1924-25*, IOR, L/P&S/10/1120, P3684, no. 80, Oct. 27, 1925.
56. *Ibid.*
57. Habibi, 1993, 233-234.
58. Ghobar, 813; `Ali Ahmad, 25.
59. Estur Palace lecture, MADK, no. 101, Oct. 22, 1928.
60. Ghobar, 813; Habibi, 1993, 191
61. Anis, *Bohran wa Nejat* 21-26; Ghobar, 797.

lishing a constitutional monarchy. Among the group's secret supporters were Prince 'Enayat-Allah Khan, the former Mo'in al-Saltana; Shah Mahmud, Nader Khan's brother; and Mohammad Wali Khan, the regent.[62] The second group was the radical leftist wing of the Jawanan-i-Afghan, also known as *Jamhuriyyat Khwahan* (Republicans). Members included 'Abd al-Rahman Ludin, Mohaiy al-Din Arti, and Mir Gholam Mohammad Ghobar (author of *Afghanistan dar Masir-i-Tarikh*), who hoped eventually for representation in the National Assembly and an impact on public policy making.

The king, on the other hand, pushed for a single party system under his own leadership. Court members and high officials such as Shir Ahmad Khan, the president of the State Council, had formed the *Hezb-i-Ashraf* (Party of the Nobility), which supported the monarch in formulating the platform of *Ferqa-i-Esteqlal wa Tajaddod* (Independence and Reform Party). Under the auspices of the regime, the *Anjoman-i-Hemayat-i-Neswan* (Association for Protection of Women's Rights) also emerged. Organized by Princess Kobra, the association had drafted a platform (*gozaresh-nama*), intending to play an important role in Afghan public life.[63]

Some liberals disapproved of the women's emancipation movement as a specific agenda for reform and openly criticized the king's stand on unveiling and other feminist issues. 'Abd-al-Hadi Dawi and 'Abd al-Rahman Ludin vociferously opposed unveiling, claiming that the unveiling of women in the capital would produce negative repurcussions in the country and would provide ample opportunity for the British to foment another popular uprising against the government.[64]

Thus by 1928, the Young Afghans, who had functioned as a vital social force during the second decade of the twentieth century and had played an important role in bringing Aman-Allah to power, were divided into moderate and radical branches, with some members of the radical branch openly expressing opposition to the king's policies. Powerful and capable men such as Mahmud Tarzi, Sepahsalar Nader Khan, and General Mohammad Wali Khan, the fulcrum of state power in the early 1920s in one way or another, dissociated themselves from the government.

THE OUTRAGE OF THE CLERGY

A decisive shift in the emphasis of the protest against the king's policies came in late September as religious forces took the lead. In the ulama's view, arbitrary use of power by the government had exceeded justification. Instead of learning from the rebellion of 1924, they thought the king had become even more extreme in his methods. This time the opposition against Aman-Allah was led by

---

[62.] Interview with 'Abd al-Hadi Dawi and Gholam Ahmad Nawid; Anis, 193. According to 'Ali Ahmad, Mohammad Wali Khan belonged to the *Jamhuriyyat-Khwahan* party.

[63.] Dawlatabadi, *Shenasnama-i-Ahzab wa Jeryanat-i Siyasi dar Afghanistan*, 27.

[64.] Habibi, *Jonbesh-i-Mashrutiyyat*, 191.

the ulama elite in Kabul, the same group that had promoted his succession to the throne. The opposition of the high ulama to the king's arbitrary use of power had begun earlier. In 1926, Mawlawi 'Abd al-Wase' Qandahari, one of the liberal ulama and a previous supporter of Aman-Allah's reforms, hinted his disagreement with the king's policies in a speech in Pol-i-Kheshti Mosque in Kabul. Qandahari was quoted to have said that the Qur'anic reference to *uli al-amr* was intended to mean "the enlightened ulama" (*'ulama-i-monawwar*) and had advised his congregation to obey the learned ulama, "because we possess the knowledge, based on which we can guide the people to the right path and deter them from iniquity (*monkar*) and debauchery (*fohasha'*)."[65] The regime construed Qandahari's sermon to mean that the king was no longer entitled to be obeyed because his policies were not in conformity with the ethical values of Islam. Qandahari was subsequently arrested on a charge of preaching against the government.[66] A year later he was released to leave Kabul for Qandahar.

Nur al-Mashayikh's Antigovernment Activities

In February 1928, Hazrat Fazl 'Omar Mojaddedi (Nur al-Mashayikh), exiled in India, began activities against Aman-Allah. On January 27 and again on February 9, Scott, the British chief commissioner in Baluchistan, reported a plot by Nur al-Mashayikh against the Afghan government.[67] A conference called by the Hazrat in Paniala to plan the defeat of the *tajaddod* movement led by the king included several *molla*s from the Southern Province and Qandahar who had fled Afghanistan. Among them were Molla Mohammad Akbar, a *qazi* from Qandahar; Molla 'Abd al-Rahim Musa Khail; Molla Karim Kharuti, and Molla Dust Mohammad, who, as is apparent in the report, served as an informant to Scott. They generated a plan to start an uprising in Khost through a network of subordinate *molla*s and tribal *khan*s in the Southern and Eastern provinces. To that end, Nur al-Mashayikh, according to this report, had enlisted the cooperation of Zadran and Mangal tribal leaders and of several prominent government officials such as the governor of Ghazni, the governor of the Eastern Province, the deputy minister of war, the minister of education, and the former governor of Qandahar (Sardar Mohammad 'Osman, a noted theologian), mostly *morid*s of Nur al-Mashayikh.[68] Mohammad Sadeq Mojaddedi (known as Gol-Agha), younger brother of Nur al-Mashayikh, and his nephew, Mohammad Sana Ma'sum (known as Miajan) coordinated underground activities in Kabul. Mohammad Akram and Mohammad A'zam, grandsons of Amir Shir 'Ali Khan, were early on suggested as possible candidates for the throne. Nur al-Mashayikh, however, refused the idea, arguing that the people of the Southern Province did not "wish

---

[65] *Ibid.,* 52.
[66] *Ibid.,* 53.
[67] For the full text of Scott's report see Appendix E.
[68] NAI, FPD, N 51-F, nos. 1-55, 1928.

any deviation from a purely religious uprising, which would be the case if any attempt were made to usurp the throne....The issue[s] would then be mixed and the support that [they] expect from the rest of Afghanistan in a religious struggle might be jeopardized."[69]

The uprising was planned for sometime in the first two weeks of the month of Ramadan (early March),[70] before the king's return from Europe. Confident of success, the group was relying on the unrest of religious forces in Qandahar and in the Eastern and Southern provinces, who were disturbed over Queen Soraya's unveiled public appearances in Europe and the anti-Soviet sentiment that had resulted from the king's visit to Russia, where, the clergy feared, the king would be influenced by atheist Marxists. The group expressed the view that Russian help to the government would be forthcoming and the belief that all Afghans would then be "cemented to their cause."[71] In a letter dated February 21, 1928, Scott hinted that the plot had a connection to an Afghan trade agent in Quetta (Baluchistan), reporting that the agent was "making purchases of all illustrated papers depicting the unveiled queen of Afghanistan and dispatching them to Kabul separately as soon as he gets them."[72]

The plot was, however, discovered before it could be carried out.[73] In mid-March, following a formal protest by the Afghan foreign office, Nur al-Mashayikh was expelled from Dera Esma`il Khan to Bombay under section 3(e) of the Frontier Security Regulation that had become effective in 1922.[74]

High Ulama's Protest against New Reforms

The official announcements made during the months of September and early October of 1928 came as a bombshell to the ulama, who were now determined to gather forces in defense of Islamic orthodoxy and their own group integrity.

An issue of grave importance to the ulama was the royal stand on the questions of female education and the unveiling of women. The ulama were genuinely offended by the queen's appearing unveiled in Europe and by the royal couple's position on unveiling, child marriage, and polygamy. The proposal to set a minimum age for marriage (eighteen for girls and twenty-two for boys) was strongly debated and defeated by the ulama in the *jerga* of 1928. Only nominally represented in the *jerga*, the ulama had been able to prevail on this

---

[69] NAI, G. I., FPD, R.N.G. Scott's Report, no. R.S.3/12/N.G.O.3., Baluchistan Intelligence Bureau, Feb. 9, 1928, secret.

[70] *Ibid.*

[71] *Ibid.*

[72] *Ibid.*

[73] According to Reshtia, the plot was revealed by the brother of `Abd al-`Aziz, the officiating war minister. Interview with Sayyid Qasem Reshtia in 1991 in Geneva.

[74] *Ibid.*

issue and on the matter of unveiling.[75] Despite the ulama's protests, after the *Loya-Jerga* the king continued to pursue the issues of child marriage and un-veiling. A month after the *jerga* was adjourned, Aman-Allah publicly forbade youthful marriages among students, and shortly afterward he issued a royal de-cree prohibiting polygamy by government officials. The emancipation of women became the immediate target of clerical protests. Deobandi ulama such as Mawlawis Ebrahim Kamawi and `Abd al-Haiy Panjshiri, members of the *Hai'at-i-Tamiz*, were distressed about the abrogation of the traditional segregation of the genders and changes in the structure of gender relations. When Kamawi at one point encountered unveiled female members of royalty at a state function, he covered his own face with the end of his turban to show his disgust.[76] Maw-lawi Fazl al-Rabbi composed a poem expressing indignation at the policy on mobilization of women. Kamawi, Fazl al-Rabbi Pakhlawi, and several other Deoband-trained ulama were ultimately imprisoned in the Arg.[77]

The ulama's major fear was the influence of atheistic Soviets. Until 1926 the state and the clergy shared common goals in foreign policy, but the king's grad-ual leaning toward Kamalist Turkey and his visit of Russia in April 1928 marked a divergence in matters of foreign policy between the state and the ulama. As a result of British propaganda or their own conjecture, the clergy attributed the king's anticlerical policies and the radical reforms of 1928 mostly to the influence of Soviet Russia.[78]

The royal visit to Turkey in May of 1928, and the subsequent conclusion of a new treaty of friendship and collaboration between Turkey and Afghanistan in 1928, which provided for the active cooperation of Turkey in Afghanistan's de-velopment, had already increased the ulama's suspicion of the king's intent to follow the lead of Kamal Ataturk. The restrictive measures taken against the Deoband-trained ulama and the imprisonment of several of their leading mem-bers appeared to the ulama analogous to the fate their counterparts suffered un-der Ataturk in Turkey. Seeing their future in danger, the clergy reacted immedi-ately. By the end of 1928, the traditional religious structure had regained its vi-tality and had asserted its historic role as custodian of religious norms and val-ues. Shortly after the adjournment of the *Loya-Jerga,* the ulama elite in Kabul began protesting against the reforms. At a gathering in the Mojaddediyya *khaneqah* in Shurbazar, the ulama discussed the situation and debated whether

---

[75.] The strong opposition expressed by the ulama on these issues was reported to have prompted an angry response from the monarch, who purportedly identified the ulama as the origin of "national calamities" and as "procurers of women." `Ali Ahmad, 18.

[76.] Musa Shafiq, Qargha, 1976.

[77.] *Tardid-i-Shayi`at-i-Batela-i-Shah-i-Makhlu`*, 17.

[78.] The theory of Russian influence over Aman-Allah, which was at the time amplified by the ulama, has been echoed in a recent work by a member of the Mojaddedi family: "Upon his return from the Soviet Union via Turkey and Iran to Afghanistan, King Aman-Allah was not the same devout Muslim. Not only had his Islamic attire changed but so had his brain, which was now expurgated of Islamic beliefs by the pernicious Leninist machine." Shah Agha Mojaddedi, 10.

to declare *fatwas* of excommunication (*kofr*) against the king and deny him *bai'at*, or to warn him first to annul the offensive social reforms. The majority deemed it advisable to proceed with the second alternative, affirming that if Aman-Allah rejected their demand an armed resistance against the regime would become necessary.[79] Sadeq Mojaddedi writes in his memoir that his request to have an audience with the king to discuss with him the ulama's concerns remained unanswered.[80] The influencial Akhudzada Hamid-Allah of Tagaw, who had supported Aman-Allah in the past, advised him to cancel radical reforms and threatened to leave Afghanistan if his demand was not met.[81] The king rejected Akhundzada's recommendation and denied him permission to leave the country.[82] Aman-Allah's abrupt response to the advice of one of the most influential religious figures in the country prompted the ulama elite in Kabul to gather forces against the regime. The clerical Mojaddedi family, particulary the Kabuli branch known as the Hazrats of Shurbazar, took the lead in invoking religious sentiment against the king.

In early September the eldest son of the Shams al-Mashayikh, Fazl al-Rahim (also known as Mia Jan Agha and Sana Ma'sum), issued a *fatwa* signed by four hundred ulama that accused Aman-Allah of reforms which violated the *shari'at*, claiming that his innovations (*bed'at*) amounted to heresy. The king, thus a heretic, was no longer to be obeyed. Mia Sana Ma'sum and his uncle Mohammad Sadeq (also known as Gol-Agha),[83] along with Qazi 'Abd al-Rahman Baiktuti,[84] Qazi Fazl al-Haqq, Qazi 'Abd al-Qader, and several other ulama carried the document to Khost, intending to inform the Mangal and Zadran tribes that the king, having violated the tenets of Islam, could no longer be obeyed. At about the same time Mawlawi Najm al-Din, an influential religious leader in northern Afghanistan, dropped the name of the king from the Friday *khotba* in Qataghan as a gesture of protest against his policies.[85]

The government reacted harshly to the activities of the Hazrats. The two Hazrats and their party of prominent ulama were arrested in Khost and brought

---

[79] Al-Mojaddedi, *Khaterat*, 4.

[80] *Ibid.*, 200.

[81] *Tardid-i-Shayi'at-i-Batela-i-Shah-i-Makhlu'*, 18.

[82] Stewart, 341-342.

[83] After the death of Shams al-Mashayikh in 1925, his younger brother Nur al-Mashayikh, then in India, became the *sajjada-neshin* ("one who sits on the prayer rug"), that is, chief successor to the leader of *tariqat-i-Mojaddediyya-i-naqshbandiyya* of Kabul; he assumed the title of Hazrat of Shurbazar. During his absence, his position was filled by his brother Mohammad Sadeq.

[84] According to 'Ali Ahmad, in an effort to preempt the ulama's challenge to the new reforms, the king had ordered Qazi 'Abd al-Rahman Baiktuti, the *qazi* of the *mahkama-i-tamiz*, or high court of appeal, who was a close associate and a *morid* of the Hazrats of Shurbazar, to issue a *fatwa* supporting unveiling and women's rights. The *qazi* had asked five days, during which he consulted with the Hazrats of Shurbazar, who advised him to flee with them to the Southern Province. 'Ali Ahmad, 29.

[85] Shah-Agha Mojaddedi, 14.

back to Kabul. The Hazrat Sadeq Mojaddedi and his nephew, along with Qazi `Abd al-Rahman and approximately thirty-five leading ulama, were imprisoned. Among them were Molla `Abd-Allah Wardaki, who had been sentenced to death after the Khost rebellion but was later reprieved; Sardar Mohammad `Osman Khan, a noted theologian linked to the Hazrats through marriage, and his son Gholam Faruq; and ten ulama from the Southern Province and about fifteen from Kohistan, including Hazrat `Abd al-Ahad, brother-in-law of the Hazrat of Shurbazar, a man of considerable influence in Kohdaman and Kohistan, and Molla Dad Mohammad of Logar, who was charged with carrying on propaganda in the suburbs of Kabul. Another member of the Mojaddedi family, the revered Hazrat of Charbagh, was arrested on the border near Parachinar.[86] The latter, outraged by the king's reforms, declared that Afghanistan under Aman-Allah was unfit for a pious Muslim.

Meanwhile, a box of leaflets authored by Indian ulama, which denounced the king's decision to move the weekly holiday to Thursday, was confiscated at Dakka by customs officials,[87] giving the government a reason to suspect a link between the protest of the Hazrats and foreign intrigue against the government. Because of their connection with the Deoband school in India, Deobandi ulama came under increased surveillance by the government. Mawlawi Fazl al-Rabbi, a noted Deobandi, was subsequently charged with having a hand in the Hazrat Shurbazar affair and was imprisoned.

In mid-September a military tribunal sentenced Qazi `Abd al-Rahman Baik-tuti and four other ulama to death and the two Hazrats to life in prison for the crime of national treachery (khiyanat-i-melli). Meanwhile, a warrant was issued for the arrest of the influential Molla of Tagaw, who was suspected of being involved in the Hazrats' conspiracy, but the forces sent for the arrest of the Molla were ambushed by the Tagawis. The Hazrats of Shurbazar were sentenced to life imprisonment but were saved from capital punishment through the intervention of `Olya Hazrat, Aman-Allah's mother, who told him that if he killed the Hazrats, he would have no chance to continue his reign.[88] However, according to Hazarat Sadeq Mojaddedi, the king postponed orders for his and his nephew's execution until the return to Afghanistan of Nur al-Mashayikh, his elder brother. Having learned about Aman-Allah's secret plan, Hazarat Sadeq Mojaddedi sent a letter with a devoted morbid to Nur al-Mashayikh, requesting that he delay his return from India.[89]

Aman-i-Afghan printed full coverage of the imprisonment of the Hazrats, providing arguments to justify the arrests:

> From the onset of his reign, His Majesty Aman-Allah Ghazi had one main objective: to free the nation from external dominance and inter-

---

[86.] *Times of India*, Sept. 13, 1928.
[87.] MADK, no. 91, Sept. 27, 1928.
[88.] Shah-Agha Mojaddedi, 15-16.
[89] F. Ghani Mojaddedi, 254.

nal oppression. In the past ten years His Majesty has concentrated his energy on fighting against despotism and arbitrary practices by limiting his own power as well as that of government officials through legislation.[90]

The editorial added that domestic oppressors included the *qazis*, who exercised unlimited power in legal matters by monopolizing the right to determine the *ta'zirat* punishments. The main purpose of the Penal Code (*Nezam-nama-i-Jaza*), it went on, was to determine a punishment for each crime in order to limit the *qazis'* discretion and eradicate a major source of corruption. According to the editorial, the transfer of the power of *ta'zirat* to the state was by no means unprecedented in Islamic tradition; the Ottoman Sultans and many other rulers have done likewise. But those who had lost the power, wished to restore it. They began to poison the people's minds by making false accusations, claiming that the *nezam-nama* violated the *shari'at*. The editorial claimed further that their agitation generated the rebellion in the Southern Province in 1924. False religious scholars took advantage of that situation to alter the *nezam-nama*s during the *Loya-Jerga* of 1924, a *jerga* composed mostly of *khans*, *sheikhs*, and *molla*s with a history of exploiting the masses. They naturally supported self-interested views of the law.

In the recent *Loya-Jerga*, the paper continued, the king's right to determine *ta'zirat* and monetary fines was restored, as was the power to pardon a criminal after signs of "reform and repentance" were observed. Angered by these changes, Qazi 'Abd al-Rahman Baiktuti, president of the Revision Court (*mahkama-i-tamiz*), and his *pir*, Mohammad Sadeq, went secretly to the Southern Province to incite the people against the government.[91] They were thereupon arrested.

Aman-i-Afghan of September 8, 1928, stated that the opposition of the clergy was based on self-interest and was directed against the *Loya-Jerga*'s decision to fix penalties for specific crimes and thereby limit the power of *qazis*. The ulama claimed that religious law does not sanction determining penalties for specific crimes before the offense is committed. The introduction of this provision to the *nezam-nama* was one of the causes of the Khost rebellion, and it was therefore dropped by the *Loya-Jerga* of 1924. The opposition had now revived because of the reaffirmation of this rule by the recent *Loya-Jerga*.

On October 7, Qazi 'Abd al-Rahman was executed on charges of treason, as were his son-in-law Qazi Fazl al-Haqq, his son Qazi 'Abd al-Hannan, and Molla 'Abd al-Qadir, a relative.[92] Meanwhile, the Afghan consul at Bombay received orders to secure the return of Hazrat Fazl 'Omar Mojaddedi to Kabul by any means possible.

[90.] *Aman-i-Afghan*, 16 *Sonbola* 1307/Sept. 8, 1928.

[91.] *Ibid.*

[92.] *Ibid.*, 20 *Mizan* 1307/Oct. 13, 1928.

Shock at the Hazrat's arrest spread throughout the country and across the border. The weekly *Sarhad* of Peshawar (September 25, 1928) expressed surprise that no one had raised a finger against the arrest of such an influential man as the Hazrat of Shurbazar and commented that no one dared to speak because of fear of incurring the king's reprisal.

These executions and imprisonments, however, cost the regime whatever support it had remaining. The policeman sent to arrest the Hazrat of Shurbazar cursed himself, according to the newspaper *Anis*, for his act, symbolic of the reaction of the police and military. The paper commented, however, that "had the man been educated, he would have at once known that the Hazrat Saheb was really an offender, and he would not have uttered such an expression."[93]

Anxiety began to escalate after the execution and imprisonment of leading clergymen. Religious protests against the king surfaced in different parts of the country with declarations of *fatwa* by the ulama, denouncing Aman-Allah as a heretic no longer fit to rule a Muslim nation. Such extreme measures could be taken against a ruler only when the political order was weak and public opinion was easily aroused against the government. The government reforms announced in the months of September and October had clearly alienated the majority of the population.

General Dissatisfaction over Reforms

General discontent in the countryside led to the success of the Islamic insurgence against the regime. In a society where modernization is introduced from the top, "the authority of the leader depends on his ablility to assure continued acceptance by social groups whose norms are undergoing significant changes."[94] Several authors have argued that authority ceases when directives from a leader are no longer accepted as legitimate.[95] In Afghanistan, where tribal democracy dominated and obedience to the central authority was in some areas only nominal, sweeping changes introduced from above along with increasing Western influence created deep resentment and resulted in a rapid breakdown of what central authority existed.

The government's efforts to introduce social reforms and cultural and behavioral patterns of foreign origin, such as the compulsory wearing of hats, and to introduce new modes of greeting, such as taking off one's hat in greeting, threatened local customs and the Islamic social order. Generally viewed as Christian ideas adopted by the king during the European tour, the reforms provoked native sensibilities throughout the country. The memory of Afghanistan's long struggle against Westerners was too strong in peoples' minds for them to allow reforms of Western origin. Unnecessary changes such as making Thursday, instead of Friday, the weekly day off and the compulsory wearing of Euro-

---

93. NAI, FPD, 4-F, 1928, no. 4062.
94. Lewis, "The Social Limits of Politically Induced Change", 2.
95. Merton, chap. 9; Easton, chap. 18; Barnard, chap. 12.

pean clothes had no significance to the people and only irritated them. Even the liberals considered the king's strategy of change grossly imprudent. According to Habibi, `Abd al-Rahman Ludin confided to a close friend that if the king's excesses were not stopped and the arbitrary power of the monarchy remained unchecked, the country would face a major disaster.[96]

The gap between the king and the grassroots population grew wider as rapid changes in the capital upset the balance between urban and peasant populations; the majority of the peasants were left outside the mainstream of social and political currents in Kabul. Dissatisfaction among the rural and tribal populations revolved around several issues: compulsory military service, now three years; compulsory wearing of suits and hats; the regime's positions on women and family matters. Due to the high illiteracy rate, it was impossible for the majority of the people to understand the purpose of the reforms or the monarch's intentions. Most saw in the costly reform program nothing more than destruction of their traditional way of life.

Tax increases and administrative abuses, however, were the major causes of discontent. Before his departure to Europe, the king ordered that tax arrears from previous years be collected immediately. During his absence, vigorous tax-collecting activity began in Bamyan, Tagaw, and Kohdaman, areas densely populated by poor peasantry, causing much suffering and anger.[97] The purchase of arms and equipment for the newly established factories, plans for the expansion of education and other development projects in 1928, and the cost of the royal tour proved burdensome to the state treasury. A massive increase in tax levies resulted. The state bore down heavily upon its main pillar of fiscal support, land revenue and livestock taxes (*maliyat-i-mawashi*). According to Gregorian, by 1928 taxes on horses and donkeys had risen 400 percent and taxes on land, 300 to 400 percent.[98] In addition, the king proposed that every Afghan male over fifteen pay five rupees and every official a month's salary in order to finance arms purchased from Europe. Heavy taxes and corruption in the administration, according to two eyewitness reporters, `Ali Mohammad and Faiz Mohammad Kateb, were the primary causes of discontentment in the countryside.[99] According to Wild, "People were fleeced of high taxes for the support by cunning old rascals in Kabul who revelled in the invention of new details to enrich their pockets."[100] In the summer of 1928, the British *chargé d'affaires* at Kabul wrote to London that as a result of high customs and the introduction of a new monetary system, the economic situation in Afghanistan had reached crisis

---

[96.] Habibi, *Jonbesh-i-Mashrutiyyat dar Afghanistan*, 233-34.
[97.] Khalili, *`Ayyari az Khorasan*, 79. Quoted in Nazif Shahrani, "State Building and Social Fragmentation in Afghanistan," 49.
[98.] Gregorian, 270.
[99.] Kateb, *Ketab-i-Tazakkor-i-Enqelab*, 1; Ali Mohammad, 22.
[100.] Wild, 50.

proportions. He speculated that if the king stayed a few months longer, "he will return only to find another established to his throne."[101]

The reforms that caused the most excitement in the rural areas were those pertaining to family law and women.[102] Changes in the status of women implied alterations in the whole system of traditions surrounding gender and the family, the basis of the social system, and threatened the traditional mores regarding tribal loyalties and family ties. The emotional response to such threats took on extreme proportions when the ulama equated women's emancipation with rejection of the Islamic social order. The ulama argued that changes in women's roles could have a grave impact on the existing social order, and they pointed to the emancipation of women as a sign of moral decay, a threat to the patriarchal structure, and a violation of *namus* (the idealized honor of women in relation to the family, and in this case, to society as a whole). Their denunciations were a major factor in encouraging mass protests against the women's emancipation movement and in arousing the people against the regime. Afghanistan's male-dominated society, where prejudice against women had been shaped over centuries, was not ready to look upon women as equals with men.

Even in Kabul many husbands who saw their traditional dominant roles in jeopardy were offended by the government's position on women's issues. These men took literally a joking remark by the king that he would provide women the weapon to shoot interfering husbands. Many husbands, angered by the king's remarks, forbade their wives to attend meetings.[103] In the months of October and November, the women's emancipation movement was the principal issue during nationwide clergy-backed riots. In mid-September, the British agent in Kurram (Khyber) reported that the Afridis greatly resented the unveiling of women.[104] Rumors were afloat in the frontier region that Aman-Allah had lost his sense of sound reasoning and that his moral and intellectual faculties had deteriorated.[105]

Another rumor emerged in the tribal region to the effect that the government required citizens to either send their daughters to Turkey for higher education or pay a fine.[106] The passing of a group of young girls through the tribal zone on their way to Turkey in October confirmed these suspicions, igniting resentment among the Shinwaris. An order requiring the tribes to send their daughters to school in Kabul incited them further.[107] Meanwhile, enemies of the king used unveiling to further disparage the image of the royal family. A picture showing the queen and other royal ladies in low-cut European evening dresses was cir-

---

[101.] Quoted in Agabekov, 160.
[102.] See for example, M. Anis, 40; Khalili, `Aiyar-i Az Khorasan, 96; Kateb, *Ketab-i-Tazakkor-i-Enqelab*, 2; `Ali Ahmad, 18.
[103.] `Ali Ahmad, 18.
[104.] IOR, L/P&S/10/1290, 5, tel. nos. 562-PN, 1847-5, Sept. 9 and 13 , 1928.
[105.] IOR, L/P&S/10/1285, K132, Simla Sept. 13, 1928.
[106.] `Ali Ahmad, 25; F. Ghani Mojaddedi, 257.
[107.] Humphrys' report, IOR, L/P&S/10/1289, P53, Pt. 6, 1928.

culated in November, making the queen "the very soul and symbol of the hated changes."[108]

Another important source of general discontent was the length of military conscription. The initial opposition against conscription had been suppressed by 1927. In fact, through the efforts of Sardar Shah Mahmud (Nader Khan's brother), who was the governor of Jalalabad and supportive of cooperative ulama, military service had become "quite popular" in the area.[109] But in the *Loya-Jerga*, the king announced an increase in the period of military service from two to three years and that there would be no exceptions. The Shinwaris and the Mohmands considered themselves a privileged warrior class and viewed military service as a religious duty during the war, but resented the government's enforcement of that duty. Discontent in the tribal area was compounded by Aman-Allah's failure to settle the question of territorial independence for the Pashtun tribes along Durand Line with the British. According to Agabekov, on his arrival in Kabul the king was received by a delegation of "independent tribes," who asked him immediately if he had a satisfactory guarantee from London about the independence of their territory.[110] Disappointed at not receiving a satisfactory response from the king, the deputies "left in a huff...[and] their rancor ceased not from this time to grow."[111]

OUTBREAK OF CLERGY-INSPIRED REVOLTS AND EROSION OF THE REGIME'S LEGITIMACY

By November 1928, King Aman-Allah had alienated many of the high ulama. In contrast to circumstances surrounding the Khost Rebellion, in which the majority of the high ulama detached themselves from the dissident *molla*s, this time the opposition was spearheaded by the high clergy in the capital and gradually attracted the ulama of all ranks in a united front against the government. The ulama were united in their demand for total allegiance to principles of Hanafi law and their denunciation of the king as the abolisher of the *shari`at* and hence unsuitable to rule a Muslim nation.

In November the historical alliance between the tribes and the ulama was revived. Religiously inspired uprisings rolled across the country in two waves.

The Shinwari Uprising

The first major revolt was started by the Sangu Khail and `Alishir Khail Shinwar tribes. On November 14, under the leadership of Mohammad `Alam and Mohammad Afzal, a former army officer in Jalalabad, the Shinwaris attacked and

---

[108.] *Daily News* (London), Oct. 19, 1928.
[109.] MADK, no. 55, July 26, 1926.
[110.] Agabekov, 163.
[111.] *Ibid.*

looted Pish Bolak and Achin and cut the telegraph lines between Jalalabad and Dakka, a border city between Afghanistan and British India.

By the end of November, the rebels reached Jalalabad and burned the winter royal palace (Seraj al-'Emarat) and other government buildings. Meanwhile, inflammatory pamphlets signed by Mohammad 'Alam Shinwari were being circulated among Afridis, Mohmands, and Shinwaris. The pamphlets accused the king of repeatedly violating Islamic precepts, including the abolition of the *hejab*, sending young women to Europe (meaning Turkey), changing the weekly day off from Friday to Thursday, forcing government officials to have only one wife and divorce others, abolishing polygamy, opening cinemas, theaters, and other places of amusement, encouraging women to cut their hair and expose their arms and breasts, and formulating codes and regulations that contradicted the *shari'at*. The king was also accused of uttering words disrespectful to the Prophet during the *Loya-Jerga*. According to the pamphlet, well-known ulama of Afghanistan had declared the king an infidel (*kafer*).[112]

The immediate causes of the outbreak were the government's attempts to enforce registration with identity cards (*tazkera*), the arrest of a local clergyman, the son of the highly revered Sufi of Faqirabad known as Hafez Saheb,[113] and the spread of a rumor among the Shinwaris that they would be required to agree to send their daughters to Turkey or pay a fine of 500 rupees to the government.[114]

Although the Shinwari revolt was a tribal uprising, the institutions of Islam became the central force behind revolutionary activities. Rebel forces in Shinwar gathered about the Hafez Saheb of Faqirabad, the *pir* of the Shinwaris and an irreconcilable opponent of the regime. Other religious leaders were Akhundzadas Mohammad Sharif, 'Abd-Allah, 'Abd al-Wahid, Fazl al-Rahim, and Mawlawi Mohammad Tayyeb.[115]

First perceived as a local religiously inspired movement, the revolt was not taken seriously in Kabul, but as the Shinwaris made advances toward Jalalabad, the government noted with alarm that within a month the protest had developed into a general uprising. Two regiments were sent against the Shinwaris under 'Abd al-Wakil Nuristani and Mahmud Yawar. The Shinwaris defeated the government forces and captured the two army commanders.[116] Soon afterwards the government dispatched the minister of foreign affairs, Gholam Seddiq Charkhi, whose father had suppressed the first Shinwari Rebellion in 1888; 'Ali Ahmad, former governor of Kabul; Shir Ahmad, former president of the State Council; and several others to the Eastern Province to negotiate with the Shinwaris. At the same time, Aman-Allah cancelled some of his most unpopular reforms to win the ulama to his side during the negotiations with the rebel leaders. Friday

---

[112] IOR, L/P&S/10/1287, 4, P6351, Nov. 27, 1928; Stewart, 431-433.
[113] IOR, L/P&S/10/1137, P6967, no. 23, Nov. 20, 1928.
[114] 'Ali Ahmad, 25.
[115] NAI, F-309, 1928, no. 23, Nov. 20, 1928.
[116] Ghobar, 820.

was reintroduced as the weekly holiday, girls' schools were closed, and regulations concerning child marriage, polygamy, unveiling, and the compulsory wearing of suits and hats were abolished. Meanwhile the Hazrats of Shurbazar, along with a half dozen religious leaders who had been jailed for inciting riots, were released after the government extracted from them letters in which they repented for past deeds and promised to never again engage in any act of malice against the government.[117] By early December, the senior Hazrat of Shurbazar, Mohammad Sadeq Mojaddedi, was negotiating with the Molla of Tagaw on the government's behalf.

By canceling certain reforms at this time, the government was able to coax a group of ulama in the capital to support the regime again. On November 26, 1928, twenty clergymen called for allegiance to the king, issuing a *fatwa* denouncing the Shinwaris as rebels.[118] Mawlawi Kamawi, who at the beginning had staunchly opposed the reforms, now softened his position and demonstrated a willingness to cooperate with the regime. Kamawi wrote a letter, suggesting that the king call a *jerga* similar to the one convened in 1924 in Paghman. He recommended that influential religious leaders of the Eastern Province, such as the Molla of Chaknawur, the Naqib of Charbagh, the Hazrat of Charbagh, and Sayyid-i-Khaksar, be invited to Kabul to discuss government policies and help remove misunderstandings in order to stop the rebellion. He mentioned at the end that he himself was ready to help.[119] But when Aman-Allah invited the ulama of the Eastern Provinces, they all claimed to be in ill health and did not attend.[120] The king sent a message to the Molla of Chaknawur requesting that he "do everything in his power to effect a peace settlement."[121] The Molla of Chaknawur, despite his refusal to appear in Kabul in November, agreed to intercede on the government's behalf on account of the king's cancellation of some of the most unpopular reforms and on the condition that the king repeal all measures relating to female education and offer amnesty for the rebels.[122] Meanwhile, he declined the Utman Khail Mohmand's invitation to leave the Afghan territory until an obvious change was noticed in the king's attitude towards the *mollas*.[123] The Hajji of Turangzai was also willing to support the government. In mid-December he sent two hundred Safis and Musa Khail Qandaharis under his son Padshah-Gol to assist the king.[124]

On December 4 and 5, a *jerga* was held at Hadda, with Shinwari, Mohmand, Khugiyani, and Afridi leaders. The Madrasa of Hadda was the most influential in the country and was where most of the influential ulama of Afghanistan, in-

---

[117] IOR, L/P&S/10/1285, G184, 6311; AWSW collections, Appendix J (4).

[118] IOR/P&S/10/1288, 1928-29, pt. 4, no. 4421-P-S, Dec. 20, 1928.

[119] See the copy of the letter in Appendix J (5), AWSW collection.

[120] NAI, 309-F, no. 21.

[121] *The Times of London*, Dec. 11, 1928; IOR, L/P&S/10/1287, pt. 3, P6652, 1928.

[122] NWFP Intelligence Bureau, IOR, L/P&S/10/1137, P152, no. 24, Dec. 8, 1928.

[123] *Ibid.*

[124] IOR, L/P&S/10/1287, pt. 3, P6755, 1928.

cluding the Molla of Chaknawur, the Molla of Tagaw, and the Padshah of Is-lampur, had been trained under the renowned Akhundzada of Hadda. The shrine to which the *madrasa* was attached was the meeting place of all the ulama of the Eastern and Southern provinces, the site of many important religious and political discussions during the first quarter of the twentieth century. The meeting was attended as well by several government officials including Foreign Minister Gholam Seddiq, Shir Ahmad Khan, and Mohammad Yosuf Khan. The dissident tribes demanded the abolition of all reforms, including compulsory conscription, the recall of Afghan female students from abroad, the abolition of female education, and no interference with the functions of the ulama. The representatives in the *jerga* took an oath to remain united, to accept no bribes from the authorities, and to make no separate peace with the government.[125]

The Kohistan (or Saqawi) Uprising

What made the situation difficult for the government was a simultaneous outbreak of clergy-backed disturbances in the north. Dissent had been simmering for some time in Kohistan, Kohdaman, and Tagaw. Riots in the north resulted from high taxes and administrative abuses. During the king's absence, the situation became alarming enough to impel `Olya Hazrat, the king's mother, to take the matter into her own hands by personally meeting with the notables of the Northern Province (Kohdaman, Kohistan, Tagaw, Nejraw, Riza Kohistan, Panjshir, and Ghorband) and listening to their grievances. According to Popalzai, by personally attending to the complaints of the dissidents, `Olya Hazrat was able to deter rioters from expanding their activities.[126] Social unrest in the Northern Province (*Samt-i-Shamali*), however, had gradually prepared the way for the emergence of Habib-Allah Kalakani, known as Bacha-i-Saqaw (son of the water carrier),[127] as a local hero who harried the government after the king's return.

Born in 1890 in Kalakan (forty-one kilometers north of Kabul), Habib-Allah had participated in the War of Independence as a soldier in the Parachinar regiment under Sepahsalar Nadir Khan and was afterwards recruited in the *Qet`a-i-Namuna* regiment, organized by Jamal Pasha. Information about the early activities of Habib-Allah is too scant to allow a rigorous analysis of his political motives. Sources disagree about his whereabouts before he became a bandit.[128]

[125.] NAI, FPD, 309-F, 1928, no. 44.

[126.] Fofalzai, *Safarha-i-Ghazi Aman-Allah Shah*, 219-221.

[127.] Habib-Allah's father had become known as *saqaw* for supplying water to the warriors during the Second Anglo-Afghan War.

[128.] According to one version, following this incident Habib-Allah fled to British India and spent three years in Solaiman Saray in Peshawar where he ran a tea house, but was arrested for breaking into a shop. It is in connection with his stay in Peshawar that it has been suggested that he had been used by the British against Aman-Allah. But according to Shah-Agha Mojaddedi, after killing the soldier, Habib-Allah fled to Parachinar and opened a tea house there.

We know that Habib-Allah and his close collaborator, Sayyid Hosain, had established a strong band of bandits in Kohistan during the king's absence and had begun harassing traffickers between the capital and the northern regions. Reports of banditry by Habib-Allah Kalakani and his gang increased in the months of September and October. By November, Habib-Allah had become known as "the hero or the villain of every fantastic tale."[129] During the revolt in Shinwar, the operations of Bacha-i-Saqaw became bolder. By then he had gained a reputation as "the defender of the oppressed," akin to Robin Hood.

Habib-Allah's movement in Kohistan did not start as an Islamic movement. Nor did it begin as an anti-Pashtun Tajek uprising, as some recent works by Afghan writers have attempted to show. Just like the revolt in Shinwar, the Saqawi uprising was provoked by local grievances of a nonreligious nature that gradually assumed religious overtones as the local ulama assumed a leadership role in the movement. A lack of information makes it difficult to understand various nuances of the rebellion in Kohistan and to determine whether Habib-Allah tried to cultivate the support of the ulama to achieve his ambitions or whether the ulama used Habib-Allah as an instrument to overthrow Aman-Allah. Two books written in recent years deal with Habib-Allah's life and activities: 1) `Ayyar-i az Khorasan*, written by the Afghan poet-scholar Khalil-Allah Khalili, which, although semifictional and biased, provides important eyewitness information about the activities of Habib-Allah; and 2) *Habib-Allah Khadem-i-Din-i-Rasul-Allah*, written by Shir Agha Mojaddedi, which contains valuable information about Habib-Allah's connections with the ulama of Kohistan, particularly the Mojaddedis. According to Shir-Agha Mojaddedi, in November 1928, a secret meeting was held in the house of `Abd-Allah Jan Mojaddedi between Habib-Allah and Bozorg Jan Mojaddedi (also known as Molla Bozorg). Bozorg Jan Mojaddedi, who was a *khalifa* of the Akhundzada of Tagaw, communicated to Habib-Allah that religious leaders at the beginning supported Aman-Allah because he declared *jehad* and launched a successful campaign against the British and that he himself was among those who endorsed him, but after returning from Soviet Russia Aman-Allah abandoned Islam and became increasingly aggressive toward the ulama. He mentioned the banishment of Hazrat Nur al-Mashayikh to India and the imprisonment of Mohammad Sadeq and Mia Sana Ma`sum Mojaddedi as two of Aman-Allah's most brazen actions against the ulama. To this end, Molla Bozorg announced that Aman-Allah had lost his legitimacy and could not be obeyed as a Muslim ruler, *uli al-amr*, and promised to support Habib-Allah so long as his actions concurred with the *shari`at*.[130] In a similar meeting, convened a few weeks later, decisions were made for a general uprising against the regime. The king's older brother, Hayyat-Allah `Azz al-Dowla, was allegedly present at the last meeting, but Sardar `Enayat-Allah Khan, the former Mo`in al-Saltana and the king's other older brother, who was also ex-

---

[129.] Letter from L. W. H. D. Best, secretary of British Legation, Kabul, to Humphrys, Dec. 31, 1928. NAI, enc. no. 1, des. no. 4., Jan. 5, 1928.

[130.] Shah-Agha Mojaddedi, 37-39.

pected to attend the meeting, did not show up.[131] Subsequently, the Mollas Shams-Allah and `Ali Shakardarayi initiated religious propaganda against Aman-Allah in Kohdaman and Kohistan.[132] Molla Bozorg Mojaddedi and his cousin, `Abd-Allah Jan, then traveled from village to village to spread the propaganda and incite the population against the government. They were soon joined in this effort by two other members of the Mojaddedi priestly family, Shams al-Haqq Mojaddedi, a highly influential cleric in Kohistan, Makhdum Ahmad Mojaddedi, and Mawlawi Mohammad Rafiq Jamalaghayi.[133] The clergy issued *fatwa*s justifying the antigovernment insurrection in Kohistan under the leadership of Habib-Allah as a *jehad* in defense of Islam in Afghanistan.

By combining local grievances with the local clergy's condemnation of government on religious grounds and by employing religious idioms that the rural population identified with, Habib-Allah evoked a sense of religious obligation for the overthrow of the regime. By November he had gained the support of all religious leaders in Kohistan, including the son of the influential Molla of Tagaw, and had established himself as the defender of Islamic values and a folk hero of Kohistan. Having gathered a large force of local dissidents under his command, Habib-Allah began to harass local authorities.

The events in Kohistan were not taken seriously until mid-November, when Habib-Allah Kalakani blocked the main road to the north between Kabul and Charikar. The government force dispatched to crush Habib-Allah and his gang, despite an initial claim of victory, made no headway against the raiders. Later in the month, the government official in Charikar found himself beleaguered by the rebel forces and was forced to agree to an armistice with Habib-Allah, promising him a position in the army in return for helping the government troops against the Shinwari rebels.

On November 8, Habib-Allah's forces attacked government posts in Sara-i-Khwaja, cut telephone lines, and closed the road between Kabul and Kohistan. On the next day he proceeded toward the capital. At this juncture Shams al-Haqq Mojaddedi issued a *fatwa* declaring that waging war without the order of an amir was against the *shari`at*. The *khotba* was read in Habib-Allah's name, and in recognition of his great service to religion, he was given the title *Khadem-i-Din-i-Rasul-Allah* (the servant of the religion of the Prophet of God).[134] The powerful Molla of Tagaw endorsed the nomination of Habib-Allah as amir.

---

[131]. Shah-Agha Mojaddedi, 42. According to Mojaddedi, the people of Kohistan later refused to acknowledge `Enayat-Allah Khan as Aman-Allah's successor for not keeping his promise to attend this meeting. *Ibid.*, 43.

[132]. *Ibid.*, 37-38.

[133]. *Ibid.*, 44-45.

[134]. Shir-Agha Mojaddedi, 46.

EVENTS LEADING TO AMAN-ALLAH'S ABDICATION

In the month of December discontent and unrest reached crises proportions as religious opposition to the regime spiraled. It was obvious that the relationship between the king and the clergy had been damaged beyond repair. Even those who were cooperative did not wholeheartedly support the government or jeopardize their relationship with the opposition. The *fatwa* of November 26 and the abolition of unpopular reforms carried no weight with most ulama; they attributed the reaction of the urban ulama to pressure from the government.

Between early December and mid-January several meetings were called in the Eastern Province to discuss the political situation. In the absence of an elected body that could be held responsible, the king was the focus of religious opposition and was held solely responsible for injudicious policies. The king's conduct, considered to contradict the *shari`at*, was deemed apostasy. His policies were characterized as *bed`at* (innovations amounting to heresy), contradicting his claim of allegiance to the *shari`at*. The ulama did not, however, agree unanimously on the issue of *takfir* (excommunication from the Muslim faith), which could lead to *khal`* (impeachment). Lobbying by Gholam Seddiq, the foreign minister, persuaded several ulama including the Molla of Chaknawur, the Hazrat of Charbagh, and Naqib of Charbagh to withhold their opinions in light of the abrogation of unpopular reforms, which they interpreted as repentance. Until mid-December, the Molla of Chaknawur was neutral. *The Times of London* reported that the Molla of Chaknawur held the key to the situation and that he had not made a declaration yet, "but his entry into the insurrection on the side of the rebels would result in a wide extension of disaffection."[135] Extremists argued, however, that as the king had already acted contrary to Islam and was thus an infidel, his repentance at this point was meaningless.[136]

On December 10, the British embassy staff reported to the viceroy as follows:

> Conservative leaders are scarcely likely now to allow *locus panilentiac* short of virtual abdication of power if not of the throne itself. Amanullah's failure to profit by lessons taught him by the Khost Rebellion must in their eyes stamp him as incorrigible.[137]

Meanwhile Habib-Allah Kalakani took advantage of the government's preoccupation with the situation in Shinwar to advance toward Kabul and demoralize the capital. News traveled among the two rebel groups by traders such as the rice dealers of Laghman and by means of ulama networks in the Eastern and Northern provinces. The binding force was the aged Akhundzada of Tagaw, the influential religious leader in the Northern Province, who as one of the disciples

---

[135] *The Times of London*, Dec. 10, 1928.
[136] *Tardid-i-Shayi`at-i-Padshah-i-Makhlu`*, 20.
[137] NAI, FPD, n. 309-F, 189, Dec. 9, 1928.

of the Molla of Hadda was linked with virtually all influential ulama of the Eastern Province.

The government's efforts to settle with the Kohistanis had only strengthened the position of Habib-Allah. His advance toward Kabul became difficult to prevent as his followers increased day by day. On December 14, the Kohistani tribesmen under the leadership of Habib-Allah, Sayyid Hasan, and Amir Mohammad Khan of Tagaw launched a surprise attack on Bagh-i-Bala in the north of Kabul and occupied two important military outposts. The situation became threatening enough that Humphrys dispatched an urgent note to London, requesting means of transportation to evacuate the women and children of the British legation in Kabul. Although the dissidents retreated after Habib-Allah was wounded during an aerial attack, in a matter of weeks, the Kohistani forces prepared themselves for a renewed assault on the capital.

For reasons still unknown, by the end of December the Molla of Chaknawur, Aman-Allah's only remaining supporter, had changed his position and had joined the opposition.[138] According to a report from the North-West Frontier Province, he had joined other ulama of the Eastern Province in declaring the king an apostate (kafer).[139] He wrote to the ulama in Kabul that "nothing short of the dethronement of the king will satisfy the tribes."[140] The Hazrat of Shurbazar (Mohammad Sadeq Gol Agha) had failed in his efforts to deter the Molla of Tagaw from fighting against the regime, but his efforts were only halfhearted to begin with.

When the situation became exceedingly dangerous for the regime, the king offered to negotiate with rebel leaders on the basis of total withdrawal of all reforms. The ban on foreign and Deoband ulama was removed, conscription was abolished, and mohtasebs were appointed to enforce the prohibition on drinking. The king also removed restrictions on the pir-morid system.[141] Late in December Aman-Allah called an ad hoc meeting of 201 influential leaders, including Mohammadzai elders, ulama of the capital, and several khans. The Aman-i-Afghan reported the king's decision to institute a senate of fifty members with legislative powers, drawn from the royal family, tribal heads, and ulama.[142] On January 6, the regime offered further concessions. Meanwhile, the king made a special request of the Padshah of Islampur, who had been restrained in Kabul since the Safi revolt of 1926, to negotiate with the rebels on the government's behalf. The

---

[138]. IOR/P&S/10/1287, 3, P6911, 1928.

[139]. Telegram from North-West Frontier to New Delhi, Dec. 3, 1928, IOR, L/P&S/10/1287, 3, P6513, 1928.

[140]. Telegram from Humphrys to the British secretary of state for foreign affairs in India, Dec. 2, 1928, IOR, L/P&S/10/1287, P53, 4, 1929.

[141]. Telegram dated Jan. 7, 1929, Humphrys to secretary of state for foreign affairs, L/P&S/10/1287, 119.

[142]. IOR, L/P&S/10/1287, P225, 3, 1929.

aged Padshah of Islampur, one of the most influential religious leaders in early twentieth century Afghanistan, died of typhoid in January on this mission.[143]

The Crisis of Legitimacy and Abdication of Aman-Allah

The new concessions completely destoryed Aman-Allah's dream of Afghanistan as a modern state, but he felt the offer was necessary to stop the rioting. Western dress, women's rights, and restrictions against polygamy, child marriage, and compulsory conscription were abolished by royal decrees. The ulama were given veto power over state legislation. However, two months of violence had so hardened the position of the regime's adversaries that Aman-Allah's attempts to reestablish Islamic order proved insufficient to restore the regime's legitimacy. Rather than being accepted as evidence of true compromise, the king's concessions were seen as a last-ditch effort to save the throne. Opposition forces became insolent in their demands. On December 29, Gholam Seddiq Charkhi returned to Kabul with a manifesto by the Shinwaris dictating the following terms for settlement: Aman-Allah's divorce of Queen Soraya, banishment of Tarzi's family, abolition of all foreign legations except the British, abolition of the new codes of law, reduction of taxes, and involvement of the ulama in government affairs.

All the cards were on the side of those seeking to overthrow Aman-Allah. Even if the ulama backed down, the political interest groups would not let the opportunity to turn the situation to their own ends slip away. As Aman-Allah's position weakened, some important high officials in the government, certain army officers, and, according to one account, even the king's older brother `Azz al-Dowla,[144] began making private accommodations with Habib-Allah in hopes of political gains in the aftermath of the rebellion. Even the Regent was suspected of supporting Bacha-i-Saqaw. In the end, however, Aman-Allah's abdication was forced not by the uprising of the Shinwaris in the East but by pressures from Kohistan. On January 13, a group of ulama of Kohistan, headed by the son of Akhundzada of Tagaw, met with Kohistani forces in Qal'a-i-Hosain Kot, the former residence of Mostawfi al-Mamalek, whom Aman-Allah had had executed for treason early in his reign. Only twenty miles north of Kabul, the area was a center of anti-Amani activity. An oath of allegiance to Habib-Allah Kalakani was also affirmed by Akhundzada of Tagaw, who proclaimed Habib-Allah *amir al-momenin*, commander-in-chief of the faithful, and urged a march toward Kabul. The meeting adjourned with a recitation of verses from the Qur'an.[145]

[143.] *Anis*, Jan. 4, 1929. The Padshah of Islampur was succeeded by his son Sayyid `Abbas Padshah.

[144.] According to Shir-Agha Mojaddedi, a secret meeting was held between `Azz al-Dawla and Habib-Allah Kalakani in the house of `Abd-Allah Jan Mojaddedi. See Shah-Agha Mojaddedi, 41.

[145.] Khalili, `*Ayyar-i az Khorasan*, 126-131.

By the next day Kohistani forces numbering about 16,000 occupied the key strongholds around the capital. The most important factor in Habib-Allah's rapid advance was the weakness of the defense forces in the capital. With a large body of government troops sent to Jalalabad against the Shinwaris, the capital was left vulnerable to the attacks of the Kohistani raiders. Dissatisfaction in the army made the situation worse for the government. The discontented, underpaid soldiers often treated brutally by high officers, had neither the will nor the strength to fight against the rebel forces. The desertion *en masse* of the troops during the assault of the Kohistani dissidents on Kabul was the result of Aman-Allah's neglect of the army, confirmed by his oft-quoted remark that his "age was one of the pen not of the sword."[146]

On January 14, when Habib-Allah was at the gates of Kabul, the king abdicated in favor of his older brother Sardar `Enayat-Allah Khan and left for Qandahar. An hour later, Sardar `Enayat-Allah was crowned king, but his authority was immediately challenged by Habib-Allah, who occupied Kabul and proclaimed himself the new ruler.

[146.] This phrase is referred to Aman-Allah's address on the occasion of `Id-i-Ozha (Feast of Sacrifice) of 1923. See Adamec, *Afghanistan's Foreign Affairs*, 81.

7

AFTERMATH OF THE ABDICATION

I make a solemn declaration to the effect that God is one and Moham-mad is his servant and his Prophet. Oh my brothers in Islam! Remem-ber that my idea was to arm with education the whole of Afghanistan so that her people might read the path of truth as taught by God and his Prophet; and that they by avoiding superstitions, bloodshed, robbery, and theft might take their rightful place among the civilized nations of the world. But now you have raised the banner of rebellion at the in-stigation of your selfish, ignorant friends, as a result of which so many brave sons of Islam have lost their lives. ....You did not ponder over the evil consequences for Afghanistan of your revolt.... As regards to those who have declared me an infidel, I leave their case to Almighty God. They cannot force me out of the fold of Islam when I am in my heart of hearts a true believer.

King Aman-Allah[1]

The oath of allegiance to a ruler is effective as long as he is committed to the conditions set forth by Islam. But once he exceeds those bounda-ries, the bai`at is automatically void. We have always extended our oath of allegiance to the rulers of Afghanistan on the condition of total adherence to the shari`at and [Islamic] ethics.

Loya-Jerga of 1931[2]

Following his abdication on January 14, 1929, Aman-Allah attempted to regain the throne. By March, he had succeeded in strengthening his position. The people of Qandahar, the Hazaras, and several tribes in the Eastern Province

---

[1] Translation of Aman-Allah's message to the Shinwari rebels, printed in the *Bombay Chronicle*, January 1, 1929.
[2] *Tardid-i-Shayi`at-i-Shah-i-Makhlu`*, 8-9.

came to his support. Also in Kabul, public opinion, again, turned in his favor, but he faced several obstacles to consolidating power.

THE ULAMA AND THE QUESTION OF LEGITIMACY

From Aman-Allah's abdication in mid-January until October 1929, the nation suffered a destructive and debilitating civil war. The clergy, joined in rebellion, were not united about how to solve the problems facing the country. Many who had assisted Habib-Allah had done so assuming that victory would be followed by the election of a ruler other than Habib-Allah. No one really expected that the former bandit would be elevated to the throne. According to Farhang, after unsuccessful negotiations with Saqawi leaders on behalf of `Enayat-Allah Khan, Hazrat Sadeq Mojaddedi proposed to Habib-Allah that a highly regarded religious scholar or a pious member of the Mohammadzai royal clan be chosen as the future ruler of the country, insinuating that he himself, or his close collaborator, Sardar Mohammad `Osman Khan, whose sister had married into the Mojaddedi family, be considered candidates for the throne. Sahebzada Shirjan,[3] a supporter of Habib-Allah, understood Hazrat's intention and asserted that Habib-Allah Khan was the most eligible candidate for the throne because of the great service that he had rendered to Islam. Shirjan preempted further discussion by extending his hand to Habib-Allah in a gesture of allegiance to him as amir.[4]

Lacking unity among themselves and a clear political agenda of their own, the ulama could not and did not claim political leadership in the aftermath of Aman-Allah's abdication. Notwithstanding, their role was important in establishing legitimacy for a future ruler. In the power struggle that ensued following Aman-Allah's abdication, the contenders allied themselves with one or more influential religious leaders. In Kabul, Habib-Allah Kalakani received the immediate support of a group of Deobandi ulama headed by `Abd al-Haiy Panshiri, an articulate `alem and former president of the *Hai'at-i-Tamiz*. Motivated by their anger toward Aman-Allah, the Deobandi ulama supported Habib-Allah with arguments based on Islamic tradition. They excused his illiteracy on the grounds that the Prophet himself was an illiterate and that literacy was not a requirement for political leadership (*imamat*).[5]

A manifesto of excommunication (*e`lan-i-takfir*) dated January 18, composed by the ulama who supported Habib-Allah and signed by practically all the notables in Kabul, declared Aman-Allah an apostate. The manifesto set forth nineteen reasons based on religion for Aman-Allah's dethronement. Attached to the manifesto was a proclamation announcing the ascendancy of Habib-Allah to

---

[3.] `Ata al-Haqq Shirjan, once a part of Na'eb al-Saltana's retinue, was one of the influential Kohistanis who were drawn to Habib-Allah. He was the son of Sahebzada Khwaja Jan. Later, he and his brother, Mohammad Seddiq, received important posts in the Saqawi regime.

[4.] Farhang, *Afghanistan dar Panjah Sal-i-Akhir*, 1:1(part 2), 539-540.

[5.] Khalili, *'Ayyari az Khorasan*, 135.

the throne of Kabul, the re-establishment of religious order, the abolition of conscription, and recision of all taxes levied by the Amani regime.[6] A subsequent proclamation in February restored the allowances to the ulama and tribal leaders that had been revoked by Aman-Allah.[7]

In Jalalabad, `Ali Ahmad, who was originally sent to Jalalabad by Aman-Allah to fight the Shinwari rebels, received the support of Sayyid Hasan Affandi (the Naqib of Charbagh), the Hazrat of Charbagh, and the Ostad of Hadda, three prominent religious leaders of the Eastern Province. He was proclaimed king in the house of Sayyid Hasan (the Naqib Saheb of Charbagh) and shortly thereafter was offered the allegiance of a group of ulama of the Eastern Province that included the Ostad of Hadda in a meeting held at the guest house (*hojra*) of the late Molla of Hadda. The following Friday, the *khotba* was recited in the name of the Servant of the Faith and Nation (*Khadem-i-Din wa Mellat*) Amir `Ali Ahmad.[8] However, according to the Naqib of Charbagh, `Ali Ahmad was never really a candidate for the Afghan throne, merely "an agent in the Eastern Province of the man who would eventually be chosen King of Afghanistan."[9]

Aman-Allah's position was more complicated, as he had been cut off from all sources of outside support. In Qandahar, he had two tasks: restore his religious image, which had been badly soiled in the course of the preceding few months, and regain legitimacy with the ulama. The religious leaders in Qandahar seemed conciliatory. Support for Aman-Allah was relatively strong in Qandahar and the northwestern provinces. On January 26, endorsed by the ulama of Qandahar, Aman-Allah reassumed his authority as king. In a meeting in Qandahar, Mawlawi `Abd al-Shakur stood up and, holding Aman-Allah's hand, declared, "I renew my allegiance."[10] Although Mawlawi `Abd al-Wase' Qandahari protested that it was illegal to renew allegiance to a former ruler once he had abdicated and the nation had largely recognized a successor, his words were "lost in the rush of men who came forward to seize Aman-Allah's hand."[11] Later, however, Mawlawi `Abd al-Wase` joined the other Qandahari ulama in rendering full support to Aman-Allah and issued a *fatwa* against Habib-Allah declaring that according to the *shari`at* a man who had once engaged in highway robbery could not be accepted as *uli al-'amr*.[12] In Ghazni, Molla Mohammad

---

6. The original text of the manifesto is in the Afghan National Archives, No 195. For an English translation, see NAI 25-F, 1929, Nos. 1-19; Stewart, pp. 481-82.

7. For an English translation of the proclamation, see IOR, L/PS/10/1287, P-1459, Feb. 16, 1929.

8. *Ghairat-i-Eslam* (Jalalabad), no. 1, 9 *Jaddyi* 1307/January 28, 1929.

9. IOR, L/PS/10/1287, 4, P-693, 1929.

10. `Ali Ahmad, 32.

11. *Ibid.*

12. After the fall of Qandahar to Saqawi forces, Mawlawi `Abd al-Wase` Qandahari was executed by Habib-Allah for issuing the *fatwa* declaring him unfit to be a Muslim ruler. See Farhang, ii, 583-584.

Esma'il, a grandson of Molla Moshk-i-'Alam, also came to the support of Aman-Allah.[13]

Several newspapers came into being at this time, each reflecting the position of a claimant to the throne. They were important inasmuch as they elevated religious values and provided the respective partisan groups vehicles with which to advocate their position. *Habib al-Islam* (the Comrade of Islam), which replaced *Aman-i-Afghan* on February 28, 1929 in Kabul, *Bidar* (Awakening) in Mazar, and *Nahzat al-Habib* (the Rise of Habib, *i.e.*, Habib-Allah) in Khanabad (in northeastern Afghanistan) promoted Habib-Allah Kalakani, extolling the glorious religious duty performed by him and the people of Kohdaman and Kohistan in saving the country from the sacrilege of Aman-Allah.

Ghairat-i-Islam (Islamic Vigor), published in Jalalabad on January 28, 1929, supported 'Ali-Ahmad on a platform of full commitment to the Hanafi creed. In its first issue, *Ghairat-i-Islam* heralded the election of 'Ali Ahmad as amir of Afghanistan and published the oath of the new amir to conduct government and religious affairs according to the *shari'at*.

Tolu'-i-Afghan of Qandahar, now replete with religious arguments, continued to support Aman-Allah, reporting the atrocities committed by the Saqawi regime of Kabul. *Tolu'-i-Afghan* challenged Aman-Allah's adversaries with reports from Indian newspapers of regiments fighting in his support and printed a proclamation by Aman-Allah declaring that "Habib-Allah has no other object than to bring about the ruin of Afghanistan and the destruction of Muslims in whatever manner possible. He has been instigated by the British, and he acts according to their instructions. This is ultimately an issue between unbelievers and believers."[14] This proclamation was the first time the British were linked in print with the revolution. Later, the newspaper reprinted an article from *Pakhtun* of Peshawar stating that "treacherous people in Afghanistan, receiving bribes from the enemies of religion and country, have brought wholesale destruction upon Afghanistan."[15]

Each group claimed strict adherence to Islamic precepts. In their efforts to placate the ulama and the dissident groups, both 'Ali Ahmad and Habib-Allah offered to abolish conscription and high taxes and restore the monetary privileges to the ulama that Aman-Allah had canceled.

Habib al-Islam, published under the supervision of pro-Habib-Allah ulama, aimed to exculpate Habib-Allah's criminal record as a highway robber. On April 26, it published an article refuting Mawlawi 'Abd al-Wase' Qandahari's *fatwa* with examples of such great kings as Aurangzib and Sultan Bayazid Yaldram, who had committed murder, and Henry of England, who was once a gambler and a highway robber, and were not punished for their crimes nor deprived of the throne, because their ancestors were kings. They had all, however, turned out to be great kings. The writer quoted Hazrat 'Ali, the fourth Caliph, who said

---

[13.] Ali Ahmad, 55.
[14.] *Tolu'-i-Afghan*, 4 *Hut* 1307/Feb. 22, 1929
[15.] *Tolu'-i-Afghan*, 1 *Sawr* 1308/May 11 1929.

that the virtue of men is determined by hard labor, not by ancestry.[16] In another article, *Habib-i-Islam* quoted passages from the Holy Qur'an and the sayings of the Prophet which enjoin Muslims to be loyal to their king no matter who he may be.[17]

According to *Habib-i-Islam*, Aman-Allah had introduced the customs of infidels into an Islamic nation, and the Muslims of Afghanistan were astonished to see that, despite the fact there had been a non-Muslim government in India for the last hundred years, the Muslims of India were not forced to give up their customs. In contrast, Aman-Allah's tendency toward heresy had resulted in the imposition of infidels' customs on the people of Afghanistan within a short period of time. *Habib-i-Islam* declared, "our devotion to Islam incited us, and we rose against him and came out victorious."[18]

The Indian newspaper *Mahajer*, published in Deoband, also sided with the Saqawi regime, arguing that Habib-Allah should not be rejected merely because he was not born a prince. It accused Aman-Allah of interfering with venerated local customs and asserted that if Aman-Allah Khan had abdicated in order to save bloodshed, he should not spell blood now in an attempt to regain power.[19]

Mohammad Ebrahim Kamawi published *Al-Iman* (The Faith) in Qal'a-i-Baburi in the Eastern Province. Although Kamawi was suspected of supporting the Shinwaris, his newspaper did not ally with any political group. *Al-Iman*'s announced goal was "to bring unity among Muslims and to counter the acts of propaganda carried out by the enemies."[20] It emphasized two major topics: principles of faith (*osul-i-iman*) and ramifications of faith (*foru`-i-iman*). It also carried domestic and foreign news.

Undeclared was also the position of the Molla of Chaknawur. He was reported to prefer no king at all and to have hoisted a new flag atop his mosque bearing the inscription: "religious law shines brightly and all other codes of law are vain."[21]

RENEWED SUPPORT FOR AMAN-ALLAH

Following the defeat of Ahmad `Ali Khan's forces in Jegdalek, the political mood in the Eastern and Southern Provinces changed. The general feeling now was decisively against elevating an ex-highway robber and a non-Pashtun to the throne.

---

[16] "*Moqayesa-i-`Alawiyyat-i-Shahan* (Comparison of the Superiority of Kings)," *Habib al-Eslam*, no. 8, 15 *Ziqa`d*, 1348/April 26, 1929.

[17] "*Enqelab* (Revolution)," *Habib-i-Eslam*, no. 6, 30 *Shawal*, 1348/April 11, 1929.

[18] *Ibid.*

[19] Reported by the North-West Frontier Intelligence Bureau, P1942, no. 3, Feb. 1929.

[20] NAI, FPD, Frontier (secret), File no. 9-F, 1929, 56.

[21] Telegram from Humphrys to the secretary of state for foreign affairs, London, April 5, 1929, IOR, L/P&S/10/1288, 289-K, April 5, 1929.

The ascendance of Habib-Allah Kalakani to the Afghan throne took the ulama of the Eastern and Southern provinces by surprise. The majority saw him as unfit to rule and was scandalized by his past acts. The tribes were equally disturbed by the occupation of the throne of Kabul by a non-Pashtun and ex-bandit. They began to reassess their attitude toward Aman-Allah.

Public opinion in Kabul was now decisively pro Aman-Allah.[22] According to Faiz Mohammad Kateb, the cordial reception Habib-Allah received at the British embassy prompted speculation that the British had had a hand in the uprising in Kohistan.

By March, general sentiment had turned in favor Aman-Allah. On March 20, 1929, the British government in India reported to London, "all sources indicate that a resurgence of feeling in favor of Amanullah is spreading in the Southern and Eastern provinces and among our own tribes."[23] Ahmadzais, Ghelzais, Logaris, and Khugiani Shi`as also supported Aman-Allah. By now, it was generally believed that Aman-Allah had repented and that the best way to get rid of Habib-Allah and the state of disorder he had created was to restore Aman-Allah to the throne. According to the Chief Commissioner of the North-West Frontier, agitation favoring the ex-king was fed mostly by distress among businessmen in Kabul, several of whom had gone bankrupt in the wake of the chaos caused by Habib-Allah's rise to power.[24]

Pro-Aman-Allah activities were already occurring in India. *Khilafat* partisans in Lahore and Peshawar held meetings demonstrating their support. On January 29, 1929, the viceroy of India reported that Afghans in Peshawar were in communication with anti-British Indian Mulsim activists and had joined them in spreading propaganda suggesting that the British government of India was involved in uprisings against the former king. The viceroy reported that supporters of Aman-Allah had published a book titled *Shari`at Orders Regarding Aman-Allah*, which declared him to be a true Muslim and Habib-Allah Kalakani a rebel to be beheaded.[25] Similarly, *fatwa*s issued by ulama on the British side of the border declared that the Aman-Allah was not a *kafer*.[26] Support for Aman-Allah was also expressed in Turkey and Iraq. A letter from Dobbs, High Commissioner for Iraq, to J. E. Shuckburg reads:

> Just before I left Baghdad I learned that the big Ulama of Karbala and Najaf, the leaders of the Shiah world, had decided to send messengers to the Hazaras of Afghanistan, who are all Shiahs, directing them to support Amanullah. The Ulama did this out of hostility to the British, whom they believe to have engineered the rebellion against Amanullah.

[22.] Kateb, *Tazakkor al-Enqelab*, 46.
[23.] IOR, L/P&S/10/1288, Part 4., telegram to the secretary of state for India, London, 1144-S, March 29, 1929.
[24.] IOR, L/P&S/10/1287, 4, P1087, Feb. 6, 1929.
[25.] IOR, L/P&S/10/1287, 4, P775, 1929.
[26.] *Ibid.*, P1087, Feb. 6, 1929.

This is a very important step, which may make all the difference to Amanullah's chances of regaining Kabul. The Hazaras, as you know, hold the whole central block of Afghanistan and reach across to Sar Sharchashma. If they have any arms (a point on which I am doubtful) they could attack Bacha-i-Saqau in the rear end, I think, ensuring Amanullah's success. They are very stout mountaineers. In any event, if they obey the Ulama's orders, as I suppose they will, it must greatly improve Amanullah's prospects and I think it might be well that the Government of India should be informed.[27]

As a result of the enthusiastic support demonstrated for Aman-Allah by Indian Muslims, particularly in the border city of Peshawar, tribal religious leaders on the British side began to back Aman-Allah. In March, the Hajji of Turangzai announced his intention to lead an expedition in support of Aman-Allah, and Akhundzada Molla Mahmud persuaded the Afridis and Mohmands to send assistance to the ex-king. Molla Mahmud later called a *jerga* to persuade Orekzai tribes to assist Aman-Allah.[28] Elsewhere, Nur Rahman (the son of the Babri Molla), with a group of other *molla*s, attempted to gain the support of the Bajauris for Aman-Allah.[29]

Meanwhile, the Safis of Tagaw had decided to raise a tribal levy (*lashkar*) against Bacha-i-Saqaw.[30] At about the same time, one of the leaders of Shinwar and his followers sent a message to Qandahar via the Afghan trade agent in Peshawar asking King Aman-Allah for pardon and pledging a renewal of their allegiance to him. The Hazaras, Ahmadzais, Logaris, and Khugiani Shi`as also supported Aman-Allah, and in Kabul public opinion definitely favored him. Inflation, disorder, and atrocities committed by Habib-Allah's officials had quickly turned the citizens of Kabul against the new regime.[31]

At this juncture, when popular support had tilted toward Aman-Allah, Nader Khan and his brothers entered Afghanistan via India with the declared intent of saving the country from a destructive civil war. It was not, however, clear at that point if Nader Khan had come to support Aman-Allah or had other intentions. In mid-March, he participated in a religious conference at Hadda called to reevaluate whether the former king was eligible to resume the throne. Representatives of the Mohmand tribes at the conference informed Nader Khan that they would only support him if he fought to restore Aman-Allah. However, the Molla of Chaknawur, who dominiated the meeting, opposed any plan to restore Aman-Allah, and the conference was adjourned without agreement on a plan of action.[32]

---

[27] IOR, L/P&S/10/1287, 4, P1682, Feb. 19, 1929.
[28] IOR, L/P&S/10/1137, NWFP, 1929, P3231, no. 8, April 6, 1929.
[29] *Ibid.*
[30] IOR, L/P&S/10/1137, P2865, no. 6, March 16, 1929.
[31] Kateb, *Tazakor al-Enqelab*, 46.
[32] IOR, L/PS/10/1288, 5, 707-S, March 16, 1929.

Meanwhile, Aman-Allah sent a message back to the Shinwaris through the Afghan trade agent in Peshawar. In the message, Aman-Allah granted the Shinwaris a general pardon, appealed to them to come forward to serve their country in its time of great danger, and asked them to get instructions from the Hazrat of Charbagh, who was acting as his agent.[33] In late March, the British viceroy in India apprised London that several Khost tribes had informed Nader Khan that they would deny him assistance unless he publicly announced support for Aman-Allah.[34]

ALLEGED BRITISH INTRIGUE

Aman-Allah's supporters suspected that the Shinwari and Kohistani revolts were part of a wider conspiracy fomented by the British, a suspicion that deepened when the government's concessions to the religious groups failed to satisfy the rebels. The general impression, was that the Shinwar revolt had been started by the British but had gone further than they wanted. On December 5, 1928, the *Daily News* of London reported that Colonel T. E. Lawrence was in India, on the Afghan border, learning Pashtu, and inferred that Lawrence intended to enter Afghanistan.[35] On the same subject, *Zamindar* of Lahore quoted the *London Weekly*: "Reforms in Afghanistan since the king's return from Europe are of special significance in regard to the political interests of Bolshevik Asiatic Russia on the north and the hills of British India in the south. Here Colonel Lawrence is watching the trouble which he has sown in Afghanistan."[36] Kabul newspapers began to print similar excerpts from Indian and other foreign presses. On December 12, *Aman-i-Afghan* reproduced an article from the *Sunday Express* of September 30 that recounted Lawrence's activities in the tribal regions against the Afghan government. The *Bombay Chronicle* also reported this story, charging that the trouble in Afghanistan had been created by enemies of the state through foreign agents to deprive Afghanistan of its independence.[37] It quoted from the Moscow version of the events in Afghanistan: "A number of leaflets containing a proclamation against the king and bearing a photograph of the queen were distributed among the tribes. ...Rebels are armed with the latest British rifles and ammunition.[38]

Earlier, on December 9, 1928, Reuters news agency had confirmed Lawrence's involvement in the Shinwari uprising.[39] *Hamdard-i-Afghan* also reported

---

[33.] Telegram, dated 17 *Saur* 1308/May 7, 1929, from the Afghan trade agent in Peshawar.

[34.] Telegram to the secretary of state for India, London, 1144-S, March 29, 1929. IOR, L/P&S/10/1288, 4.

[35.] *Daily News*, December 5, 1928, quoted in Adamec, *Afghanistan Foreign Affairs*, 152; see also NAI, FPD, 5-F, 1929, no. 2.

[36.] *Zamindar*, Dec. 15, 1928; NWFIB, P992, no. 1, January 5, 1929.

[37.] IOR, L/PS/10/1288, 5, no. 240-A.

[38.] *Bombay Chronicle*, January 19, 1929.

[39.] NAI, FPD, no. 309-F, 1928, d. 200.

that Colonel Lawrence, using the epithet Pir Karam Shah, had entered Afghanistan in the midst of the rebellion.[40] The paper printed letters to the Molla of Chaknawur criticizing the policy against Aman-Allah adopted by the ulama of Afghanistan.[41] The fact that the rebellion had started in the vicinity of the Durand Line strengthened the suspicion that Colonel Lawrence and the British were involved. It was rumored that religious groups had been secretly infiltrated by British agents. Another popular view suggested that the Hazrat of Shurbazar was behind the rebellion and that Humphrys, the British minister in Kabul, was behind the Hazrat.[42] Later, the extraordinary move of the Hazrat of Shurbazar (Mohammad Sadeq Mojaddedi), seeking help from Humphrys and the British legation to arrange a truce and the evacuation of the royal party and foreigners from Kabul, caused the European and Indian presses, as well as Soviet authorities, to raise questions about Humphrys' role in the events that led to Aman-Allah's downfall.[43]

The role the British may have played in the defeat of Aman-Allah has been debated. While acknowledging other factors, the Afghan historians Ghobar and Reshtiya, as well as Mohaiy al-Din Anis, an eyewitness journalist, have emphasized the role of the British in the overthrow of Aman-Allah. They have, however, not provided corroborating evidence. More recently, the theory of British intrigue has been refuted by the Afghan poet-scholar Khalil-Allah Khalili in his semi-fictional work `*Ayyari az Khorasan* and by Shir Agha Mojaddedi in *Amir Habib-Allah Khadem-i-Din-i-Rasul-Allah*. Both argue that the ulama and the people of Afghanistan, who had fought against the British for decades, had sense enough not to be used by them.[44] Farhang discounts possible involvement by Lawrence in the rebellion, claiming that Lawrence had retired from political activity by the time of the rebellion in Afghanistan. Moreover, speaking neither Pashtu nor Persian, it is unlikely that he could have been effective in stirring up the tribes.[45] Poullada has also rejected the theory of British involvement in the overthrow of Aman-Allah, basing his conclusion on the absence of documents in the British archives revealing that they were.[46]

The British had plenty of reasons to oppose Aman-Allah. From the beginning of his reign, Aman-Allah had taken a strong position against the British. His support of anti-British activities in India and the demand of the Pashtun tribes for reunification of Pashtunistan, which was divided between Afghanistan and British India by the Durand Line, as well as his friendly relations with Moscow, gave the British cause for misgivings about Aman-Allah's intentions.

---

[40] *Hamdard-i-Afghan*, April 8, 1929.
[41] *Ibid.*
[42] IOR L/P&S/10/1287, P1156, Feb. 8, 1929.
[43] Gregorian, 267.
[44] Khalili, `*Ayyari az Khorasan*, 101; Shah Agha Mojaddedi, 17.
[45] Farhang, vol.1 (part 2), 551-552.
[46] Poullada, 260-262.

Some observers even predicted that an invasion of India was among Aman-Allah's plans:

> The Afghans are a young nation.... In spite of their youth they already have military traditions behind them of which they are justly proud. They were once masters of Northern India.... Even shrewd and matter of fact Afghans are looking forward eventually to annexing India's northwest provinces, which are inhabited almost exclusively by people of Afghan blood.... This may be visionary, or it may sometime prove to be a practical political programme.[47]

Aman-Allah's visit to England in March 1928, despite its apparent success, did not improve his relations with Great Britain.[48] In an earlier interview with an English correspondent, he had openly stated that his upcoming interview in London with Sir Austin Chamberland, the British secretary of state for foreign affairs, was going to determine whether or not he would consider Britain a friend of Afghanistan.[49] Chamberland's refusal to discuss with him the question of the independent tribes along the border and the question of occupied Pashtun land in the North-West Frontier increased Aman-Allah's resentment toward the British.[50] Despite the grand hospitality extended him by the British government during his visit, Aman-Allah turned his back on the British by proceeding to Moscow in April 1928. The establishment of a closer relationship between Afghanistan and the Soviet Union as a result of this visit and plans for construction of a railway in Afghanistan that would link Chaman in India to Koshk on the border of the Soviet Union, raised anxiety in Great Britain for India's security. Great Britain feared that construction of such a rail line would "remove from India the protection of Afghanistan's status as a buffer state."[51] Humphrys wrote to London, "We should at this stage neither obstruct nor encourage any of the foreign [French and German] prospectors, but if necessary exercise diplomatic pressure to defer as long as possible the construction of a railway likely to threaten Indian security."[52]

However, as Poullada has pointed out, British archival records provide no evidence that the British were involved in a plot to overthrow Aman-Allah. Either such documents never existed, or documents relating to British involvement in anti-government uprisings in Afghanistan have been removed or de-

---

[47]. L. Weiss, "Russia's March Toward India," *The Living Age*, vol. 332, 1927, 109-110.

[48]. Following his return from Europe, Aman-Allah allegedly become even more anti-British and blatantly expressed his feelings. He reportedly offended Humphrys by making negative remarks about the British publicly during a speech at Estur Palace. Mohammad 'Osman Khan Amir, Aman-Allah's chief of protocol, confided to friends concern about possible consequences of the king's anti-British rhetoric.

[49]. *Times of London*, January 23, 1928.

[50]. Agabekov, 161.

[51]. Stewart, 407.

[52]. *Ibid.*, 408.

stroyed. There is, however, evidence of British efforts to frustrate Aman-Allah's attempts to regain the throne.

After his arrival in Qandahar, Aman-Allah sent a message to Great Britain via the Afghan minister in London, requesting arms and ammunition with which to fight the rebels. In a telegram to the secretary of state for foreign affairs, Humphrys apprised London that the majority of Afghans would support Aman-Allah in his struggle to regain power, if he were able to obtain assistance from Great Britain or the Soviet Union.[53] Humphrys advised London to refuse to provide any kind of assistance to Aman-Allah and, at the same time, to deny official recognition to the Afghan minister in London, as he no longer represented an official government. Humphrys suggested further that "H. M.'s Government should communicate a warning to Russia of 'Hands Off' as regards supplying troops or war materials [to Aman-Allah]."[54]

Great Britain denied assistance to Aman-Allah by declaring a policy of non-intervention in Afghanistan. However, if the British did not intervene, they did interfere at great cost to Aman-Allah. The viceroy of India relayed a recommendation from Humphrys to London regarding the delivery of arms: "It is requested that arms and ammunition purchased by the Afghan Government from Europe and already landed at the Indian ports...may at present be detained at their respective ports."[55] In effect, the British deliberately delayed the delivery of arms through India to Afghanistan, at a time when Aman-Allah was in desperate need of munitions. These two policies of the British, non-intervention and detention of arms, greatly strengthened Habib-Allah's position.

ABORTIVE ALLIANCE WITH THE SOVIET UNION

Aman-Allah's only hope for outside help was now the Soviet Union. Gholam Nabi Charkhi, the Afghan minister in Moscow, contacted Soviet authorities for help. In a meeting in Moscow attended by Stalin, Charkhi, and Primakoff, the Soviet military attaché in Kabul, it was decided that Primakoff and Charkhi should lead an expedition against the Saqawi regime from the north.[56] The plan received the support of Akhund Babayuf, the president of Uzbekistan, who was quoted earlier in *Yangi Turkistan* of Constantinople as having blamed the British for the rebellion in Afghanistan and having requested arms from the Soviets to assist Aman-Allah.[57]

Aman-Allah's plan was to regain control of the capital by launching simultaneous attacks against Habib-Allah from three fronts—Nader Khan from the

---

[53.] Quoted by Stewart, *ibid.*

[54.] Telegram from the minister in Kabul to the secretary of state for foreign affairs, London, no. 71, January 20, 1929, NAI, FPD, File no. 137-7, serial nos. 1-182.

[55.] Telegram no. 1687, May 16, 1929, from the viceroy to the secretary of state for India, London. Quoted in Marwat and Kakakhel, 57.

[56.] Agabekov, 166-167.

[57.] IOR, L/P&S/10/1137, P1942, no. 3, Feb 2, 1929.

south, Gholam Nabi Charkhi from the north, and Aman-Allah himself from the southwest. However, personal differences between Nader Khan and Aman-Allah Khan, on the one hand, and between Nader Khan and Charkhi, on the other, made it questionable whether Nader Khan could be counted on to cooperate. Intertribal rivalries, now overshadowing religious issues, were additional obstacles to this plan. In the end, Gholam Nabi Charkhi's overtures to the Soviets did more harm than good, providing little aid and giving Aman-Allah's enemies ammunition to discredit him as a friend of atheist Russia.[58]

Late in April, forces under the leadership of Gholam Nabi Charkhi occupied Mazar. Simultaneously, a mission of the Saqawi regime arrived from Kabul and quickly spread word that the Soviets were united with Aman-Allah and his representative, Gholam Nabi Charkhi. Members of the Saqawi mission built upon earlier rumors of Aman-Allah's close ties with the nonconformist Turks and atheist Soviets and fueled fears that the Soviets were paving the way to establish themselves in Afghanistan. The Saqawi mission succeeded, thereby, in securing the support of Damolla Adina ʿArab, who was the most influential religious leader in northern Afghanistan, along with his disciple Mawlawi Gholam Haidar Mazari, and Khalifa Qezel Ayaq, a highly revered religious leader in Balkh, and in obtaining from them a *fatwa* of *jehad* against the expedition led by Charkhi.[59]

The Soviet support of Aman-Allah destroyed what little legitimacy he continued to enjoy and weakened his position in the northern regions and in Herat. The proclamations of *jehad* issued by the religious leaders of Mazar and Balkh produced the effect desired by the Saqawi mission. The soldiers revolted against their officers and submitted papers of allegiance to the mission from Kabul.[60] Gholam Nabi Charkhi's advances in the north were checked by Habib-Allah's forces with support from Khalifa Qezel Ayaq, whose followers, numbering twelve thousand men, joined the Saqawi forces. Meanwhile, in Herat, Molla Mohammad Seddiq and Mofti Seraj al-Din Saljuqi set about turning public opinion in Herat in favor of Habib-Allah. However, Charkhi's campaign was haulted, not by these encounters, but by Aman-Allah's departure from Afghanistan.

NUR AL-MASHAYIKH AND THE TRIUMPH OF NADER KHAN

In April, Nur al-Mashayikh, Aman-Allah's powerful rival, returned to Afghanistan. His arrival at this sensitive time destroyed any chance of Aman-Allah's

---

[58.] Poullada, 182-190.
[59.] Khalili, *Nokhostin Tajawoz-i-Rusiya dar Afghanistan*, 15-16. The author, a renowned Afghan poet and the son of Mostawfi al-Mamalek, who was executed by Aman-Allah immediately after Aman-Allah acceded to the throne, was a member of the mission from Kabul. Then a young unknown writer, Khalili played an important part in drafting the *fatwa* of *jehad* against Gholam Nabi Charkhi and Aman-Allah. This was the first time, he wrote, that "my humble pen was introduced to drafting a proclamation." *Ibid.*
[60.] *Ibid.*

return to power. Earlier in October 1928, the Hazrat had refused Aman-Allah's invitation to return to Afghanistan but had continued activities against the regime from exile. In November, the Afghan foreign minister requested that the government of India remove Nur al-Mashayikh from Katiwar to someplace where he would be innocuous, claiming that the Hazrat was "collecting large sums from Seths for propaganda" against the regime.[61]

Having returned to Afghanistan, Hazrat Nur al-Mashayikh now held the key position. As *pir* of the Ghelzais, one of the two largest tribes in Afghanistan, and as a religious leader highly respected throughout Afghanistan, his endorsement could determine the future of political leadership in Afghanistan. Nur al-Mashayikh had one main goal, to overthrow Aman-Allah. His strategy was to let Habib-Allah do the job of overthrowing Aman-Allah, and then support as ruler a man of his own preference. Although he did not openly support any candidate, he was in close communication with General Nader Khan. By mid-April, Nur al-Mashayikh was reported to have come to an agreement with Nader Khan,[62] who had by then enlisted the support of the Naqib of Chaharbagh as well, and was correspondening with Padshah Gol, the son of the Hajji of Turangzai.[63]

With the legitimacy of Aman-Allah in question and the rule of Habib-Allah not accepted by the majority of population, Nader Khan became a viable candidate for the Afghan throne. He was a hero of the War of Independence and a military figure much respected by the tribes. He made Jaji in the Southern Province the center of his activities and managed gradually to turn the tide of anti-Saqawi feeling in the tribal area and in Kabul to his benefit. The newspaper *Eslah*, originally published in Khanabad under his direction, resumed publication in Jaji with the objective of turning the tribes of the Eastern Province against Habib-Allah and in support of Nader Khan. Articles in the paper disparaged Habib-Allah as a murderer and notorious highwayman, who had taken advantage of the weakness of Kabul during the Shinwari revolt to usurp the throne, destroy the national treasure, and disgrace Afghanistan in the eyes of the world.[64] *Eslah*, purposely, did not back a candidate, but aimed to "correct the ideas of the people and put a stop to the disturbance and destruction of the revolution."[65] Its policy was to "serve the nation and side with Islam and the truth."[66]

Eslah implicitly promoted the cause of Nader Khan. In its first issue, it enumerated the qualities of political leadership: "A king or *imam* is required to have good manners and good qualities. He should be a learned and a practical man. He ought to be religious, pious, and patriotic, and must have a special

---

[61.] IOR, L/PS/10/1288, 4, tel. 322-F, Nov. 21, 1928.

[62.] *Ibid.*

[63.] IOR, L/PS/10/1288, 885-P, April 9, and 56-C, April 5, 1929.

[64.] *Eslah*, Jaji, no. 1, *Asad* 15/August 7, 1929.

[65.] *Eslah*, no. 1, *Asad*, 15/August 7, 1929; NAI, 9-F, 1929, 71.

[66.] *Ibid.*

knowledge of government and politics. He should have sympathy for the nation, and should always place the interests of his nation above his own."[67]

By the end of May, Habib-Allah had the upper hand. In Ghazni, the advance toward Kabul of Aman-Allah's joint force of Abdali and Hazara tribes was prevented by a surprise attack of Ghelzai tribesmen, long-standing enemies of the Dorranis, instigated by Nur al-Mashayikh, their spiritual leader (*pir*). The Ghelzais' ostensive support of Habib-Allah's forces in Ghazni was based on an understanding that Nader Khan would become the next ruler of Afghanistan.[68]

Aman-Allah realized that he was now in for a fight on two fronts—Saqawi forces from Kabul and the Ghelzai tribes. With his funds depleted, he had no choice but to accede to Nader Khan's advice that he leave the country. On May 23, following the defeat of his forces in Herat and Ghazni, Aman-Allah left Afghanistan for India and then Rome, his final destination.

On June 14, 1929, shortly after Aman-Allah's departure, Nur al-Mashayikh issued a religious decree (*fatwa*) against Habib-Allah, blaming him for a reign of tyranny that had brought unrest, anarchy, and bloodshed to the country.[69] The *fatwa* significantly strengthened Nader Khan's position, bringing him the support of the Hazrat's large following in the tribal area at a time when repeated requests for help from the British had been refused based on the British policy of noninterference. Now joined by his third brother, Shah Mahmud from Kabul, Nader Khan gained influence with Mohmand, Afridi, Jaji, and Waziri tribal leaders and with the ulama of the Eastern Province. In contrast, Habib-Allah's supporters were deserting. Hazrat Sadeq Mojaddedi, Habib-Allah's main advisor, sent to negotiate with Nader Khan, joined his brother (Nur al-Mashayikh) instead against the Saqawi regime. On July 7, the ulama and the leaders of Kohistan, Kohdaman, and Kabul held a meeting with Habib-Allah and advised him to settle with Nader to stop further bloodshed. However, since Nader Khan had refused earlier overtures for compromise, Habib-Allah decided to fight to the bitter end. During the months of July and August, his forces succeeded in repelling several attacks on Kabul. By September, however, his position had weakened considerably. On October 13, Shah Wali Khan, a younger brother of Nader Khan, occupied Kabul.

On October 15, 1929, Nader Khan was proclaimed king. In the tradition of the Dorrani rulers whose names were followed by the appellation *shah,* he took the name Nader Shah. His future policy was spelled out in the *farman* of appointment of Hashem Khan as prime minister:

> As God has now saved Afghanistan from the fire of revolution, and as the nation has selected me as their king, I wish that hereafter Afghanistan should be a progressive state staunchly adhering to Islamic doctrines, and that the country be ruled better than ever before and

---

[67.] *Ibid.*; Adamec, *Afghanistan's Foreign Affairs*, 177-178.

[68.] IOR, L/P&S/10/1137, P3523, no. 10, April 20, 1929.

[69.] IOR, L/PS/10/1288, 338, telegram 35, June 22, 1929.

that heads of departments should be responsible to the nation and that reforms should be carried out easily and without disturbances, I have, therefore, in accordance with the orders of Islam and principles enforced in other civilized countries decided to appoint a premier who should form his cabinet.[70]

Following his accession to the throne, Nader Shah used the familiar religious slogans of his predecessors to legitimize his rule. He tried to cultivate the good will of the two most powerful groups in Afghanistan, the tribal *khans* and the religious leaders. The Mohmand, Ahmadzai, and Jaji tribes were exempted from military service in return for the great service they had rendered in defeating Habib-Allah, and the ulama were included in the government.

In December 1929, the Society of the Ulama of Afghanistan (*Jam`iyyat-i-`Ulama-i-Afghanistan*) was established by Nader Shah within the state machinery.[71] The society's platform, which was promulgated on December 17 of that year, stipulated a membership of individuals appointed from among top religious leaders. Its functions included everything from implementation of the *al amr bi al-ma`ruf* to supervision of every detail of public and private religious life.[72] So at the end of the 1920s, the role of the ulama in government was stronger than ever. The appointment of Nur al-Mashayikh and his brother, Sadeq Mojaddedi, as minister of justice and Afghan minister to Cairo, respectively, suggested that the ulama would play a significant role in Nader Shah's government.

On November 14, the British recognized Nader Shah as the new king of Afghanistan.[73] The *Tribune* of Lahore commented that Great Britain's recognition of Nader Shah as the king of Afghanistan finally extinguished all chances of ex-king Aman-Allah's returning to the throne or of any member of his family taking his place. In September 1931, a *Loya-Jerga* of five hundred ten representatives refuted any further claim Aman-Allah might have to the throne. The major argument against the ex-king was that he had abrogated his right to the throne by overstepping the *shari`at.*[74] In effect, the announcement of the *Loya-Jerga* of 1931, was the official declaration of deposition (*khal`*) of King Aman-Allah.

---

[70] *Eslah,* Kabul, no. 6, `Aqrab, 22, 1308/November 14, 1929.

[71] *Salnaman-i-Kabul,* 1311/1932, 107.

[72] *Maram-nama-i-Jam`iyat-i-`Ulama-i-Afghanistan,* 3-5.

[73] Adamec, *Afghanistan's Foreign Affairs,* 185.

[74] The arguments of the *jerga* against the ex-king were published in a booklet titled *Refutation of Rumors by the Deposed King (Tardid-i-Shayi`at-i-Shah-i-Makhlu`).*

8

SUMMARY OF THEMES AND ISSUES

> I have had many occasions to observe [King Aman-Allah's] contempt
> for fanaticism and his passionate desire for the progress of his country
> on modern lines. It appears however that circumstances are still too
> strong for him to enforce his personal wishes....
>
> One cannot help admiring the courage of a man who thinks that he sees
> what is best for his country and is determined to have it at all costs.
> Francis Humphreys[1]

The reign of King Aman-Allah was a period of Afghan history in which the
ulama were deeply involved in national politics. By analyzing original Afghan
sources, as well as British archival materials, I have attempted to clarify several
of the dimensions of the conflict between the monarchy and the clergy in Afghanistan during the 1920s.

In *Reform and Rebellion in Afghanistan*, Leon Poullada attributed Aman-
Allah's problems in implementing reforms and his ultimate demise to the tribal
nature of Afghan society. The intent of this inquiry is not to challenge Poullada's
analysis, but rather to shed greater light on the one facet of the opposition to
Aman-Allah's reforms in the 1920s that was underrated in Poullada's work. I have
examined the doctrinal and the practical dimensions of the clerical opposition to
King Aman-Allah's development policies and the pivotal role played by the
religious leaders in the peasant revolts that eventually resulted in Aman-Allah's
downfall.

King Aman-Allah's abortive efforts to introduce social reforms in
Afghanistan in the 1920s provides an early example of the problem of legitimizing
social reform in the modern Muslim world. The growth of Islamic movements in
opposition to modernizing regimes in the last two decades indicates that the clash
between traditionalist and modernist Muslim leaders is ongoing. The core of the

---

[1] Kabul despatch, 12, February 14, 1925 (A.S. XVII, 160), cited in Maconachie, 4; IOR,
L/P&S/10/1285, 1929, P53, 1 and 2, no. 107.

186

problem, according to Dekmajian, is the failure of intellectual modernizing Muslim elites to find a secular ideology of legitimation to substitute the traditional Islamic legitimacy. As in most other Islamic countries, Afghanistan lacked the hallmark of the modern nation-state--a political order based on popular consent. Nationalism was a strong stimulus for change in Afghanistan. The government that Aman-Allah forged after independence was a modernizing despotic monarchy, but unlike his contemporaries, Kamal Attaturk and Reza Shah, who relied on strong and loyal army to maintain legitimacy, Aman-Allah, declared the period following the independence to be the era of the pen and not of the sword,[2] and he tried to find support for his policies among the people by promoting social justice and equality before the law in the name of Islam. He saw himself as a benevolent monarch and servant of the nation, *khadem-i-mellat*, protecting the suppressed and leading his nation in progress.

> On ascending to the throne he continued to bestow attention to popular aspirations, and perceiving that the people were fretting under the yoke of the nobles, he yielded to the rising tide of Afghan public opinion. He emphasized the view which disgusted the nobility--that he was the representative of the masses, a king risen out of the humble ranks of his kinsmen....[3]

The egalitarian and emancipating aspects of Aman-Allah's early reforms, such as the abolition of slavery and forced labor, and his attention to the interests of the oppressed in other regards, did, in fact, increase his popularity among the masses. However, the initial popular support for reforms dwindled quickly as the state began to interfere in traditional way of life. Conflict between the regime and the ulama emerged as Aman-Allah's policies diverged from orthodox practices and threatened personal interests of members of the clergy. On two occasions the ulama's challenges to the regime's social and legal reforms created serious crises of legitimacy and without a strong army, Aman-Allah was not able to forestall the growing tide of resistance to his regime.

In contrast to the situation in Turkey and Egypt, two other Sunni Muslim countries where the power of the clergy was greately reduced during the nineteenth century, in Afghanistan the influence of the ulama pervaded all levels of Afghan culture. After the disintegration of the Dorrani empire, the autonomy of religious groups increased considerably in Afghanistan. The *qazi*s assumed unlimited power in judicial matters in urban centers, and the lower clergy and the *sheikh*s of the *tariqa*s controlled religious and social life in the countryside. The British invasions of Afghanistan during the nineteenth century had the effect of increasing the political autonomy of religious leaders. Also, as a result of frequent wars of succession, the authority of the throne became increasingly subject to challenge. The power of the ulama to bestow political legitimacy increased

---

[2.] Quoted by Adamec, *Afghanistan's Foreign Affairs to the Mid-Twentieth Century*, 81.
[3.] Iqbal Ali Shah, "Young Afghans on Trek", p. 369.

commensurately in the course of the nineteenth century. As the clergy gained increasing political power in their roles as mobilizers and leaders of *jehad* against the British, they also began to exert greater influence in legitimizing and controlling the rulers. Legitimacy of authority depended in considerable degree on the ruler's acceptance and approval of values and behavior that conformed to Islamic precepts and to a lesser degree, to the mores of *pashtunwali*. As the result of actions of the ulama, commitment to *jehad* in defense of Islamic territory and the Islamic way of life became a requirement for political legitimacy in Afghanistan, and the rulers' policies toward the British continued to affect state-clergy relations for years.

In the last quarter of the nineteenth century, King `Abd al-Rahman was able to break down the political power and economic independence of the clergy by force of arms. He brought the institution of *jehad* under the state's control and made the clergy more dependent economically on the state. He implemented order and strengthened the role of the state in the realm of religion by establishing a hierarchy of highly qualified ulama subordinate to the state. Keenly aware that the legitimacy of his leadership was based on Islam, `Abd al-Rahman justified his absolute authority by adhering to the *shari`at* and strict orthodoxy.

`Abd al-Rahman's success in crushing the power of the clergy was, however, temporary and limited to his reign. Lax policies toward the religious establishment on the part of his son and successor, Amir Habib-Allah, along with political developments inside and outside of Afghanistan, afforded the members of the clergy opportunities to reassert themselves within a few years after Amir `Abd al-Rahman's death. Under the leadership of Nasr-Allah Khan Na'eb al-Saltana, the political influence of clergy, particularly in the tribal region bordering India, increased considerably. The rise of Afghan nationalism, pan-Islamism, and the entry of Turkey into the Great War generated strong religious feelings in support of the caliphate and brought religious leaders back to the forefront of Afghan politics, as *jehad* once again became a major political issue. At the same time, nationalism became a progressive force for change.

King Aman-Allah rose to power in circumstances of crisis following the sudden death of his father, Amir Habib-Allah. At that time he seemed keenly aware of the power of the ulama and knew that his claim as Habib-Allah's rightful successor could be approved or contested by clerical forces. He succeeded in displacing his uncle Sardar Nasr-Allah Khan, the leader of traditional forces in Afghanistan, by responding immediately to the general demand for independence and by declaring *jehad* against the British. The achievement of independence in the name of *jehad* earned him the support of the ulama, and a leadership status reserved for heroes.

After the War of Independence Aman-Allah pursued pam-Islamic goals in alliance with the Afghan ulama and with the leaders of the *khilafat* movement in British India. His call for Islamic solidarity and his support of the cause of Muslims outside Afghanistan, particularly his support of the *khilafat* movement in India, further strengthened his relations with the clergy. The ulama were pleased with his policies, which contrasted sharply to the pro-British tendencies of his father, Amir Habib-Allah, and his grandfather, Amir `Abd al-Rahman. However, when Aman-Allah embarked on his nation-building program, members of the clergy soon found themselves at odd ideologically with many of the government's policies.

The first stage of the Amani reforms was based on precepts of late nineteenth-century Muslim reformers elaborated by the Afghan intellectual, Mahmud Tarzi, in the pages of *Seraj al-Akhbar*. Although Tarzi was the catalyst in redefining Islamic tenets in more dynamic nation-building terms in Afghanistan, like many other nationalist Muslim reformers, he failed to establish a strong legitimizing basis for change. The presumption that Aman-Allah could shift the religious fervor generated in support of the War of Independence to support a program of social reform proved to be mistaken. Instead, Aman-Allah's attempts to create a new social order and a new Afghan identity based on a fresh interpretation of Islam had the contrary effect of increasing the leverage of the clergy and propelling them into the center of politics. As a consequence, there was a sudden rise in the political influence of the religious establishment during the reign of Aman-Allah in comparison to the relative weakness of the clergy in relation to the state during reign of `Abd al-Rahman, and even of Habib-Allah.

King Aman-Allah used tradition symbolicly to generate support and instill loyalty, but in general the policy of his government were of Western origin. His modernization program began with reform of the judiciary, a sensitive area of conflict between the state and the clergy in modern Islam. Insofar as many functions of the clergy were closely tied to the legal system, reform of the judiciary jeopardized their status and prerogatives and ultimately their power. The transfer to the state of the power to determine discretionary punishments (*ta`zirat*) and the introduction in 1923 of the Fundamental Law (*nezam-nama-i-asasi*), based on positive law, eventually aroused resentment among the orthodox clergy. For political reasons, the high ulama did not actively resist these changes initially. They were either dependent on the state as government employees or simply continued to support the regime because Aman-Allah had achieved Afghanistan's independence from Great Britain and had supported Muslims outside Afghanistan. Although the liberal faction of the high ulama in Kabul, the capital, initially endorsed Aman-Allah's reforms and even participated in codifying new laws, the more orthodox members of the high clergy, who formed the majority, were disturbed by the government's alleged tampering with the *shari`at* and the adverse impact of certain reforms on their own positions. As opposed to the high ulama, who were enmeshed in politics at the state level and were dependent on the regime for employment or monetary grants, the lower-ranking rural clergy were deeply involved in the affairs of the local population on whom they depended for their livelihood. Directly threatened by the reforms, they were the first to challenge the government's reform policies. Opposition to the reforms first surfaced in the Pashtun tribal regions, where parochial autonomy was greatest. General discontent then erupted in the Khost Rebellion. Typical of the Third World rebellions, the uprising in Khost was a peasant-tribal insurrection which found expression in religious terms by local *mollas*.

The interests of religious and tribal leaders coalesced during the Khost uprising. As the rebellion progressed, individuals in the ranks of high clergy, who had tacitly opposed the rebellion for political reasons, began to sympathize with the insurgents. When King Aman-Allah convened the *Loya-Jerga* of 1924 in the midst of the rebellion to seek the support of the high ulama for his reforms, the high clergy were given an opportunity to openly criticize and force revisions of controversial reforms. In matters of administration the high ulama did not oppose modernization, and they endorsed such unpopular reforms as military conscription and new taxes. On the other hand, they adamantly resisted social and legal reforms that they deemed contradictory to the *shari`at.* The fact that the regime succeeded in suppressing the rebellion by yielding to religious rather than to tribal demands was a clear indication that the political power of religious leaders in Afghanistan was expanding.

When Aman-Allah announced unprecedented new reforms in 1928, he precipitate a new crises of legitimacy for his regime. Although he never renounced his role as a proponent of Islam, his policies became increasingly heretical to the ulama. In many ways the reforms of 1928 threatened the prerogatives of the high clergy. Aman-Allah's bureaucratization program in the second stage included the seizure of religious endowments and explicit intrusion upon of the power and the prerogatives of the high clergy. Assaults on the *pir-morid* system and denigrations of the Mojaddedi *sheikhs* of Kabul (the Hazrats of Shurbazar) were among the serious offenses that turned the most powerful segment of Afghan clergy against the Amani regime.

This time *sheikhs* of the Sufi orders and senior members of the ulama provided essential leadership in starting the agitation. General discontent over the scope and the radical nature of reforms strengthened the position of the clergy against the regime. Aman-Allah's development plan covered far-reaching administrative reforms that challenged the traditional family structure, the village, the tribe, religious values, and customary practices all at once. The villages that contained the majority of the Afghan population were self-sufficient entities where tribal units co-existed with agricultural communities under a village head and a spiritual leader. Previously there had been little interference from a central government beyond periodic tax assessments.

As the result of Aman-Allah's push for centralization, the government bureaucracy became more invasive than any that had gone before, with more deeply felt consequences. Functions that the family, the tribal leader, the village head and the religious authorities had performed for centuries now tended to be gathered in the hands of the state. A Western-styled penal code was to replace familiar customs, which had evolved with the *shari`at* over centuries to deal with serious crimes. Social institutions such as tribal and subtribal *jergas*, which performed much of the work of the legal system, were to be replaced by a formal state judiciary. In addition, military service became compulsory and universal, and people were forced to obtain identity cards for business and legal transactions. Attempts such as these to restructure rural society produced general discontent and heightened susceptibility to nativist sentiment, which the clergy succeeded in mobilizing.

In his desire to push Afghanistan rapidly into the twentieth century, Aman-Allah failed to give sufficient attention to the social, political and economic realities of his country. He was driven by the idea that Afghanistan as a newly independent country had to go through a rapid reform program in order to catch up with the rest of the world. Otherwise, he felt that Afghanistan would fall far behind other countries, lose what it had fought for, and never achieve its proper place among civilized nations. In contrast to Turkey and Egypt, where the grounds for change had been prepared by earlier reforms in the nineteenth century, the experience of modernization in Afghanistan under Aman-Allah was sudden. Civil and dynastic wars, and the two British invasions retarded Afghanistan's progress during the nineteenth century. Unlike India and Egypt, which benefitted from British colonialism, Afghanistan experienced only the negative aspects of British imperialism. The imposition of protectorate status on Afghanistan in 1880, which brought the country's foreign relations under British control, blocked free access to the outside world and forced Afghanistan further into isolation. Centralization of state under Amir `Abd al-Rahman and a moderate reform program introduced by Amir Habib-Allah in the early twentieth century, brought a few changes, particularly in the areas of administration and education, but did not prepare the country for Aman-Allah's ambitious social transformation program.

As the result of his Grand Tour, Aman-Allah's urge to rapidly change the medieval picture of Afghanistan increased. His development program at this stage concentrated heavily on social and cultural reforms, but it also included projects for the growth of Afghan economy. In fact, as Poullada and Rubin have shown, important strides were made toward economic development during the first stage of reform and more projects were underway. Afghanistan did enjoy a degree of economic growth as a result of expansion of domestic and foreign trade, and serious efforts by the government to attract foreign capital and technical skills after the independence. During the Grand Tour, Aman-Allah concluded several commercial treaties to attract foreign investment and also purchased machinery for industrial projects.[4] However, neither offered immediate benefit to the rural population which carried the greater burden of reforms and taxes. These burdens along with corruption in the bureaucracy added to general dissatisfaction, permitting the dissident clergy to rally massive peasant support.

Among the reforms of 1928, the most controversial were those pertaining to the status of women. Aman-Allah's policies regarding women were integral to the larger goal of nation-buiding and dealt with female education, the abrogation of forced marriage, child marriage, discouragement of polygamy, veiling, and segregation of the sexes—all of which were issues of extreme sensitivity for pious Muslims, because family law constitutes the core of the *shari`at* and the veiling and seclusion of women are central to the traditional Islamic notion of morality. With the exception of Turkey, and to some extent Egypt, no other Islamic country

---

[4.] See Adamec, *Afghanistan's Foreign Affairs to the Mid-Twentieth Century*, 113-132.

had yet dared to address openly issues relating to the family and the veil. The opposition of the Egyptian and Iranian governments to Queen Soraya's appearing unveiled in Cairo and Tehran was a clear indication of the prevailing conservative attitude toward the *hejab* and women's issues in the Middle East during the 1920s. It was not surprising, therefore, that the Afghan ulama should find their most ready weapon against Aman-Allah in the polemic over polygamy, child marriage and the unveiling of women. Many of the reforms of 1928, such as changing the sabbath day from Friday to Thursday and and requiring the wearing of Western hats and suits in the capital, increased the misgivings and suspicions of the clergy that the regime intended to diminish Islamic culture in Afghanistan and replace it with non-Muslim Western culture. As the result of the agitation by the ulama, these issues, along with the government's interference in family matters and the practice of *hejab,* became dominant factors in the uprising that eventually brought about the collapse of the Amani regime.

Although the members of clergy played a pivotal role in legitimizing the insurgence against Aman-Allah, they were unable or unwilling to dictate its outcome. The Islamic resurgence in Afghanistan in the 1920s did not include an ideology or stratagem to place the clergy in power. The clergy-backed uprising against the regime was led by two opposing forces, the Shinwari Ghelzai Pashtuns from the south and the Kohistani Tajiks from the north, neither of which was willing to accept supremacy by the other. The rebellion was successful in overthrowing the Amani regime, but it failed to provide a basis of legitimacy for alternative clerical or popular political leadership. In the political chaos that ensued, General Mohammad Nader rose to power. His leadership strategy included close cooperation with the ulama and removal of Aman-Allah from the scene. So the clergy-inspired rebellion of 1928-1929 ended with an official declaration of *khal`* (removal from office) of Aman-Allah by the *Loya-Jerga* of 1931.

The theory that the British were involved in the uprising of 1928 against Aman-Allah received a great deal of credence in the Turkish, Soviet, Egyptian, and Muslim Indian press during and after the 1928 uprising. To what extent, if any, the British actually played a role in the overthrow of Aman-Allah, remains unclear. Although official correspondence among British officials reveal their intent to block Aman-Allah's return to power after his abdication, there is no evidence in official correspondence in British archives to suggest their involvement in the insurgence of 1928. It is certain, however, that if the British or any other foreign government were interested in deposing Aman-Allah, the unstable political environment created by sudden changes provided ample opportunity for meddling.[5]

Although King Aman-Allah was not able to balance the disparate political forces in Afghanistan, his reforms have historical significance. He created an

---

[5.] Several scholars of modernization theory have noted the possibility of foreign intervention in the turmoil caused by the clash between the forces of tradition and modernity.M.I.T. Study Group, "The Transitional Process," in Welch (ed.), *Political Modernization*, 31.

Afghan national identity, and many of the reforms he instigated survived. He was responsible for opening Afghanistan to the outside word, reorganizing the national bureaucracy along Western lines, overhauling the Afghan economy, and introducing order and discipline into the military. His educational reforms produced an educated middle class that played an important role in the future development of the nation, and despite the apparent failure of his campaign to emancipate women, the effort had long-range effects on the condition of women in Afghanistan. The opportunity for education was eventually extended to women, and mandatory veiling was ended in 1958, when the shock of unveiling women had subsided and efforts to unveil women had began in other parts of the Muslim world. With the exception of the penal codes, the Marriage Law, and the Constitution of 1923, which were the major focus of religious opposition, all other *nezam-nama*s of the Amani period, including those pertaining to conscription and identity cards, were reintroduced with slight changes in the name and context by the regime that followed.

Amir 'Abd al-Rahman (1880-1901)

Amir Habib-Allah (1901-1919)

King Habib-Allah with his wife Nur al-Haram olya Jenab in 1910

'Olya Hazrat Seraj al-Khawatin,
King Aman-Allah's mother, with her daughters

Traditional veil, preparing to go out

Aman-Allah 'Ain al-Dawla at the age of 9

Sardar Nasr-Allah Khan Na'eb al-Saltana
during his visit to London in 1896

Mahmud Tarzi as Afghan Minister to France (1922-1924) with the staff of Afghan delegation in Paris, 1923

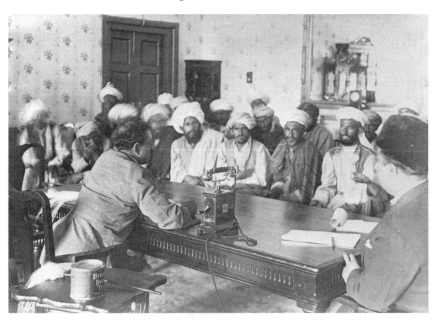

King Aman-Allah conferring with tribesmen in Jalalabad, 1926

King Aman-Allah wrapped in the Iranian flag. On his right is Ettela' al-Molk, the Iranian Minister to Afghanistan wearing the Afghan flag to demonstrate unity and brotherhood between the two neighboring Muslim countries.

The Afghan Foreign Minister, Mohammad Wali Khan, in the center, being greeted in Bombay by delegation of the Khilafat Conference. On his right is the mother of Shawkat Ali and Mohammad 'Ali, leaders of the Khilafat Movement.

King Aman-Allah and Jamal Pasha during the latter's visit to Kabul in 1921

Sir Francis Humphrys, the British Minister in Kabul (January 1922-February 1929)

King Aman-Allah addressing the congregation at the
'Idgah Mosque in Kabul in 1926

Courtesy of *The Illustrated London News Picture Library*, London.

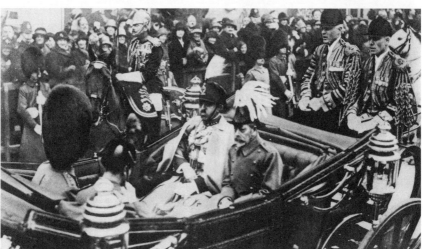

King Aman-Allah and Queen Soraya with King George VI and
Queen Mary in London, March 1928

Courtesy of *The Illustrated London News Picture Library*, London.

Queen Soraya during her visit in London, March 1928

King Aman-Allah lecturing during the European Tour, 1928

Courtesy of *The Illustrated London News Picture Library*, London.

King Aman-Allah with Kamal Attaturk during the former's
visit to Ankara, June 1928

Courtesy of *The Illustrated London News Picture Library*, London.

Royal ladies in viol veils watching tennis in Paghman, October 1928

King Aman-Allah introducing Soraya as the official queen of Afghanistan and Prince
Rahmat-Allah as his heir to delegates in the *Loya-Jerga* of 1928

King Aman-Allah and Queen Soraya upon their return to Kabul in September 1928

روز یکشنبه ۹ میزان ۱۳۰۷ ساعت ۴ و ۹ صبح روانه اروپا ...

First Afghan girls to study abroad, October 1928

Nur al-Mashayikh in later years

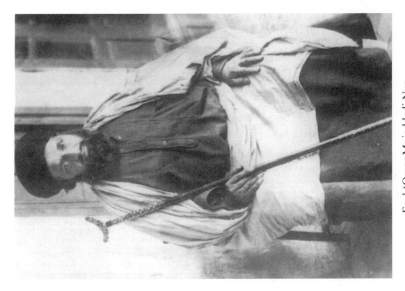

Fazl 'Omar Mojaddadi Nur
al-Mashayikh

Mohammad Sadeq Mojaddadi, the Hazrat of Shurbazar, also known as Gol-Agha in 1930

Akhundzada Amir Mohammad, known as the Molla Saheb of Chaknawur

Habib-Allah Kalakani, known as Bacha-i-Saqaw, at the time of his accession to the throne in 1929. Sayyid Hosain, Habib-Allah's brother, is standing.

'Ali Ahmad Khan (Loynab), the Governor of Kabul in 1928. He was executed by Habib-Allah Kalakani in July 1929.

King Nader Shah (1929-1933)

Table 1

Lineage of the Clerical Barakzai Family of Qandahar

Akhunundzada Mohammad Esma'il Barakzai

Akhunundzada Mohammad Sa'id (Khan Molla Khan under Shah Mahmud Saduzai)

Qazi 'Abd Al-Salam (Khan Molla Khan under Amir Shir 'Ali)

Akhunundzada 'Abd al-Rahman (Khan Molla Khan under Amir 'Abd al-Rahman)

Akhunundzada Sa'd al-Din (Governor of Herat and the Qazi al-Quzat under Amir Habib-Allah)

Akhunundzada 'Abd al-Karim

Akhunundzada 'Abd al-Shokur (Qazi al-Quzat under King Aman-Allah)

Akhunundzada Ahmad 'Ali (Qazi of Herat under King Nader Shah and King Zaher Shah)

Table 2

Genealogy of the Mojaddadi Sheikhs of Kabul

Imam Rabbani Sheikh Ahmad Faruqi Mojaddad Alf Al-Sani (d. 1034/1624)

Mohammad Ma'sum 'Orwat Al-Wusqa (d. 1079/1661)

Mohammad Sebghat-Allah Qayyum Jahan (d. 1122/1710)

Imam Mohammed Ma'sum Sani Qutb al-Aqtab (d. 1161/1748 in Peshawar), Contemporary of Ahmad Shah Dorrani

Shah Saffi-Allah Qayyum Jahan (d. 1212/1798 in Hejaz) Established the Mojaddadi *khaneqah* in Kabul, Contemporary of Timur Shah and Zaman Shah

Mian 'Abd al-Baqi (d. 1287/1870) Contemporary of Amir Dust Mohammed and Shir 'Ali

Mian Gholam Seddiq (d. 1305/1888) Contemporary of Amir 'Abd al-Rahman

Gholam Qayyum also known as Qayyum Jahan (d. 1329/1913) Contemporary of Amir Habib-Allah

Fazl Mohammad Shams al-Mashayikh (d. 1342/1925)

Fazl 'Omar (Nur al-Mashayikh d. 1371/1953)

Mohammad Sadeq (Afghan Minister in Cairo) d. 1974

Fazl 'Osman

Mohammad Harun

Sana' Ma'sum (Sabajan or Mianjan (d. 1971)

Mohammad Ebrahim Shir Pachajan (Ziya al-Mashayikh), arrested in 1978, whereabouts unknown

Hashem, 'Abd-Allah

Sebghat-Allah (Shahzadajan, the leader of the National Liberation Front, *Jabha-i-Melli-Afghanistan*, 1979-   )

Table 3

Pir-Khalifa Lineage of the Qaderiyya Warrior Tribal Sheikhs of the Eastern Province

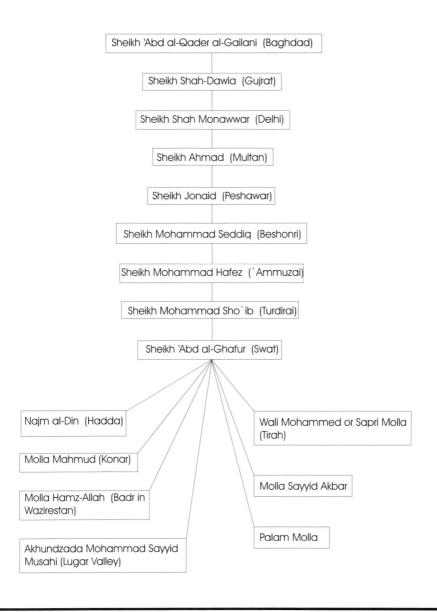

Table 4

The influential Disciples of the Molla Najm al-Din of Hadda

Padshah Saheb of Islampur (Mir Mohammad Saheb Jan, d. 1928), inherited the benefits of the shrine of Hadda at the death of Molla Najm al-Din. He was influential among the Mohmand and Safi tribes, succeeded by his son Sayyid `Abbas Bacha.

Ostad Saheb of Hadda (Molla Payenda Mohammad) from Kabul of the Reka tribe, the custodian of the shrine at Hadda.

Molla Saheb of Chaknawur (Akhundzada Amir Mohammad, d. 1930) from Chaknawur, in Jalalabad, was influential among the Khawazai and Baezai Mohmands.

Hajji Saheb of Turangzai (Fazl-i-Wahed), influential among all followers of the Molla of Hadda.

Akhundzada Saheb of Tagaw (Hamid-Allah d. 1929, son of Mir `Osman, a prominent religious leader and a participant in the Second Anglo-Afghan War,) influential among the Safi tribemen of Tagaw, Laghman and Jalalabad, succeeded by his son Mian Gol who was also known as the Akhundzada of Tagaw.

Hazrat Saheb of Charbagh (Mohammad Amin Zia al-Ma`sum Fida'i Ma`Sum Jan, related to the Mojaddadis of Kabul, d. 1919), influential in Jalalabad and Kabul, was the *pir* of Amir Habib-Allah and Nasr-Allah Khan, succeeded by his son Shahzada Jan.

Mian Saheb of Hessarak, influential among the nomadic Ghelzai tribes at the border.

Sufi Saheb of Baiktut (Molla `Alam-gol Faqir Mohammad) of Sangak Kheil tribe from Mazina, influential in Rudat, Shinwar and Mohmand.

Mian Saheb of Baru (Akhundzada Qamar al-Din), influential throughout Nangarhar or Eastern province.

Mian Saheb of Sarkani (Jan Mohammad `Abd al wadud), influential among the Mohmands in Konar.

Lala Pir (Sayyid La`l Shah) was influential among Khostwalis, Wazirs and Mahsuds (Mas`uds).

Hazrat Saheb of Botkhak (`Abd al-Shokur), a cousin of Zia al-Ma`sum, influential among Ahmadzai Ghelzais.

Babri Molla (Sayyid Ahmad Shakar Gol) influential among the Mohmands.

Mowlawi `Abd al-Wadud, known as Molla Galai or Garai, fom Mazina in Jalalabad.

Sayyid `Abd al-Karim, known as Pacha Saheb, from Mazina of Rodat in Jalabad.

Sheikh Saheb of Nazian (Akhundzada `Abd al-Hamid), from Nazian in Laghman, resided in Kabul, was influential among the Afridi and Orakzai tribes and in Qandahar.

Molla Saheb of Dawlatzai (Ahmad Jan) from Chapalhar near Jalalabad.

Padshah Saheb of Tirgari (Sayyid Hazrat Shah also known as Baba Saheb) in Laghman, near Jalalabad was succeeded by his brother Sayyid Ziwar Shah, influential in Laghman among the Safi tribes.

Table 5

Prominent Government-employed Ulama (1901-1929)

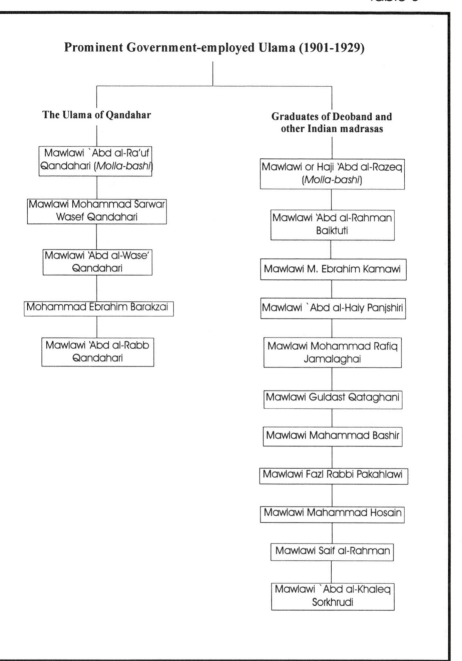

The Ulama of Qandahar

Mawlawi `Abd al-Ra'uf Qandahari (*Molla-bashi*)

Mawlawi Mohammad Sarwar Wasef Qandahari

Mawlawi `Abd al-Wase' Qandahari

Mohammad Ebrahim Barakzai

Mawlawi `Abd al-Rabb Qandahari

Graduates of Deoband and other Indian madrasas

Mawlawi or Haji `Abd al-Razeq (*Molla-bashi*)

Mawlawi `Abd al-Rahman Baiktuti

Mawlawi M. Ebrahim Kamawi

Mawlawi `Abd al-Haiy Panjshiri

Mawlawi Mohammad Rafiq Jamalaghai

Mawlawi Guldast Qataghani

Mawlawi Mahammad Bashir

Mawlawi Fazl Rabbi Pakahlawi

Mawlawi Mahammad Hosain

Mawlawi Saif al-Rahman

Mawlawi `Abd al-Khaleq Sorkhrudi

Table 6

Genealogy of Afghan Royal Dynasties (1747-1973)

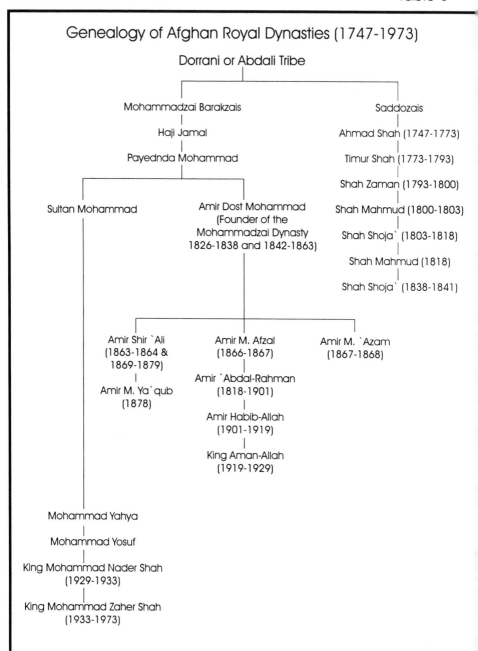

Dorrani or Abdali Tribe

Mohammadzai Barakzais

Haji Jamal

Payednda Mohammad

Sultan Mohammad

Amir Dost Mohammad
(Founder of the
Mohammadzai Dynasty
1826-1838 and 1842-1863)

Saddozais

Ahmad Shah (1747-1773)

Timur Shah (1773-1793)

Shah Zaman (1793-1800)

Shah Mahmud (1800-1803)

Shah Shoja` (1803-1818)

Shah Mahmud (1818)

Shah Shoja` (1838-1841)

Amir Shir `Ali
(1863-1864 &
1869-1879)

Amir M. Ya`qub
(1878)

Amir M. Afzal
(1866-1867)

Amir `Abdal-Rahman
(1818-1901)

Amir Habib-Allah
(1901-1919)

King Aman-Allah
(1919-1929)

Amir M. `Azam
(1867-1868)

Mohammad Yahya

Mohammad Yosuf

King Mohammad Nader Shah
(1929-1933)

King Mohammad Zaher Shah
(1933-1973)

APPENDIX A

Afghanistan and Russia

Having in view the reforms which were needed in our military forces in the provinces and in the improvement and re-organization which the ministry for war had previously planned, our government, acting on the advice of its counsellors, was obliged to send some of the ministers to Mazar-i-Sharif, Qataghan, Badakhshan, Herat, Jalalabad and Kandahar to organize the civil administration, reform the military forces and discharge old and unfit soldiers. But the steps for the improvement of our forces in the North have appeared to the people as an indication of some secret or open difference between the Russian and Afghan governments and they are spreading and publishing rumors so that I have been obliged to make known the policy of my government in order to remove existing doubts. Afghanistan in no circumstances wishes to create trouble for her friendly neighbors Russia and Bokhara. Since the Afghan government regards Bokhara as an Islamic state, and her people as their brothers, how can they possibly be desirous of creating trouble and difficulties for them? In fact Afghanistan is a supporter of the independence and complete freedom of Bokhara and any infringement of the rights of Bokhara is a source of grief for her.

The Russian Republic, in accordance with the Treaty between the two states, accepted the independence of Bokhara with all the conditions of self-government.

Accordingly, the present disturbances in Bokhara are regarded by Afghan statesmen as a kind of internal disorder, in which the Russian and Afghan governments have no right to interfere. Afghanistan, disapproving particularly of this kind of internal strife, remains neutral.

The government of His Majesty Our King is making the utmost efforts to improve its internal administration and to strengthen the friendly relations which exist with neighboring states.

The idea of world conquest, or of trampling on the rights of others, does not enter into our policy, but rather we look on such actions as evidence of moral turpitude.

I have full confidence that relations between Afghanistan will, day by day, be more surely directed towards, and will strengthen, the welfare and freedom of Bokhara and Khiva.

Mohammad Wali

Source: *Aman-i-Afghan*, July 29, 1902; also NAI, File 378-F, sec. 1923

APPENDIX B

*Nezam-nama*s Promulgated Between 1919 and 1928

Central Government Organization:
I. Ministries:
    Post Office, 1921-22
    Constitution, 1923
    Central Organization, 1923-24
    Ministry of Finance, 1920
    Ministry of Education, 1923
    Ministry of Foreign Affairs, 1923
    Ministry of Justice, 1923
    Publication, 1924
    Ministry of War, 1923
II. Sub-Ministries:
    1. Inspections, 1920
    2. Sale of State Land, 1920
    3. Government Buildings, 1922
    4. Buildings in Paghman, 1922
    5. Buildings in Laghman, 1923
    6. Afghan Government Consulates, 1923
    7. Accounting Office, Ministry of Foreign Affairs, 1923
    8. Personnel Offices in Ministries, 1923
    9. Offices of Archives and Correspondence, 1923
    10. Construction of the City of Dar al-Aman, 1923
    11. Sale of Government Property, 1923
III. Civil Servants:
    1. Attendance, 1922-23
    2. Leave, 1923
    3. Resignation, 1924 & 1928
IV. Finance:
    1. Finance, 1920
    2. Inspection of Finance, 1920
    3. Accounting Office, 1920
    4. Clearance of Past Accounts, 1921
    5. Job Description for Finance, 1921
    6. Tax Collection, 1920
    7. General Budget, 1922

Provincial Administration and Economics:
I. Definition of Jurisdiction:

      1. Provincial and District Boundaries, 1921
      2. Municipalities, 1924
      3. Village Administration, n.d.
II. Duties of Administrators:
      1. Governors and Subordinate Officials, 1921
      2. District Officials, n.d.
      3. Provincial Finance Officials, 1923
      4. Agricultural Officials , 1923
III. Provincial Economic Policy:
      1. Livestock Tax, 1922
      2. Dry Farming, 1923
      3. Food Supplies, 1927
      4. Land Settlement (Qataghan), 1923

Military:
I. Organization
      1. Penal Code, 1921-22
      2. Uniforms, 1920
      3. Duties of Clerks, 1920
      4. Compulsory Military Service, 1926
      5. Ranks, 1927-28
II. Training
      1. Noncommissioned Officers, 1922-23
      2. Superior and Junior Officers, 1927-28

Citizenship and Civil Status:
      1. Medals (Decorations), 1920
      2. Official Titles, 1921
      3. Identity Cards, Citizenship, Passports, 1922
      4. Immigrants, 1923
      5. State Decorations, 1925
      6. Residence of Foreigners in Afghanistan, n.d.

Changes in the Law:
      1. Handbook for Judges, "Tamassuk al-Qozat," 1921
      2. Legal Rights of Civil Servants, 1921
      3. Prisons, 1923
      4. Life Imprisonment and the Death Penalty, 1924
      5. General Penal Code, 1920 and 1924
      6. Laws Concerning Criminal Cases in *Shari`at* Courts, 1927
      7. *Fatawa-i-Amaniyya*, 1925

Education:
      1. Ministry of Education, 1923
      2. Teachers' Training Colleges, 1923

3. Medal of Education, 1923-24
4. Publishing Department, 1923-24
5. Engineering School, n.d.
6. Private Schools (Mosque Schools), 1923
7. Dormitories, 1924
8. Secondary Education, 1923-24

Social and Cultural:

1. Marriage, 1920 (Child marriage and extravagant expenses of weddings abolished) Marriage, 1923 (Polygamy discouraged)
2. Funerals, 1922
3. Abolishment of Slavery, 1919 (by Royal Decree)
4. Abolishment of Forced Labor, 1920 (by Royal Decree)
5. Prohibition against wearing *kollah* (cap) or *dastar* (turban), 1928 (by Royal Decree)
6. Western Dress Required in Kabul, 1928 (by Royal Decree)

Public Welfare:

1. Welfare and Training of Orphans, 1926
2. Administration of Home for Indigents, n.d.

APPENDIX C

Royal Proclamation

To my dear sisters, the inhabitants of Kabul and its vicinity:
The following provisions have been ratified for your welfare and that of your daughters and are herewith announced for your information.

Every one knows that mankind originated from one man and one woman. Had there been only one man and not a woman or visa versa the human race would have been quickly extinguished from the surface of the earth. Therefore, by strict definition, neither a man nor a woman alone can be regarded as a complete human. A man and a woman together form the complete human being, as the survival of both is essential for the continuation of the human race. Thus, the responsibilities of life have been divided between men and women. Women are in charge of raising children, preparing food and managing the household, and men are responsible for earning a living and providing for the family. If we examine their respective roles carefully, we see that the responsibilities of women are even more difficult than those of men, particularly in the area of child care, which means that without acquiring proper education herself, it is virtually impossible for a woman to properly fulfill this most important responsibility in life. Women are in charge of bringing up the future generation, the most important responsibility in life. If we deprive women of education, we have, in effect, incapacitated half of our body and have destroyed our subsistence with our own hands.

It was not in vain that Hazrat Mohammad (may peace be upon him) made the acquisition of knowledge obligatory for both men and women without ascribing any special privilege [to men] when he said, "to gain knowledge is the religious duty of all Muslim men and women." The Mohammadan law (*shar`-i-mostafawi*) allows a woman to become a *qazi*, and it is obvious that in order to reach that rank one has to go through years of study with a great master and acquire a great deal of knowledge. This proves that [in Islam] education is considered equally important for women. In the days when literacy had become common among Muslims and educational centers were established throughout the Muslim world, many women like men became famous scholars, *mohadithas* (specialists of *hadith*), literary persons, and artists. We all know that the *sahaba* and *tabe`in* consulted the Hazrats Om al-Momenin `Ayisha Seddiqa, Om Salma and Hafasa and sought their *fatwa* on difficult matters. Asiya bint Jar al-Allah was one of the great scholars of *hadith*. Jalal al-Din Saiyuti, the great Muslim scholar, took lessons from her. Ay Malak, the sister of Sheikh Jamal-al-Din Shara`i, was a contemporary of Ibn `Ajaz `Asqalan, the great scholar of *mohadith*, with whom she had many scholarly debates. Asma' bint Mohammad, the sister of Qazi al-Qozat Najm al-Din, was acclaimed as a pious woman and a

221

scholar of *hadith.* She studied and taught many books on the *hadith* of Makki. Imam Saiyuti studied the *Thalathiyat-i-Mosnad* under Alef bint al-Jamal. There are many examples of highly educated and famous women scholars, teachers, and saints in Islamic history, and there are many examples of women who demonstrated great bravery in war. In short, it is rational and legally proper for women to acquire knowledge.

In response to an urgent need, two girls schools, Maktab-i-Masturat and Maktab-i-'Asmat, were established last year in Sara-i-'Olya and Qal`a-i-Baqer Khan in Kabul. However, since neither of these schools could accommodate more students, and the first one was a little too far from the city, both schools were merged in Golistan Saray, which has superior rooms and can house 800 students. In this way all female students will be able to meet in one place, where their expenses for clothing, food, veils, and books will be paid by the government on an equal basis. A number of skilled teachers will be recruited from inside the country and from abroad to teach classes in home economics, child development, sewing, knitting, and cooking. Since the regular girls' school will recruit only young girls between the ages of six and ten, a vocational school has been established for adult women to provide professional training in sewing, cooking, and making artificial flowers. The purpose of this school is to help women learn new skills and become financially independent in order to release themselves from total financial dependence on their husbands or their families. By the end of the year 1301 [1922], the students who graduate with the first, second or third rank in any of the above professions will receive awards of 1000, 700, and 400 rupees, respectfully. If a student ranks first in all three, she will receive 1,500, and if she ranks second in all three, she will receive 1000 rupees. In addition, by learning a skill that will help them earn money, women will become assets to their husbands. The vocational women's school (Maktab-i-Sanayi`-i-Onathia) is also housed in Golistan Saray and is awaiting the attendance of ambitious and high-minded sisters.

Qualified teachers will receive good salaries and, in addition, will render a service to the educational program of our beloved country.

By means of this proclamation, I inform you that whosoever wants to register in Maktab-i-Masturat or Sanayi`-i-Onathia or would like to apply for a teaching position should send her resume to the director of Maktab-i-Masturat for permission and benefit from sources of knowledge and information. At this stage, students will be placed in different classes according to the level of their achievement.

The supervisor of women's schools
Seal of Queen Soraya
(signed) Shahzada Khanom

Source: National Archives of Afghanistan (*Archif-i-Melli-i-Afghanistan*), no. 197, 37.

APPENDIX D

The Platform of *Ferqa-i-Esteqlal wa Tajaddod*

The platform for the Party of Independence and Reform (*Ferqa-i-Esteqlal wa Tajaddod*) reads as follows:

1. The Party of Independence and Reform is a legal national political party with its headquarters in Kabul.

2. The goal of the Party of Modernity is to elevate the Afghan nation to the highest possible stage of progress and to prevent all types of authoritarianism in the administration. The Party proclaims the custody of Afghanistan's independence as its primary goal and duty for the present and for the future.

3. The Party will try to remove from politics all superstitions which are not in conformity with Islam but have become a part of religious practices through old customs. It is the aim of the Party to establish political, social, and economic laws that will meet popular needs and that conform to the requirements of contemporary civilization.

4. The Party will exert its energy and effort for the welfare and sovereignty of the Afghan people. It recognizes the equality of individuals before the law and rejects all kinds of class, group, family, and individual privilege. It is the moral duty of each member of the Party to avert all kinds of maltreatment and injustice.

5. The Party will foster ideological unity among the citizens. It will apply this principle to all aspects of its activities. The Party's primary objective is to establish the authority of enacted law throughout the nation.

6. The Party will attempt to gain electoral votes with programs and activities that guarantee the welfare of the people.

7. The organization of the Party will begin in the capital and extend throughout the country to the smallest village.

8. The members of the Party will pay a small membership fee.

9. His Majesty the King is the president and the founder of the party.

APPENDIX E

Secret
Baluchistan Intelligence Bureau
Quetta, January 27, 1928

My Dear Colonel,

I have obtained a certain amount of information concerning a gathering which is proposed to be convened in Dera Ismail Khan under the leadership of the Hazrat Sahib of Shor Bazaar, Kabul-Fazli Umr [Omar] by name-who's who 498 of 1922. As will be seen further on, this meeting may have concerned the party in Kandahar [Qandahar] which came into evidence in the beginning of last year.

In August last year I obtained information concerning the Hazrat Sahib. I was informed that he was in regular correspondence with the following important men in Afghanistan:

Abdul Aziz Khan	Acting War Minister
Abdul Usman Khan	Who's Who No. 834 of 1927
Sher Ahmad Khan	Who's Who No. 773 of 1927
Abdul Hakim Khan	Who's Who No. 50 of 1927
Mohd Yaqub Khan	Sulaiman Khel of Gardiz
Malik Zalmai	Mangal, Who's Who No. 877 of 1927
	(arrested by the King during his Gardiz tour)

The above men are said to be "murids" of the Hazrat Sahib. It was hinted to me that the Hazrat Sahib was perhaps trying to engineer a plot against the Afghan Government.

Quite recently a mullah named Abdul Rahim, Musa Khel, a resident of Zana khan (38 c.c.2) in the vicinity of Ghazni arrived in Quetta. This man is said to have escaped being arrested when the King was in Gardez owing to timely warning having been conveyed to him by Ali Ahmad Khan. He left Quetta in the company of a mullah named Haji Dost Mohd residing in the Toba. The latter is the source of information received by me.

Both of the above mullahs are the "murids" of the Hazrat Sahib. They have both proceeded to D.I.K. [Dera Ismail Khan]

According to information, the following mullahs are also to be present in D.I.K.:

Said Amir of Zarmat; A mullah relative of mullah Jangi Khan; The mullah of the Gurbaz clan; Mullah Karim Khan, Kharoti, Mullah Khan Mir.

The following maliks are also to be present at the meeting:

Malik Baland Khan .. Zadran. This man also effected his escape.
Malik Mangal, son of Malik Khohi Dad, who is at present a prisoner in Kabul.

Possible connection with the Kandahar party

In addition, Qazi Mohammad Akbar of Kandahar, whose recent dismissal was reported in my Diary No. 5 of 1928, and whose arrival in Chaman with Civil Brigadier Abdul Ali (see Kandahar Conspiracy Case) was also reported, Diary No. 55 of 1928, left Quetta for Lahore on the 25th instant. While in Quetta he inadvertently mentioned the fact he intended to see the Hazrat Sahib either at Lahore or in D.I.K. In order to watch his movement I was able to get a man of mine to accompany him as a servant.

The presence of Qazi Akbar at the meeting may indicate the existence of an understanding between the Simat-i-Janubi [Samt-i-Jonubi] party and the Kandahar party. Mohammad Akbar realized that he had made a slip in mentioning his intended visit to the Hazrat Sahib as he subsequently tried to eradicate the impression that he had given.

If there is any such understanidng I would say that the Afghan Trade Agent in Quetta, Mirza Khuda Dad Khan, is also concerned as he is with the party to which Mohammad Akbar, Abdul Ali and Mastaufi Saiyd Habib belong.

Reason for calling the meeting

My informant states that the reason of the calling of meeting is to formulate plans whereby the "Jadid Party" [*Modernist Party, Firqah-i-Esteqlal wa Tajaddud*] or new party in Afghanistan can be overthrown. He stated that the "ulema" [`ulama] and the common people of Afghanistan were entirely opposed to the new party in the plans for which they see only disaster for Afghanistan and Islam. They are not actively against the King but they desire to bring off a coup during his absence by obliterating the new party and with this as a *fait accompli*, to force the king to break away from his present attitude as regards the tenets of Islam. If, however, he refuses to do so they are prepared to set up a republic.

Haji Dost Mohammad is expected back as soon as the meeting is over and further information will, it is hoped, become available.

Place of meeting

As far as I can gather, the probable place of meeting will be at **Paniala** near Paharpore (38 L.D.4.)

If not too late, I would suggest that the D.I.B. be informed in order that the proceedings may secretly be watched.

***

Secret
No.R.S.3./12/N.G.O.3.
Baluchistan Intelligence Bureau

My Dear Colonel.

As reported in my telegram of yesterday, Mullah Haji Dost Mohammad has returned from D.I.K. and I have interviewed him. He travelled with Mullah Abdul Rahim (see previous letter) whose real name is Mullah Mohammad Hassan, to Harnai with the intention of proceeding by car to D.I.K. via Loralai and Duki but information received on the state of the road caused them to change their minds and they proceeded by train.

In D.I.K. they met the Hazrat Sahib. There were several other mullahs present and the discussion centered around the proposed rising in the Khost. Also the inclusion, or other wise, of one or more of the sons of the late Sardar Ayub Khan. From what I have gathered of late the latter part of the scheme has been thrust on the Hazrat Sahib. That he is against it, as also are his mullahs, was made clear to me. The Simat-i-Janubi do not wish any deviation from a purely religious rising which would be the case if any attempt were made to usurp the throne from Amanulla [Aman-Allah]. The issue would then be mixed and the support that the Simat-i-Janubi expects from the rest of Afghanistan in a religious struggle might be jeopardized if there were an attempt at the same time on the throne.

To begin with the plot centering around the sardars. Apparently two men whose names are not known, arrived in D.I.K. They are Ahmedzais and have met Mohd Akram in Bans Bareilly, and Abdul Kadir in Lahore and are said to have come with the express purpose of aiding the two above mentioned men to escape into Afghanistan. The original idea was that one should find his way into the Simat-i-Janubi, the other into the Simat-i-Mashriqi. They met the Hazrat Sahib and propounded their proposal and asked for his aid. He refused to have anything to do with their entry into the Simat-i-Janubi. He told the two men that they should obtain their entry into the Simat-i-Mashriqi. The date apparently had been fixed for the attempted escape. The night of the Shab-i-Barat. Messengers were sent in order to effect the necessary change in their plans consequent to the refusal of Hazrat Sahib to allow any entry to Simat-i-Janubi. (As explained there is no desire on the Hazrat's part to have them mixed up in his own particular show). These two men have also, it is said, obtained the promise of cooperation from the Mullah of Chaknaur. The latter has stated that he is ready. The mother of Mohd. Akram is a Mohmand or has Mohmand blood and the tribe is ready to help. This woman apparently travelled from Bans Bareilly to the Sirhand Sharif shrine to interview the Hazrat and finding him gone to D.I.K. wrote him a letter to the effect that as she had permission to travel as far only as Sirhand Shariff, requested that he should come and see her. He refused....

I will now deal with Hazrat's own show. After many discussions and having satisfied themselves that they were acting in accordance with the Shariat a decision was reached that a rising should take place. With this object in view two mullahs, Mohammad Hassan, alias Abdul Rehim, and Mohd Jan, have left for the Simat-i-Janubi in order to prepare the Mangal and Zadran tribes. Malik Biland has also left for Zadran. Malik Ghulam Khan, son of Malik Sardar of the Gurbaz clan, has left for Gurbaz. (Note, Malik Sardar of the Gurbaz is dead and his son is now malik).

The maliks of the Ghilzais in the D.I.K. district apparently all met the Hazrat Sahib in secret conferences and have promised their clans on his behalf.

The following maliks were in D.I.K. when the informant left: Id Mohd Khan, Mallakhel; Zarin Khan, Khwajak.

When the show is started Haji Mullah Dost Mohammad (the informant) is to be informed by the Hazrat Sahib and he has been deputed to travel via Duki, Loralai and Thal to stir up the returning Ghilzais.

The following men are also in the plot: Abdul Hakim Khan, Governor of Ghazni; Abdul Aziz Khan, Officiating War Minister; F.M. Shah Mahmud, Governor of Semit-i-Mashriqi; Faiz Mohammad Khan, Wizarat-i-Muarif [Minister of Education]; Mohammad Usman Khan, previous governor of Kandahar.

The Hazrat Sahib was expecting a Qazi from Kandahar to attend the conference (Mohd Akbar). The informant did not know his name. He sent him a telegram addressed to Sardar Zakariya in Lahore requesting his attendance. He, however, did not arrive.

The date fixed for the rising to come off was any time up to the 15th of Ramadan (8th March).

The conspirators feel confident of success and expect the active co-operation of Zimindawar [Zamindawar]. The informant stated that two of Hazrat's relatives were working in Kabul. They are Mohammad Sadiq, younger brother called Gul Agha; Masum, the nephew.

Note. The elder brother of Fazil Umar the present Hazrat Sahib was named Fazl Mohd, called Shah Agha. Died in 1925.

As far as I could gather there is a decided opinion against Amanullah. The Ghilzais are against "hasht nafari" which has been forced upon them. Reported by me in paras. 392, 586 of 1927. They are also angered by the oppression of Afghan troops (see para 433 of 1927). The mullahs have their own axe to grind. They are very anti Russian and hope that Russian help will be forthcoming to the Government as they then consider that all Afghanistan will be cemented to their cause. At present I have no further information but hope that I have given sufficient to go on with.

Yours sincerely,
R.N.G. Scott.

***

Secret
No. R.S./10/NGO.Baluchistan Intelligence Bureau
Quetta, February 21, 1928
My Dear Colonel:

The following may be of some interest to you in connection with the movement reported by me against the Young Afghan Party and King Amanullah.

(i).The Afghan Trade Agent, Quetta is cognisant of some movement and in my opinion is anti-Amanullah. For (a) he, in course of conversation with my Indian officer, when told that the period of Amanullah's stay in England was to be of about three weeks duration, remarked that it was quite a possibility that Amanullah would be a State guest for the remainder of his life: (b) he is making purchases of all illustrated papers depicting the unveiled Queen of Afghanistan and despatching them to Kabul separately as soon as he gets them. His attitude on this account towards the Queen is one of hatred: (c) he suspects Mohd. Wali—the Regent in Kabul—to be secretly in favour of disaffection against Amanullah hoping that luck may be on his side to step into his shoes should Amanullah be deposed. The latter he says may depend on Nadir Khan should he ever come into the field.

(ii).Nadir Khan has been mentioned as being behind the Hazrat Sahib should his schemes go wrong, then Nadir Khan would be blamed, and, as he is in Switzerland, he cannot be harmed. Nadir Khan is also a murid of Fazli Umar.

(iii).A man who has previously worked for me has arrived from D.I.K. and has informed me that Fazli Umar is "courting" the Hazrat Sahib of Paniala. The latter is paramount among the Gilzais. Fazli Umar has himself been frequently visiting the Ghilzais.

My man who has no knowledge of facts as I know them said that undoubtedly something was on foot in D.I.K. What it was he did not know. But the Hazrat Sahib has mixed you in it. As he put it "even a man who knew nothing about intelligence work could realize that something was being hatched." I hope that I shall be able to utilize his services in order to get some further information from D.I.K.

Yours sincerely,
Sd/ R.N.G. Scott.
Intrigue to create trouble in Afghanistan during the King's absence in Europe.
NAI, F&PD, File No. 51-F, Secret, 1928.

APPENDIX F

A pir who has been expelled from Afghanistan is living in Dara Ismail Khan since some time. He is called pir Fazl and the Pawindas visit him. People look upon him with great suspicion. It is said he is the son of a well known deceased pir of Afghanistan in whom Amir Habibullah Khan had great faith. He took a leading part in the backward movement against the *nezam-namas* in spite of Amir Aman-Allah Khan's advice and the movement resulted in a rebellion. His Majesty simply expelled him from his dominions and gave him no further punishment out of respect for his father. After coming away from Afghanistan this pir went to different places in India and at last settled in Dera Ismail Khan where the political agent allotted two big houses to him. It is thought that Dera Ismail Khan has been selected to carry on propaganda against the government of Afghanistan and the reforms as the Pawindahs pass this way and it is somewhat obscure as compared with independence-loving Pashawar. His having no ostensible standard of livelihood, his standard of life, the visit of Pawindahs to him, Dera Ismail Khan's situation in the way of Pawindas and his getting two houses from the political agent are not facts that can be regarded as accidental.

Excerpt from the *Tarjoman-i-Sarhad* dated February 23, 1928

APPENDIX G

Servant of Nation and Faith, Amir 'Ali Ahmad Khan and Allegiance by the Ulama and Notables of Samt-i- Mashriqi

All *'alim*s, notables and inhabitants of the Samt-i-Mashriqi know that Amir 'Ali Ahmad Khan has been courageous and religious. He has rendered valuable services in and outside Afghanistan for the advancement of Islam and the Muslims. His enlightened thoughts have always been engaged in reforming the nation and the country. For these reasons it has been thought that he will be a great king. When His Majesty reached Jegdalek from Kabul, the ulama, *sheiks* and the notable of Khugiani, Surkhrud, and the neighborhood of Jagdalak went to his presence and offered allegiance. From Jegdalek he came to Chaharbagh-i-Safa to the house of Hazrat Naqib Sahib where the allegiance was renewed. After reaching Jalalabad on Friday he went to the house of the Akhund-zadah Sahib of Hadda. Here a body of ulama and *mashayikh*, including the Ustad of Hadda Mullah, Tuti Akhund-zada, Mian Sahib of Qilghu, and other ulama of Shinwar, Chaparhar and Khugiani offered allegiance to him as king. In the *hujra* (chamber) of the Akhund-zada Sahib of Hadda out of regard for its sanctity. On the next Friday the ulama, notables and the people assembled in the Masjid-i-Shahi, Jalalabad, and the *khutba* of the Friday service was in the name of the Servant of the Nation and the Faith, Amir 'Ali Ahmad Khan, the King of Afghanistan. After the prayer the ulama and the notables renewed their allegiance and the allegiance deeds were read amid sincere and enthusiastic cries of congratulation from all directions. His Majesty was given the title of the Servant of the Nation and the Faith.

His Majesty then delivered a speech which was full of national and Islamic sentiments, and in the course of the speech promised the following reforms based on the *shari'at* as the basis his government:

1. All *nezam-nama*s that were enforced in Aman-Allah's reign are abolished. All government affairs will be carried with full accord to the tenets of the *shari'at* and the Qura'n.

2. Conscription has been abolished. Men will, however, however be recruited on Rs. 20 per month for the defence of the country on their own will, according to the *qawmi* system.

3. Arrears of revenue etc. outstanding against the subjects for the period of Amanullah's reign and before that are remitted. Loans taken by government servants during Aman-Allah's reign will, however, be recovered by installments.

Reliable news as been received from Jegdalek that the Mullah Sahib of Tagaw and the *ulama* and people of most of the districts of Kabul have offered allegiance to His Majesty.

Source: *Ghairat-i-Islam*, Jalalabad, no. 1, January 28, 1929, editor `Abd al-Halim, NAI, F&PD, File 9-F, 1929.

APPENDIX H

Nader Khan's letter to the Jaji Tribe:

I am a servant of the Faith and the Kingdom of Islam and consider myself a well-wisher of the Afghans. In Paris I heard the dreadful news of Afghanistan. Although I was very ill at the time, my duty to Afghanistan came first, so with all haste I traveled to Peshawar.... God willing and with the unity of high-minded tribes of the Eastern and Southern provinces, we will proceed to Kabul and, after dethroning the tyrant robber [Habib-Allah] who has usurped the Kabul throne, will elect as king, with the consent and unity of the tribes, a man able to serve the Faith, the country of Afghanistan, and the nation....

(Translation of Nadir Khan's open letter to the Waziri Tribe, dated Ramadan 27, 1347/March 18, 1929, NAI, 302-G, 1929, p. 8; IOR., L/PS/10/1288, 5. 703-PS, March 19, 1929)

232

APPENDIX I

My dear gallant Tanni tribes, You are fully aware that Kabul, the center and capital of Afghanistan, has been raided and occupied by one Bacha Saqao, a man of low origin and famous only as a thief. His behavior must bring ruin and disaster to Afghanistan. He has taken from the treasury the savings of the past fifty years, and does not hesitate to kill the weak, to pillage property, or to violate the honor of noble families. He has closed the roads by which grain and firewood were taken to Kabul, and every day hundreds of men die of starvation. He has no other object than to bring about the ruin of Afghanistan and the destruction of the Musselmans. It has come to my attention that he has been encouraged by the English, and that he acts under their instructions. Evidently this is a situation of *kafer*s (unbelievers) against Islam—so much so that on the 9th day of Hut, by the grace of God, I, together with the army and all the Ghelzais and the Duranis of Kandahar, will move on Kabul. If I were to send for all of you, it would be inconvenient. So at present intelligent men of your tribe should come to see me at Ghazni so that I may interview them, and if God wishes, we will join hands and clear out of the country the unclean bodies of the enemy, removing this blot from the name of the Afghans. When, by the grace of God, this is done, a general *jerga* will be held and questions affecting the prosperity and welfare of the country will be discussed. I will then do what is best for the country.

> No. 130, dated the 4th Hut 1307/February 24, 1929. Page 67 of
> the Register of Royal Correspondence:
> Aman-Allah

6th Dalw 1307

To my dear sons, the inhabitants of the Southern Province

Internal disturbances began in the Eastern Province and, while these had not yet been settled, a party from the north suddenly marched upon Kabul.

These internal intrigues and dissensions are based solely upon the machinations of the enemies of the progress of Afghanistan. They have, however, put questions into the mouths of the public and of the ignorant [and have brought forward] certain unfounded objections to my person. I gave them fatherly advice, but as the fire of mischief and of their ignorance increased every moment and as I did not wish the fight and the quarrel to continue on account of me, or that Moslems should be killed and the nation ruined, or that strength collected for defense against enemies should be exhausted in a civil war, and also because of the fact that I do not attach importance to my personal rule (having taken up this heavy burden only for the sake of the prosperity of the country and the progress of the nation) I decided to ask my elder brother, the Moinal Sultanat, to accept the throne for the sake of public peace. The Moinal Sultanat did not agree at first, but when I insisted he accepted it for my sake. The people of the city made submission to him. Hoping that my departure from Kabul might end the civil war and the mischief, I decided to go to Kandahar and proceeded to that place. I explained this to the Kandahar citizens on my arrival there. These people, who represented all classes and communities, wept and cried and stated that they would have me only as their King. I did my best to explain the advantages of my idea, but the people did not accept it. I was also eagerly awaiting news of the state of affairs in Kabul. It appeared, however, from the development of the situation in Kabul that the mischief was not limited to the collection of objections against my person, but that on account of the intrigues of the enemies there was a desire to ruin and destroy unity. The sum total was that the fire was not extinguished and as the mischief makers had forces also, they did not accept the Moinal Sultanan. The Moinal Sultanat also came to Kandahar and again discussions were held with the entire population of Kandahar. Moinal Sultanat in the presence of all expressed a desire to be relieved of the throne and stated "I had no desire originally and have none now and I resign." The entire population of Kandahar unanimously came to me and said that I should not give up the kingship of the Musselmans of Afghanistan as long as one of them was alive. They said that their patriotism, their honor, and the fact that they were Afghans made it impossible to agree to the rule of a man like Bacha Saqao, who had spent his life as a murderer and a raider of the property of the Moslems and who was not even an Afghan. They cannot agree that he should be their King. The people of Kataghan, Mazar, Maimana, Herat, Farah, and Hazarajat have the same views as the people of Kandahar. I therefore, in accord with the desire of my dear nation and for the sake of saving the country from becoming a toy in the hands of the people of mean birth, accepted the throne. You, my dear children, the inhabitants of the Southern Province, are informed by means of this Firman, and I am sure that your noble Afghan sentiments cannot agree that a menial of no position should occupy the throne and make a toy of this sacred country and gallant nation for his personal desires. You have some tribal feuds and family dissensions, but a grave national problem has arisen and you should unite for the welfare and organization of the State and the country. I pray God to help me so that our enemies may not succeed. You should bravely carry out the administration and maintain peace in your territories.

Aman-Allah

APPENDIX J

Document 1
Sepahsalar Nader Khan's letter to His Majesty the Ghazi [Aman-Allah] reporting the situation in Central Asia, Qataghan, *Saratan* 2, 1301/June 23, 1922. AWSW Collection.

۳- سنع زمانی که در وقتِ لشکرکشی خدمت مردم نباشد چون به آنکا بنا بر گله و رفع گذشته غفل ای اند این ربره شته اعلیٰ ان که نباشد که دولت به تدبیر رعایت خاطر خوانند که تلافی اصلاح آن نماید.

۴- لشکرگیر از داده عنی سپاهی که صلاحیت ثبت عهده حق نباشد و گشت و از راه اموز ملک و وزن لشت و اسم رابی در قانون نامت دور نباشد و قوت سیت قوام به صلاح رای آن سپه مقدم گردد که اگر آن لشکر تایاق رعایت علیم شده و گمان مرد که ما خبر نیست بید که آن نایه دولت به و سپه منفی سر بری از خدمت یاقی نما و درایی نیست یا نباشد خوانند بر بنت وزین این لشت و خدمت یاقی به پیش نتایجا نایی آن حال بر آن نداشت. دشند قوت این را به زیر قط بخوت بدان مردوست.

نبید برابی نبت بخیل ساب عنی برای کتب وقت لانی لگری درین مدد شمهد دولت نباشد وارکمه برسان روز که کراشی بر خانک اردبر ۵- وقت نب و بر زار آر ۱۲ می نشک آت در سانه کر نباشد فوق درکای نم خلفد دربار سمیه عفل مدارس بنی آب ماخ مرتب بری این دودم ولع دفتر ربا گرکبت از ایان وشن رضای بر گذگ این بد و گذگ دفع کای لید آت نباشد که بد شمد لندروپ ولیاق لنشوری و شد گذگ آن دام در مع کگیه خلط آنه که بی لی بر و لدام نبرد دمکت نما معه و فوت نب دو گاه لاب وقتی در دفوت نبت آن قا لغل قط قط موبنه بداقیاد لغلم آرم برسدانا نثا آئو نبرگ قوت عام رعای نبت بال نه جنت مدرست از زدق آت فاریت. زاده قرای این وقت ملک رافع مدام بر نبر

۱- چیا قمت در ای ای ماده محروره

۲- لغیم قط مفتی آن الآ دنی قوت آین نتاری بیت معیدبست بر ای ای نبت وقتی آین نتاری بیت معیدبست آین اتین ای نبت آ نبت آزی قای آ ای آ

۳- نبت آ آن آ نبت آ ای آ نبت آ نیت آ ای آ - ای آ نبت آ نبت آ آ ای آ نبت آ

۴- بی آ نبت آ ای این قوت آین نتاری بیت معیدبست. بر ای ای نبت آ آ آ آ ای آ نبت آ آ آ آ ای آ آ آ آ آ آ آ آ آ آ ای آ.

خطاب وظفه و ماموریته را یک حکومت نیز خان ... از نایب دوم راه مقام از دولت جنوه یکجا... جمع تفقیم اوری ...
بسر متابا رایج سیاست اوفا بهم درج . در فقو معدن ... خفلک - نیر بیطر ... بند ... بطوع غلام ...
خور نایز معدنی خیز زوده خور دن ای اله سوار خالو گفتیس ... و بایگر خور نایب داری علمیه بنوه ... بر دو علم که از خیز یک حق ...
از نواره ام برق رسم راه را دولتما رو خفوعة و بیت ... خان زواد و خفوعة از دره بی لیت - ...
مدنیت کم در از نا ... مک دوی اساس ساطع امضه زواکه مک بند کمیته ... پ مقید و بلوه ای برق تقیم دائج اوکوته ...
در خان اوم اس سه و نیب تقب - و نیر و بوس و بوسه ... خال دار وبکه کندای نام ... وبکه کندگ خطعه کم ... مدسه و نیب تو و دم ای اش ... در دور ...
و کب کندک نام ... و بکبیر و خطعه بانه مدسه و برخیز ... دم بیگ ... خان وادم بی یت بردسا ای نو .
جد برای نام ... از ربنی بیاد پیاده بانید ... بیت ... بی مفود دری ... مدت بر خیله و کو تف نیدر ویکه بیتل ...

... زان فداحیث کسم درجب نواره که از ... سعیت - رجه ... درستم کمای رعایا خون وتاز وزه وتا ... به رطقه ... رفنه ای خون ...
به جمع این امدک در مستغو ... لعوبست قد جر رتبا ... عله ... بانت دائ از دیم ... مقه ... کمک در مست نا لوجد بنی نوراس ای قبته وان ...
فودکیت - جمع بانج نام بکتا ... بیوا کبدای مو در مرتب ای ... بلو دیدید ... خان زلایک پ ... بل سار دبا خون کو دیدره راری خان نم ... خرا ...
دبنه زار نا معدین این در بست اور ... درنت کبا خو د برای بند منذوره دارنه مصفار ... طرح ... رو دوله ماور رای برای داری دیک خو دارای ...
نارچه معوفت فواکسد ... ما بتادن فق ... و بدیم ... کب ... آبع اوئ نه وای ... بخیبتک ... در نا نارخ رساند کو و داره ... در نا عوفت خی ...

۸ جوزا ۱۳۰۵   فرمان پادشاهی

ع۱۱۵

فضایل مآب مدظله حکمنفذ !

اطاعت و رسم درباریان ... کی لوٹ در دوران وفاء پیشگان بزل نا لکرنت کده موجب افضل ...

ازارزو نا را جنار نحمه ام دلع نمی حت ... امرنی ... دلکی تحقیقت حضور درحدیل آمد ملل نجم کایا ...

... به تحقیقت و دقیقات نشدن در اجرا نمم برات ... تا به کهنرم نا ... به نا شد ... ارازو مبنع نجزل ...

... باعی مانج نفزٹ حج نیا علا ونمم ... نا راح مبنع نجبزد ... افتح لعتم مشتری باعی مشترمعت نا ...

حضرت نا نیا ... برودزه .

... درخصم مم تی نا ... غبرت ... از دوراره ... رمم بلو حضرت صایه لم باطنار نا ... دم ... نگذہ نحمت ... نا بعده ...

جاد رشب عیاد نمم لبرتشه ... اوزں دعی نعت نرتی ... امر مبانی دملعزی ... ابراز دلعم ...

الہ کا فرب لت ... نیعت لندر ... دین و نمعایی ... رست ... منع افن نون نشمل یعه نکا ...

اکجی

Document 2
Royal decree (no. 115, *Jawza* 8, 1305/May 29, 1926) by King Aman-Allah granting the Molla of Chaknawur annual allowance and subsidy for pilgrimage (*hajj*). Chaknawuri Letters.

فس ملا ما ... حکمنور !

از طرف مخفی برای ما شنیده شده که در اقامتگری شما برای نفع در علاوه و قری ها شخصیت کرده و عزم

میری تقریر زیاد با شما شنیده که اندر زمان تغری میت شما یک نوع تکلیف برای لیا وارد مگر در

میان برای شما امر معروف زبان حکومت دارد متی رعیتشیان نهین شهر بلکه بقیه رعایا

با این تو ظیفش گردید اگر شما بدرست منصب یعنی باتج رفیش تغری با ... شنبل بوا کریس را ...

در تو بیست ساعتی است ، زیرا دینا با یک نوع لکن ... ایل تو ... حی میتیشی بحل و مردمها

کلیفست شمید ، باطیر تجوید نگرند ، اگر حکومت علاوه رعیتشیان علاوه بقتشیان در یک نه علاوه زبان با شما آب

برای شما بیند لعلاج لزوم ندارد و شما را امر فرشان بنج ، آتوق محارج تغریم دارد خواهم

وما اگر خدا ناکرده شما در کدام محل رفتن خودرا علاوه بقتشیان لزوم شمرم قبل از حرکت ، از مقام آتیسها

حال دارم و احکم .... خواهم منع شفری شما را انتر و برخی خدا تکلیف زحمت دارد

گردد کا به ...

Document 3
Royal decree (no. 190, *Jawza* 15, 1305/June 6, 1926) from King Aman-Allah to the Molla of Chaknawur on prohibiting him from touring villages with large number of followers to preach the *amr bi al-ma'ruf wa nahy 'an al-monkar*. Chaknawuri Letters.

Document 4
Mawlawi Mohammad Ebrahim Kamawi's letter to King Aman-Allah proposing a *jerga* of ulama in Kabul to negotiate a peace settlement between the government and the rebel forces in Jalalabad. No date, AWSW Collection.

Document 5
Letter of appeal for amnesty and pledge of loyalty by Mohammad Sadeq and Zia Ma'sum Mojaddedi to King Aman-Allah dated *Rajab* 12, 1347/December 20, 1928. AWSW Collection.

وملحق خودم بود در این خدمت اگر برد رنی بینا نداریا روولت من فرماییم حاضر و منتظریم که یک قطره خون خود دراین

مبارزه برای حمایت ترقی وحفظ ملت تا وطن بریزیم — المدعا بع دارم واوکدودارم برد وزنبع با دنیا کلام لا ذنبع بنا

۲۳) چون اقوام شندگان کا مولوده در هر خدمت کی اللہی کومی بقیت حاصل کرده وغندکا رن برا دولت متقبل

کرده در صورت عدم قبول الاصلاح فورا شکے اپائے آم هربکزدآم مشرقی یو به تبلیغ حقی در مسبر مبارزه جمع کرده

با شنز جها واکبرم اعلان حرب دقتل باعنان احفظ خود یع گردیده وجا وحالوا والدحذوا فورای ترقی وآتا وطن

بالنیر امر ومر آیت اعلوقت عازی خوا بدکندم این خدمت حر یی نیز علاوا عاده وفرمیکنم اگر جیو دالا وبا لالظهور

این وقوجهالت کدر باحمیم مشرقی رخ داده ومن نیز منقلب پریح حصو مشرقی دیده ام حمالات کشیده باشر منده بک

٩) مروضه فوق راعرض وهدایت کا می واجبا زه خدمت اصلاح درصورت اول ومبارزه درصورت ثانی میری

اگر طالع من این بیدار نش بمرضای اطعمت کدر زر مرضای خدا اورکوار است خدمت جا لفت فی دی نشان روفزت

را کا خودم بیدا رم این بودعین وریش ایا دیش خیار با نقص الفکر که اظها رکرده مشرع بردن دعا لقادرجودذات عزیز

قدر رهیم کا مون —

روبا دائم صیس عاجز نارین

بسم الله الرحمن الرحیم

نومره: (۹۷۱)
۳۹۹۳

فرمان پادشاهی

عزیزانم پسران و باقی متعلقین جناب ملا صاحب چکنور !

از ضیاع اسفناک جناب فضایل مآب ملا صاحب مرحوم که داعی اجل را لبیک گفته اند : حضور من اطلاع سید : از نهایت جناب معنوی

یگانه عالم متبحر و بهی خواه عالم اسلام و مجاهد فی سبیل الله بودند و بندوره زندگانی خود نیز دیهود مسلمانان بندلغز و رشته

و دررهوال اتفاق و اتحاد اقوام بذل مساعی مینمودند و وجود شان برای شما خانواده و ملت افغانستان خیر مقتضی فیض

در برکت بود حضور با جنبه بنا تر گردید ؛ چون بموجب امر الهی که اذا جاء اجلهم لا یستاخرون ساعة

و لا یستقدمون " هیچ فردی را از اجابت جشیدن دایقه موت چاره نیست و جناب موصوف که شخص صالح

خداجوی و خیرخواه عمومی بودند فی الواقع مرده و زنده جاوید گردیده اند ؛ بنابران شما باز ماندگان و تمام

خلاص کیشان و علاقه مندینکه از فیوضات مرحومی مستفیض بوده اند تسلیت داده ؛ از خداوندیا تبار

توفیق میخواهم که به پیروی اصلات و نظریات پاک ملا صاحب مرحوم موفق دیابندبرده نام او را زنده درج

شاد و خورسند د شته باشید .

GLOSSARY

'adat [*'adāt*]   customs
'adalat [*'adālat*]   justice
al amr bi al-ma'ruf [*al 'amr bi al-ma'rūf*]
                                                enjoining the good (verse from the Qor'an)
al-nahy 'an al-monkar [*al-nahy 'an al-munkar*]
                                                forbidding evil (verse from the Qor'an)
'alem [*'ālim*]   a man learned in the religious law of Islam
                                                (pl. *'ulama'*)
akhlaqiyat [*akhlāqīyāt*]   ethics
akhund [*ākhūnd*]   religious teacher
akhundzada [*ākhūndzāda*]   an honorific used before the name of a
                                                religious leader who claims noble lineage
amir al-mo'menin [*amīr al-mu'minīn*]
                                                commander of the faithful
amwal-i-khalesa [*amwāl-i-khālisa*] state land
'ashura [*'āshūrā*]   the day of the commemoration of the
                                                martyrdom of Imam Hosain
awqaf [*awqāf*]   religious endowments (s. *waqf*)
azadi [*azādi*]   freedom
azadi-i'aqida [*āzādi-i-'aqīda*]   freedom of belief
azan [*āzān*]   call for the five daily prayers
bad-dadan [*bad-dādan*]   the custom by which a woman was given
                                                away in marriage to compensate for a crime
badal [*badal*]   the Pushtun law of revenge
bai'at [*bai'a*]   the act of rendering an oath of allegiance to
                                                the ruler
bed'at [*bid'a*]   reprehensible innovation; mode of action
                                                which is not in accord with traditional Islamic
                                                sources
borqa [*burqa'*]   extreme type of veiling practiced in
                                                Afghanistan
chadari [*chādari*]   a type of veil
chadari-i-maktabi [*chādari-i-maktabi*]
                                                a special type of veil designed for female
                                                students

chars [chars]   Indian hemp
dar al-harb [dār al-ḥarb]   "abode of war," a country which is actually or
                                       potentially a seat of war for Muslims
darugha-i-'adalat [dārūgha-i-'adālat]
                                       prosecutor of justice
dastar-bandi [dastār-bandi]   wrapping the turban, the traditional ceremony
                                       performed upon accession of a new king or
                                       graduation of a religious student to the status
                                       of 'ālim
dawlat [dawla]   state
Deobandi [Deobandi]   that faction of the ulama trained in the Muslim
                                       religious seminary in Deoband, India
din [dīn]   religion
diwan-i-'ali [dīwān-i-'āli]   high court
e'ana [i'āna]   voluntary contributions
e'dam [i'dām]   capital punishment
'Ed-i-Fitr ['Id-i-Fiṭr]   religious feast following the month of
                                       Ramadan
'Ed-i-Ozha ['Id-i-Uẓḥā]   the feast of sacrifice commemorating
                                       Ibrahim's sacrifice of his son
ejtehad-i-moqayyad [ijtihād-i-muqayyad]
                                       restricted interpretation of the shari'at
'elm ['ilm]   knowledge or science
emam [imām]   a religious leader
emamat [imāmat]   leadership of the community of believers
ejtehad [ijtihād]   the application of the mind to the verses of the
                                       Qur'an and hadith for the purpose of applying
                                       them to a particular situation
ertedad [irtidād]   apostasy
eta'at-i-ulu al-'amr [itā'at-i-ulū al-'amr]
                                       the doctrine of obedience to political authority
ettehad-i-islami [ittiḥād-i-islāmi]   Islamic unity
'ezzat ['izzat]   honor
far' [far']   a subdivision or derivative (pl. furu')
fatawa [fatāwā]   legal decisions pronounced by the mufti; law
                                       digests including the, farāyiż (farayez) usually
                                       bearing the name or names of the authors or
                                       ruler to whom the work has been dedicated
fatwa [fatwā]   a ruling by a jurist or a formal interpretation
                                       of a directive of the sharī'at which is binding
                                       on those who accept the authority of the
                                       issuing scholars (pl. fatāwā)
farz [farz]   religious obligation (pl. farayez/farāyiż)
feqh [fiqh]   Islamic jurisprudence

gair-i-moqadara [*ghair-i-muqadara*]
    legal punishments which are not prescribed in the Qur'an
ghaza [*ghazā*]   a type of holy war
ghazi [*ghāzi*]   a champion who repels infidels
habs [*habs*]   imprisonment
hadd [*hadd* (pl. *hudū d)*]   fixed penalty for major offenses, prescribed in the Qur'an
Hai't-i-Tamiz [*Hai'at-i-Tamīz*]   Religious Council
hai'at-i-wozara [*hai'at-i-wuzarā*]   cabinet
hadith [*hadīth*]   a dictum or example attributed to the Prophet
Hanafi [*Hanafi*]   the school of law founded by Abu Hanifa (699-767)
Haramain [*Haramain*]   the holy cities, Mecca and Madina
hasht-nafari [*hasht-nafari*]   a system of recruitment for the army whereby one man was selected out of eight
hazrat [*hazrat*]   an honorific used before the name of great spiritual leaders; the title of the leaders of the Naqshbandiyya Mojaddedis in Afghanistan
hejab [*hijāb*]   seclusion or veil
hejrat [*hijrat*]   migration modeled on the Prophet's migration from Mecca to Medina
hoquq [*huqūq*]   rights (s. *haqq*)
hoquq al-'bd [*huqūq al-'abd*]   individual rights
hoquq- Allah [*huqūq-Allāh*]   God's rights
hoquq al-nas [*huquq al-nās*]   the rights of society
hoquq-i-zanan [*huqūq-i-zanān*]   women's rights
iman [*imān*]   faith
jam'iyat [*jam'iyat*]   association
jaza [*jazā*]   punishment
jaza-i-naqdi [*jazā-I-naqdi*]   monetary punishment
jehad [*jihād*]   a war in the cause of Islam
jenayat [*jināyat*]   crime
jerga [*jirga*]   a tribal council
jezya [*jizya*]   poll tax on non-Muslims
kafer [*kāfir*]   infidel
khadem-i-mellat [*khādim-i-millat*]   nation's servant
khal' [*khal'*]   deposition
khalifa [*khalīfa*]   caliph, vice-regent, delegated to enforce divine law
khan [*khān*]   a tribal chief; a general title of respect
khaneqah [*khāniqāh*]   sufi headquarters
khan molla khan [*khān mullā khān*]
    see *molla-bashi (mulla-bāshi)*

khan-i-'olum [*khān-i-'ulūm*]	supervisor of religious instruction and the supreme judge
Kharafat [*kharāfāt*]	superstition
Khatib [*khaṭīb*]	deliverer of the *khutba*
Khelafat [*khilāfat*]	caliphate
Khishi [*khīshi*]	establishing a relationship through marriage
Kofr [*kufr*]	denial or disbelief, interpreted as an act that causes a person to be excommunicated from Islam
Lashkar [*lashkar*]	tribal levy (of troops)
Loya-Jerga [*Luya-Jirga*]	Grand Tribal Assembly
ma'aref [*ma'ārif*]	education
madani [*madani*]	civil
madrasa [*madrasa*]	religious school
Mahfel-i-Mizan wa Tahqiq [*Mahfil-i-Mīzān wa Tahqīqat*]	
	High Religious Council
mahkama [*maḥkama*]	law court (pl. *mahā kim*)
mahkama-i-'liya-i- tamiz [*mahkama-i-'ālīya-i-tamīz*]	
	supreme court
majales-i-mashwara [*majālis-i-mashwara*]	
	advisory committees
makateb-i-alsana [*makātib-i-alsana*]	
	language schools
maktab [*maktab*]	school
maktab-i-hokkam [*maktab-i-ḥukkām*]	
	school for the training of civil servants
maktab-i-qozat [*maktab-i-quẕat*]	school for the training of *qazi*s
maktab-i-masturat [*maktab-i-mastūrāt*]	
	girls' school
maliya [*mālīya*]	tax
maliya-i-jensi [*mālīya-i-jinsi*]	tax payment in kind
maliya-i-naqdi [*mālīya-i-naqdi*]	tax payment in cash
ma'murin [*ma'mūrīn*]	civil servants (s. *ma'mur*)
mashayikh [*mashāyikh*]	plural of *sheikh*
mashruta-khwahan [*mashrūṭta-khwāhān*]	
	constitutionalists
mashwara [*mashwara*]	consultation
mawlawi [*mawlawi*]	a master of theology, an honorific applied to eminent religious scholars
mellat [*millat*]	nation
mir-wa'ez [*mīr-wā'iż*]	head preacher in the capital
mo'zzen [*mu'azzin*]	a caller to prayer
modarris-bashi [*mudarris-bāshi*]	head master of the major religious school
mofti [*mufti*]	a legal religious advisor

mohadeth [*muḥaddith*]	the reciter or scholar of *hadith*
molk [*mulk*]	state
molla [*mullā*]	a learned man; once used as an honorific for all religious scholars, it was later degraded to denote mosque functionaries only
molla-bashi [*mullā-bāshi*]	the head *molla (mulla)* or the chaplain of the royal house
mohtaseb [*muḥtasib*]	"a calculator," the supervisor of public morality
moqtada-beh [*muqtadā-bih*]	a model to be followed
mosaddeq [*muṣaddiq*]	attesting authority
motawalli [*mutawālli*]	custodian of a shrine
morid [*murīd*]	an aspirant
nekah [*nikāḥ*]	marriage
nekah-i-saghira [*nikāḥ-i-ṣaghī ra*]	child marriage
nezam-nama [*niẓam-nā ma*]	a code of law
padshah [*pādshāh*]	king, also an honorific used with the name of eminent tribal religious leaders who claimed to be descendent of the Prophet
padshah-enqelabi [*pādshāh-i-inqilābi*]	
	revolutionary monarch
parda [*parda (purda)*]	veil, seclusion
pashtunwali [*pashtunwāli*]	Pashtun code of ethics
peshk [*pishk*]	lottery—a system of recruitment in the army
paizar [*paizār*]	traditional shoes
pir [*pīr*]	leader of sufi order; spiritual leader
qabahat [*qabāha*]	petty misdemeanors
Qadiyani [Qādīyāni]	a follower of Mirza Ghulam Ahmad Qadiyan, the founder of the Qadiyani or Ahmadiyya sect in India
qanun [*qānūn*]	secular law, as distinct from the *shari'at*
qarya-dar [*qarya-dār*]	the village head
qarya-dari [*qarya-dāri*]	a system whereby a *qarya-dā r* is in charge of assessing and collecting the taxes
qatl [*qatl*]	homicide
qatl-i-'amd [*qatl-i-'amd*]	deliberate homicide
qawanin [*qawānīn*]	plural of *qanūn*
qawmi [*qawmi*]	tribal
qazi [*qāẓī*]	a religious judge
qazi al-qozat [*qāẓi al-quẓāt*]	the supreme judge
qimat-i-'awazi [*qīmat-i-'awaẓī*]	exemption fee
qesas [*qiṣāṣ*]	retaliation for homicide
qozat [*quẓāt*]	plural of *qazi*
ra'iyat [*ra'īya*]	subjects

rajm [*rajm*]	stoning
rawaj [*rawāj*]	custom
rawayat-i-za'ifa [*rawāyāt-i-za'īfa*]	obscure rules
ruh [*ruḥ*]	spirit
ruhaniun [*rūhānīūn*]	spiritual leaders
sadat [*sādāt*]	plural of *sayyid*
sadr-i-shahr [*ṣadr-i-shahr*]	a high clerical position whose holder was in charge of supervision of eligious endownment and the supervision of the administration of the religious law
sardar [*sardār*]	a title used by the Barakzai nobility
saheb [*sāḥib*]	master; used as an honorific
satr-i-'awrat [*satr-i-'awrat*]	seclusion of women; veiling
sayyid [*sayyid*]	a direct descendant of the Prophet
shahi [*shāhi*]	royal
shahid [*shahīd*]	martyr
shari'at [*sharī'a*]	social-religious law of Islam
sheikh [*sheikh*]	an elder; a learned man; the leader of a *tariqa*
shura-i-dawlat [*shūrā-I-dawlat*]	State Council
shura-i-melli [*shūrā-I-milli*]	National Assembly
sufi [*ṣūfi*]	Islamic mystic
sonnat [*sunna*]	the tradition of the Prophet's behavior and practice
tafsir [*tafsīr*]	commentary on the Qur'an
tajaddod [*tajaddud*]	renewal or reform
takfir [*takfir*]	the formal denunciation by the ulama of an individual as an infidel
taleb [*ṭā lib*]	student of a *madrasa*
taqlid [*taqlīd*]	"imitation;" strict adherence to the interpretation of authoritative medieval jurists
tashhir [*tashhīr*]	public exposure of a criminal
tariqat [*tarīqa*]	mystical order
ta'zir [*ta'zīr*]	deterrence; discretionary punishment as opposed to *ḥadd* (pl. *ta'zirat)*
tazkera [*tazkira*]	citizenship or identity card
tollabt [*tullāb*]	plural of *ṭālib*
ulama ['*ulamā*']	plural of '*ā lim*
ulu al-'amr [*ulū al-'amr*]	"those in authority;" the rightful ruler
'*olum wa fonun* ['*ulūm wa funūn*]	arts and sciences
'*orf* ['*urf*]	customary law
osul [*uṣūl*]	the principles of Islamic jurisprudence
wa'ez [*wā'iż*]	preacher
wafd [*wafd*]	delegation

BIBLIOGRAPHY

Archival Materials

Afghan National Archives, *Archif-i-Melli-i-Afghanistan* (AMA)
No. 195
No. 197

National Archives of India (NAI), Government of India, Foreign and Political Department

H.R.C. Dobbs, Chief British Representative, "Report on the Kabul Mission," 9 January 1922, Secret Book Copy A 194
File No. 2-F, 1922
File No. 233-F, 1923
File No. 224-F (confidential), 1923
File No. 224-F (secret), 1923
File No. 621-F (secret), 1925
File No. 46-F, 1928
File No. 51-F, 1928
File No. 56-F, 1928
File No. 163-F, 1928
File No. 309-F, 1928
File No. 335-F, 1928
File No. 380-F, 1928
File No. 523-F (secret), 1928
File No. 1(2)-F, 1929
File No. 9-F, 1929
File No. 190-F, 1929
File No. 137-F, 1929
File No. 302-G/29 (secret), 1929

Archives of the India Office Records, London (IOR)

L/PO/214-16 Afghanistan Affairs, 1922-24.
LPS/10/18, file 281, 1904 Afghanistan: HMG Relations.
LPS/10/22, file 281, 1904, Afghanistan: Plot against the Amir, pt. 8.
LPS/10/808, file 1061, 1919, The Third Afghan War.
LPS/10/813, 1919 North-West Frontier: Intelligence Bureau Diaries (FIBD).

LPS/10/836, 1919 Bolshevik Activities in Central Asia and Afghanistan.
LPS/10/196, 1921 General Situation Reports.
LPS/10/967, 1921 North-West Frontier: Intelligence Bureau Diaries (FIBD).
LPS/10/961, 1925 Sir Humphrys' Summary of Events, Oct. 1924-Feb. 1925.
LPS/10/1015, file 4700, Education of Afghan Youth in Europe and Turkey.
LPS/10/1019, file 5243, 1921 Haji Abdul Razaq [Razeq].
LPS/10/1081, file 477, 1923 North-West Frontier: Intelligence Bureau Diaries (FIBD).
LPS/10/1112, 1924, The Khost Rebellion.
LPS/10/1120, 1924 Military Attache's Diary in Kabul (MADK).
LPS/10/1137, file 393, 1925 North-West Frontier: Intelligence Bureau Diaries (FIBD).
LPS/10/1207, 1922-25 Military Attache's Diary in Kabul (MADK).
LPS/10/1207, file 627, 1927 Diaries of Military Attache in Kabul, 1927-29.
LPS/10/1170, 1926 Military Attache's Diary in Kabul (MADK).
LPS/10/1285, 1929
LPS/10/1286, 1929
LPS/10/1287, 1929
LPS/10/1288, 1929
LPS/10/1289, 1929
LPS/10/1290, 1929
LPS/12/197, 1930 (secret, n. 26s)
Military Attache's Diary in Kabul, (MADK) 1922-1928
LPS/11/161, 1919, Pan-Islamic Movement
LPS/11/273 D 4664/ 1923 Opposition to Conscription in Kandahar
R/12/162/4/42, Notes on the Young Afghan Party, Republican Party and Pro-Amanullah Party

Unpublished Manuscripts, India Office Records, London

Ali Ahmad, "Fall of Aman-Allah."
Biographical Accounts of Chiefs, Sardars, and Others in Afghanistan (confidential file published by British government in India), 1888.
Dundas, A.D.F., "Precis on Afghanistan, 1927-36." Government of India, 1938.
Maconachie, R.R., "Precis on Afghan Affairs, 1919- 1927." Government of India, 1928.
Who's Who of Afghanistan (confidential file, compiled by General Staff, British Government in India), 1914.
Who's Who of Afghanistan (confidential file, compiled by General Staff, British Government in India), 1920.

German Documents

Auswartiges Amt: Buro des Reichemin, Akten Afghanistan, Band-1, 1920-1929, Band-2, 1929-1933, D624799-D625157. University of Michigan, Ann Arbor.

Afghan Government Publications

Afghanistan dar Penjah Sal-i-Akhir (Afghanistan during the Last Fifty Years). Kabul: Government Press, 1347/1968.

Layiha-i-Taraqiyat-i-Panj-sala (Five-year Development Report). Kabul: Sherkat-i-Rafiq, 1307/1928.

Maram-nama-i-Jam`iyat-i-`Ulama-i-Afghanistan (The Platform of the Association of Ulama in Afghanistan (The Kabul: Matba'ah-i-'Omumi-i-Sarkari (Government Press), Qaws 25, 1308/November 17, 1929.

Monasebat-i-Afghanistan wa Ettehad-i-Shurawi, 1919-1967 (Afghan-Soviet Relations, 1919-1967). Compiled jointly by the Afghan and Soviet Foreign Departments. Kabul: Government Press, n.d.

Nezam-nama-i-Amwal-i-Mawashi (Grazing Land Law). Kabul: Government Press, 1301/1922.

Nezam-nama-i-Asasi-i-Dawlat-i-`Aliyya-i-Afghanistan (The Fundamental Law of the Exhalted Government of Afghanistan). Kabul: Government Press, *Mizan* 1302/ October 1923.

Nezam-nama-i-Forush-i-Amwal-i-Sarkari (Regulations regarding the Sale of State Land). Kabul: Government Press, 1302/1923.

Nezam-nama-i-Jaza-i-`Omumi (General Penal Code). Kabul: Government Press, 1300/1921, 1302/1923, 1305/1925.

Nezam-nama-i-Ma`aref (Law of Education). Kabul: Government Press, 1302/1923, 1305/1926.

Nezam-nama-i-Makateb-i-Khanagi (Regulations regarding Private or Mosque Schools). Kabul: Government Press, 1302/1923.

Nezam-nam-i-Maliya (Tax Law). Kabul: Government Press, *Hamal* 1299/March 1920.

Nezam-nama-i-Maliya-i-Shesh Koruhi-i-Kabul (Tax Law of Kabul and Its Vicinity). Kabul: Government Press, [1298/1919].

Nezam-nama-i-Mohajirin-i-Hindi (Regulations concerning Indian Immigtants). Kabul: Government Press, 1302/1923.

Nezam-nama-i-Nekah, `Arusi wa Khatna-suri (Law of Marriage, Wedding and Circumcision Ceremonies) Kabul: Government Press, 1300/1924, 1302/1923, *Sonbola* 1303/September 1924.

Nezam-nama-i-Osul-i-Mohakemat-i-Jazaiyya-i-Ma'murin (Law of Civil Court Procedures). Kabul: Government Press, 1302/1923.

Nezam-nama-i-Tashkilat-i-Asasi (The Fundamental Organizational Law). Kabul: Government Press, 1302/1923.

Nezam-nama-i-Tazkera-i-Nofus (Identity Card Law). Kabul: Government Press, 1301/1922.

Ruydad-i-Gozareshat-i-Loya-Jerga-i-Dar al-Saltana-i-Paghman, 1303 (Report on the Loya-Jerga of 1303/1924). Kabul: War Ministry Press, 1303/1924.

Ruydad-i-Diwan-i-`Ali-i-Hokumat-i-Shahi Raje` ba Kha'enin Mellat wa Ghadaran-i-Mamlakat, Mohammad Wali wa Mahmud-i-Sami (Afghan Royal Government's High Court Report on the Trial of the Traitors of the Nation and the Government, Mohammad Wali and Mahmud Sami). Kabul: Government Press, *Hamal* 1309/March 1930.

Taftish-i-Welayat-i-Qandahar (The Inspection of the Province of Qandahar). Kabul: Matba'ah-i-Rafiq, 1304/1925.

Tamassok al-Qozat al-Amaniyya (The Amani Handbook for Judges). Kabul: Government Press, 1300/1921.

Tardid-i-Shaye`at-i-Batela-i-Padsha-i-Makhlu`: Faisala-i-Loya-Jerga 1309 (Refutation of Rumors by the Deposed King: The Resolution of the Loya-Jerga of 1309/1930). Kabul: Government Press, *Hamal* 1310/March 1931.

Private Documents

Chaknawri Letters (Ch. L.)
`Abd Al-Wali Sorush Wali Document Collection (AWSWD).

Newspapers

Afghan (Kabul)
Azadi-i-Sharq (Berlin)
Aman-i-Afghan (Kabul)
Anis (Kabul)
Bombay Chronicle (Bombay)
Daily News (London)
Daily Telegraph (London)
Eblagh (Kabul)
Emruz (Lahore)
Ershad-i-Noswan (Kabul)
Eslah (Jaji)
Eslah (Kabul)
Eslah (Khanabad)
Ettehad-i-Mashriqi (Jalalabad)
Gairat-i-Eslam (Jalalabad)
Habib al-Eslam (Kabul)
Habl al-Matin (Calcutta)
Hamdard-i-Afghan (Peshawar)
Haqiqat (Kabul)
Iman (Jalalabad)

Izvestiia (Moscow)
Izvestiia (Tashkent)
Literary Digest (New York)
Masawat (Kabul)
Mo`rref-i-Ma`aref (Kabul)
Nohzat a-Habib (Khanabad)
Phukhtun (Peshawar)
Pioneer (Allahabad)
Seraj al-Akhbar (Kabul)
Times (London)
Tolu-i-Afghan (Qandahar)
Zamindar (Lahore)

Personal Interviews

`Azimi, Mohammad `Aziz, headmaster in Khost during the 1928 rebellion. Tucson: June 1987.
Chaknawuri, G. Nabi, former senator and son of the Molla of Chaknawur. Peshawar: September 1994.
Fofalzai, `Aziz al-Din Wakil, Afghan historian. Kabul: July 1976.
Ghobar, Mir Gholam Mohammad, author of *Afghanistan dar Massir-i-Tarikh*. Kabul: July 1976.
Majrooh, Shams al-Din, former president of the Department of Tribes (*riyasat-i-qabayel*) and son of Padshah Saheb of Tirgary, a disciple of the Molla of Hadda. Atlanta: October, 1995.
Naim, M. `Aziz, former professor at Kabul University and grandson of King Nader Shah. London: Summer 1991.
Nawid, Gholam Ahmad, poet-diplomat, sympathizer of the Mashruta Khwahan party. Kabul: Summer 1976.
Reshtia, Sayyid Qasim, Afghan historian. Geneva: July 1991.
Sayyid `Abd al-Qayyum, known as Hajji Pacha Saheb, Qadereiyya *sheikh* in the line of the Molla of Hadda. Peshawar, September 1994.
Shafiq, Musa, last Afghan prime minister under King Zaher Shah, the son of Mawlawi `Abd Hai Kamawi and an expert in Islamic law. Qargha: Summer 1976.
Shahrani, Ni`mat-Allah, former professor of theology, Kabul University. Tucson: November 1976.
Sorkhabi, Tahera, one of the female students who accompanied the conciliatory mission to Khost; also selected to pursue higher education in Turkey. Kabul: August 1976.

Secondary Sources

`Abd al-Haiy. *Afghanistan aw Sarhad (Afghanistan and the Frontier)*.
Peshawar: Hajji Faqir Mohammad, 1987. (Pashtu)

`Abd al-Mohammad. *Aman al-Tawarikh*, 9 vols. New York University Library,
New York (unpublished manuscript).

`Abd al-Qader, Qazi (compiled by order of Amir Shir `Ali). *Wa`z-nama: Tohfat
al-`Ulama* (Book of Admonitions: The Gift of the Ulama). Kabul: Gov-
ernment Printing House, 1292 h.q./1874.

`Abd al-Rahman (Amir).  *Haza Bayan Al-Nas*.  Kabul:  Matba`a-i-Dar al-
Saltana-i-Kabul, 1311/1893.

`Abd al-Rahman (Amir). *Taj al-Tawarikh (Crown of History)*. Lahore:
Matba`a-i-Islamiyya-i-Lahore, n.d.

Abdul Ghani, Dr. *A Review of the Political Situation in Central Asia*, 2nd
edition. Lahore: Aziz Publishers, 1980.

_____. *A Brief Political History of Afghanistan*. Lahore: Najaf Publishers,
1989.

Abdul Karim et. al. "The Flight of Aman-Allah from Afghanistan." In F. R.
Marwat and Kakakhel (eds.) *Afghanistan and the Frontier*. Peshawar:
Emjay Books International, 1993, 56-68.

Adamec, Ludwig W. *Afghanistan, 1900-1923: A Diplomatic History*. Berkeley:
University of California Press, 1967.

_____. *Afghanistan's Foreign Affairs to the Mid-Twentieth Century: Relations
with the USSR, Germany and Great Britain*. Tucson: University of Arizona
Press, 1974.

_____. *Who's Who of Afghanistan*. Graz-Austria: Akademissche Druck-u.
Verlagsanstalt, 1975.

_____. (ed.) *Historical and Political Gazetteer of Afghanistan*, Vol. 6. Graz-
Austria: Akademische Druck-u. Verlagsanstalt, 1985.

Afghani, Mohammad Taj al-Din. *Tohfat al-Amir fi Bayan-i-Soluk wa al-Tadbir*
(The Gift of the Amir on Rules of Administration). Kabul, n.d.

Afghanpur, Amin. "*Sheza aw tolena*" ("Women and Society"). *Jamhuriyyat*
(Kabul Daily), 9, no. 2, 1353 /1974, p.3. (Pashtu)

Agabekov, Georges. *OGPU: The Russian Secret Terror*. Translated by W.H.
Bunn, 2nd ed. Westport: Hyperion Press, 1975.

Ahady, Anwar al-Haq. "Afghanistan: State Breakdown." In J. Goldstone and R.
Gurr (eds.) *Revolutions of the Late Twentieth Century*. Boulder: Westview
Press, 1991, pp. 162-193.

_____. "Conflict and Post Soviet Occupation of Afghanistan." *Journal of
Contemporary Asia*, 21, no. 4, 1991.

_____. Contending Theories of Legitimacy in Afghanistan" Paper presented at annual meeting of Middle East Studies Association, Portland, Oregon, October 28-31, 1992.

Ahang, M. Kazim. *Sayr-i-Zhornalism dar Afghanistan* (Development of Journalism in Afghanistan). Kabul: Anjoman-i- Tarikh wa Adab (Historical and Literary Society), 1349/ 1970.

Ahmad, Akbar S. "Emergent Trends in Moslem Tribal Society: The Wazir Movement of the Mullah of Wana in North-West Frontier Province of Pakistan." In said Amir Arjomand (ed.) *From Nationalism to Revolutionary Islam.* Albany: State University of New York Press, 1984, pp. 71-93.

_____. *Religion and Politics in Muslim Society.* Cambridge: Cambridge University Press, 1983.

_____. *Post Modernism and Islam.* London: Routledge, 1992.

Ahmad, Akbar S. and David H. *Islam in Tribal Societies: From the Atlas to the Indus.* London: Routledge and Kegan Paul, 1884.

Akbar, Shah Mian. *Azadi Ke Talash (Struggle for Freedom).* Islamabad: Tribal Bureau of Historical and Cultural Research, 1989. (Urdu)

Akhawi, Sharough. *Religion and Politics in Contemporary Iran.* Albany: SUNY Press, 1982.

Alekozai, Ahmadjan. *Asas al-Qozat (Handbook for the Judges).* Kabul: Government Press, 1311/1891.

Ali, Muhammad. *A Cultural History of Afghanistan.* Lahore, 1964.

_____. *Afghanistan: The Muhammadzai Period.* Kabul, 1959.

_____. *Afghanistan: The War of Independence, 1919.* Kabul, 1960.

_____. *Manners and Customs of the Afghans.* Lahore: Punjab Educational Press, 1958.

Al-Marghinani, Burhan al-Din. *The Hidaya.* Translated by Denis Ogdeb and Charles Hamilton, 2nd ed. Lahore: Premier Book House, 1957.

Al-Mojaddedi, Mohammad Sadeq. "Khaterat (Memoirs)." Unpublished manuscript.

_____. *Mokhtasar al-Baiyan dar Tarikh-i-Shahid-i-Elm wa Iman Mawlana `Abd al-Rahman (A Short Account of the History of the Martyrdom of Mawlana `Abd al-Rahman).* Peshawar, n.d.

_____. *Rahnoma-i-Tariq: dar Tariqa saiyyedena Abu-Bakr Seddiq (Quide to the Tariqa of Abu-Bakr Seddiq).* Peshawar, 1376/1996.

Amedroz, H. F. "The Office of Qadi in the Ahkam Sultania." *Journal of the Royal Asiatic Society,* 1911, pp. 735-774.

_____. "Recent Developments in Shari`a Law" (a series of five articles in successive issues). *The Muslim World,* Oct. 1950-Oct. 1951.

Amir Mohammad, Hafiz. *Zohur al-Aman (Emergence of Peace).* Kabul: Government Press, 1302/1923.

Anderson, J. N. O. *Islamic Law in a Modern World.* New York: New York University Press, 1959.

Anis, Mohaiy al-Din. *Bohran wa Nejat (Crisis and Deliverance)*. Kabul: Anis Printing House, 1310/1931.

Arakzai, Wahid-Allah. "A`la Hazrat Aman-Allah-I-Ghazi (His Majesty Aman-Allah Ghazi)." Kabul: Faculty of Law, Kabul University (unpublished monograph), n.d.

`Aref, `Osman. "Sayyid Jamal al-Din Afghani Pishahang-i-Nahzat-i-Azadi Bakhsh-i-Ma (Sayyid Jamal al-Din-i Afghani, the Forerunner of our Liberal Movement)." *Zhuwandun*, nos. 47-48, *Dalwa*, 1353/March 1974, pp. 35-40.

Arjomand, Said Amir (ed.). *From Nationalism to Revolutionary Islam*. Albany: State University of New York, 1984.

_____. *The Political Dimensions of Religion*. Albany: State University of New York, 1993.

`Azim Khan, Mir Mohammad and Dehlawi `Abd al-Razaq. *Taqwim-i-Din (Straightening of Religion)*. Kabul: Government Printing House, 1306/1884.

_____. *Al-Jehad: Al Targhib ela fi Amir al-Balad (Jehad at the Instigation of the Ruler of the Country)*. Kabul: Government Printing House, 1304/1882.

Aziz Ahmad. *Islamic Modernism in India and Pakistan, 1857-1964*. London: Oxford University Press, 1967.

Baer, G. "The Ulama in Modern History." *Asian and African Studies*." 7, 1971, pp. 94-98.

Banuazizi, Ali, and Weiner, Myron. *The State, Religion, and Ethnic Politics: Afghanistan, Iran, and Pakistan*. New York: Syracuse University Press, 1986.

_____. *The Politics of Social Transformation in Afghanistan, Iran and Pakistan*. Syracuse: Syracuse University Press, 1994.

Barnard. C.I. *The Function of the Executive*. Cambridge: Harvard University Press, 1938.

Bart, Fredrik. *Political Leadership Among Swat Pathans*. London: Athlone Press, 1970.

Barthorp, Michael. *The North-West Frontier: A Pictorial History, 1859-1947*. Bristol: Blandford Press, 1982.

Beattie, Hugh. "Effects of the Saur Revolution in the Northern Area of Northern Afghanistan." In N. Shahrani and R. Canfield (eds.). *Revolutions and Rebellions in Afghanistan: Anthropological Perspectives*. Berkeley: University of California, 1984, pp. 184-208.

Beck, von Sebastien. "Das Afghanisch Strafgesetzbuch vom Jahre 1924 mit dem Zusats vom Jahre 1925." *Die Weld des Islams*." Band 11. 1928, Heft 1/2, pp. 67-157.

Berkes, Niazi. *The Development of Secularism in Turkey*. Montreal: McGill University Press, 1964.

Binder, Leonard. *Religion and Politics in Pakistan*. Berkeley: University of California Press, 1961.

Bullard, G. "The Power of Menace: Soviet Relations with South Asia, 1917-1974." *British Journal of International Studies*. 2, no. 1, 1976, pp. 51-66.

Caroe, Olaf. *The Pathans, 550 B.C.- A.D. 1957*. Karachi: Oxford University Press, 1976.

Costagne, J. "Le Mouvement d' Emancipation de la Femme Musulmane en Orient." *Revue des Etudes Islamiques*. 1929.

Cumming, Sir John, Sir Richard Dane, Sir Patrick Fagan, and Sir George McMunn. "Some Features of the Afghan Problem." *The Asiatic Review*, July 1929.

Curzon, Marquess of Kedleston. *Tales of Travel*. New York: George H. Doran, 1923.

Dari, Gholam M. *Hoquq-i-Famil dar Islam* (Family Law in Islam). Kabul: Government Printing House, 1971.

Das, Taraknath. "Afghanistan in World Politics." *The Modern Review*. May 1929.

Dawlatabadi, Basir Ahmad. *Shenasnama-i-Ahzab wa Jeryanat-i-Siyasi dar Afghanistan* (An Account of Political Organizations and Trends in Afghanistan). Qom: Dawlatabadi, 1371/1992.

Dekmajian, Hrair. "The Anatomy of Islamic Revival: Legitimacy Crisis, Ethnic Conflict and the Search for Islamic Alternatives." *Middle East Journal*, 34, Winter 1980, pp. 1-12.

Dupree, Louis. *Afghanistan*. Princeton: Princeton University Press, 1973.

_____. "Islam in Politics: Afghanistan." *The Muslim World*. 56, no. 4, 1966, pp. 269-276.

_____. "Mahmud Tarzi: Forgotten Nationalist." *American University Field Staff Reports*, South Asia Series, 8, no. 1, 1964.

_____. "The Political Uses of Religion: Afghanistan." In K. H. Silevert (ed.), *Churches and State: The Religious Institutions and Modernization*. New York: AUFS, 1967, pp. 195-212.

_____. "Tribal Traditions and Modern Nationhood." *Asia*, 1, 1964, pp. 1-12.

Dupree, Louis, and Albert, Linette (eds.). *Afghanistan in the 1970s*. New York: Praeger Publishers, 1974.

Dupree, Nancy H. "Revolutionary Rhetoric and the Afghan Women." *The Asian Society, Afghan Council*, no. 23, 1981.

Easton, David. *A Systems Analysis of Political Life*. New York: Wiley, 1965.

Eisenstadt, S. N., *Modernization: Protest and Change*. New Jersey: Englewood Cliffs, 1966.

El-Awa, Muhammad. "Ta`zir in the Islamic Penal System." *Ahmad Bello University*, 6, 1976, pp. 41-57.

Elphinstone, Mountstuart. *An Account of the Kingdom of Cabul*. London: Richard Bentley, 1839.

Enayat, Hamid. *Modern Islamic Political Thought*. Austin: University of Texas Press, 1982.

Esposito, John L. *Islam and Development of Religion and Sociopolitical Change*. New York: Syracuse University Print, 1980.

_____. *Islam and Politics*. New York: Syracuse University Press, 1984.

_____. *Voices of Resurgent Islam*. Oxford: Oxford University Press, 1983.

Fakhri, Majid. "The Theoretic Ideas of Islamic States in Recent Controversies." *International Affairs*, 30, 1954, pp. 430-463.

Farhadi, Rawan A.G. *Maqalat-i- Mahmud Tarzi dar Seraj al-Akhbar-i-Afghanistan (The Ariticles of Mahmud Tarzi in Seraj al-Akhbar)*. Kabul: Baihaqi Printing Institute, 1355/1976.

_____. "Jonbesh-i-Qanungozari dar Aghaz-i-Esteqlal-i-Afghanistan" ("Legislative Movement at the Dawn of Afghanistan's Independence"). In *Afghanistan dar Penjah Sal-i-Akhir*. Kabul: Mo'assesa-i-Tab`-i Kotob, *Sonbola* 1347/September 1968, pp. 8-34.

Farhang, Mir Mohammad Seddiq. *Afghanistan dar Panj Qarn-i-Akhir (Afghanistan in the Past Five Centuries)* 3 vols. Qom: Esma`iliyan Publishing Institute, 1371/1992.

Farrokh, Sayyid Mahdi. *Tarikh-i-Siyasi-i-Afghanistan (Political History of Afghanistan)*. Qom: Ehsani, 1371/1992.

_____. *Korsi-nishinan-i-Kabul (Those in High Positions in Kabul)*. Tehran: Mo'assesa-i-Pozhohesh wa Motale`at-i-Farhangi, 1370/1991.

Faruki, Kamal. *The Evolution of Islamic Constitutional Theory and Practice*. Karachi: National Publishing House Ltd., 1971.

Faruqi, Zia ul Hassan. *The Deoband School and the Demand for Pakistan*. London: 1963.

Faushet, Maurice. *Notes sur l'Afghanistan, Oeuvre Posthume*. Paris: Maisneuve Press, 1931.

Fazl-Allah, Mohammad. `Omdat al-Moqamat. Kabul: Ketab-khana-i-No`mani, 1355/1914.

Ferrier, Joseph P. *History of the Afghans*. London: J. Murray, 1858.

Fofalzai, Aziz al-Din Wakil. *Timur Shah Dorrani*. Kabul: Anjoman-i-Tarikh (Publication of Afghan Historical Society), vol. 1, 1346/1967.

_____. *Dorrat al-Zaman fi Tarikh-i-Zaman Shah (History of Zaman Shah)*. Kabul: Publication of the Afghan Historical Society, 1959.

_____. *Dar al-Qaza' dar Afghanistan az Awayil-i-Islam ta `Ahd-i-Jamhuriyat (Justice Department in Afghanistan from the Early Days of Islam to the Time of the Republican Government)*. Kabul: Government Printing House, 1369/1990.

_____. "Dar al-Qaza'-i Hozur-i Lame` al-Nur Fakhera-i Ahmadshahi dar Qandahar" ("The Luminous Ahmadshahi Justice Department in Qandahar"). *Aryana*. 30, no. 4, 1351/1972.

_____. *Negahi ba Tarikh-i-Esterdad-i-Esteqlal-i-Afghanistan* (A Glance at the History of Restoration of   Independence of Afghanistan). Kabul: Government Printing House, 1368/ 1989.

_____. *Safarha-i-Ghazi Aman-Allah Shah dar Dawazda keshwar Asia wa Orupa, 1306-1307 (The Tours of Ghazi King Aman-Allah to Twelve Asian and European Countries, 1927-1928).* Kabul: Government Printing House, 1364/1985.

Forbes, Archibald. *The Afghan Wars, 1839-42 and 1878-80.* 4th ed. London: Seely & Co., 1906.

Fraser, David. *Proceedings of the Central Asian Society* (London) June 12, 1907.

Fraser-Tytler, Sir W. Kerr. *Afghanistan: A Study of Political Development in Central Asia.* London: Oxford University Press, 1953.

Gailani, Sayyid Mahmud. *Tajalli-i-`Orfan-i-Qaderiyya* (The Manifestation of the Qaderiyya Path). Islamabad, 1366/1987.

Ghani, Ashraf. "Islam and State-building in a Tribal Society: Afghanistan 1880-1901." *Modern Asian Society,* 12, no. 2, 1978, pp. 269-284.

Ghobar, M.G.M. *Afghanistan dar Massir-i-Tarikh* (Afghanistan in the Process of History). Kabul: Mo'assesa-i-Chap-i-Kotob (Book Printing Institute), 1346/ 1967.

Ghosh. N. N. "The Afghan Civil War, 1928-1929." *The Modern Review,* February, 1930.

Gibb, H.A.R. "Al-Mawardi's Theory of the Khalifa." *Islamic Culture,* 11, July 1937, pp. 291-302.

_____. "Constitutional Organization: The Muslim Community and the State." In M. Khaddori, and H.J. Liebeany, (eds.), *Law in the Middle East.* Washington, D.C., 1955, pp. 15-27.

_____. *Modern Trends in Islam.* Chicago: University of Chicago Press, 1947.

Gibb, H.A.R., and Bowen, H. *Islamic Society and the West.* Oxford: Oxford University Press, 1960.

Gibb, H.A.R, and Kramers, J. H. (eds.). *Shorter Encyclopedia of Islam.* Ithaca: Cornell University Press, 1953.

Gladmeck, Johannes and Kircheisen. *Turkey und Afghanistan.* Berlin: Veb Deutscher Verlag Der Wissenschafteb, 1986.

Gordon, Richard. "Non-cooperation and Council Entry, 1919-1920." *Modern Asian Studies,* 12, July 1973, pp. 443-473.

Grassmuck, G., Adamec, L. W., and Irwin, F. H. *Afghanistan: Some New Approaches.* Ann Arbor: University of Michigan Press, 1969.

Gray, A. J. *At the Court of the Amir: A Narrative.* London: Richard Bentley, 1895.

Gregorian, Vartan. *The Emergence of Modern Afghanistn: Politics of Reform and Modernization, 1880-1946.* Stanford: Stanford University Press, 1969.

_____. "Mahmud Tarzi and Saraj-ol-Akhbar: Ideology of Nationalism and Modernism in Afghanistan." *Middle East Journal,* 21, 1967, pp. 345-368.

Guha, A. "The Economy of Afghanistan during Amanullah's Reign, 1919-1929." *International Studies,* 9, 1967-68, pp. 161-182.

Habib-Allah (Amir of Afghanistan). *My Life from Brigand to King.* London: Marston & Co., 1936.

Habibi, 'Abd al-Haiy. *Tarikh-i-Mokhtasar-i-Afghanistan (A Short History of Afghanistan),* 2 vols. Kabul: De Ketab Chapawulu Mo'assesa, 1346/1967.

_____. *Jonbesh-i-Mashrutiyyat dar Afghanistan (Constitutional Movement in Afghanistan),* 3rd ed. Qom: Isma`iliyan, 1372/1993.

Hagger, Robert. "State, Tribe, and Empire in Afghan Inter-policy Relations." In R. Tapper (ed.). *The Conflict of State and Tribe in Afghanistan.* New York: St. Martin Press, 1983, pp. 83-114.

Hamilton, Angus. *Afghanistan.* London: W. Heinemens, 1906.

_____. "Indo-Afghan Relations under Lord Curzon. *Fortnightly Review,* December 1906.

Haqshenas, S. N. *Dasayes wa Jenayat-i-Rus dar Afghanistan az Amir Dust Mohammad Khan ta Babrak (Russian Conspiracy and Crimes in Afghanistan from the Time of Amir Dust Mohammad Khan to the Time of Babrak).* Tehran: Jam'iyat-i-Eslami Afghanistan, 1363/1984.

Hardi, M. J. L. *Blood Feuds and the Payment of Blood Money in the Middle East.* Beirut: 1963.

Hashemi, Sayyid Sa`d al-Din. Jonbesh-i-Mashruta Khwahi dar Afghanistan (The Constitutional Movement in Afghanistan). Kabul University, unpublished monograph, 1354/1975.

Hensman, H. *The Afghan War of 1879-80.* London: H. Allen, 1881; Lahore: Manzar Printing Press, 1978.

Hepper, Metin, and Israeli, Raphael (eds). *Islam and Politics in the Modern Middle East.* London: Groom Helm, 1984.

Hidayat, Hamid. *Modern Islamic Political Thought.* Austin: University of Texas Press, 1982.

Holdich, Sir Thomas H. "The Influence of Bolshivism in Afghanistan." *New Europa,* December 4, 1919.

Iqbal, Muhammad. *The Reconstruction of Religious Thought in Islam.* Lahore: Ashraf Press, 1968.

Ishaque, Khalid M. "Al-Ahkam al-Sultaniyah: Laws of Government in Islam." *Islamic Studies,* 4, 1965, pp. 340-365.

Ka Ka Khel, Nazeer M. "Bay`a and its Political Role in the Early Islamic State." *Islamic Studies* (Islamabad), 20, no. 3, 1981, pp. 227-238.

_____. "The Theory of Impeachment in Islamic Polity." *Islamic Studies* (Islamabad), 17, no. 2, Summer 1978, pp. 93-103.

_____. "Legitimacy of Authority in Islam." *Islamic Studies* (Islamabad), 19, no. 3, Autumn 1980, pp.167-181.

Kakar, Hasan Kawun. *Government and Society in Afghanistan: The Reign of Amir `Abd al-Rahman Khan.* Austin: University of Texas Press, 1979.

_____. "Trends in Modern Afghan History." In Dupree, L. and Albert, A. (eds.), *Afghanistan in the 1970s.* New York: Prager Publishers, 1974, pp. 13-33.

Kamali, Hashim M. *Law in Afghanistan: A Study of Constitutions, Matrimonial Law and the Judiciary.* Leiden: E. J. Brill, 1985.

Karim, Sahebzada M. "Yad-Dashtha (Memoirs)". University of Nebraska (unpublished monograph).

Kateb, Faiz Mohammad. *Seraj al-Tawarikh (The Torch of Histories).* 3 vols. Kabul: Government Press, 1332/1915.

_____. *Tazakkor al-Enqelab (Notes on the Rebellion).* Unpublished manuscript.

Kaufeler, Heinz. *Modernization, Legitimacy and Social Movement: A Study of Socio-cultural Dynamics and Revolution in Iran and Ethiopia.* Ethnologisches Seminar der Universitat Zurich. Paris: Sipa-Press, 1988.

Keddie, Nikki R. (ed). *Scholars, Saints, and Sufis: Muslim Religious Institutions in the Middle East since 1500.* Berkeley: University of California Press, 1972.

Kepple, Arnold. *Gun-Running and the Indian North-West Frontier,* 2nd ed. Quetta: Gosha-e-Adab, 1977.

Kerr, Malcolm H. *Islamic Reform: The Political and Legal Theories of Muhammad Abduh and Rashid Rida.* Berkeley: University of California Press, 1966.

Khalil, Ebrahim. *Tarikh-i-Mazarat-i-Kabul (History of the Mausoleums of Kabul).* Kabul: Anjoman-i-Tarikh, 1339/1960.

Khalili, Khalil-Allah. `Ayyari az Khorasan: Habib-Allah Khadem-i-Din-i-Rasul-Allah (A Hero from Khorasan: Habib-Allah Khadem Din-i-Rasul-Allah).* n.p., 1983.

_____. *Nokhostin Tajawoz Rusia dar Afghanistan (The Fist Russian Aggression in Afghanistan).* Islamabad, 1363/1984.

_____. *Dastani az Dastanha-i-Qahraman-i-Kohistan (One of Many Stories of the Herao of Khorasan).* Islamabad, 1363/1984.

Khan, Ghulam-Mustafa. "The Naqshbandi Saints of Sind." *Journal of the Research Society of Pakistan* (Lahore), 13, no. 2, April 1976, pp. 19-47.

Labonne, R. "La Revolution Afghane. Le Duel Anglo-russe en Asie Centrale." *Le Correspondant,* April 25, 1930.

Lambton, Ann K. S. *State and Government in Medieval Islam: In Introduction to the Study of Islamic Political Theory.* Oxford: Oxford University Press, 1981.

Lee, Dwight. "The Origins of Pan-Islamism." *American Historical Review,* October 1941 and July 1942. 2 parts.

Lerner, Daniel. *The Passing of Traditional Society.* Glencoe: The Free Press, 1958.

Lewis, John W. "The Social Limits of Politically Induced Change." In J. Lewis and D. Ashford (eds.), *Modernization by Design.* Ithaca: Cornell University Press, 1969, pp. 1-33.

Maley, William. *Afghanistan: Politics and Government.* Boulder: Westview Press, 1991.

Marin, L. "L' Afghanistan et la France." *Bulletin Asie Francaise.* July 1923, pp. 221-224.

Marwat, Fazal-il-Rehim, and Kakakhel, W.A. Shah (edts.) *Afghanistan and the Frontier,* Peshawar; Emjay Books International, 1993.

Maududi, S. Abdul A'ala. *The Islamic Law and Constitution,* 5th ed. Lahore: Islamic Publications, 1957.

Massel, Gregory J. *The Surrogate Proletariat: Muslim Women and the Revolutionary Strategies in Soviet Central Asia, 1919-1929.* Princeton: Princeton University Press, 1972.

McMahon, A.H. and Ramsay, A.D.G. *Report on the Tribes of Dir, Swat and Bajour Together With the Utman-Khel and Sam Ranizai.* Reprint from the 1901 original text. Peshawar: Saeed Book Bank, 1981.

Meron, Ya'akov. "The Development of Legal Thought in Hanafi Texts." *Studia Islamica.* 30, 1969, pp. 73-118.

Merton, Robert K. *Social Theory and Social Structure.* New York: The Free Press, 1957.

Minault, Gail. *The Khilafat Movement: Religious Symbolism and Political Mobilization in India.* New York: Columbia University Press, 1982.

Mir Munshi, Sultan Mahomed (ed.). *The Life of Abdur Rahman: Amir of Afghanistan,* 2 vols. London: John Murray, 1900.

_____. *The Constitution and Laws of Afghanistan.* London: John Murray, 1900.

Modarres, Molla Gol Ahmad et al. *Seraj al-Ahkam fi Mo`amelat al-Eslam (The Rulings of Seraj on Islamic Settlements*: Vol. 1, *Adab al-Qazi*; Vol. 2, *Ketab al-Wekala.* Kabul: Matba'a-i-Shahi, 1323 h.q./1905.

Mohammad, Taj al-Din. *Tohfat al-Amir fi Bayan Soluk al-Moluk wa al-Tadbir.* Kabul, n.d.

Mohan Lal. *Life of the Amir Dost Mohammad Khan of Kabul,* 2 vols. Karachi: Oxford University Press, 1978.

Mojaddedi, Fazl Ghani. *Afghanistan dar `Ahd-i-Saltanat-i-`Alahazrat Aman-Allah Khan, 1919-1929 (Afghanistan during the Reign of His Majesty Aman-Allah Khan, 1919-1929.* 1997.

Mojaddedi, Shah-Agha. *Habib-Allah Khadem-i-Din-i-Rasul Allah.* Lahore: Al-Jedda Printers, 1984.

Molesworth, G. N. *Afghanistan 1919: An Account of Operation in the Third Afghan War.* New York: Asia Publishing House, 1962.

Mottahedeh, Roy. *Loyalty and Leadership in Early Islamic Society.* Princeton: Princeton University Press, 1980.

Mott-Smith, M. "Behind the Purdah in Afghanistan". *Travel,* 54, Dec. 16, 1929, pp. 12-51.

Nawid, Senzil. "Comparing the Regimes of Amanullah (1919-1929) and the Afghan Marxists (1978-1990): Similarities and Differences," *Critique,* 1, no. 2, 1993, pp. 15-31.

_____. "The Feminine and Feminism in Tarzi's Work." *Annali*, 55, no. 3, 1995, pp. 355-366.

_____. "The Khost Rebellion: The Reaction of Clerical and Tribal Forces to Social Change," *Annali.* 58, no.3, 1966, pp. 311-319.

_____. "Political Advocacy in Early Twentieth Century Afghan Poetry," *The Afghanistan Studies Journal*, 3, 1992, pp. 5-17.

_____. "The State, the Clergy, and British Imperialism in Afghanistan during the 19th and Early 20th Centuries." *International Journal of Middle East Studies*, 29, no. 4, Nov. 1997, pp. 581-605.

Nikitine, B. L' Afghanistan dans la Politique Internationale. *Revue des Sciences Politiques*, 50, 1927, pp. 593-611.

Nizam al-Mulk. *The Book of Government or Rules of Kings: Siyar al-Muluk or Siyasat-nama of Nizam al-Mulk,* translated by Hubert Drake. Persian Heritage Series, vol. 32. London: Routledge and Kegan Paul, 1978.

Olesen, Asta. "Afghanistan: The Development of the Modern State." In K. Ferdinand and M. Mozzafari (eds.), *Islam: State and Society.* Studies on Asian Topics, no. 12, Scandinavian Institute of Asian Studies. Riverdale: Curzon, 1988.

_____. "The Political Use of Islam in Afghanistan During the Reign of Amir `Abd al-Rahman." In C. Baraae, and K. Ferdinand (eds.), *Contributions to Islamic Studies: Iran, Afghanistan and Pakistan.* Studies of Contemporary Islam. Armus: Armus University Press, 1987.

`Omarjan, Mohammad. *Hedayat al-`Erfan: Dar Baiyan-i-Azkar-i-Tariqa-i-`Aliyya-i-Naqshbandiyya (A Guide to the Naqshbandiyya Order).* Kabul: No`mani Publishers, 1940.

Pazhwak, `Abd al-Rahman. "Ta'amolat-i-Hoquqiyya wa Jaza'iya-i-Melli" ("National Legal Transactions"). *Salnama-i-Kabul* (Kabul Almanac), 1318 Sh.H./1939, pp. 241-258.

Pernot, M. "La Situation en Afghanistan: Le Cause de la Revolte Contre le Roi Amanoullah." *Europe Nouvelle*, January 5, 1929, pp. 15-16.

_____. "Les reformes en Afghanistan." *Journal des Debats*, July 10, 1925.

Poullada, Leon B. *Reform and Rebellion in Afghanistan: King Amanullah's Failure to Modernize a Tribal Society.* Ithaca: Cornell University Press, 1973.

_____. "The Pushtun Role in the Afghan Political System." *The Afghanistan Council of the Asian Society.* Occasional Paper no. 1 (1970).

_____. "Problems of Social Development in Afghanistan." *Royal Central Asian Journal*, 49, 1962, pp. 33-39.

_____. "The Search for National Unity." In Louis Dupree and Albert Linette (eds.), *Afghanistan in the 1970s.* New York: Praeger Publishers, 1974, pp. 34-49.

Pratap, Mahendra. "My German Mission to High Asia." *Asia*, May 1925.

_____. *My Life Story of Fifty-Five Years.* Delhi, 1947.

Qureshi, Ishtiaq Hussain. *Ulema in Politics: A Study Relating to the Activities of Ulema on the South-Asian Subcontinent from 1556 to 1974*, 2nd edition. Karachi: Ma'aref Limited, 1974.

Rahman, Fazlur. *Islam and Modernity*. Chicago: University of Chicago Press, 1982.

Raveraty, Henry G. *Notes on Afghanistan and Baluchistan*, reprint from 1878 ed. Lahore: Manzoor Printing Press, 1976.

Reshtiya, Sayyid Qasim. *Afghanistan dar Qarn-i-Nozda* (Afghanistan in the Nineteenth Century). 3rd ed. Kabul: Government Printing House, 1346/1967.

Rosenthal, Irwin I. J. *Islam in Modern Nation States*. Cambridge: Cambridge University Press, 1965.

_____. *Political Thought in Medieval Islam*. Cambridge: Cambridge University Press, 1962.

Roy, Olivier. *L'Afghanistan: Islam et Modernite Politique*. Paris: Editions Du Seuil, 1985.

_____. *Islam and Resistance in Afghanistan*. Cambridge: Cambrige University Press, 1986.

Rubin, Barnett R. *The Fragmentation of Afghanistan*. New Haven: Yale University, 1995.

Sabet, Amr. "Islamic Iran: A Paradigmatic Response to Modernity." *The Iranian Journal of International Studies*. 7, no. 1, pp. 59-88.

Saljuqi, Fekri (ed.). *Resala-i-Mazarat-i-Herat*. Kabul: Government Press, 1967.

Sale, Lady. *A Journal of the Disasters in Afghanistan, 1841-42*. London: John Murray, 1843.

Schacht, Joseph. "Problems of Modern Islamic Legislation". In R.H. Nolte (ed.), *The Modern Middle East*. New York: Atherton Press, 1963, pp. 172-201.

_____. *An Introduction to Islamic Law*. Oxford: Corlendon Press, 1964.

_____. "Problems of Modern Islamic Legislation. *Studia Islamica*, 12, 1960, pp. 99-129

Schinasi, May. *Afghanistan at the Beginning of the Twentieth Century: Nationalism and Journalism in Afghanistan--A Study of Siraj al-Akhbar, 1911-1918*. Naples: Instituto Universitario Orientale Seminaro di Studi Asiatici, 1974.

_____. "Italie-Afghanistan, 1921-1941: De l 'Affaire Piperno a l'Evacuation de 1929." II, *AION* (Naples), 50, no. 2, 1990

_____. "Italie-Afghanistan, 1921-41," III, *AION* (Naples), 52, no. 2, 1992.

_____. "Siradj al-Akhbar: l'Opinion Afghane et la Russie." *Afghanistan*. 25, no. 2, 1972, pp. 29-41.

Shah, Iqbal Ali. "Afghanistan and the War." *The Near East*, February 15, 1918, pp. 324-30.

_____. *Afghanistan of the Afghans*. London: Diamond Press, 1928.

_____. "The Afghan Revolt and After." *Asia*, September 1934, pp. 828-30.

_____. "Bolshevism in Central Asia." *Edinburgh Review*, 1921.

_____. "The Federation of the Central Asian States under the Kabul Government." *Journal of Central Asian Society*, 8, no. 1, 1921, pp. 29-48.

_____. "The Meeting of East and West." *Criterion.* 8, June 1928, pp. 37-53.

_____. *The Tragedy of Amanullah.* London: Alexander Ousely, 1933.

Shah, Wali Khan Sardar. *My Memoirs.* Lahore: Punjab Educational Press, 1970.

Shahrani, M. Nazif, "State Building and Social Fragmentation in Afghanistan: A Historical Perspective," in A. Banuazizi & M. Weiner. *The State, Religion and Ethnic Politics: Afghanistan, Iran, and Pakistan.* New York: Syracuse University Press, 1986, pp. 23-74.

Shahrani, Nazif, and Canfield, R. (eds.). *Revolutions and Rebellions in Afghanistan: Anthropological Perspectives.* Berkeley: University of California Press, 1984.

Siddiqi, Amir H. *The Caliphate and Kingship in Medieval Persia.* Philadelphia: Porcupine Press, 1977.

Siddiqi, Muhammad Iqbal. *The Penal Law of Islam.* Lahore: Kazi Publications, 1979.

Smith, Dennis. *The Concept of Social Change.* London: Routledge and Kagen Paul, 1973.

Smith, Donald (ed.). *Religion and Political Modernization.* New Haven and London: 1974.

Smith, Wilfred C. *Islam in Modern History.* Princeton: Princeton University Press, 1957.

Stewart, Rhea T. *Fire in Afghanistan, 1914-1929: Faith, Hope, and British Empire.* New York: Doubleday, 1973.

Tapper, Nancy. "Marriage and Social Organization among Durrani Pashtuns in North Afghanistan." Unpublished Ph.D. Dissertation. University of London, 1979.

_____. *Bartard Brides: Politics, Gender, and Marriage in Afghanistan.* Cambridge: Cambridge University Press, 1991.

Tapper, Richard (ed.). *The Conflict of State and Tribe in Afghanistan.* London: Croom Helm, 1983.

Tarzi, Mahmud. *Watan wa Ma`ani-i-Motanawe`a wa Mahakemat-i-Hokmiyya-i-An.* Kabul: Kabul Printing House. 1335/1916.

Tillardat, F. "La Fin du Voyage du Roi Aman Ullah." *Bulletin Asie Francaise,* October 1928, p. 326.

_____. "La Revolte Afghane." *Bulletin Asie Francaise,* 1929, pp., 15-20.

_____. "Le Roi Aman Ullah en Angleterre." *Bulletin Asie Francaise,* May 1928, pp. 184-188.

_____. "La Voyage du Roi Aman Ullah." *Bulletin Asie Francaise,* February 1928, pp. 67-69.

_____. "Nadir Khan, Emir du l'Afghanistan." *Bulletin Asie Francaise,* 1930, p. 313.

Utas, B. "Notes on Afghanistan: Sufi Orders and Khaneqahs." *Afghanistan Journal,* 7, no. 2, 1980, pp. 60-67.

Vigne, G. T. *A Personal Narrative of a Visit to Guzni, Kabul and Afghanistan and of a Residence at the Court of Dost Mohammad.* Delhi: Gian Publishing House, 1986.

Viollis. A. "L'Agonie de la Rebellion Afghane." *Europe Novelle,* December 20, 1930, pp. 1831-1833.

Voll, John D. "Renewal and Reform in Islamic History: Tajdid and Islah." In J. L. Esposito (ed.), *Voices of Resurgent Islam.* Oxford: Oxford University Press, 1983, pp. 32-47.

Warburton, Sir Robert. *Eighteen Years in the Khyber, 1879-1898,* 3rd ed. Karachi: Oxford University Press, 1975.

Wheeler, Talboys J., *Memorandum on Afghanistan Affair from A.D. 1700.* Calcutta: Office of Superintendent of Government Printing, 1869.

Wilbur, Donald. "The Structure and Position of Islam in Afghanistan." *Middle East Journal,* 6, no. 1, Winter 1952, pp. 41-48.

Wild, Donald. *Amanullah: Ex-King of Afghanistan.* Quetta: Nisa Traders, 1978.

Woodsmall, Ruth. *Muslim Women Enter A New World.* New York: Round Table Press, 1936.

Yusufi, Allah Bakhsh. *Maulana Mohammad Ali Jauhar: The Khilafat Movement.* Karachi: Mohammad Ali Educational Society, 1980.

Zadran, A.S. "Marriage Principles and Customs Among the Pushtuns of Afghanistan," *Afghanistan Quarterly,* 33, no. 3, 1980, pp. 52-67.

Zahir, P.M. and Elmi, S.M. *De Afghanistan de Ma`aref Tarikh (History of Education in Afghanistan),* 2 vols. Kabul: Ministry of Education Press, 1960 (Pashtu).

Zalmai, Mohammad Wali. *Mojahed Afghan (The Afghan Mojahed).* Kabul: Government Press, 1346/1967 (Pashtu).

Index